NEIGHBORHOOD PATRIOTS,
BACKCOUNTRY REBELS,
— *and their* —
UNDERDOG CRUSADES
— *to* —
REDRAW AMERICA'S
POLITICAL MAP

— *by* —

Bill Kauffman

CHELSEA GREEN PUBLISHING
WHITE RIVER JUNCTION, VERMONT

Excerpt from "The Mad Farmer, Flying the Flag of Rough Branch, Secedes from the Union," by Wendell Berry, used by kind permission of Wendell Berry.

Lyrics from "Two Hundred Years Is Long Enough" by Pete Sutherland. Copyright © 2008 by Pete Sutherland, Epact Music, BMI. Reprinted by kind permission of Pete Sutherland.

Project Manager: Patricia Stone
Developmental Editor: Joni Praded
Copy Editor: Laura Jorstad
Proofreader: Nancy Ringer
Indexer: Peggy Holloway
Designer: Peter Holm, Sterling Hill Productions

Printed in the United States of America
First printing June, 2010
10 9 8 7 6 5 4 3 2 1   10 11 12 13

Our Commitment to Green Publishing
Chelsea Green sees publishing as a tool for cultural change and ecological stewardship. We strive to align our book manufacturing practices with our editorial mission and to reduce the impact of our business enterprise in the environment. We print our books and catalogs on chlorine-free recycled paper, using vegetable-based inks whenever possible. This book may cost slightly more because we use recycled paper, and we hope you'll agree that it's worth it. Chelsea Green is a member of the Green Press Initiative (www.greenpressinitiative.org), a nonprofit coalition of publishers, manufacturers, and authors working to protect the world's endangered forests and conserve natural resources. *Bye Bye, Miss American Empire* was printed on Natures Natural, a 30-percent postconsumer recycled paper supplied by Thomson-Shore.

Library of Congress Cataloging-in-Publication Data
Kauffman, Bill, 1959-
  Bye bye, miss American empire : neighborhood patriots, backcountry rebels, and their underdog crusades to redraw America's political map / Bill Kauffman.
      p. cm.
  Includes bibliographical references and index.
  ISBN 978-1-933392-80-6
  1. Secession--United States. I. Title.

JK311.K38 2010
320.473'049--dc22

                                        2010016118
Chelsea Green Publishing Company
Post Office Box 428
White River Junction, VT 05001
(802) 295-6300

www.chelseagreen.com

To Carlos Narvaez (1959–1997)
In the prayerful hope that you knew how much you were loved
Rest peacefully, old buddy

CONTENTS

There is only one of him, but he goes.
He returns to the small country he calls home,
his own nation small enough to walk across.
He goes shadowy into the local woods,
and brightly into the local meadows and croplands.
He goes to the care of neighbors,
he goes into the care of neighbors.
He goes to the potluck supper, a dish
from each house for the hunger of every house.
He goes into the quiet of early mornings
of days when he is not going anywhere.

> —Wendell Berry, from "The Mad Farmer, Flying
> the Flag of Rough Branch, Secedes from the Union"

I believe that our country is too large for its own good. Great countries . . . are a menace to themselves and everyone else. People are not meant to live in such vast, impersonal political communities.

> —George F. Kennan, *Democracy and the Student Left*

I was born, like other men, in a spot of the earth which I loved because I had played boys' games there, and fallen in love, and talked with my friends through nights that were nights of the gods. And I feel the riddle. These little gardens where we told our loves. These streets where we brought out our dead. Why should they be commonplace? Why should they be absurd? Why should it be grotesque to say that a pillar-box is poetic when for a year I could not see a red pillar-box against the yellow evening in a certain street without being wracked with something of which God keeps the secret, but which is stronger than sorrow or joy? Why should any one be able to raise a laugh by saying 'the Cause of Notting Hill'?—Notting Hill where thousands of immortal spirits blaze with alternate hope and fear.

> —G. K. Chesterton, *The Napoleon of Notting Hill*

To the States, or any one of them, or any city of the States,
Resist much, obey little,
Once unquestioning obedience, once fully enslaved,
Once fully enslaved, no nation, state, city of this earth, ever afterward resumes
  its liberty.

> —Walt Whitman, "To the States"

ACKNOWLEDGMENTS

For the chance to treat these subjects in their pages, I thank editors Hal Clifford, Karl Zinsmeister, Erich Eichman, Scott McConnell, Thomas Fleming, Kara Hopkins, Steve Fraser, Terry Golway, Dan Hall, Jeremy Beer, and Marty Zupan. Effusive thanks to John S. Whitehead for his thoughtful responses to my questions on Alaska and Hawaii. I am grateful to Joni Praded and John Barstow for their editorial advice. And I salute my friends in Vermont, who are an inspiration, a lesson in the rejuvenescent possibilities of small things in our age of Bigness run riot. Come Independence Day, I hope you'll locate your New York embassy in Genesee County instead of the Imperial City.

Wherein We Meet Genial Radicals by the Shores of Lake Champlain

*T*he American Empire is dead. That gathering murmur you hear is not sobbing: Good riddance to the damn monster. Rather, the noise is the sweet hum of revolution, of subjects learning how to be citizens, of people shaking off (or flipping off) their Wall Street and Pentagon over-lords and taking charge of their lives once more, whether as members of verdant countryside or the sodality of the city neighborhood.

Oh, the empire's corpse may yet wander the desert sands, rattling chains in Marley-like clangor, but the thing itself, as a breathing and vascular entity with its own tomorrows, is dead. An expiry long past due, I might say. Senator J. William Fulbright, the only good Bill ever to exit Arkansas for the national political stage, said in the 1960s that "the price of empire is America's soul and that price is too high."[1] He was right. The American Empire, that cold-eyed death machine that ground American boys into fodder to spit out into the frozen Chosin of Korea, the rice paddies of Southeast Asia, the dunes of Mesopotamia, has run out of money, out of even the fig leaf of moral justification, out of any international sanction save the specious pule of the coerced and the fraudulent. The empire—what Edmund Wilson called "a huge blundering power unit controlled more and more by bureaucracies whose rule is making it more and more difficult to carry on the tradition of American individualism"[2]—always was the enemy of the true America, the America of Mark Twain and Levon Helm, Henry Thoreau and Zora Neale Hurston. The empire demanded that we pledge allegiance to the distant over the near, to the abstract over the real, to perpetual war over peace and harmony.

The Crash of 2008 and its salutary humbling of the hubristic was only the overture. The dissolution is yet to be played out, though the plot thickened and union thinned early in the first year of the presidency of Barack Obama, who continued the Bushian policy of socializing risk and privatizing reward in his series of bailouts of corporate entities that were, in the obscenely inverse phrase of the mass media, "too big to fail." The phrase reeked of wishful thinking, though it conveyed with great effectiveness the mind-set of those who run the empire. Bigness is next to godliness, which is in turn a subsidiary of Goldman Sachs; smallness is mingy and negligible; and modesty is for losers. Ten thousand corner delis must die so that AIG can live. The political corollary is that Xenia, Ohio, and Fairbanks, Alaska, are nothings, fit only to send tribute in the form of taxes to Washington and future corpses to the war of the hour. The fifty stars of Old Glory are no more than smudge marks on a wet rag; what counts is the octopus in the District of Columbia whose tentacles curl out to smother and strangle and steal from the nether provinces.

As the empire accelerates through its welcome decline, real patriots of all shades and shapes will hold with renewed and redoubled fastness to the cherishable pieces of our lorn and lovely land: its little places, its accented regions, its history-echoing, blood-seeded grounds.

The times—the *Times*, too—push me to the rocks off Lake Ontario's Point Breeze, where I sit licking an ice cream cone and pondering Brooklyn's Good Gray Poet, for I love Old Whitman so, to borrow Allen Ginsberg's line (via James Whitcomb Riley—how do you like *that* triple play?). Saith Walt as his America was rent asunder:

> *I listened to the Phantom by Ontario's shore,*
> *I heard the voice arising demanding bards*
> *By them all native and grand, by them alone can these States be fused into the*
>   *compact organism of a Nation.*
> *To hold men together by paper or seal or by compulsion is no account . . .*[3]

Paper, seal, compulsion: These are the ties that strangle, not bind. I love America deeply but the country I love is far too small to show up on a television screen. The idea of "citizenship" has been diluted from one of membership in an organic body in which each person matters and takes part in civic affairs to the current condition, in which you are a cog in a machine, just another brick in the wall. The role of an American citizen, as viewed by our rulers in Washington, DC, is to pay your taxes, cast a meaningless vote every four years, and shut the hell up.

The anti-Obama reaction of 2009 was like a controlled burn that blew past its carefully constructed boundaries. Republican operatives had hoped to exploit popular unhappiness over the new president's (typical, even Bush-like) acts of aggrandizement and power grabbing to set up the GOP for a rebound in 2010. But the rubes wandered off the reservation, past the barbed-wire fences of Responsible (which is to say eunuchlike) Dissent and into the Forbidden Zone of revolution, refusal, even . . . secession.

By spring 2009 radicalism spiced the air. States from Michigan to New Hampshire were considering "state sovereignty" resolutions that audaciously reasserted the Tenth Amendment to the US Constitution: "The powers not delegated to the United States by the Constitution, nor prohibited by it to the States, are reserved to the States respectively, or to the people." Since both parties—two wings of a single bird of prey—and the corporate media that serve them regard anyone who quotes the Bill of Rights as a militiaman (occupying the same rung of the social ladder as a white-trash meth head), this seemingly innocuous act—declaring, in the face of all evidence, that the US Constitution is operative—had the flavor of sedition. And the sovereignty resolutions, once unpacked, left a great question hanging in the air: What if Washington tells the states to shove off? Don't mind your own business, Montana and Oklahoma: Uncle Sam will mind it for you. What then? The choices, it would seem, are two: submission or secession. And given that choice, what man or woman of hale and hearty spirit would not choose secession?

Even dullard politicians caught the fever, or at least mimicked its symptoms. On Income Tax Day, April 15, 2009, that annual reminder of our serfdom, the empty-suited Governor Rick Perry of Texas, a man theretofore so unremarkable as to have languished in the shadow of his predecessor, George W. Bush, addressed a raucous crowd in Austin (many shouting "Secede!") and later told reporters, "We've got a great union. There's absolutely no reason to dissolve it. But if Washington continues to thumb their nose at the American people, you know, who knows what might come out of that. But Texas is a very unique place, and we're a pretty independent lot to boot."[4]

Inarticulate, to be sure. And where was Perry when President Bush and Dick Cheney were shredding the Constitution for the previous eight years? But still: Something was abrew. Our birthword and birthgift—secession, which had been removed from our vocabulary when we were but a young country—was on the tongues of the unregulated, the unbossed, the unruly.

Perry was pilloried, naturally. No unapproved opinion may be expressed in the land of the free without earning the sayer thereof his time on the cross. Who should come to Perry's defense but the most radical and honest presidential hopeful of the prior year, Representative Ron Paul (R-TX), the libertarian scourge of war, militarism, statism, and Big Brother? "Secession is an American tradition—it's how we came into being," said Paul, standing by Perry in the eye of the storm. "A free society means you can dissolve." Conceding that the Civil War, er, complicated matters somewhat, Paul opined that had secession remained a vital principle in American life, "the federal government would have been restrained" throughout our history, as the threat of states breaking away would have acted as a brake on the runaway national juggernaut.[5]

If secession today has a vaguely naughty, even disreputable sound, owing to that war which Gore Vidal called "the great single tragic event that continues to give resonance to our republic," that only means we need to throw away our social studies textbooks and relearn, or learn for the first time, history as it is not dictated by the winners to the stenographers.[6]

Talk of breaking up our increasingly fractious and unhappy union predated the presidency of Barack Obama. In fact, it gained voice largely due to the man who made possible the Ovalization of Mr. Obama: George W. Bush.

In the wake of the egregious Bush reelection in 2004, frustrated liberals talked secession back to within hailing distance of the margins of national debate—a place it had not occupied since 1861. With their praise of self-rule and the devolution of power, they sounded not unlike many conservatives had in the days before Bush & Cheney & Limbaugh welded the American Right to the American Empire. While certain proponents of the renascent secessionism were motivated by spite or pixilated by whimsy or driven by the simpleminded belief that these United States can be divided into blue and red—as though our beautiful land can be painted in only two hues!—others argued with cogency and passion for a disunionist position that bordered on the, well, seditious. Emphasizing both culture ("Now that slavery is taken care of, I'm for letting the South form its own nation," said Democratic operative Bob Beckel) and economics (Democratic pundit Lawrence O'Donnell noted that "ninety percent of the red states are welfare clients of the federal government"), writing in forums of neoliberalism (*Slate*) and venerable liberalism (*The Nation*), liberals helped to disinter a body of thought that had been buried at Appomattox. And—surprise—the corpse has legs.[7]

Secession is the next radical idea poised to enter mainstream discourse—or at least the realm of the conceivable. You can't bloat a modest republic into a crapulent empire without sparking one hell of a centrifugal reaction. The prospect of breaking away from a union once consecrated to liberty and justice but now degenerating into imperial putrefaction will only grow in appeal as we go marching with our Patriot Acts and National Security Strategies through Iraq, Iran, Afghanistan, and all the frightful signposts on our road to nowhere. The liberals who considered secession while tossing and turning in the fever dreams of the Bush nightmare may back off, for the nonce, mollified by the honeyed cadences of the savior Obama. But he is no less a servitor of Wall Street and the American Empire than are the Republicans, and when President Obama dispatches troops to Georgia (the land of Joseph Stalin, not Ray Charles) or Somalia or bombs Iran, in fulfillment of John McCain's campaign jingle, they may be jolted once more into a radical and clear-eyed wakefulness.

Some of the contemporary secessionists are puckish and playful; others are dead serious. Some seek to separate from the main body of a state and add a fifty-first star to the American flag, while others wish to leave the United States altogether. Some proposals are so sensible (the division of California into two or three states) that in a just world they would be inevitable. Others are so radical (the independent republic of Vermont) as to seem risibly implausible—until you meet the activists and theoreticians preparing these new declarations of independence.

For these movements are, in the main, hopeful and creative (if utopian) responses to the Current Mess engulfing our land. They are the political antidote to the disease of giantism. We are a nation born in secession, after all, and of rebellion against faraway rulers. Ruptures, crackups, and the splintering of overlarge states into polities of more manageable size, closer to the human scale, are as American as runaway slaves and tax protesters.

⤙⤚

"Secession," says Rob Williams—Vermont filmmaker, songwriter (of the MTV-unfriendly "Kill Your Television"), radio host (of *Green Mountain Globa-Local*, which spotlights Vermont artists), and professor of history and media education at Champlain College—"is every American's birthright."[8]

It's been almost a century and a half since any significant number of Americans believed that, but in November 2006 Williams's cranny of New England hosted the first-ever nationwide conference of those who wish to make the nation a little less wide.

Yeah, sure, I know: Breaking away is impossible. Quixotic. Hopeless. So was dancing on the Berlin Wall.

The historic Vermont gathering was convened by Kirkpatrick Sale, founder in 2003 of the Middlebury Institute, a secessionist clearinghouse whose "ultimate task" is "the peaceful dissolution of the American empire." The 2004 Middlebury Declaration, drawn up by Sale at the first confer-ence his outfit hosted, committed itself to the promotion of "all the forms by which small political bodies, dedicated to the precept of human scale, distance themselves from larger ones, as in decentralization, dissolution, disunion, division, devolution, or secession, creating small and indepen-dent bodies that rule themselves."[9]

Sale is the author of the decentralist compendium *Human Scale* (1980) and books on the Luddites and Students for a Democratic Society. So that agents of the Department of Homeland Security won't have to pore over his works, he offers this description of his political vision: "I am an anar-chist who wants to see society organized on a small, human scale, based on self-determining communities."[10]

Sale scheduled the confab for just three days before the 2006 election, not for any symbolic reason but because it was "the first cheap weekend after the fall foliage season."

So upon Burlington converged the divergent. Forty-three delegates from eighteen states met around a long table in the Lake Champlain Salon of the Wyndham Burlington. I saw ponytails and suits, turtlenecks and sneakers, an Alaskan gold miner and one delegate from the neo-Confederate League of the South who wore a gray greatcoat, as if sitting for a daguerreotype just before the battle. When Sale called the gathering to order at 9 AM, more or less sharp, the delegates did not begin the meeting with the Pledge of Allegiance.

The Puerto Rican Independence Party sent supportive greetings but no delegates, though the Puerto Ricans—like the Hawaiians—denied that they need to secede from anything. Rather, they consider themselves an occupied country. Hell, they *are* an occupied country. Despite his best efforts, Sale was unable to attract Mexican American delegates from the Southwest or representatives of the original conquered people, American Indians. These absences were sorely felt.

The location might seem, at first, thuddingly inappropriate. Why hold a secession conference in New England: cradle of unionism, bête noire of the Confederacy, source of the "Battle Hymn of the [indivisible!] Republic"? Yet no region of the country has been as fertile a ground for secessionist thought as New England.

Yankees threatened to leave the Union in 1803 when, with his constitutionally dubious Louisiana Purchase, Thomas Jefferson doubled the American realm, and the cries of separation once again rang through the Northeast in 1814, when New Englanders, appalled by the War of 1812, met at the Hartford Convention to discuss going their own way.

The subject of an amicable divorce was raised in the 1840s, during the debates over the annexation of Texas and the Mexican War. In each instance, New England had a strong moral case for secession. A practical one, too: The country had gotten too damn big to govern from a swamp on the Potomac. The godlike (on his good days) Daniel Webster argued in 1846 that "there must be some limit to the extent of our territory, if we are to make our institutions permanent. The Government is very likely to be endangered . . . by a further enlargement of its already vast territorial surface."[11]

By the 1850s New England, with its courageous defiance of the Fugitive Slave Act, had become the epicenter of states' rights—the logical end of

which is secession—and of localist defiance of tyrannical central government. Yes, a century later racist governors poached the phrase, but why
should the fact that some Southern politicians used "states' rights" to justify
segregation in the 1950s forever discredit the philosophy of Jefferson and
Patrick Henry? I mean, look: Neoconservative chickenhawks use the word
freedom as often as Richard Pryor used to say "fuck." Does that mean we
ought to junk *freedom*? Or should we reclaim it?

∽◉∾

My sympathy for the secessionists bleeds all over the page. I am native to
and still a citizen of rural Western New York, which is about as close as
one can find to a powerless colony. And yet it is a sign of our debilitation
that the most robust calls for two New Yorks have come from Gothamites
(William Randolph Hearst, Norman Mailer, Bella Abzug).

Still, a state of West New York would be a new star on Old Glory. So
would the felicitously named State of Jefferson (marrying far Northern
California to Southern Oregon) or the Upper Peninsula of Michigan. The
secessionists assembled in Burlington want, for the most part, out of the
union altogether. They wish to be lone stars. Or if that sounds too grand—
for a star, up close, is burning and blinding and unfit to love—maybe we
should just say that they want to be, like demoted demotic Pluto, "dwarf
planets" whom the giants disdain to notice. Or attack.

For men (only two women delegates were present) who want no part
of union, the Burlington delegates were awfully solicitous. Intersectional
amity was the order of the day—rather as though a roomful of wives were
seeking divorce from the same polygamous spouse, and whatever differences they might have among themselves paled before their agreement
that Big Daddy is a real louse.

"This isn't right or left," said one New Hampshirite, setting a theme
for the conference. Peaceful hippies, whimsically radical Vermonters, and
anti-corporate leftists broke bread with Southern Christians and men
wearing Confederate flag lapel pins, and the skies did not darken nor the
earth crack. In fact, the most striking feature of the conference was that if
an auditor closed his eyes and could block out the accents, it was hard to
tell who was the "leftist" and who was the archconservative.

I heard mentioned, as heroes, Saul Alinsky, Robert E. Lee, strategist of nonviolence Gene Sharp, Thomas Jefferson, and Martin Luther King Jr. Denunciations were made of corporate greed, federal empire, television, the Iraq War, and the Patriot Act.

Were there fruits and nuts? Sure, a few. But just as cranks keep this country turning, so, too, are fruits and nuts a sapid alternative to Wonder Bread. The furry, troll-like man who proclaims himself King of Kansas is imaginative and harmless; the shaven men in tailored suits who call themselves president of the United States have been, of late, unimaginative and grossly harmful. I'll take the King of Kansas, thank you very much.

If some secessionists are woolgathering gnomes, the best of them are patriots in the truest sense: They cherish the music, literature, accents, agriculture, history, and quirks of their places.

Secessionists—most of them, anyway—are all too aware that what they seek (the dissolution of the mightiest empire on the planet Earth) borders the inconceivable. But they have made peace with its implausibility, and moved on. Reform they scorn; he who works within the system is swallowed by the system. Taking up arms is madness. "Rebellion and revolution are useless," says Sale. "You would be crushed." If you want out of a bloated empire and dehumanizing system, secession is the path.

In its latest incarnation, secession has something of a greenish cast. It was made in Vermont, and if it has not yet proven as exportable as, say, Vermont Teddy Bears or Cherry Garcia, well, give it time.

Thomas Naylor is the gentle godfather of the Vermont independence movement. Naylor taught economics at Duke for thirty years before, in best contrarian fashion, he and his wife, Magdalena, did a reverse snowbird and moved north in retirement to Charlotte, Vermont. In October 2003 he founded the hopefully named Second Vermont Republic (SVR). (The first one lasted from 1777 to 1791, before the Green Mountain Boys threw in with the United States.) Naylor proposed separating from the United States, he says, almost as an afterthought. He was delivering an antiwar speech when "I said that if we stop this war there will only be another one. Whenever Bush or Slick Willie or Reagan need to improve their popularity they'll bomb someone." He came to a realization: A citizen of an independent Vermont might hope to live in a free and peaceful republic; a subject of the American Empire is doomed to watch helplessly as her taxes feed an unquenchable war machine. So why not leave the empire and pledge allegiance to Vermont?

Naylor's call struck a chord. A minor chord, perhaps, but a chord that has reverberated since 1776.

Because the Vermont secessionists were not sallow ideologues but rather men and women deeply in love with their state, they gained a foothold. The state has, perhaps, the most well-developed sense of itself of any state in the Lower 48, and the SVR is awash in Vermontishness, from maple syrup to Robert Frost.

Member Jim Hogue delivers hortatory speeches dressed as the state's rollicking founder, Ethan Allen. Rob Williams, editor of the superb pro-secession bimonthly *Vermont Commons*, seeks to "create a visual iconography of Vermont secession" as a means of making secession "sexy—an attractive, interesting, viable political option."

Vermont Commons is a gem: a literate, polemical, thought-provoking, radical newspaper that has featured contributions from the likes of Wendell Berry, Bill McKibben, James Howard Kunstler, Burlington mayor Peter Clavelle, and a cast of politically uncategorizable Vermonters. For the stream of secession is fed by many American springs: the participatory democracy dreams of the New Left, the small-is-beautiful ethos of the greens, the traditional conservative suspicion (nearly rubbed out by the Bush eraser) of big government and remote bureaucracy, and that old-fashioned American blend of don't-tread-on-me libertarianism with I'll-give-you-the-shirt-off-my-back communalism.

The *Vermont Commons* contributors ask and sometimes even answer the hard questions about secession: How would a local currency work? How do we revive town-meeting democracy? How does Vermont achieve a sustainable food system? How does it encourage community-supported agriculture, organic farms, co-ops, roadside markets, and backyard gardening? What would an independent Vermont energy policy look like? How feasible is local clothing production? With whom would Vermont trade?

"The left–right thing has got to go," declares Ian Baldwin, co-founder of Chelsea Green Publishing and publisher of *Vermont Commons*. "We're decentralists and we are up against a monster."

What might replace left and right, liberal and conservative, as useful political bipolarities? Globalist and localist, perhaps, or placeless versus placeist. Owing to economic exigencies, Baldwin expects that the "world economy will relocalize." Dismissing homeland security as "fatherland security," Baldwin says we need "homestead security": sustainable agriculture, small shops, a revival of craftsmanship, local citizenship, communal spirit. The vision is one of self-government. Independence from the empire but interdependence at the grassroots. Neighborliness. The other American Dream.

Why should Vermont (or Kansas or Mississippi) be compelled by strangers in Washington to implant computer chips in its cattle and send its state militia (now known as the National Guard) to fight in overseas wars and register its firearms and subject its children to standardized tests and participate in federal farm programs that privilege corporate agribusiness? Aren't Vermonters, guided by their intimate knowledge of local conditions, capable of fashioning their own laws (or nonlaws) on such matters?

Step back and it sounds so fantastical: little Vermont wanting out of the United States. But secessionists are fond of the Soviet example. If, in 1985, you had stood on a platform and predicted that within a lustrum the Soviet Union would be all but dissolved, the snickers would have filled a candy factory. Kirk Sale also likes to point out that the United Nations, founded with 51 members in 1945, now has 192. Why not 193? A *Newsweek* poll in 1995 found that only 41 percent of blacks, 61 percent of whites, and 54 percent of Hispanics believed that a century hence the United States would "still exist as one nation."[12] It doesn't take a weatherman (or Brookings fellow) to know which empire the wind is gonna topple next.

Still, the s-word has, to some, a treasonous taint. It's not that Americans see it as a black-and-white issue; no, they see it through a haze of blue and gray.

"Abraham Lincoln really did a number on us," admits Naylor. "He convinced the vast majority of Americans that secession is illegal, immoral, and unconstitutional."

Naylor's frustration over Lincoln's giant shadow is shared by Donald Livingston, a philosopher at Emory University, noted scholar of David Hume, and the "guru" of the new secessionists, as Naylor calls him.

"Historiography in America is based on the fundamental postulate that the Union should have been preserved at all costs," says Livingston. He proposes to challenge that assumption; to inspire students and colleagues and those tired of the consolidationist consensus to write history from a decentralist perspective. Livingston's educational foundation, the Abbeville Institute, takes as its motto "Divided We Stand; United We Fall." The USA, he believes, no longer works; why not try the Disunited States of America? (Livingston belongs to the Second Vermont Republic but not to the League of the South. More on that anon.)

Critics of secession wonder if devolving power might not empower local tyrannies. For instance, the Vermonters have taken flak for cooperating with the League of the South, which is either a Southern cultural organization with an official commitment to equality before the law or an unsavory group nostalgic for the Confederacy, depending upon whom you believe. Yet the range and potential of oppressive government has natural limits in a small jurisdiction. If a town in Alabama—or an upscale precinct in Manhattan—falls under the sway of knaves or crooks, abused minorities can remonstrate, face-to-face, with the authorities. They can organize resistance on a human scale. Or, if all else fails, they can leave. Even at the state level, redress is not impossible. Subjects of a large empire have no such option (other than expatriating). And unlike the Alabama town or Manhattan block, the US government can wage wars, fill prisons, and curtail liberties on a scale undreamed of by petty tyrants. I suppose it comes down to this: Do you trust your neighbors, or do you trust Barack Obama and Newt Gingrich?

The Kentucky essayist Katherine Dalton, writing on the decentralist Web site Front Porch Republic, responds to the charge that local control leaves the door open to local oppression in this way: First, "that there are many examples of centralized injustice and we will live to see more, and, second, that we are going to have to tolerate local mistakes and injustices, at least in communities that are not ours (we can holler like anything at home), if we are going to trust people to govern themselves rather than be ruled from afar. Will children ever grow up if not given the leeway to fail?"[13]

Amen, Sister Kate, amen.

⤬

"Secession in the twenty-first century is not a racist plot," says Ian Baldwin. "The myth of Lincoln," he continues, "has erased secession from the consciousness of people in the North." It is as if the Civil War settled for all time the question of whether a state might withdraw from the Union.

"This is not a North–South issue," insists Walter Donald "Donnie" Kennedy, author of *The South Was Right!*, a popular work of Confederate apologetics. It is here that a Northerner like myself gets stuck in the briar patch, confounded by what the Drive-By Truckers call "the duality of the Southern thing."

Most of the Southerners present at the Burlington conference were associated with the League of the South, which was founded in 1994 and seeks "to advance the cultural, social, economic, and political well being and independence of the Southern people by all honourable means." (That English *u* in *honourable* is no misprint: The LOS disdains the Yankee lexicographer Noah Webster's orthography.)

I know Southerners who were members of the league in its early years but later dropped out because they were "uncomfortable" with some others who had joined. The league has repudiated overt racists such as the ex-Klansman David Duke, but I'm told that it has attracted its share, or more, of racist assholes, and it has done a piss-poor job of attracting black members. Judge for yourself at www.dixienet.org.

The Northerners in Burlington are wary of the delegates from the land of cotton.

"What do you think these Southerners are up to?" Sale asks Naylor the night before the convention.

"They're coming to deal," replies Naylor. The Southerners, he suggests, want legitimacy. Were they on tiptoes, not saying things that should have been said? Perhaps. Or maybe the stakes have become so high, the costs of empire so crushing—spiritually and socially as well as financially—that cultural differences just don't matter anymore.

League director Franklin Sanders, a gold and silver dealer from Dogwood Mudhole, Tennessee, delivers an anti-corporate stemwinder that denounces Walmart, McDonald's, and the way that "local economies have been bled dry by corporations." He calls for a relocalization of the economy. He speaks with great hope of the homeschool and whole foods movements, of "local purchases with local money."

I ask Sanders about the cultural differences between the Southerners, who in the straitjacket taxonomy of the age are "ultra-conservative," and the "leftists" of New England.

"What you're seeing graphically demonstrates the breakdown of the left–right distinction," says Sanders. "What you're seeing is the failure of American politics."

"We are about liberty and home rule," adds Donnie Kennedy. "Let's defeat the empire."

I tell Kennedy that I have heard rumors that he intends to run as a Southern Pride candidate in the 2008 Republican presidential primaries. He doesn't deny it. The plan, he tells me as we walk the busy streets of human-scale Burlington, is to win a few delegates, unfurl the Confederate flag at the national convention, and get tossed out on their Dixie asses. It didn't pan out. But I liked the rebel spirit of the thing, even though as a New York Democrat I pulled the lever for Obama (the anti-Hillary) in the primary and Ralph Nader in November.

Kirk Sale asks the Southrons, point-blank, if they condone racial discrimination.

"If you're gonna be a racist, you can't be for liberty," replies Kennedy, but the best defense is always a good offense, and nothing so grates upon a proud Southerner as the rasp of New England sanctimony. "I haven't seen but one black person since I've been here," continues Kennedy, "so I won't be lectured on race by Vermonters." Touché: The Green Mountain State has a minuscule (0.5 percent) black population. And dig this: The founder and president of the League of the South, Alabaman Michael Hill, taught for many years at Stillman College, a historically black school.

"We are a biracial culture," says Sanders, "and we kinda like it that way. Equality before the law is what we want." Zora Neale Hurston and Ray Charles are as Southern as Jefferson Davis, and there ain't no Allman Brothers without the Delta Blues. Southern culture, as writers from William Faulkner to Shelby Foote have proclaimed, is, indissolubly, African American.

Thomas Moore, representing the Southern National Congress

Committee, which in 2008 would convene a congress of Southern citizens that sought to provide an "alternative, legitimate structure" to the "over-extended empire" that the SNC believes to be on the verge of collapse, spoke of "holding hands together in harmony and friendship" with "our black brothers and sisters" in an independent South. The Southern secessionists tend to speak the language of Christianity, but then the tradition of Christian resistance to unjust or arbitrary power is in the same American grain as anarchistic abolitionists and lunch-counter sit-ins.

Look. Who can ever really know what is in another's heart? The LOS likely contains some scoundrels and scumbags. But I do know this. The men at this conference were not the sort of careerist apple-polishers who go around kissing Yankee ass. Thomas Naylor, who as a young Mississippi liberal took pride in refusing to stand for "Dixie" when his beloved Ole Miss Rebels played, told me that he was so disarmed upon attending the 2006 League of the South convention that for the first time since before the civil rights movement he actually sang the words to that tuneful ode to the land where old times are not forgotten.

To my mind, the strongest—irrefutable, really—case for secession from the United States belongs to those two most recent additions to the indivisible but addable union, Alaska and Hawaii.

Dexter Clark, a quinquagenarian gold miner and co-proprietor of "Mining Our Own Business," is vice chairman of the Alaskan Independence Party, and boy does he look the part. Wisconsin native Clark, who plays Santa Claus in the sun-starved Alaskan Decembers, came to Alaska in 1973 to work on the pipeline and "get rich quick." He didn't get rich but he stayed. He and his wife, Lynette, "Yukon Yonda," live in Fox, ten miles outside Fairbanks. He is the only delegate with clothes fastened by reindeer buttons.

Clark reaches into his pocket and fishes out five gold nuggets, one shaped like Pegasus. My daughter, then twelve, is delighted; she has met a real Alaskan. At the conference, Clark recites a Robert Service poem ("Yellow") about a man who watches another shoot a dog. In conversation, he quotes the unlikely duo of Mahatma Gandhi and Ayn Rand, but then incongruities, even mesalliances, pervade the weekend.

Like the other delegates—and like most Americans before the First World War—Clark thinks of himself as a citizen of his state and not of the USA! USA! "Name a country," he says. "If I go there and they ask me where I'm from, I say, 'Alaska.' I see a smile. If I say 'the United States,' I get . . . the glare."

"Statehood for Alaska and Hawai'i had been an integral part of the Cold War," wrote historian John S. Whitehead in *Completing the Union* (2004), his thorough account of the transformation of these two far-flung territories from "Cold War defense installations" into states forty-nine and fifty.[14] These territories were pawns in a geopolitical game, and after half a century of being pushed around the board, the pawns are restless. Disputes with Washington over matters from oil extraction to hunting point to a larger truth: People ought not to be ruled by a capital thirty-four hundred miles away. Alaskans want to be "masters in our home," says Clark. In the late 1970s he attended a rally of Alaskans for Independence, which in time begat the Alaskan Independence Party. The party's history is as colorful as you would expect: Its founder, gold miner Joe Vogler, was murdered in 1993 under circumstances that remain contested. Ambitious lawyers seldom vie for the AIP gubernatorial nomination; typical was the 2006 ticket, which consisted of a native chief and a reindeer herder. In 2008 former AIP member Todd Palin's wife ran for vice president of the United States, though Sarah shed the vestments of Alaskan independence as quickly as John McCain had shed his crippled first wife.

Statehood for Alaska and Hawaii never made sense in a republic: Their admission violated the contiguous integrity of the Lower 48. But the opposition to stitching stars forty-nine and fifty to Old Glory came only from a handful of Southern Democrats, Taft Republicans, and independent liberals. Representative Woodrow Jones (D-NC) raised the specter of empire: "If Hawaii is admitted, the next step will be Alaska, and after these will come Puerto Rico, the Virgin Islands, Guam, Wake Island, and on down the line. Where is the line to be drawn? Where shall we stop? Shall we spread the American States over two or three continents? Have we learned nothing from the lessons of the old Roman Empire?"[15]

Ku Ching, a native Hawaiian, speaks in Burlington on behalf of independence for the Aloha State. "We're not for secession," he says, "because we feel we were never in the United States." Queen Liliuokalani was deposed in 1893 by a US-backed coup, and in 1898 the erstwhile Kingdom of Hawaii was annexed—illegally, contend the Hawaiian patriots, because it was by resolution rather than treaty. (Allow me to venerate my fellow Upstater, President Grover Cleveland, perhaps the most formidable anti-imperialist ever to occupy the White House. Cleveland said that he was "ashamed" of the subterfuge and shenanigans of the Hawaii-coveting presidents Benjamin Harrison and William McKinley.)

Hawaii became an exotic garrison of the aborning American Empire. Statehood came in 1959, and with it Jack Lord and many bad jokes about getting lei'd. Dreams of an independent Hawaii, it seemed, had sunk at Pearl Harbor. But a rejuvenescent independence movement centered in the native population gained momentum when in 1993 the US Congress apologized for the theft of the islands a century earlier. (As Ku Ching speaks, a Southern delegate interjects, "They apologized but they didn't give it back.")

Deploring a colonial economy based on "militarism and tourism," Ku Ching explains that Hawaiian patriots are "pro-peace, antiwar, and anti-violence." They differ on the form of government that a free Hawaii might take: Some prefer a constitutional republic, others the restoration of a queen. But that is a decision best reserved for Hawaiians, not politicians five time zones distant.

Donnie Kennedy asks Ku Ching the question that he is no doubt asked daily himself: "How would people who do not look like you be treated" in an independent Hawaii?

Ku Ching replies, "The Hawaiian kingdom was never a racial kingdom. We welcomed people of all nations. 'Aloha,' the genuine kind, says that if you want to, you and I can be brothers."

Amity: a horror to some but not to these divisors.

Thomas Naylor suspects that the outposts of resource-rich Alaska and strategically located Hawaii are the last states Washington would ever let go. Give up oil and the Pacific? Not on your conscript son's life! Vermont, on the other hand, is so lacking in the sort of strategic assets that register with Serious Men that its absence, while slicing a piece of the American soul, would mean nothing to the bottom line. The dispatch of US troops to fight another Battle of Bennington seems unlikely, and as for the effectiveness of US economic sanctions on an independent Vermont, "Canada did not honor the anti-Cuba embargo and would not honor a Vermont embargo," says Naylor. An independent Vermont, he believes, need be no more heavily armed than army-less Liechtenstein or Costa Rica. For legitimate defense needs, the Vermont Guard, freed of its "national" obligations in distant places, would suffice.

～◎～

The crimes and follies of the Bush-Cheney administration boosted their fortunes on the left, admit secessionists, just as the statist lunges of Barack Obama energized independence sentiment on the right, but no matter which party lays claim to leviathan, the case for radical devolution loses none of its cogency. The problem with the United States is one of scale, and it cannot be solved simply by electing new or different or better people to public offices. As Donald Livingston says, "The public corporation known as the United States has simply grown too large for the purposes of self-government, in the same way that a committee of 300 people would be too large for the purposes of a committee. There needs to be a public debate on the out-of-scale character of the regime and what can be done about it."[16]

The average congressional district now contains 647,000 persons. And this is the "people's house," thought by the Founders to be the most responsive and grassroots of federal institutions. How is anything like representative government possible on such an enormous and impersonal scale?

Decentralizing power would have the additional virtue of localizing those coalition splitters known as "social issues." Case in point: When one of the Southern delegates at the Burlington conference calls abortion a heinous crime, I sit back to watch the fireworks. The sparklers are doused in the fresh waters of federalism. There is general agreement on a mind-your-own-damn-business principle. If Marin County wants to serve joints with school lunches and Tupelo, Mississippi, wants the Ten Commandments in the classroom, well, that's up to the people of Marin and Tupelo. Ain't none of my business. Yours, either.

"I detest homosexuality," says Donnie Kennedy over lunch in gay-friendly Burlington, but if other states—or nations—wish to grant marriage licenses to homosexual couples, he has no objection. (One suspects, however, that the independent South of Kennedy's dream might well refurbish the closet—setting off, perhaps, a second Battle of New Orleans.)

Let Utah be Utah, and let San Francisco be San Francisco. The policy will drive busybodies mad with frustration, but for the rest of us, it just might be the beginning of tolerance.

There is no reason why this kind of hands-off mutuality requires secession—they didn't used to call the US system "federalism" for nothing—but the urge to intervene is so irresistible to noxious nannies and moralizing marplots that states and cities and towns have been deprived of the right to make their own laws, shaped by local circumstances, on such matters as the legality of marijuana and abortion and the proper way (if any) to define marriage. Does anyone really think that the Christian Right or feminist Left will ever agree to de-nationalize such issues and trust local people to make their own laws?

Trust local people. That, really, is the soul of the case for secession. Bringing it all back home, as a small-town Minnesota boy who took the name of Bob Dylan once titled an album. For home is where secession must be rooted. Ideology of any sort is not so much a dead end as it is a road without end that carries the enthusiast far from anyplace resembling home. It unmoors him, it leaves her without anchorage, quick to blame societal ills on outsiders, on dark alien forces. I know: We lived through eight years of the bloody and dark Bush Octennium. If Dick Cheney isn't a dark alien force I don't know what is. But a healthy secessionist movement must be founded in love: love of a particular place, its people (of all ethnicities and colors), its culture, its language and books and music and baseball teams, and, yes, its beer and flowers and punk rock clubs.

The wine flowed at the Burlington conference's concluding banquet, and your author, I am afraid, drank freely of the vine. (It ought to have been, but was not, a Vermont vintage. But then chain hotels tend not to pay attention to such things.)

Maybe the Burlington conference was a sideshow, an amusing tour of the more outré precincts of American politics. But I think it was a harbinger. The delegates ratified a "Burlington Declaration" that echoed the Declaration of Independence in asserting, "Any political entity has the right to separate itself from a larger body of which it is a part and peaceably to establish its independence as a free and legitimate state in the eyes of the world."

Jason Sorens, a political scientist at SUNY Buffalo, while acknowledging that the dis-United States are not in the immediate offing, urged the delegates to "move ahead with political party infrastructure to have it in place" in case of an upsurge of separationist sentiment. (He instances the Scottish National Party, which for years ran candidates without hope of winning but today is Scotland's second largest party.) Sorens has run a regression analysis to determine "the predicted secessionist vote share" in the states and territories. Puerto Rico and Alaska top the list; no other place is even close, though Hawaii and Texas are a distant third and fourth.

As a Yale graduate student, Sorens founded the Free State Project, a plan to move twenty thousand libertarians to New Hampshire. Eight thousand have made the pledge, but only five hundred have moved, and the disabling flaw in the plan is that it elevates ideology over place. Jason Sorens is an impressive scholar, and I like him. I like libertarians, too. Hell, I'm one myself, more or less. But if I were a Granite Mountain Boy and saw twenty thousand libertarians massing 'long the Monadnock I'd grab the flintlock, bar the door, and barricade myself in for a *Night of the Living Dead* siege. (The Free Staters take no position on secession, though a faction thereof desires an independent Republic of New Hampshire.)

"And the movement now begins," announced Sale at the banquet. They agreed to meet again next year, perhaps in the South. (In Chattanooga, as it turned out.) Sale wanted to put secession "on the national agenda as a legitimate thing to think about."

Think what you will. This is radicalism deep-dyed in the American grain. "The military-industrial-energy-media complex is running an empire on the ruins of the republic," said Rob Williams, who does not think that simply putting Democratic hands on the levers of power solves anything. It's the levers themselves that have to be removed.

Would the union miss Vermont? Sure. But as a young John Quincy Adams said, "I love the Union as I love my wife. But if my wife should ask for and insist upon a separation, she should have it, though it broke my heart."[17]

Besides, Vermont's not going anywhere. Even if she were to secede, the Green Mountains will not be moved, the sap will still flow, the novels of Howard Frank Mosher and Dorothy Canfield Fisher will remain. Hell, even Ben & Jerry's will keep dishing it out. But why shouldn't Vermonters run Vermont? Why should President Barack Obama or Senator John McCain have even a whisper of a say in how Vermont orders her affairs?

"I want to leave my country," said Kirk Sale, "without leaving my home." That line packed a jolt, at least for this Little American. I'm not sure what I think about that. But isn't it time that we gave the matter some thought?

Cards on the table, shall we? I am Genesee County, New York, to the marrow. My politics are localist, decentralist, libertarian. I am wholeheartedly in favor of such states as New York and California birthing smaller states wherein democratic self-government might better be practiced. I am a patriot of the old contiguous forty-eight, so I would eagerly bid adieu to Alaska and Hawaii (and of course Puerto Rico). As for Vermont . . . well, I'm an American sentimentalist so I'd want to keep Upstate New York in the union, but I'd not lift a finger to keep neighbor states from going their own way. Thus the paradox within this book: We need more states—and we need fewer states as well.

I have a deep and abiding love for these United States, unlike Sale and Naylor. If I see a little flag blown off a soldier's gravestone when I walk past the Pine Hill cemetery every morn, I replace it, or fold it tenderly. The flag is not a rag, as Jack Kerouac would angrily declare when Ginsberg or one of his hippie friends was fooling with Old Glory. I believe that, too. I sing along with the Star-Spangled Banner and my favorite patriotic verse, "America the Beautiful." (But not "God Bless America," which after 9/11 became a kind of second-string national anthem. It is tuneless and its banal lyrics say nothing about America.)

Hell, I even have a soft spot for Abraham Lincoln—not the War

President, but the wrestler of Jack Armstrong, the awkward and tentative wooer of Mary Todd, the gutsy Illinois congressman denouncing the Mexican War. My Lincoln is an amalgam of fact and fiction, of myth and speeches, of Henry Fonda and Gore Vidal and Billy Herndon and Raymond Massey and Walt Whitman and David Herbert Donald and, yes, I confess, Carl Sandburg. In the eternal flame department, I'll take Ann Rutledge over Durie Malcolm any day.

The camp guards of contemporary politics will tell you that secession is based in fear or isolation. I say it flows from love and from hopefulness, from the belief that ordinary people, living in cohesive communities, can govern themselves, without the heavy hand of distant experts and tank-and-bomb-wielding statesmen to guide their way. The secession of which I write with (sometimes qualified) admiration is Norman Mailer in love with Brooklyn, native Hawaiians hearing ancestral echoes, Vermonters who think that Robert Frost and George Aiken are wiser men than Barack Obama and Joe Biden. There are, sitting beady-eyed before their computers, a few "secessionists" whose goad is hatred; they want to separate as a means of saving the white race, or La Raza, or pure Hawaiian blood, or whatever their ethnic obsession happens to be. I don't write about them. Life is too short to waste words on assholes. Moreover, political secession in America is an expression of a community of shared geography, which the race-crazed certainly are not.

Secession is blowing in the wind. Sale and Naylor count at least twenty-eight US secessionist movements active everywhere from Alaska and Hawaii to Staten Island and Queens.

Will America go fission? Is there any reason not to?

More Thomas Jefferson than Jefferson Davis: A Brief and Digressive History of Secession That Is Not Tinctured in Shades of Gray

*N*orman Mailer, the novelist and pugilist whose 1969 campaign for mayor of New York City was the most articulate and pugnacious and inspiring secession episode of the twentieth century, called himself a "left conservative." He was not playing the goofy juxtaposition game. Rather, Mailer acknowledged that "the Left has been absolutely right on some critical problems of our times, and the conservatives have been altogether correct about one enormous matter—which is that the federal government has no business whatever in local affairs."[1]

We shall revisit Mr. Mailer in chapter 2, but for now we take his point that secession is neither left nor right but a vivifying amalgam of both. Or maybe it is a refreshing embrace of neither. One cannot, after all, stand on two feet while listing badly to either side.

From Greenwich Village to Canarsie, Mailer preached the righteousness of local self-government to bemused urban leftists, who were not always receptive audiences. "Radicals seem forever unable to understand that states' rights can be invoked and honored to create a Socialist community as well as to defend slavery (or other conservative and reactionary objectives)," wrote William Appleman Williams, exasperation rising from the page.[2] So wed has the modern left been to centralized authority that it hesitates to use the most efficacious tools at hand to Fight the Power on a variety of fronts, from the deployment of oxymoronical state National Guards to desert sands to the federal nullification of state drug laws.

In the 1990s, inspired by the magnificent dissolution of the Soviet Empire, Americans started asking hard but edifying questions about self-determination for places as diverse as Northern California, West Kansas, and Upstate New York. These corners of America were not seeking to leave the country. Instead, they wanted to redeem certain American promises whose redemption was not possible for citizens in, say, Yreka (population seven thousand), in a California of thirty-five-million-plus people.

Establishment liberals and empire-minded conservatives—which is to say the entire spectrum of permissible opinion in the land of the fee—were not amused. Secession, lectured Peter Overby of *Common Cause*, "leads down a dead-end alley, falsely promising escape from a world plagued by lousy schools, higher taxes, rising crime and racial tensions." The compulsively coercive communitarian sociologist Amitai Etzioni said that secessionists "selfishly promote a smaller community."[3] Only a man who is part of no community at all would use such phraseology.

Yet if the captive nations of the Eastern Bloc could throw off centralized tyranny, why not Chemung County, New York? The Soviet Constitution had provided that "each Union Republic shall retain the right freely to secede from the USSR." This was the meaningless paper guarantee to end all meaningless paper guarantees, but the fifteen Soviet republics did indeed secede in 1990–91. Gorbachev was no Abe Lincoln, that's for sure. Lithuanians are forever grateful.

Somehow the fact that Latvia and Estonia and the Soviet Muslim-stans *seceded* from the USSR never quite penetrated the American dome. After all, secession is *bad*. Besides, other red devils had learned well the lessons of the Civil War. Zhu Rongii, Chinese premier, responding to a question about China's intentions toward Taiwan at an April 8, 1999, press conference with President Clinton, said, "Abraham Lincoln, in order to maintain the unity of the United States . . . resorted to the use of force . . . so, I think, Abraham Lincoln, president, is a model, is an example."[4] *That* is a jujitsu master.

Secession may be an act of desperation but at its best it is animated by passion and enlivened by wit. For what good is ever accomplished without laughter and joy? Grave ideologues and humorless commissars of acceptable thought will never be among secession's constituency. They are the prison guards keeping the rabble from watering the tree of liberty with the blood of tyrants, in Mr. Jefferson's sanguinary and sanguine image.

We are a country born in secession against a distant colonial power. The

Declaration of Independence asserts that "Governments are instituted among Men, deriving their just Powers from the Consent of the Governed," and that "whenever any Form of Government becomes destructive of these Ends, it is the Right of the People to alter or to abolish it." This does not imply the perpetuity of established states; should a government commit "a long Train of Abuses and Usurpations," the people have not only the right but the duty to throw it off.

To secede means to withdraw. It is not self-effacement; the seceding party does not disappear. It simply removes itself from an arrangement it no longer finds satisfactory and sets up another.

While the Constitution does not expressly forbid the secession of a state from the union, it doesn't make a provision for breaking away, either. The Berlin-born legal scholar Francis Lieber told the people of his adopted state of South Carolina in 1851 that the "absence of all mention of secession" in the Constitution "must be explained on the same ground on which the omission of parricide in the first Roman penal laws was explained—no one thought of such a deed."[5] Perhaps. Or maybe the entrance into a compact implies the right of exit, which need not be codified.

Thus the legal confusion, not to mention carnage, of 1861, when the Civil War erupted over the South's desire to secede—in order, it must be said, to protect slavery. Happily for the future states of West New York and Jefferson, however, Article IV, Section 3, of the US Constitution makes state partition a straightforward affair:

> New states may be admitted by the Congress into this union;
> but no new state shall be formed or erected within the jurisdic-
> tion of any other state; nor any state be formed by the junction
> of two or more states, or parts of states, without the consent of
> the legislatures of the states concerned as well as the Congress.

Four states have been formed in this way: Vermont out of New York, Kentucky out of Virginia, Maine out of Massachusetts, and, most recently, West Virginia, which was sliced from the Old Dominion in 1863. The birth of West Virginia was problematic, if illuminating. Shall we take a quick spin down those country roads toward Almost Heaven?

The western part of Virginia, mountainous and inhospitable to slavery, was conservative unionist territory. Neither abolitionist nor secessionist, its "peasantry of the West" had voted by a margin of about three to one against the Virginia Ordinance of Secession.[6] (The margin of rejection was closer—34,000 to 19,000—in the counties, not all of them northwestern, that eventually made up the state of West Virginia.)

Western Virginia unionists organized a ramshackle government and sent representatives and senators to the US Congress, which recognized them as the rightful delegates from Virginia. The mountaineers petitioned Washington for admission as a new state. The proposed boundaries were highly questionable: Half the counties of what became West Virginia had supported the secession ordinance and therefore belonged in the Confederate State of Virginia.

Attorney General Edward Bates advised President Lincoln that the creation of West Virginia was clearly unconstitutional, for the legislature of Virginia had not given its consent. Thaddeus Stevens, the South-hating Pennsylvania Radical Republican who got off one of the all-time deathbed lines ("It is not my appearance but my disappearance that troubles me"[7]), agreed with Attorney General Bates but supported admission: "I say then that we may admit West Virginia as a new state, not by virtue of any provision of the Constitution but under our absolute power which the *laws of war* give us. I shall vote for this bill upon that theory and upon that alone, for I will not stultify myself by supposing that we have any warrant in the Constitution for this proceeding."[8]

The "absolute power which the laws of war give us": Muzak to imperial ears! War is a warrant—a limitless warrant. Abraham Lincoln took the Stevens view. When bullets fly, constitutional niceties go with them. "The division of a state is dreaded as a precedent," explained the president—but why? Two states instead of one made sense. Surely God intended West Virginia, else He would not have put the Allegheny Mountains betwixt it and Virginia. Moreover, if Virginia's rebellion against the union were successful, its western counties would have been transferred, against their will, into a confederacy to which they had not given their assent.

"It is said that the admission of West Virginia," wrote President Lincoln, "is secession, and tolerated only because it is our secession. [Undeniably true, by the way.] Well, if we call it by that name, there is still difference enough between secession against the constitution, and secession in favor of the constitution."[9] This is Abe at his most, ah, flexible.

West Virginia came into the union as the thirty-fifth state on June 20, 1863, "the bastard child of a political rape" as former Virginia governor and Confederate general Henry A. Wise crudely observed.[10] It wasn't pretty, but if mountaineers could do it, why not Yoopers and other outnumbered outliers today?

Contra Lincoln, the scission of states is a profound affirmation of the American ideal of local self-government. Bigness is just not compatible with self-rule. Thomas Jefferson wrote James Monroe in 1786: "Considering the American character in general . . . a State of such extent as one hundred and sixty thousand square miles [roughly the size of California] would soon crumble into little ones."[11] That California, for example, has not crumbled suggests a sorry decline in the "American character in general" to which Jefferson adverted.

Now, as for states leaving altogether . . .

Just what is so eternal about the American union anyway? As Paul C. Nagel wrote in his study of the idea of union in antebellum America, "What Americans of the late eighteenth century considered to be simply one means for confronting common problems gradually became an end, an ultimate, an embodiment of society."[12] Union began as a strategic imperative. It became, in President Lincoln's seraphic design, a perpetual design to be preserved by "the better angels of our nature."

Nary a cherubim had been present three-quarters of a century earlier at Independence Hall in Philadelphia. The undying and indivisible nature of the American union was not a subject anyone at all dwelled upon during the Constitutional Convention of 1787, when fifty-five delegates convened to revise the Articles of Confederation—the first American constitution, the "firm league of friendship" that the thirteen American states had formed during the Revolution—but scrapped the Articles altogether in favor of the Constitution, which Patrick Henry called "the most fatal plan that could possibly be conceived to enslave a free people."[13] The brilliant and bibulous Maryland delegate Luther Martin, appalled at the consolidationist scheme offered by James Madison and the Virginians, said that "he had rather see partial confederacies take place, than the plan on the table."[14]

Madison replied that partial confederacies or a "total separation" from one another "would be truly deplorable, & those who might be accessory to either, could never be forgiven by their Country, nor by themselves." Piling on, New York's Alexander Hamilton added that one consequence of "a dissolution of the Union" would be a North America forever at war with itself, as its various confederacies made alliances with rival European powers.[15] As if to validate Hamilton, Gunning Bedford of Delaware warned the larger states that unless they acquiesced in the matter of equal representation of states in the national legislature, "the small ones will find some foreign ally of more honor and good faith, who will take them by the hand and do them justice."[16]

A North America of two or more confederacies was not regarded on all hands as a dread eventuality to be avoided at all costs, but the overwhelming sentiment of the Constitutional Convention was for a union of the thirteen states as well as the inevitable western additions. The matter of a state withdrawing from the union was never brought up in Philadelphia. Yet to assert the union's perpetuity would have seemed risibly presumptuous. As Richard Weaver wrote of the states, "Had they been told they were entering a door which could never be opened again, it is questionable whether a single one would have entered."[17]

Nathaniel Gorham of Massachusetts, an advocate of the new Constitution, conceded that "the States as now confederated have no doubt a right to refuse to be consolidated, or to be formed into any new system." He hoped they would see the light and come together, but such linkage could hardly be expected to last until the end of time. He asked the Constitutional Convention on August 8, 1787, "Can it be supposed that this vast Country including the Western territory will 150 years hence remain one nation?"[18] Impossible! Surely the continent would fracture into republics of a manageable size; no leviathan could span the endless America. It did remain one nation, of course—but at the cost of half a million dead.

The state conventions ratifying the document were filled with skeptical Anti-Federalists who thought the scale of the new government was all wrong. Melancton Smith, the pseudonymous "Federal Farmer" who in a series of essays warned his countrymen against the adoption of the new Constitution, pleaded with the New York ratifying convention of 1788 to consider "the impracticability of governing a free people on such an extensive plan. In a country where a portion of the people live more than twelve hundred miles from the centre, I think that one body cannot possibly legislate for the whole."[19] Yet Smith would not have broken up the union; rather, he favored a gentle confederation similar to the one that had existed under the Articles.

I suppose I am one of the handful of extant Americans who has read through not only the variorum accounts of the Constitutional Convention of 1787 (by James Madison, Robert Yates, and John Lansing) but also the entire five volumes of *The Debates in the Several State Conventions on the Adoption of the Federal Constitution* (1827), edited by Jonathan Elliot. (I did so while writing a biography of my favorite besotted Anti-Federalist, published in 2008 as *Forgotten Founder, Drunken Prophet: The Life of Luther Martin*. Surely you have committed it to memory.)

I slipped back into 1787–88 expecting that I would find, among other things, abundant confirmation of my anti-nationalist prejudices. Surely Madison, et al., envisioned these United States as a compact, created by the states and dissolvable by those same states when, as Jefferson wrote in 1776, the regnant "form of government becomes destructive."

I found no such thing. The convention of 1787, which with equal accuracy might be termed the counterrevolution of 1787, established a unitary national state with federal features. Madison and the Framers did not believe the Union to be a compact of equal sovereign states that reserved the right to withdraw from that compact at any time and for reasons of their choosing. Except for the Anti-Federalist dissenters in Philadelphia (notably Martin) and at the ratifying conventions, the consensus among those who wrote and ratified the document was that the states were clearly subordinate to the national government.

We will find precious little support for multiple confederacies in the ranks of the Federalist winners of that first and defining contest over the shape of the American republic. Hark, instead, to the losers. To George Mason, for instance, oft-credited as the father of the Bill of Rights, who in the Virginia ratifying convention asked with incredulity, "Does any man suppose that one general national government can exist in so extensive a country as this?"[20] Or listen to Patrick Henry, who in that same convention declared: "A great deal is said about disunion, and consequent dangers. I have no claim to a greater share of fortitude than others; but I can see no kind of danger."[21]

If Northern states combined into one confederacy, and Southern states did likewise, so be it. Why should Virginia declare war upon Pennsylvania just because they do not answer to the same central authority? And why should Pennsylvania have any say whatsoever over the laws under which Virginians live?

Henry and Mason suited up for the losing team, but the vote for ratification in the Virginia convention was a tantalizingly close 89–79. As in Massachusetts, North Carolina, New York, New Hampshire, and Rhode Island, the Constitution's opponents were almost as numerous as its supporters.

From the start, there were doubts and challenges to the irrefrangibility of the union. As the great toponymist George R. Stewart wrote in *Names on the Land* (1945), "The very plurality of States . . . was a standing suggestion that what had once been united could equally well be taken apart; in the very name, the seeds of nullification and secession lay hidden."[22]

The prospect of a President Thomas Jefferson roused in some New England Federalists the republic's first real secessionist reveries. "I wish the Northern States would separate from the Southern, the moment that event [Jefferson's election] shall take effect," wrote Connecticut lieutenant governor Oliver Wolcott Sr. in 1796.[23] He was echoed by a correspondent in the *Hartford Courant*, who insisted that "the Northern States can subsist as a Nation, as a Republic without any connection with the Southern."[24]

Jefferson was not elected in 1796; John Adams was, and he made Massachusetts hash of the First Amendment with his Alien and Sedition Acts. Under the Sedition Act, a man who wisecracked when President Adams was saluted by cannonfire that he wished the "wadding might hit the President's backsides" was arrested and fined $100. Congressman Matthew Lyon of Vermont was thrown in jail for four months for saying that Adams had "an unbounded thirst for ridiculous pomp, foolish adulation, or selfish avarice."[25] (Lyon was an interesting case. A "localist par excellence," in his biographer's words, Lyon's Vermont First sentiments had led him to oppose absorption into the union in 1790–91.[26] He was reelected to Congress easily from his jail cell in 1798.)

This high-handed pseudoroyalism was not what the Revolution had been fought for. Who was John Adams to think that his ass was sacrosanct? You might think that this called for the American Civil Liberties Union, but remember that America *was* a civil liberties union.

Defiance of Adams's Alien and Sedition Acts led Thomas Jefferson and James Madison to ghost, respectively, the Kentucky and Virginia Resolutions of 1798. As Jefferson wrote in the former, "whensoever the General Government assumes undelegated powers, its acts are unauthoritative, void, and of no force."[27] Jefferson was not enjoining secession but rather nullification, the last best option for a state unwilling to prostrate itself beneath the national boot heel. It is a measure of Jefferson's timelessness that state-level activists in 2010 are exhuming nullification as a way to thwart the feds from sending state guardsmen and -women to Afghanistan, disarming citizens, and otherwise trampling old liberties into dust.

By 1798 rumor had Virginia and North Carolina ready to buck the "domination" of the New England states by creating their own confederacy.[28] Vice President Jefferson, writing on the sly to his fellow Virginia agrarian John Taylor on June 4, 1798, admitted that the Old Dominion was "compleatly under the saddle of Massachusetts & Connecticut," which "ride us very hard, cruelly insulting our feelings as well as exhausting our strength and substance." But he counseled patience, not disunion, and made this trenchant criticism of secession: "If on a temporary superiority of the one party, the other is to resort to a scission of the union, no federal government can ever exist. If to rid ourselves of the present rule of Massachusetts & Connecticut, we break the union, will the evil stop there? Suppose the N. England states alone cut off, will our natures be changed? Are we not men still to the south of that, & with all the passions of men? Immediately we shall see a Pennsylvania & a Virginia party arise in the residuary confederacy, and the public mind will be distracted with the same party spirit.

"A little patience," Jefferson advised, "and we shall see the reign of witches pass over."[29]

It did. And Federalists and Adams men would find Jefferson to be just as odious a tyrant as the Jeffersonians had found Adams to be. The new boss is ever the same as the old boss.

Jefferson lost no sleep over a bisected America. "The future inhabitants of the Atlantic and Missipi [*sic*] states will be our sons," he wrote John C. Breckinridge on August 12, 1803. "We leave them in distinct but bordering establishments. We think we see their happiness in their union, & we wish it. Events may prove it otherwise; and if they see their interest in separation, why should we take side with our Atlantic rather than our Missipi descendants? It is the elder and the younger son differing. God bless them both, & keep them in union, if it be for their good, but separate them, if it be better."[30]

The historian Gordon Wood says of Jefferson: "At times he was remarkably indifferent to the possibility that a western confederacy might break away from the eastern United States."[31] Que sera sera. If they go they go. "Those of the western confederacy will be as much our children & descendants as those of the eastern," he wrote to Joseph Priestley in 1804.[32] The bonds of kinship and culture were far stronger than political ties.

If Jefferson, with his adoration of liberty and parti pris for the parts of republic against the whole, was temperamentally and intellectually inclined to provincial resistance, the buckram sons of Puritan New England were no less so.

Sour, splenetic, headstrong Timothy Pickering, secretary of state under Presidents Washington and Adams and inflexible Federalist senator from Massachusetts during what he regarded as the Jefferson disaster, was at the vortex of the storm. Poor Pickering has not proved a favorite of historians. Edward Payson Powell, for instance, says that Pickering was "always careful to be on the wrong side" and was also "the only member of an American cabinet who ever died in his bed that deserved to be hanged."[33] (You must recall that Powell wrote before Janet "The Witch of Waco" Reno and Donald Rumsfeld, maestro of shock and awe.)

Here is Senator Pickering writing to federal judge Richard Peters on December 24, 1803: "Although the end of all our Revolutionary labors and expectations is disappointment, and our fond hopes of republican happiness are vanity, and the real patriots of '76 are overwhelmed by the modern pretenders to that character, I will not yet despair: I will rather anticipate a new confederacy, exempt from the corrupt and corrupting influence and oppression of the aristocratic Democrats of the South. There will be— and our children at farthest will see it—a separation. The white and black population will mark the boundary. The British Provinces, even with the assent of Britain, will become members of the Northern confederacy."[34] Submit to mud-spattered slavocrats? Never!

Pickering writes former senator George Cabot, a Massachusetts Federalist, on January 29, 1804, to complain that Jefferson is wrecking the republic. The Wretch of Monticello even has the gall to remove Federalist appointees from sinecures! Pickering will take no more: "And must we with folded hands wait the result, or timely think of other protection? This is a delicate subject. The principles of our Revolution point to the remedy,—a separation. That this can be accomplished, and without spilling one drop of blood, I have little doubt . . . The people of the East cannot reconcile their habits, views, and interests with those of the South and West . . . I do not believe in the practicability of a long-continued union. A Northern confederacy would unite congenial characters, and present a fairer prospect of public happiness; while the Southern States, having a similarity of habits, might be left 'to manage their own affairs in their own way.' If a separation were to take place, our mutual wants would render a friendly and commercial intercourse inevitable. The Southern States would require the naval protection of the Northern Union, and the products of the former would be important to the navigation and commerce of the latter . . . But *when* and *how* is a separation to be effected? . . . It must begin in Massachusetts. The proposition would be welcomed in Connecticut; and could we doubt of New Hampshire? But New York must be associated; and how is her concurrence to be obtained? She must be made the centre of the confederacy. Vermont and New Jersey would follow of course, and Rhode Island of necessity."[35]

Pickering introduces an uncharacteristic note of hesitancy at the end of his letter. "Are these ideas visionary or impracticable? Do they not merit consideration?" Well of course they do, Terrible Tim. Cabot, while not favorable to Pickering's plan, admits that "a separation at some period not very remote may probably take place."[36]

Pickering became a proselyte, spreading the good news of sectional divorce, which he insisted would be amicable. To Theodore Lyman he writes on February 11, 1804, that "all the advantages which have been for a few years depending on the general Union would be continued to its respective portions, without the jealousies and enmities which now afflict both, and which peculiarly embitter the condition of that of the North. It is not unusual for two friends, when disagreeing about the mode of conducting a common concern, to separate, and manage each in his own way his separate interest, and thereby preserve a useful friendship, which without such separation would infallibly be destroyed."[37]

A friendly separation based on mutual respect, even love: how deliciously incongruous that the choleric Pickering understood that affection can breed secession.

Not that Pickering was a fountain of love. His hatred of Jefferson, whom he compares to a "Parisian revolutionary monster," was so all-consuming it's a wonder he had time to eat, drink, shave, or piss. But he operates out of more than pettiness. He is a patriot of his state and region, concerned with their survival in a union soon to be dominated by the South and West. "How many Indian wars, excited by the avidity of the Western and Southern States for Indian lands, shall we have to encounter, and who will pay the millions to support them?" he asks despairingly.[38]

Pickering was practical enough to include the Middle Atlantic states in his revised confederacy, with New York at its head, if not heart. He and his separationist Federalist colleagues feared democracy, the mob, and the slavocracy; and they were assuredly not Jeffersonian democrats. No one will nominate them for the libertarian hall of fame. But they had grasped, quite early, the absolute necessity of devolution if these United States were not to become a ravening and militarized unitary state, dangerous to other nations and oppressive to the liberties of its own people.

Despite the 1804 prediction of Senator James Hillhouse (F-CT) that the United States, bloated beyond recognition by the constitutionally dubious Louisiana Purchase of President Jefferson, "would soon form two distinct and separate governments," the anti-purchase New England Federalists were weak and in no real position to press the point.[39] But the point was indisputably pressable. Writes Edward Payson Powell: "It must be borne in mind that not once in the plotting of 1803–4 was the right of a State or of a group of States to secede questioned."[40]

It fell to Jefferson's saddle sore Aaron Burr to give separation the taint of disloyalty. The demonization of Aaron Burr, the suave New York descendant of Jonathan Edwards, vice president under Thomas Jefferson, murderer of Alexander Hamilton (twenty years too late!), and would-be emperor of the West, which he dreamed of detaching from the United States, has been two centuries in the making. Despite Gore Vidal's exercise in high wit and patriotic reclamation in his 1973 novel *Burr*, he remains, in the popular mind—to the extent that such antediluvian characters as Burr remain even motes in that mind—a scoundrel. His prime crime? Encouraging "the country west of the [Appalachian] mountains to seek a separation from the Atlantic States in a peaceable and constitutional manner," as Burr's associate (or dupe) Harman Blennerhassett, the incestuous Irish immigrant who lived on an island in the Ohio River with his niece, wrote in 1806 in the *Ohio Gazette*.[41] Some dared call this treason.

The ragtag army of insurgents Burr may or may not have put together was wholly incapable of effecting such a separation. Nothing came of Burr's plotting, and at his treason trial the sly old Anti-Federalist tosspot Luther Martin spat back the government's feeble case like a mouthful of 3.2 beer and won for his rapscallion client the grimacing verdict of not guilty "by any evidence submitted to us."

Burr's Western Empire came a cropper, so secession talk returned to its natural home, its ancestral hotbed, New England.

As the trade embargoes imposed by the Jefferson and Madison administrations in response to British depredations on the high seas bottled up marine commerce, New England's voices of protest grew clamant. Timothy Pickering wrote Edward Pennington on July 12, 1812: "I would preserve the Union of the States, if possible . . . [Say what?] . . . To my ears there is no magic in the sound of Union. [That's more like it.] If the great objects of union are utterly abandoned,—much more, if they are wantonly, corruptly, and treacherously sacrificed by the Southern and Western States,—let the Union be severed. Such a severance presents no terrors to me."[42] His disunionism flares as the bombs burst in air. He writes George Logan on July 4, 1813: "I believe an immediate separation would be a real blessing to the 'good old thirteen States,' as John Randolph once called them."[43]

Correspondents in the Middle States, too, entertained such notions. Maryland Federalist A. C. Hanson, already sick and tired of growth, wrote Pickering that with "the creation of so many new States," he had "become heartily sick of the Union. For my part, I say without reserve that *the Union was long ago dissolved*; and I never thought it criminal to compass a dismemberment of the States, although we have been educated with that belief."[44]

I pile quote upon quote not to try the patience of the reader—I do appreciate you sticking with me, and when this chapter's done it's local beers and beef jerky for the house—but rather to demonstrate that secession is as American as the sacrifice bunt, and that it is of Yankee conception, if not immaculate then at least wholly untainted at birth by the smear of racism.

Let us now choose as our cicerone from Hartford to Eternity that rara avis: an unjustly obscure Massachusetts man. (They write the histories, you know. As the Upstate New York novelist Harold Frederic once had a character complain, "I cannot read or listen to the inflated accounts" of the role played in the Revolution by Massachusetts and Virginia "without smashing my pipe in wrath.")[45]

If you can know a man by his pseudonyms, then John Lowell (1769–1840) was worth knowing. The inveterate pamphleteer—during the War of 1812 there was seldom a moment when he didn't feel a discourse coming on—wrote as Yankee Farmer, a Friend to Peace, a Bostonian, a citizen of Massachusetts, a New England Farmer, an Old Farmer, a Massachusetts Lawyer, and Nobel-espirit. His primary sobriquet was the Rebel, but when in the grip of his Big Idea of 1813–14, he sometimes went by the superhero name of The Refederator. Others, undazzled, called him Crazy Jack.

He was the son of John "The Old Judge" Lowell, progenitor of the line that includes the poets James Russell and Amy and Robert Lowell; the eccentric discoverer of life—or at least canal-like lines—on Mars, Percival Lowell; and the Harvard president Lawrence Lowell, who thought the Rebel the most brilliant of his forebears. The family did not exactly swim in the pool of demos; as doggerel sometimes attributed to the Reverend Samuel Clarke Bushnell had it:

I come from good old Boston
The home of the bean and the cod
Where Cabots speak only to Lowells
And Lowells speak only to God[46]

The Rebel—oh, let's make like saucy washerwomen on Beacon Street and call him Crazy Jack—had a wider circle of speaking acquaintances than is contained in the Holy Trinity, but he was emphatic that it not include persons resident in states numbered fourteen and higher. For Crazy Jack was a union originalist.

The season of Crazy Jack's discontent began under President Jefferson, whose Louisiana Purchase, as he wrote in a letter of July 5, 1804, "had no merit in it whatsoever."[47] The embargoes of Presidents Jefferson and Madison he reviled, as he did Mr. Madison's War of 1812 and the conscript army raised to fight it. As if anticipating the Old Right historians of the late 1940s, Lowell titled one anti-Madison broadside "Perpetual War, the Policy of Mr. Madison." His words speak to us through the centuries: "From the moment war was declared those who had conscientiously opposed its declaration have the right, and to preserve consistency are bound, to endeavor to bring about a peace by showing the folly, the wickedness and the evils of the war."[48]

The Rebel never was more rebellious (his critics would say Crazy Jack never was crazier) than when, under the bucolic quill name "A Massachusetts Farmer," he published the verbosely titled "Thoughts in a Series of Letters, in Answer to a Question Respecting the Division of the States" (1813), in which he proposed, as one appalled historian writes, to "kick the West out of the Union!"[49]

The war with England, the embargo, the scuttling of maritime commerce—young America is under a "fatal spell . . . hurried along to destruction," writes Lowell. All is despondency; all is dolor. Look through any window and see "our frontier settlements drenched in the blood of its [*sic*] inhabitants; our commerce swept from the ocean; our merchants made bankrupt, while our seacoasts are blockaded from Rhode Island to the Mississippi." No one's getting fat except "army contractors, our navy agents, our military officers and salary men, together with a host of tidewaiters, pimps, and spies." Placemen and scamps have throttled "the farmer, the merchant, the tradesman, and the mechanic." What is to be done?

Divide to reconquer. Break up the union. But Crazy Jack emphasizes that "the division here advocated is not a division of the original thirteen United States. No; palsied be the hand that would attempt to hold the pen to effect so vile a purpose." (If a man uses not an exclamation point after that last sentence, he's never gonna use one.) What he is proposing, explains Lowell, "is a division of the illegitimate states beyond the Allegany mountains and Louisiana, which are adverse to our prosperity; whose interests, habits, and pursuits are diverse from ours and never can coalesce." Nice touch, that "illegitimate states." As if Ohio were a bastard to be cut on the street!

The growth spurt in the wake of Mr. Jefferson's purchase of Louisiana, asserts the Massachusetts Farmer, has found the Constitution inadequate to the task; one thinks of the Hulk bursting from his pitifully small human garments—buttons popped, sleeves torn. "The thirteen states are quite large enough for a republican government," announces Lowell.[50]

Toward the South he bears no animus, though he uncordially despises Madison, Jefferson, and "the peculiar institution," as euphemists once called slavery. He cherishes the "great variety of climate" of the original thirteen states, praising the "unbounded fisheries on the New England coast," which are productive of "a hardy race of men," and while he stints on Southern rhapsodies he does appreciate the "bread stuff" Southrons trade northward to sustain those hardy men of New England. The South bakes Yankees cakes. The regions are bound by mutual interest if not affection: "The south cannot say to the north, I have no need of thee, neither can the north say to the south, I have no need of thee; but each" acknowledges the "irresistible evidence that it was designed to constitute one great whole, and that any addition would be redundant, and any diminution would effect [*sic*] its symmetry."[51]

The handiwork of Providence is visible in the original design of the republic. The "stupendous mountains" to the west form a "national line of demarkation"—beyond them is barbarity and emptiness and "not an individual article that we want." The frontier families make their own clothing, distill their own spirits: leave them be, and they will make their way. Even if a few wretches in the East covet such items, the mountains are insurmountable. Cheaper it is to buy European. There would be no coming together in the future, either. The base of the western economy would be "agricultural and manufacturing," while New England (he has long since forgotten the Southern states in these essays) prospers by "maritime and commercial" pursuits. Lowell desires a navy to protect these interests; he suspects that frontiersmen will not wish to be mulcted by the tax collector to support a fleet of dreadnoughts.

But aside from the paucity of desirable goods in the West there is the matter of size. "A republican government," says Lowell, "the nature of which being mild, is much less calculated for a very extensive country than any other." (Arch-Federalist Lowell is here echoing the most cogent Anti-Federalist argument of 1787–88.) "A more despotic [government]," he continues, "where the remote parts are governed by viceroys or satraps, is better suited to such a vast territory; but in ours, where general opinion governs, it is necessary that the people should be less extended, and more enlightened, and that there should be some similarity in their manners, habits, and pursuits."[52]

Are these the foaming delusions of a crazy man? Or did the Rebel, stuck in the mud of Massachusetts, have a truly grounded understanding of the practical limits of the commonweal?

Lowell prophesies that sooner rather than later the new states will force the removal of the national capital to some dark vale over the mountains, "perhaps on the river Ohio."[53] (If only! Imagine the national capital in Louisville, city of baseball bats and the long shadow of Wendell Berry.)

It is time, Lowell says in 1813, to "shake off immediately this unnatural connection." Write off the $15 million Louisiana Purchase as a Jeffersonian folly; "sound policy," he says, "would dictate the parting with it, as a man would part with a gangrene limb to save his life."[54]

The country or countries that will grow beyond the mountains will pose little threat to the thirteen United States. "Having little, or no competition, in those pursuits wherein we acquire wealth," comity should rule the continent. Oh, the occasional quarrel may break out back east, but it's all in the family, for "the states on this side of the mountains, who resemble a large family, [are] bound together by consanguinity."[55]

He concludes in a dire key that "uniting, in sentiment and pursuit, the original thirteen states" is "the last hope of our country."[56]

Samuel Eliot Morison, the Brahmin court historian of the US Navy, mocked Lowell's "extremist proposal" as "so idiotic that it would hardly be worth serious consideration, had it not come from a high source and been promoted in the Federalist press." Morison—a pompous ass who liked to be called "the Admiral," an honorific he was given for his official histories of naval operations in the Second World War—in the next paragraph called Lowell's plan "unrealistic to the point of imbecility."[57] Okay, Admiral, we get the point: You don't like it!

Lowell's contemporaries were less contemptuous. His plan won wide support in the New England Federalist press. Disunion, many Massachusetts Federalists believed, was essential to the preservation of the republic, which could not survive the strain of continual expansion. Or continual war. A Newburyport editor wrote in 1813, "We have always been led to believe that a separation of the States would be a great evil. We still think it an evil. But rather than prosecute the present war, which will eventuate in the ruin of the Northern and Eastern States . . . we think it by far the least of the two evils."[58]

The Federalists of Massachusetts, wrote historian James M. Banner in *To the Hartford Convention* (1970), "envisaged a republic bound to the ocean." The party and doctrine appealed to "a special sort of farmer: resistant to change, unventuresome, satisfied with a static life, unmoved by the spirit of agrarian enterprise, fearful of competition, and not yet taken by land speculation."[59] These were the fixed, not the wanderers.

Among those who looked kindly on the shedding of excess states were a pair of non–New England Founding Fathers: Gouverneur Morris, who represented Pennsylvania at the convention, and Maryland's Charles Carroll of Carrollton.

Morris, the penman to blame for the leaden prose of the Constitution, had lost faith. The consolidationist roué of Philadelphia was flirting with secession. He wrote Timothy Pickering on October 17, 1814: "I should be glad to meet with some one, who could tell me what has become of the union, in what it consists, and to what useful purpose it endures."[60] Pick was the wrong guy to ask. He replied, "Union is the talisman of the dominant party; and many Federalists, enchanted by the magic sound, are alarmed at every appearance of opposition to the measures of the faction, lest it should endanger the Union. I have never entertained such fears. On the contrary, in adverting to the ruinous system of our government for many years past, I have said, let the ship run aground. The shock will throw the present pilots overboard, and then competent navigators will get her afloat and conduct her safely into port."[61]

On November 1, 1814, Morris wrote Rufus King (who had represented Massachusetts at the convention): "A union of commercial States to take care of themselves, leaving the war, its expense, and its debt to those choice spirits, so ready to declare and so eager to carry it on, seems to be now the only rational course." That same day he wrote Congressman Lewis B. Sturges, a Connecticut Federalist: "New England will, I trust, continue true to herself. The oppressive course pertinaciously pursued must open the eyes even of the wilfully blind. You will unite with Massachusetts, and New York must connect herself, whether she will or no, with New England. The question of boundary to be solved, therefore, is the Delaware, the Susquehanna, or the Potomac. *Medio tutissimus ibis.* Better preserve principle, than extend dominion."[62]

Better to preserve principle than extend dominion. Talk about the credo that failed!

This was no foul-breathed scandalmonger casting murrains from the gutter. Twenty-seven years after writing the Constitution, Gouverneur Morris was telling friends to wake up to the breakup. Do not, however, count on the vox populi to steer statesmen down the right course. For as Morris wrote Benjamin Walker, "The people must feel before they can think. Expect heroism from a sheep, charity from a wolf, and music from a crow, and perhaps you may not be disappointed; but do not expect, or even hope for reason from the populace."[63] No sentimental populist was he!

The "Reunion of the Original Thirteen States" movement of Lowell caught on in New England, hotbed of antiwar dissent (though its patriots point out that the region provided the union with more regiments in the War of 1812 than did either the Middle Atlantic or Southern states). His radical proposal hardly made Lowell an outcast: Crazy Jack was given an honorary degree in 1814 from Harvard, whose corporate leadership was "100 percent anti-war."[64] He was lionized by Timothy Pickering, who wrote Lowell that "in this wicked world, it is the duty of every good man, though he cannot restore it to *innocence*, to strive to prevent its *growing worse*. This has been your course."[65]

Of the Hartford Convention, the outstanding display of New England regional discontent during the War of 1812, Lowell had little good to say. The seeds of this convention had been sown in December 1813, when Federalist Hampshire County, Massachusetts, decided to propose a gathering of New Englanders "to consider what action could be taken in the 'awful crisis.'"[66] The fever spread, fanned by Noah Webster, the lexicographer who knew the meaning of the word *agitation*.

Twenty-six New England men met in Hartford over three weeks in December and January, seeing 1814 out and 1815 in. Delegations from Massachusetts, Connecticut, and ever-fractious Rogue Island were sent by the legislatures of those states, while "irregular delegates" from counties in New Hampshire and Vermont also attended. Conventioneers hoped to plot a course for New England, which had had just about enough of Jeffersonian expansion, Madisonian warfare, and Republican disregard of Yankee commerce.

New Englanders marched boldly up to the precipice. They spoke of tax resistance, negotiating a separate peace with England, declaring neutrality. Some took the final step and counseled secession. After all, insisted the editor of the *Salem Gazette*, "the federal constitution is nothing more than a treaty between independent sovereignties."[67]

The Hartford delegates, however, twenty-one of whom were lawyers, were more circumspect. Shunning disunion, they nevertheless begat a lode of proposed constitutional amendments, most of them in an anti-expansion or antiwar vein. To wit: They would require a two-thirds congressional vote to declare offensive war; a two-thirds vote to admit new states; and a two-thirds vote to impose embargoes, which were limited to sixty days; and they would bar naturalized citizens from serving in Congress and the president from succeeding himself or hailing from the same state as his predecessor. Take that, Virginia!

A blanket of secrecy was thrown over the convention, as it had been a generation before in Philadelphia, but whereas the Constitutional

Convention conspirators were praised by posterity for the cloister, the Hartfordians were condemned. For his part, Jack Lowell thought the conventioneers slumbered beneath the blanket anyway. To Pickering he wrote, "I was opposed sincerely and most zealously to the [Hartford] Convention because I found no man among its advocates prepared to *act*." Lowell sought in vain for a "bold and ardent man" in the Massachusetts delegation. He found only timid temporizers, mewling moderates, pusillanimous pulers. In any event, thought Lowell, the convention was premature: Secession would come in its own good time. The union had overexpanded; dissolution was inevitable. Neither Pickering nor Lowell was at Hartford. Their epistolary exchange reflects, perhaps, the temperamental differences between the worlds of politics and letters.

Lowell expected nothing. Indeed, he had opposed the participation of Massachusetts because "I was convinced that the Convention would not go far enough." To hell with diffident recommendations and finely phrased proclamations: Northern states must present a series of demands—"a *treaty*, not a *constitution*"—for greater self-rule, no slave representation, and stricter controls on declaring war.[68] Lowell was speaking the language of the Jefferson and Madison of 1798, of interposition and the Virginia and Kentucky Resolutions.

Pickering, for once, was the Pollyanna. On November 28, 1814, he told Lowell that the Hartford Convention is "the best hope of our best men." He went on to recommend an amendment requiring a two-thirds or three-fourths vote for the declaration of war. (Note well: Secession has walked hand in hand with peace and anti-militarism since the republic's youth.) Pickering thought the bell was about to toll. The most outright disunionist in antebellum American politics, he waited on the British navy to deliver New England from bondage. "From the moment that the British possess New Orleans, the Union is severed," he wrote.[69] Andrew Jackson smashed that hope to bits in the Battle of New Orleans. The Hartford Convention would ever after carry the fetor of disloyalty. And the next time men would speak seriously of disunion, they would do so in accents of the American South.

By 1815, the Reunion of the Original Thirteen States movement was dead. Oblivion beckoned. Jack Lowell was headed for the footnotes. Yet we do Lowell an injustice if we ascribe his Refederator fantasy to snobbishness or dyspepsia. For he was, first and foremost, a Bostonian. He was a Harvard man, as Lowells are, a director of the First National Bank of Boston, president of the Boston Athenaeum, and a passionate horticulturalist convinced that none were so fragrant as the flowers of Eastern Massachusetts.

The "Boston Rebel" of Essex County, to use yet another of his aliases, was intensely loyal to his home ground. He was part of the notorious "Essex Junto," an informal collection of Boston-area merchants and politicos (including Timothy Pickering) who were at once ultra-Federalist yet rooted in the Bay State. In Pickering's sensible formulation, his loyalties were "in what you will deem their natural order—toward Salem, Massachusetts, New England, the Union at large."[70]

"Provincialism marked this Junto," huffed Admiral Morison disapprovingly. Lowell, although he "made the grand tour of Europe," is indicted by Morison, with the others, by a borrowing from Horace: "They changed their sky, not their dispositions, by travel, returning to Boston as bigoted as when they departed."[71] Well, this is what cosmopolitan travelers would have you believe, but Emerson, Massachusetts-man that he was, had his doubts: "I am not much an advocate for traveling," wrote the Concordian, "and I observe that men run away to other countries because they are not good in their own, and run back to their own because they pass for nothing in their new places. For the most part, only the light characters travel. Who are you that have no task to keep you at home?"[72]

Crazy Jack had tasks, which he performed on a seventeen-acre hilltop estate in Roxbury. He had given up the law in 1802, the year his father died and one year after his failure to save the life of a client he regarded as innocent of murder. Lowell was every bit the shopaholic and mad planter of seeds that Jefferson was. In his European sojourns he shipped home statues and furniture and horticultural oddments. His orchards were famed; he endowed the Harvard Botanical Garden and helped to found the Massachusetts Horticultural Society. In Jack Lowell, we have the Federalist as localist patriot. As he told the horticultural society in an 1830 speech, the United States were "too long accustomed to rely upon foreign nurseries for fruit trees and other plants. We should depend on our own resources and learn to appreciate them. It has been the prevailing fashion to underrate everything of domestic origin and to attach value to exotics . . . everything that bore the impress of a foreign original was sought after and admired . . . [but] these prejudices are fast receding before the beaming light of intelligence and patriotism." You may hear his echoes at your local farm market.

Lowell died in 1840, shortly before the second great spasm of expansion would englut Texas and the lands of the Southwest. It's just as well. He never could see that far anyway. The *New England Farmer* eulogized him: "The agriculture of Massachusetts was indebted to him more than to any other living individual."[73]

We should all be so crazy.

Chapter One and a Half: Well, Okay, Maybe Just a *Touch* of Gray

The cross, or perhaps crowbar, of disunion would soon be passed. The men of Hartford, New Englanders who in the face of nationalist war hysteria had sought to assert their pacific regional interests, were reviled throughout the land. Down Virginia way, the *Richmond Enquirer* huffed on November 1, 1814: "No man, no association of men, no State or set of States *has a right* to withdraw itself from this Union, of its own accord."[74] Less than half a century later the *Enquirer* would be whistling a different tune.

Massachusetts ceded its role as the epicenter of states' rights. Yet even as the discordant notes of Hartford faded, many were still deaf to the mystic chords of memory that in twoscore years Abraham Lincoln would hear so poetically in the great heartsong of union. John Randolph of Roanoke, the brilliant Virginia statesman and savagely eloquent critic of war and expansion, declared that union was "the *means* of securing the safety, liberty, and welfare of the confederacy and not itself an end to which these should be sacrificed." If the means were no longer adequate, then by all means dispense with them. "There is no magic in the word union," said Randolph. "I value it as the means of preserving the liberty and happiness of the people."[75] Should it fail at such duty, then other expedients must be sought. In 1820, Thomas Jefferson heard the "fire bell in the night," the clanging chimes of doom sounding from the halls of Congress. The debate was over Missouri's admission as a slave state, and though it was settled by the famous Missouri Compromise—the Show-Me State came in slave, Maine entered free, and slavery was henceforth barred in the northern stretch of the Louisiana Purchase—Jefferson heard in its peals "the knell of the Union."[76]

That same year, even the son of the father of the Sedition Act pondered separation without calling for smelling salts. John Quincy Adams, recording a conversation with John C. Calhoun in his diary, opined that a "dissolution, at least temporary, of the Union, as now constituted, would be certainly necessary" if the United States were to wash clean "the great and foul stain upon the North American Union"—slavery. Adams neither relished nor dreaded the severance.[77]

Had the time come to put the quietus to the Philadelphia experiment? Adams also confided to his diary: "Perhaps it would have been a wiser as well as a bolder course to have persisted in the [slavery] restriction upon Missouri, till it should have terminated in a convention of the States to revise and amend the Constitution. This would have produced a new Union of thirteen or fourteen States unpolluted with slavery, with a great and glorious object to effect, namely that of rallying to their standard the other States by the universal emancipation of their slaves."[78]

Adams understood renewal of the union, and ablution of its soul, as the work of the states, acting with individual agency yet also in concert. He looked not for direction from the federal city, from the archons of Washington, from a national state backed by a national military that would bend the Carolinas and Marylands to its will.

The Constitution was barely into a man's middle age when its genesis and eschatology became matters of immediate concern.

The question that once bedeviled American politics (though it has long since been replaced by more pressing matters, such as whether senators should wear flag pins on their lapels every day or only on holidays) was this: Did the states precede and create the United States without forfeiting their own sovereignty, or, by ratification of the Constitution, did the states subordinate themselves for all time to an indissoluble union of which they are constituent but not independent pieces?

The polymathic Philadelphian William Rawle—Federalist Quaker abolitionist, distinguished member of the bar, US attorney for Pennsylvania by appointment of George Washington, theologian, and poet—capped his career with *A View of the Constitution of the United States of America* (1825), which became the standard textbook on the subject. In it, Rawle—without apoplexy, or conjuring the garrote—reasoned: "The states . . . may wholly withdraw from the Union," though the "secession . . . should be deliberate, clear, and unequivocal," for "to withdraw from the Union is a solemn, serious act," not to be done on a whim or a fit of pique.

Rawle was no disunionist. "We feel the deepest impression of a sacred obligation to preserve the union of our country," he wrote, but he recognized that compacts outlive their usefulness, and that there was nothing in the Constitution that explicitly forbade separation. If the thing needs be done, it would be done.[79] (West Point cadets Jefferson Davis and Robert E. Lee had studied Rawle's book in class, a conjunction that West Point critics would make much of in later times.)

Rawle's work represented a kind of high-water mark of the confederacy concept, which soon suffered a series of sharp and even humiliating defeats.

Kenneth M. Stampp, in his monograph on "The Concept of a Perpetual Union," locates the "explosion of unionist rhetoric" in the nullification debate that began in 1828.[80] Congress had enacted the Tariff of 1828, known by its Southern detractors as the Tariff of Abominations for its high duties on imports. The act was a piece of sectional legislation designed to protect Northern industries; the agrarian South, traditionally in favor of freedom of trade and minimal duties, was aghast.

South Carolina was the locus of the revolt. Its favorite son and paladin, Vice President John C. Calhoun, asserted the right of "nullification." States, argued Calhoun, possess "the right of judging" acts of the "General Government." A state may declare an obnoxious federal law "null and void" and therefore disregard it. Calhoun assured his audience that such "interposition" would be rarely exercised, but his doctrine amounted to a kind of state veto over national laws.[81] Those who make national laws were not amused. Not then, and not now, when decentralists and radical democrats propose that their states nullify the national call-up of state guard units.

Nullification was a weapon used by those who wished to preserve the union. Secession, by contrast, is a withdrawal, a dissolution of the union, and thus represents the final act, when all hope is gone.

In January 1830 the Expounder and Defender of the Constitution, Senator Daniel Webster of Massachusetts, cast his anathemas upon nullification in his two replies to Calhoun's South Carolina ally Senator Robert Y. Hayne. Once staples of a schoolboy's recitative chores, Webster's orations are full of magnificent bombast. Yet he demolished the pedestrian Hayne. (Had Calhoun been a member of the Senate rather than wasting away in the vice presidency we might have seen a duel of equals.)

Senator Hayne, in his half of the debate, carefully makes the case that the states preceded the union, and that although they delegated certain powers to the federal government they "remained equally sovereign and independent" within the union. The Constitution is a "compact between sovereigns," he gamely asserts, and the states retain the right to interpret the proper limits of national authority.[82]

Even this reader of the colloquy, whose sympathies lie Hayneward, waits impatiently for the South Carolinian to finish so that he may hear, in his mind's chamber, the Websterian cadences. Webster's peroration in his second reply to Hayne is so lovely that I quote the entire paragraph, fully aware that it contradicts my own meager theses. I bow to genius:

> I have not allowed myself, Sir, to look beyond the Union, to see what might lie hidden in the dark recess behind. I have not cooly weighed the chances of preserving liberty when the bonds that unite us together shall be broken asunder. I have not accustomed myself to hang over the precipice of disunion, to see whether, with my short sight, I can fathom the depth of the abyss below; nor could I regard him as a safe counsellor in the affairs of this government, whose thoughts should be mainly bent on considering, not how the Union may be best preserved, but how tolerable might be the condition of the people when it should be broken up and destroyed. While the Union lasts we have high, exciting, gratifying prospects spread out before us, for us and our children. Beyond that I seek not to penetrate the veil. God grant that in

my day at least that curtain may not rise! God grant that on my vision never may be opened what lies behind! When my eyes shall be turned to behold for the last time the sun in heaven, may I not see him shining on the broken and dishonored fragments of a once glorious Union; on States dissevered, discordant, belligerent; on a land rent with civil feuds, or drenched, it may be, in fraternal blood! Let their last feeble and lingering glance rather behold the gorgeous ensign of the republic, now known and honored throughout the earth, still full high advanced, its arms and trophies streaming in their original lustre, not a stripe erased or polluted, not a single star obscured, bearing for its motto, no such miserable interrogatory as "What is all this worth?" nor those other words of delusion and folly, "Liberty first and Union afterwards" but everywhere, spread all over in characters of living light, blazing on all its ample folds, as they float over the sea and over the land, and in every wind under the whole heavens, that other sentiment, dear to every true American heart—Liberty *and* Union, now and forever, one and inseparable![83]

What cold heart is unwarmed by such ardent expression?

As the debate raged, Dr. Thomas Cooper of South Carolina explained to Martin Van Buren the likely consequence of the tariff: "We shall separate in all amity; and assume conscientiously our share of the national debt; we have and shall have with you, no quarrel or dispute."[84] It sounded cut and dried, and no messier than the divvying up of the spoils after a bank heist.

The South Carolina legislature declared null and void the Tariff of 1828 and the succeeding Tariff of 1832. Contra Thomas Cooper, quarrel and dispute ensued. In response, on December 10, 1832, President Jackson issued his Proclamation to the People of South Carolina, which Kenneth Stampp describes as "close to being the definitive statement of the case for perpetuity."[85] Jackson invidiously compares South Carolina's defiance and the implied threat of separation with New England's policy of objecting to the War of 1812 but staying within the union. Brother Jonathan the Yankee, suggests Jackson, behaved honorably, while the cavaliers traffic in perfidy. Jackson, or rather his secretary of state, New Yorker Edward

Livingston, who drafted this statement, dallies with metaphysics when he notes the Constitution's preambulary pledge to form "a more perfect Union" and suggests that this grammatically shaky ("more" perfect?) locution is a kind of guarantee of eternal life. That union which is "more perfect" (as opposed to merely "perfect"?) is not divisible. Right?

Whether one calls our system a league, a confederation, or a union of states, the bond of the Constitution is unbreakable, said Jackson/Livingston. From the moment of ratification, "each State having expressly parted with so many powers as to constitute jointly with the other States a single nation, cannot from that period possess any right to secede, because such secession does not break a league, but destroys the unity of a nation, and any injury to that unity is not only a breach which would result from the contravention of a compact, but it is an offense against the whole Union. To say that a State may at pleasure secede from the Union, is to say that the United States are not a nation because it would be a solecism to contend that any part of a nation might dissolve its connection with the other parts, to their injury or ruin, without committing any offense. Secession, like any other revolutionary act, may be morally justified by the extremity of oppression; but to call it a constitutional right, is confounding the meaning of terms . . ."[86]

Jackson carried the day. He threatened the use of force and received congressional authorization for it, though wise heads in Congress also moderated the tariff. South Carolina backed down. "Our Union—it must be preserved!" Jackson had declaimed in a famous toast at a Jefferson birthday celebration in 1830. Calhoun's response—"The Union—next to our liberties, most dear"—somehow lacked oomph.[87] The nationalists were ascendant.

Union had achieved an almost religious significance. No longer was it simply mutually advantageous for the states to confederate under one government: No, it was written in heaven's book. Skeptics were skewered. As the historian Paul C. Nagel, author of *One Nation Indivisible* (1964), put it, by the 1830s "blasphemy had now joined insanity and treason as impulses for those wretched challengers of Union."[88]

The firebell's clang grew louder.

In the North, frustration over the constitutional obligation to return runaway slaves nagged at men and women of conscience. "Union," wrote

Ralph Waldo Emerson in 1851 in protest of the Fugitive Slave Act, "is a delectable thing, and so is wealth, and so is life, but they may all cost too much, if they cost honour." If the Southern states wish to detach, then good riddance! For "the worst mischiefs that could follow from Secession and new combination of the smallest fragments of the wreck were slight and medicable to the calamity your Union has brought us."[89]

From the South, too, came blasts at the mystical oneness of America: "Is my State, a free State, to lie down and submit because political fossils raise the cry of the glorious Union?" asked an exasperated Georgia Democratic senator Robert Toombs in 1856.[90]

The United States had been cleaving along the fault line of slavery since their birth. Madison did his best to quell discussion of the peculiar institution in the Constitutional Convention, though that reliably uncouth teller of truth Luther Martin proclaimed that "it was inconsistent with the principles of the revolution and dishonorable to the American character to [protect the slave trade] in the Constitution."[91] The document barred the Congress from prohibiting the import of slaves—or "such persons as any of the states now existing shall think proper to admit," in the vapid phrase of the Constitution—until 1808. It also provided, in Article IV, Section 2, that "no person held to service or labour in one state, under the laws thereof, escaping into another, shall, in consequence of any law or regulation therein, be discharged from such service or labour, but shall be delivered up on claim of the party to whom such service or labour may be due."

In plain words, a slave who slips his master's leash is still a slave of that same master, no matter where he may roam or under whose guardianship he may lodge himself. The Fugitive Slave Act of 1793 gave the clause teeth. Northern states were not permitted to offer shelter or, heaven forfend, freedom to runaways. The act was upheld by the Supreme Court in *Prigg v. The Commonwealth of Pennsylvania* (1842), which sanctioned "recaption," as it was called, in the face of a Pennsylvania law punishing slave catchers. But Justice Story, in his opinion, left unlatched a trapdoor through which states could safeguard runaways.

In response, Vermont and Massachusetts enacted in 1843 personal liberty laws "forbidding the State officers, under severe penalties, to assist in the capture of fugitive slaves, and prohibiting the use of the

State jails for their detention."[92] The feds might have the legal warrant to enforce the fugitive slave laws, but the Green Mountain and Bay States were not going to help them do it. Others followed. In fact, the only long-established Northern state that did *not* adopt a "personal liberty law" protecting runaway slaves was Lincoln's Illinois, the most anti-black of the free states.

In his poem "Massachusetts to Virginia," John Greenleaf Whittier celebrated his state's defiance of fugitive slave laws:

> *But for us and for our children, the vow which we have given*
> *For freedom and humanity is registered in heaven;*
> *No slave-hunt in our borders,—no pirate on our strand!*
> *No fetters in the Bay State,—no slave upon our land!*[93]

Personal liberty laws varied. Some guaranteed escapees from bondage "the right to a writ of habeas corpus and to jury trial"; others punished kidnapping or guaranteed counsel for captured runaways; some barred the use of state jails to incarcerate those accused of being runaway slaves; others forbade state officials from cooperating with the federal laws requiring return of fugitives.[94]

Clear-cutting these proliferating personal liberty laws in one fell swoop was the Compromise of 1850, that last-ditch effort to glue together the jigsaw puzzle of the states. Under the compromise, California was admitted as a free state, the slave trade was abolished in the District of Columbia, and a new fugitive slave law overrode, with crushing authority, the separate laws of the states.

Overturning state personal liberty laws betrayed the states' rights principles avowed by many Southerners. A few honest men of the South, among them Jefferson Davis, acknowledged, even rued this, but most Southern fire-eaters were situational states' rights men.[95] For hard-core defiance of centralized authority, one had to journey by the North Star.

Consider *Ableman v. Booth* (1859), which grew out of a Wisconsin case in which anti-slavery editor Sherman M. Booth led a party trying to free a captured fugitive named Joshua Glover. Booth was arrested by a US Marshal for violating the Fugitive Slave Act. The Wisconsin Supreme

Court declared this act unconstitutional and freed Booth. He was rearrested and the case went to the US Supreme Court, whose Chief Justice Roger B. Taney was always willing to forget his bias toward the states when slavery was at stake. Taney upheld the supremacy of the fugitive slave law over state efforts to impede its operation.

Wisconsin may not have been one of Jack Lowell's prized original thirteen but it had the fighting spirit. On Wisconsin! The state legislature thumbed its nose at the Supremes: Stop—in the name of Glover! The Wisconsin legislators declared that "the several states which formed that instrument [the Constitution] being sovereign and independent, have the unquestionable right to judge of its infraction, and that a *positive defiance* by those sovereignties of all unauthorized acts done, or attempted to be done, under color of that instrument is the right remedy."[96]

Abolitionists not only dallied with secession; they embraced it. William Lloyd Garrison, the Liberator, was by the 1840s a vocal disunionist. But then what would you expect, given whom he had chosen as his hero as a boy? As biographer John L. Thomas writes, "In 1845, at the height of the slavery controversy in Massachusetts, he would argue for separation from the Union in terms which were essentially those of his spiritual guide and mentor, Timothy Pickering."[97]

Pick lives!

In a March 1842 letter Garrison announced himself as "for the repeal of the Union between North and South. We must dissolve all connexion with those murderers of fathers, and murderers of mothers, and murderers of liberty and traffickers in human flesh, and blasphemers against the Almighty, at the South." He believed that once North and South were separate, the latter would hemorrhage runaways, for "how would she be able to prevent the escape of any indefinite number of her slaves to the new republic?" Secession would be the instrument by which slavery was not preserved but *abolished*, as border states, one by retreating one, emancipated their fast-disappearing slaves. The result: "a general and peaceful abolition throughout the entire South."[98]

Impracticable? Maybe not. The historian Jeffrey Rogers Hummel, in his provocative *Emancipating Slaves, Enslaving Free Men: A History of the American Civil War* (1996), takes seriously the Garrisonian strategy of draining the South of slaves via personal liberty laws. Writes Hummel: "Slavery flourished because the country's political and legal structure socialized its enforcement costs . . . The economic viability of the peculiar institution rested on political power. Removing the free states out from under the Constitution's fugitive slave provision would at first undermine slavery in the upper South. But the lower South faced a potentially fatal domino effect. Once the supports provided by local, state, and central governments were knocked out, a combination of market forces and a black thirst for liberty could bring the system down."[99]

Would not a "general and peaceful abolition" have been preferable to the bloodbath of 1861–65? Are we so gone in war-worship that the question is unaskable? At all events, Garrison, once the smell of gunpowder was in his nostrils and the screams of gut-shot rebels filled his ears, whooped it up for war. As biographer Thomas writes, "The Christian anarchist in him yielded to the super-patriot who discovered traitors and treason everywhere."[100] Isn't it ever thus?

Confederates did enjoy tweaking abolitionists for their hypocrisy. Those damn Yankees were in 1862 mouthing oily platitudes about the sacred Union when just a few years earlier the American Anti-Slavery Society was passing resolutions declaring:

> Resolved, "That secession from the United States Government is the duty of every Abolitionist, since no one can take office or deposit his vote under the Constitution, without violating his anti-slavery principles, and rendering himself an abettor to the slave-holder in his sin."
>
> Resolved, "That years of warfare against the slave power has convinced us that every act done in support of the American Union rivets the chain of the slave—that the only exodus of the slave to freedom, unless it be one of blood, must be over the remains of the present American Church and the grave of the present Union."
>
> Resolved, "That the Abolitionists of this country should make it one of the primary objects of this agitation to dissolve the American Union."[101]

Oh you pluperfect hypocrites! I can still hear you saying/You would never break the chain.[102]

Before the fields ran red with consecrating blood, most abolitionists thought peaceful separation a better option than regimentation and death. Among them was the Boston lawyer and fiery orator Wendell Phillips. As the Union tottered in the interregnum between Lincoln's election in November 1860 and his inauguration the following March, Phillips did his manly best to push it over the edge. In a speech boldly titled "Disunion," Phillips scoffed at those nationalists who would uphold union at sword's point. "A Union is made up of willing States, not of conquered provinces," he declaimed. "There are some rights, quite perfect, yet wholly incapable of being enforced. A husband or wife who can only keep the other partner within the bond by locking the doors and standing armed before them, had better submit to peaceable separation."

Spare him tears over this divorce, said Phillips. "Let us not, however, too anxiously grieve over the Union of 1787. Real Unions are not made, they grow. This was made, like an artificial waterfall or a Connecticut nutmeg. It was not an oak which to-day a tempest shatters. It was a wall hastily built, in hard times, of round boulders; the cement has crumbled, and the smooth stones, obeying the law of gravity, tumble here and there. Why should we seek to stop them, merely to show that we have a right and can?"[103] Few agitators have ever been quite so agitated as Phillips—"he cannot conceive of a tempest outside of a teapot," jibed Horace Greeley— but Boston and its purlieu was big enough for him.[104] He was of his place, and he knew that his place was different from other places.

A unitary state misfits our continent. "Remember," Phillips urged, "that homogeneous nations like France tend to centralization; confederacies like ours tend inevitably to dismemberment." We are, by nature, cohesionless; no amount of stickum can keep disparate states together.

This was not to say that the disjoined states of America would be enemies. Explained Phillips, "I would make [Massachusetts], in relation to South Carolina, just what England is."[105] That is to say, a trading partner, a commercial relative, a cousin with whom one shares a tongue and fraternal memory but no political bond. A common ruler is weak ligature anyway.

Abraham Lincoln rejected Phillipsian nuance in his first inaugural address, when he said that "the Union of these States is perpetual." It was no mere "association of States" from which the parties might withdraw. "Universal law" commanded its eternality.

"Plainly the central idea of secession is the essence of anarchy," declared Lincoln, though it is no such thing: To secede from a larger political entity is not the same as denying the sovereignty of *any* political entity, as anarchists do.[106] (I say this as a quasi-anarchist, or anarcho-localist, or whatever compound word leaves me wiggle room enough to accept the authority of locally constituted and democratically elected bodies in certain narrowly defined circumstances.)

Disunion or fratricidal war? Radical critics of slavery had the guts to ask.

Horace Greeley, editor of the *New York Tribune*, was, like many abolitionists, inclined to permit the South to leave the union in peace. He editorialized in the *Tribune* of November 9, 1860: "We hold, with Jefferson, to the inalienable right of communities to alter or abolish forms of government that have become oppressive or injurious; and, if the cotton States shall decide that they can do better out of the Union than in it, we insist on letting them go in peace. The right to secede may be a revolutionary right, but it exists nevertheless; and we do not see how one party can have a right to do what another party has a right to prevent. We must ever resist the asserted right of any State to remain in the Union and nullify or defy the laws thereof; to withdraw from the Union is quite another matter. And, whenever a considerable section of our Union shall deliberately resolve to go out, we shall resist all coercive measures designed to keep her in. We hope never to live in a republic whereof one section is pinned to the residue by bayonets."[107]

Nullification, no; secession, if you insist. (Soon enough, the tolerant tone would be replaced by war cries and bloodlust.)

Greeley, as historian Thomas N. Bonner noted, would not scruple to coerce "one or two States" to remain—sorry, Second Vermont Republic—but come the flood tide he would stand aside. As he told Lincoln, should eight or ten states want out, he would say, "There's the door—go!"[108] In orderly fashion, of course. No running in the halls.

The good-riddance interval between Lincoln's election in November 1860 and his inauguration in March of the following year abounded with proposals to politically reorganize the North American continent. Abolitionists were not the only creative thinkers. Men of the border states, too, uncomfortable with both the fire-eaters of the Deep South and the righteous crusaders of New England, looked upon the world afresh.

John Letchner, governor of Virginia, suggested in December 1860 that "not two, but four political entities would replace the Old Union. The New York–New England area and the Pacific states would each form a separate nation, and the deep South would form a third entity. The rest of the old Union, the border states, Pennsylvania, New Jersey, and the northwestern states, would be the mighty fourth force that would entice Louisiana, Texas, and Mississippi away from the deep South. Finally this growing giant would wrest Pensacola from the dwindling cotton kingdom, and a rough equilibrium would be established."[109]

Before war and its attendant gore, there was considerable discussion in Maryland, Delaware, and New Jersey about throwing in with the Confederacy or, more likely, breaking off to form a subunion of the central states. By December 15, 1860, Albany, New York's *Atlas and Argus* was stating that when "the Southern States become *de facto* a separate Confederacy, we shall consider the present Union at an end in all its parts. Then New York will seek to gather around her, in mutual relations of friendship, the States that will naturally seek her alliance, and will open her ports and offer her internal lines of communication to their use. She will preserve her own freedom and give to her sister confederates and to the world the boon of freedom of trade."[110]

Monmouth, New Jersey's *Democrat*, which had supported Stephen A. Douglas, also beat the drum for a central confederacy. Above all, however, it insisted that war was not the answer: "We are in favor of peaceful dissolution, and opposed to all measures of coercion. If the Union cannot be preserved without shedding the blood of our brethren, it cannot be preserved at all."[111]

Such opinions were repeated in hundreds of newspapers across the North, where the vast majority of Democrats and a substantial number of Republicans, judging by newspaper comments, wished to let the South go, unmolested. Even Republican congressmen, at least those not blinded by gunsmoke and deafened by cannonblast, preferred peace to war. As

Representative Alfred Wells (R-NY) of Ithaca protested, "I never can give up the conviction of my mind that it would be brutal and inhuman butchery . . . I would rather make a peaceful division than shed a drop of blood . . . Let her go . . . Peace! wait; shed not blood. Let not these cannon that run along our streets send forth their showers of grape and canister."[112]

Then Fort Sumter changed everything. The South had fired first; the benediction "depart in peace" was lost amid the din of war fever. Mars deranges. Did then, does today. But I have laid this cairn of quotes (and left many others in the discard pile) to show that Americans have considered, calmly and with favor, the prospect of letting states go. Live and let live. Once upon a time in America that phrase meant something.

Just four months before that first bloodshed, Congressman Daniel Sickles (D-NY), whom we will meet again in our next chapter, insisted that secession "is the highest constitutional and moral guarantee against injustice; and therefore, if it had been always and universally acknowledged as a rightful remedy, it would have contributed more than all else to perpetuate the Union, by compelling the observance of all their obligations on the part of all the States."[113] The threat of severance encourages conciliation.

The 1860 Republican Party platform would have nothing of it. The GOP denounced the threat of disunion "as denying the vital principles of a free government, and as an avowal of contemplated treason, which it is the imperative duty of an indignant People to rebuke and forever silence."

A bit intemperate, wouldn't you say? "Rebuke," maybe, but "forever silence" has an ominous ring, and would seem to run contrary to "the vital principles of a free government."[114] *Forever silence* sounds a lot like *murder*—but that verb is reserved for the crimes of individual persons. Governments are above that, surely.

Secession was treason, or revolution, if you prefer. Seeing no contemplated right of secession in the proceedings of the Constitutional Convention of 1787 and the ensuing state ratifying conventions, I incline more to the view of Senator Alfred Iverson Sr. (D-GA), who said, "I do not myself place the right of a State to secede from the Union upon Constitutional grounds. I admit that the Constitution has not granted that power to a State." Rather, says this nineteenth-century gunning Iverson, "the secession of a State is an act of revolution." And "while a State has no power under the Constitution conferred upon it, to secede from the Federal Government or from the Union, each State has the right of revolution, which all admit."[115] So dash these legalistic claims: Revolt! Pass out the arms and ammo, because there's something in the air . . .

That something was dissipated at Vicksburg, Gettysburg, Appomattox.

The Civil War, it seemed, had driven the legal question to a condition of almost perfect mootness. Even Confederate apologists no longer bandied about secession as a "right."[116]

Might makes right—or at least it made law.

"There are no angels/There are devils in many ways," shrieked LA punk Exene Cervenka, and while I have seen far more of heaven than of hell in this brief life, hers is a useful caution when writing of public men. Not every secessionist is noble; not every consolidationist is a blackguard. Theorists of the Confederacy defended not only the right to secede but the noxious right to own other human beings. The fact ought to intrude now and then upon any discussion of the Civil War. I admire few American presidents *as men* as much as I do Lincoln—even while I deplore his presidency as catastrophic. Lincoln, at his best, spoke in a poetry of brotherhood. Yes, I know about his skepticism that blacks and whites might live together as equals. What man of his time did not so believe? I don't go for cheaply bought expressions of moral superiority to our ancestors—Union *or* Confederate.

My daughter and millions of other schoolchildren begin the weekday with a recitation of the Pledge of Allegiance. As Vermont patriot Thomas Naylor notes, "While much attention has been paid in recent years to the phrase 'under God' in this declaration, far too little has been paid to the word 'indivisible.'"[117]

One nation, indivisible. Other than Lincoln, says who?

Says the Reconstruction-era US Supreme Court, for one, which in *Texas v. White* (1869) held that the Lone Star State never seceded from the union since such an act is a constitutional and metaphysical impossibility. The case centered on the legitimacy of bonds issued by the Confederate-era Texas government, but the decision, written by Chief Justice Salmon Chase, spoke to far more fundamental questions.

Chase was the anti-slavery Ohio Free Soil stalwart who served as Lincoln's secretary of the Treasury. He was substantial and in many ways admirable, a fact of which he was not unaware. "Chase is a good man," said his fellow Ohioan Ben Wade, "but his theology is unsound. He thinks there is a fourth person in the Trinity."[118]

Chase was always more favorably inclined toward a limited view of government power than many of his Lincolnian colleagues. His unsuccessful pursuit of the 1868 Democratic presidential nomination was a missed opportunity for the faltering republic. The basis of Chase's reconstruction policies, as historian Harold M. Hyman writes, was a triad of "race- and gender-blind equal civil rights, a recommendation for universal male suffrage, and total amnesty for former Confederates."[119] It was neither punitive toward the South nor pettily partial in its conferring of civil rights upon African Americans. It was a higher road than that chosen by Grant spoilsmen, Radical Republican vengeance seekers, and Klansmen.

In *Texas v. White*, Chief Justice Chase rejects "the theory that the rights of a State under the Constitution might be renounced, and her obligations thrown off at pleasure." The bond between the individual states and the United States is unbreakable. "The Constitution," he avers, "in all its provisions, looks to an indestructible Union, composed of indestructible states." He adverts to the Articles of Confederation, the original charter for a federal government, though one much despised by consolidationists and supplanted by the Constitution. But, you see, their official title was the Articles of Confederation and Perpetual Union, and that word *perpetual* comes in handy when cobbling a case for constitutional immortality. (The second Article stipulated, "Each State retains its sovereignty, freedom and independence . . ." Although Article 13 stated that the "union shall be perpetual," it didn't last ten years. The document was junked in Philadelphia in 1787. Perpetuity was briefer in those days.)

Skipping lightly from the Articles crematory, *Texas v. White* adduces the Constitution's preambulary promise to form "a more perfect union." Writes Chase, "It is difficult to convey the idea of indissoluble unity more clearly than by these words. What can be indissoluble if a perpetual Union, made more perfect, is not?"

Fixing his eye on eternity, Chase continues, "When, therefore, Texas became one of the United States, she entered into an indissoluble relation. All the obligations of perpetual union, and all the guarantees of republican government in the Union, attached at once to the State. The act which consummated her admission into the Union was something more than a compact; it was the incorporation of a new member into the political body. And it was final. The union between Texas and the other States was as complete, as perpetual, and as indissoluble as the union between the original States. There was no place for reconsideration, or revocation, except through revolution, or through consent of the States."[120]

Hmm. Come again? "Except . . . through consent of the States." The window is left open just a crack. The ordinance of secession ratified by a three-to-one popular vote in Texas in 1861 is "null," but if Texas had received the "consent of the States"—all of them? a majority acting in Congress assembled?—then perhaps its departure would have been legal. Was Chief Justice Chase being inconsistent? Or was he just committing an act of honesty? *Texas v. White* left open the question: If her sister states consented to, say, Vermont taking her leave, would the perpetual and more perfect union be any less so? From a distance of sevenscore years, Salmon Chase lights the way out.

Indivisibility was also the promise of Francis Bellamy, author of the American oath of allegiance. Francis, cousin of novelist Edward Bellamy of *Looking Backward* (1887) fame, is the reason that indivisibility has been on every American schoolboy's lips for upward of a century.

But let us first consider cousin Edward, the finest example I know of how one man's heaven can be another man's hell.

In *Looking Backward*, the publishing phenomenon of the Gilded Age, Bellamy envisaged an America of the year 2000 in which all have been drafted into an "Industrial Army." Individual liberty has been extinguished. Toil is compulsory, as "every able-bodied citizen [is] bound to work for the nation, whether with mind or muscle."[121] Cooking is done only in public kitchens, music is performed only by conscripted professionals, and even rain is a thing of the past, as cities are guarded by enormous tarps. "In the nineteenth century," explains one character, "when it rained, the people of Boston put up three hundred thousand umbrellas over as many heads, and in the twentieth century they put up one umbrella over all the heads."[122] Consider it a metaphor for localism versus centralism.

Under the One Big Umbrella, separate states have disappeared, for "state governments would have interfered with the control and discipline of the industrial army."[123] Bellamy called his jackbooted philosophy—whose horrifying implications he draws out, with pride—"Nationalism." Historian Arthur Lipow notes, "Bellamy's authoritarian socialist views were an historical precursor of totalitarian collectivist ideological currents."[124]

This is as close to a novelistic prescription for mass slavery as has ever been written. To Edward Bellamy, it was utopia.

Looking Backward sold more copies than any novel since *Uncle Tom's Cabin*. Across the land irrupted 150 Nationalist Clubs, dedicated to regimenting America.

In an 1889 Nationalist manifesto, Bellamy stated that patriotism must be co-opted to achieve Nationalist goals. He urged his followers to "identify themselves with National traditions and aspirations."[125] Enter cousin Francis and the indivisible union.

Francis Bellamy, born in Mount Morris, New York, to an itinerant Baptist preacher, was in the process of losing his religion. He had been a minister and Prohibition Party speaker before turning to "Christian Socialism" and delivering such sermons as "Jesus the Socialist."

Francis was a charter member of the First Nationalist Club of Boston. He promoted the Nationalist creed in the populist magazine *The Arena*, whose editor Benjamin Flower wrote scornfully of Nationalism: "All individualism would be surrendered to that mysterious thing called government."[126]

Looking for practical ways to advance his causes, Francis Bellamy became an editor with *Youth's Companion*, a popular children's magazine.

Bellamy took a lead role in promoting the National Public School Celebration of Columbus Day in October 1892. His address upon the quadricentennial contained a frank dismissal of religious schools: "The training of citizens in the common knowledge and the common duties of citizenship belongs irrevocably to the state."[127]

The centerpiece of Columbus Day was to have been the flying of US flags above every schoolhouse in the land. But a twenty-three-word oath written by Bellamy for the September 8, 1892, edition of *Youth's Companion* stole the glory.

Bellamy called it a "Pledge of Allegiance," probably choosing the word *pledge* because it smelled of the temperance movement. His single felicitous sentence—"I pledge allegiance to my Flag and to the Republic for which it stands, one nation, indivisible, with liberty and justice for all"—was published anonymously, which enabled various liars to later claim the Pledge as theirs.

For an editor, Bellamy hated to be edited. He was indignant when in 1923 and '24 the National Flag Conference expanded "my flag" to "the flag of the United States of America." In 1929 he ridiculed an effort to add a line to the Pledge vowing adherence to Prohibition. A lapsed Baptist, he would have opposed the 1954 addition of "under God."

The Pledge has proved an invaluable tool of indoctrination. You can't say that something is "indivisible" thousands of mornings of your life and not accept, at some subdermal level, the truth of the statement.

Indivisible? We'll see. As Kirk Sale of the Middlebury Institute says, all that is necessary is for one state—Vermont, Alaska, Hawaii—to act: "Secession would simply come before the state legislature; both houses would pass it with big majorities; and the governor would send a letter to the US secretary of state saying that the state is now independent and would be pleased to have diplomatic relations with Washington."[128]

Washington could consent, opening Chief Justice Chase's escape hatch; or it could clamp the vise of economic embargo; or it could rain down bombs upon the village squares of Vermont, the caribou of Alaska, the sullen native precincts of the Hawaiian Islands. Weapons of mass destruction would be alleged; methamphetamine production, too, and for good measure sexual misconduct by independence leaders.

When in the course of human events . . .

CHAPTER TWO

Start Splitting the State:
New York, New York

The feeling between this city and the hayseeds . . . is every bit
as bitter as the feeling between the North and South before the
War . . . Why, I know a lot of men in my district who would like
nothin' better than to go out gunnin' for hayseeds.
—GEORGE WASHINGTON PLUNKITT, Tammany Hall, 1905[1]

*A*s a defiant and proud native son of Batavia in Genesee County,
cradle of Western New York, onion basket of the world but
voiceless helot in the politics of the Empire (yech!) State, I came to think
about secession early on. Not seceding from the Union—for I have kindly
feelings toward North Dakota and Maine and Mississippi—but the separation of Upstate New York from the city four hundred miles distant that
effectively controls state government. I was not the first to have such
notions, though to my surprise, those who have raised the flag of Two
New Yorks have been, in the main, from *their* New York. Maybe this is
more complicated than my simple morality play would have it?

Sectional enmity in New York used to be served with a wink and a
smile. The Downstaters were slickers, the Upstaters were appleknockers;
they were swells, we were yokels. Stanley Walker of the *New York Herald
Tribune* could call Upstaters "earthbound clodhoppers, with inferiority
complexes dating from a boyhood passed in shoveling out the barnyard,"
and no great offense was taken.[2]

At the great junctures in American history, Upstate had acted nobly,
Downstate ignobly. Our patriots, the Gil Martins later fictionalized by our
historical novelist Walter D. Edmonds, consecrated the Revolution with
blood, while Tories and cowards sought haven in Manhattan. After the
war, Downstate money interests and Hamiltonian centralists rammed the

new Constitution through, over the protests of the farmers and artisans who had shouldered the muskets.[3]

The marvelous idea of divorce—of two New Yorks—was advanced at our ratifying convention in June and July 1788. Ten states had already assented to the new Constitution, but New York, led by such Upstatesmen as Melancton Smith and the "Rough Hewer," shoemaker's apprentice Abraham Yates Jr., held out. Downstate Federalists resorted to threats: If New York did not ratify, its largest city would split off and join the union anyway. As John Jay wrote George Washington, "An idea has taken air that the southern part of the State will at all events, adhere to the Union; and if necessary to that end, seek a separation from the northern."[4]

To our everlasting regret, several Upstate delegates caved in, and we entered the United States as one.

There would be many through the years who did not regard that one as indivisible. Exhibit A: a thoughtful rogue of a mayor.

If Mayor Fernando Wood had had his way in 1861, Michael Bloomberg, Katie Couric, and the Yankees would be crammed into the "International News" section of your local Gannett rag. If only . . .

First, about that name. Wood was of Welsh-Prussian stock, but his mother was reading a lurid Spanish novel while gravid, so Fernando it was.

The enterprising young Fernando sold grog and "segars" with a notable lack of success until his smooth manner and honeyed tongue led him into a political career whose highlight was three tumultuous terms as Democratic mayor of New York City.

Fernando Wood eventually became rich in the tried-and-true manner of American statesmen: real estate speculation and marrying wealth. (His third wife was a sixteen-year-old heiress who immediately became stepmother to two sons her senior. Oedipus, we may be sure, ran riot in that household.) Tammany Hall's legendary Boss Tweed marveled of his rival, "I never went to get a corner lot, that I didn't find Wood had got in ahead of me."[5]

Wood was equal measures of charm and knavery, principle and deceit. Even a fairly sympathetic biographer, Jerome Mushkat, concedes that Wood "took duplicity to an extreme and made it an integral part of his operations."[6] His most loyal supporters were Irish and German immigrants—yet he was a secret member of the anti-immigrant American

Party, or the Know-Nothings. When his inconsistency was discovered, he calmly swore out an affidavit denying his membership.

In the dukes-up age of antebellum American politics, Wood's more ardent fans included the Dead Rabbits, the brawling Irish gang that was in philosophical agreement with the mayor's refusal to enforce the statewide prohibition law of 1855. He had the common touch and was said to be on speaking terms "with every longshoreman in his district."[7]

But for all his picturesque qualities, Fernando Wood was no mere scamp. This rascal had a vision. In his dissoluteness he also stood for dissolution. On January 7, 1861, as the federal union verged on collapse, Mayor Wood suggested that New York City go it alone—seceding not only from the rest of New York but from the United States themselves.

He was motivated, in part, by antipathy toward the Republicans who ran Albany and were about to take over Washington. The New York State government meddled intolerably in city affairs, even assuming control of the city's police department during the "Municipal Revolution" of 1857. "Our city occupies the position of a conquered province, entirely dependent on the will of a distant indifferent and alien government," said Wood—and that was only Albany that he was talking about.[8] Yes, we good country folk have played the oppressor, too. Upstate Republican busybodies, sneered the *Herald*, "daren't trust themselves alone with a loaded pistol, or a gin bottle, or a pretty girl, or a steam hammer without a good stout law to protect them and keep them in bounds . . . Therefore they like prohibitory laws, and license laws, and blue laws against kissing, and other pleasant little abridgements of natural liberty. We city folk, on the contrary, can stand a good deal of freedom without making wry faces."[9]

Touché, my urban friends!

The Municipal Revolution provoked a secessionist counterrevolution. A (Wood-less) assembly of fifteen hundred New Yorkers that gathered in Hamilton Square in July 1857 resolved "that the time has come when it is expedient to consider whether the political connection between us and those who tyrannically assume to be our masters should not be severed, and all proper and legal measures adopted to erect the lower counties of New York into a new State, and thus add a new star in the East to our glorious national constellation."[10]

Wondered Wood: Why not a lone star?

Like many New York merchants, Wood had Southern sympathies: The mayor and his brother Benjamin supported Kentucky Democrat John Breckinridge over Abraham Lincoln in the 1860 presidential election. Fernando averred that "with our aggrieved brethren of the slave states we have friendly relations and a common sympathy. We have not participated in the warfare upon their constitutional rights or upon their domestic institutions."[11] The latter term was code for slavery—if you're looking for a libertarian hero, Wood ain't it.

But Wood's free-city proposal was not simply the pipe dream of a pro-Confederate tobacconist. Mayor Wood envisioned New York City as a capitalist oasis, a nineteenth-century Occidental Hong Kong. He wanted New York to be a free port, trading with both North and South, making money, not war. He told the city council: "As a free city, with but a nominal duty on imports, [New York's] local government could be supported without taxation upon her people. Thus we could be free from taxes, and have cheap goods nearly duty free."[12]

They would also be rid of the New York State legislature, which "has become the instrument by which we are plundered to enrich . . . speculators, lobby agents, and Abolition politicians."[13]

"The South is our best customer," he reasoned, and isn't the customer always right?[14] Why war upon your most lucrative trading partner? A free nation of New York City would enjoy "uninterrupted intercourse with every section."[15] Gunfire, cannonade, and the weeping of bereft widows and mothers might fill the air of the disunited states, but the dominant sound in New York City would be the cheerful sough of money changing hands. Maybe it wasn't a sublime vision, but no nineteen-year-old boy would get his head or legs blown off by enemy fire in the New York of Fernando Wood's dream.

Rather, New York City would serve as a beacon during the Cimmerian blackness of war: "Amid the gloom which the present and prospective condition of things must cast over the country, New York, as a free city, may shed the only light and hope for a future reconstruction of our once blessed confederacy."[16]

He saw one, two, many secessions, and he welcomed them: "California and her sisters in the Pacific will no doubt set up an independent republic, and husband their own rich mineral resources. The Western States, equally rich in cereals and other agricultural products, will probably do the same. Thus it may be said why should not New York City . . . become also equally independent?"[17]

Wood was howled down, as prophets, whether sage or crazed, usually are. His strongest support came from the *New York Daily News*, edited by brother Benjamin. The paper, in which Wood had a controlling interest, was deemed treasonous in August 1861 by the US Circuit Court grand jury for the Southern District of New York because of its "frequent practice of encouraging the rebels" by "expressing sympathy and agreement with them."[18] The post office then barred the paper from the mails in one of the Lincoln administration's numerous offenses against traditional American liberties. (Ben Wood was no less colorful than Fernando: He ran lotteries, wrote the pro-secession 1862 novel *Fort Lafayette: or Love and Secession*, and helped inspire the city's anti-draft riots.)[19]

A Free New York was not without appeal to the city's mercantile class. One anonymous merchant asked the *Journal of Commerce*, "If I believe that as a free port New York would become the greatest city on the globe, am I a traitor because I assert such an opinion?"[20]

From the South, the pro-slavery sociologist George Fitzhugh called the idea of a "Republic of New York" the "most brilliant that these eventful times have given birth to," throwing in a sidewise sneer at "the immoral, infidel, agrarian, free-love Democracy of western New York."[21] Well, we takes our compliments where we gets 'em.

Horace Greeley's *Tribune* raged, "Fernando Wood evidently wants to be a traitor; it is lack of courage only that makes him content with being a blackguard."[22] It is, of course, a Greeley's prerogative to change his mind, but the vehemence with which he moved from a "you can go your own way" policy to scourging traitors is startling.

While the dithering lame-duck Democratic president James Buchanan fretted over Mayor Wood's threat, Abraham Lincoln brushed it off with the remark that it would be "some time before the front door sets up housekeeping on its own account."[23]

Whatever glimmer of hope the free city had was snuffed at Fort Sumter. New York City was in the union, and in the war.

Fernando Wood endured. Elected to Congress in 1862 as a Peace Democrat, he became the most respectable of rogues, with a nine-term congressional career culminating in his chairmanship of the House Ways and Means Committee. Chairman Wood was a passionate free-trader who spent the postbellum years trying to do for his country what he had failed to do for his city: keep open its ports, and thrash the dreaded tariff as soundly as his Dead Rabbits used to the Bowery Boys.

Historian Tyler G. Anbinder notes that the handful of scholars who have paid any attention at all to Wood's free-city plan have followed the lead of Marxist Philip Foner in ascribing it to the Southern interests of the merchant class. But this crude ideologizing, he reminds us, "ignore[s] the long history of antipathy which has characterized the relationship between New York City and the rural portions of the state since the seventeenth century." Just weeks before Wood floated his plan, Democratic congressman Daniel Sickles had predicted that New York City, "a subjugated dependency of a fanatical and puritanical State government, that never thinks of the city except to send its tax gatherers among us, or to impose upon us hateful officials, alien to our interests and sympathies, to eat up the substance of the people by their legalized extortions," would take a cue from the Deep South and "free herself from the hated Republican State government."[24] That's telling 'em, Dan. Oh, for a Sickles today to hammer our heads! (Sickles made Wood look like Ward Cleaver. He had recently been acquitted, by reason of insanity, of killing the man who had cuckolded him—Francis Scott Key's son!)[25]

Fernando Wood's trial balloon of an independent city-state of New York was punctured, and over the next century not even William Randolph Hearst could set aloft the more moderate and infinitely just idea of two New York states. Hearst proposed a split in 1921, when it became obvious that he could never win the governorship if yokels had the franchise. Hearst demanded a state of Manhattan whose boundaries extended through all five boroughs and included Westchester County and Long Island.

Upstate blocked Hearst from the governorship as effectively as it did Mayor Ed Koch in 1982, after Hizzoner imprudently told *Playboy*: "This rural America thing—I'm telling you, it's a joke." Behind the pastoral facade lurked a truly nightmarish reality: "wasting time in a pickup truck when you have to drive twenty miles to buy a gingham dress or a Sears, Roebuck suit."[26] Not exactly Jackie Mason, but still, a pretty harmless jest. Rural York, alas, had lost its sense of humor. We rejected Koch for Mario Cuomo.

I was among the affronted rural New York Democrats who voted for that sanctimonious windbag Cuomo. Stupid me. I hadn't the wit to understand Koch's bluster as a sort of charmingly abrasive Manhattan provincialism. (This is not to say that Koch would have been a good governor. Only an amusing one.)

Governor Cuomo spoke of a "family of New York," its branches stretching from the Upper West Side to Massena to Buffalo. But he never did explain what qualities, other than our common humanity, these far-flung brothers and sisters shared. What familial tie binds a Wyoming County deerhunter to an East Village scenemaker? The fact that their taxes are poured into one huge coffer? Big deal. How is an Elba onion farmer kin to Maureen Dowd or Rudy Giuliani? David Leavitt, Manhattan's erstwhile golden boy of letters (before he swiped Stephen Spender's life), looked beyond the Hudson and saw "a scrubbed, manicured neighborhood . . . The music is by Wayne Newton, the paintings are by Norman Rockwell, and sex takes place only between married men and women in beds at night."[27] The details are all wrong, of course, except maybe for Norman Rockwell and the bed, but that's to be expected of Leavitt, who knows less about my country than I do about the Pet Shop Boys. No matter. This is how the *New York Review of Books*, *National Review*, and everything in between see us, and this is why some sharp Upstate pol, maybe a demagogue and maybe not, will one day tap into the populist potential and try to set this house on fire. Our call to battle could come from William Jennings Bryan's Cross of Gold speech: "Our war is not a war of conquest. We are fighting in the defense of our homes, our families, and posterity. We have petitioned, and our petitions have been disregarded; we have begged, and they have mocked when our calamity came. We beg no longer; we petition no more. We defy them."[28]

The train of abuses and usurpations snakes into eternity. We are taxed to subsidize their squalid subway system, their welfare industry, and those artistic expressions deemed pleasing by the heirs to the longtime New York State Council on the Arts culture czarina—and former squeeze of the artless Thomas Dewey—Kitty Carlisle. Rural and working-class folk are harassed by an array of city-driven restrictions on gun ownership, education mandates, and extortionate regressive levies and licenses for every human activity beyond breathing.

Our family of New York is rent by misunderstanding, suspicion, and mutual hostility. Downstaters regard us as hicks and philistines with calluses hardened by pulling the lynch rope. Contrariwise, Upstaters see New York City as a distant Babylon, violent and gaudy, disrespectful of tradition and simple human decency. Each of us may be wrong—*each of us is wrong*—but that is how we have viewed each other for centuries, and those who speak of common ground inevitably wish to reach it through the medium of commercial culture, which only degrades all involved.

Remember, the two sides of a partitioned New York would still be part of the same union. No Fernando Woods are on the horizon—yet—and no one wants to erect a Yonkers Wall. Visitors—even immigrants—are always welcome. Relations between the two states would doubtless be marked by comity, perhaps even a newfound goodwill. (Nah, not really, but isn't it pretty to think so?)

In fact, we'll even let Downstate keep the name New York. Some sharp lawyer has probably copyrighted it anyway. A plebiscite can determine our name; I'd vote for Iroquois, in homage to the Indian confederacy that once overspread this land. It may have been, as David Hackett Fischer writes, "a French understanding of an Algonquian version of two Basque words that meant 'killer people,'" but hey, better a fierce name as deterrent than a standing army.[29]

By what right does a Midtown state senator dictate the speed limit on Route 5 between LeRoy and Caledonia? Why should Finger Lakes assemblymen have a say over housing policies in the Bronx? Why let Tuxedo Parkers force irradiated waste on Allegany County?

The practical effect of New York's excessive size and centralization is captured by the Kentucky poet-farmer Wendell Berry's lament that "everywhere, every day, local life is being discomforted, disrupted, endangered, or destroyed by powerful people who live, or who are privileged to think that they live, beyond the bad effects of their bad work."[30]

Case One: in 1987, Albany's bureaucrats, obsessed as they are with the clank and smoke of Progress and making our national product even grosser, betook to force—right down their throats—the fifty-two-mile supercollider project on Ontario and Wayne Counties, public opinion be damned. The supercollider would have destroyed apple orchards and encroached on the Hill Cumorah, cradle of Mormonism, as well as hundreds of *homes*, places where real people live and love, all for the fool's prestige of federal pork and Big Science.

Governor Mario Cuomo was baffled by the spirited grassroots protest to save Wayne and Ontario. He did not understand that rural people might love their homes more than they love money. There are, believe it or not, people who care about more than high wages and endless construction, who do not want to live in the vast metal and concrete prison of urban America.

At the same time as the appleknockers were thwarting the supercollider, a state-regents-appointed committee of library bureaucrats almost shut down hundreds of our rural libraries by imposing unmeetable staffing requirements. The implication was that we are too stupid to oversee our local libraries; we need educated Downstate Big Sisters to help us out. The committee's purported aim was to "improve services" to the hicks. Why, some of these small-town gal librarians were so backward they actually filled their bibliotheca with Shakespeare and Hawthorne and Tolstoy instead of the prescribed workout videotapes and computers. Some of those crazy old spinsters actually shushed noisy patrons and pushed *Penrod* onto brainy boys![31]

These and a hundred other bitter conflicts rage in schizophrenic New York. Why not separate the clashing personalities? Relations between our Iroquois and their New York would be cordial. Trade, travel, and all forms of legal intercourse would continue unabated. The only change would be *political*: Downstate would no longer be able to push us around. It's akin to having the class bully transfer to another school. Ah, to breathe fresh and free air!

Viewed through the Big Picture—which leaves out all the enlivening detail—the vitality is gone up here: no ferment, no foment, no nothing. Or so it appeared to Governor Cuomo, who seriously overplayed his hand and touched off a rural rebellion that for one brief brilliant moment showed us What Might Be.

In 1989 the governor determined to locate a low-level nuclear waste dump in rural, money-poor Allegany County. Most of New York's waste is generated around the city, but, well, you know: mustn't rouse the righteous dander of E. L. Doctorow and Christie Brinkley. It would be so much easier to steal land in our godforsaken region. The *Times* wouldn't make a peep.

Imagine Cuomo's surprise when his likeness was hung in effigy across the Southern Tier of Western New York. Protesters—not stoned college kids but natives, many with roots generations deep—kept state inspectors off the threatened property. Raucous rallies recalled Whiskey Rebels and Daniel Shays. Guitar slingers who'd take Johnny Cash over Joan Baez any day sang rousing songs. Top of the pops: "Allegany County is full of nasty boys/Shotguns is their favorite toys."

The anti-nuke firestorm whipped up a great new cloud of anti-urbanism. Most Upstaters, at least in my neck of the woods, have never even been to New York City, four hundred miles distant. Nevertheless, as Norman Mailer has said, "the good farmers and small-town workers of New York State rather detest us."[32] And why not? You send your murderers and rapists and howling Son of Sam lunatics to Attica, and you want to bury your waste in our woodlands. Like a boorish suitor who has already been to the mountaintop, you don't even flatter us into submission. You just seize the land by eminent domain, all the while crowing about how green thou art. (The upper-middle-class environmentalist groups, so exercised over plastic trash bags and snowmobiles, were shamefully silent on the attempted rape of Allegany. After all, Cuomo appeared White House–bound, and why piss off the man who might appoint you deputy assistant administrator of something-or-other?)

The anti-Cuomo, anti-NYC sentiment churned to a roiling boil, but to outside eyes it seemed diffuse and unchanneled. It had no public outlet. The parties, the chain papers, the TV and radio stations owned by absentee corporations: The New York establishment really is one big happy family. Agrarian and small-town dissent embarrasses Upstate elites, who have been to college and met people from all over the world and learned never to trust their own judgments or those of un-degreed, untraveled neighbors.

While Allegany burned in 1990, the Republicans ran for governor a Manhattan millionaire economist named Pierre Rinfret, chosen for his bulging purse. Rinfret yammered about the death penalty and the fool drug war, as though serial killers and white powder are what ailed us. He called his Upstate campaign trips a waste of money. He squandered the rural vote with a remarkable proposal that counties bid for the privilege of *not* hosting waste dumps—thus ensuring that our poorest, most verdurous, least populated shires would become the Metropole's latrine. Westchester would go scot-free, while Allegany would be forever despoiled. Despairing Yorkers cried that the Cuomo–Rinfret contest proved that the system no longer worked, but I suspect that this long-forgotten race proved just the opposite: The system by which Cities and Money keep us in vassalage works all too well.

A quadrennium passed, and the Republicans nominated an obscure politico from the borderlands to take on Cuomo: George Pataki, the former mayor of Peekskill in Westchester County. Pataki's campaign was vapid and gray. He and Cuomo never bothered to appear in thirty-eight of the state's sixty-two counties between Labor Day and Election Day, but come the second Tuesday in November a massive Upstate turn-out produced a regional Pataki landslide that overwhelmed the governor's Downstate stronghold and delivered us, for a dozen years, from the latest in a long line of governors (Dewey, Harriman, Rockefeller) whose disdain for rural York is exceeded only by their ignorance of it. Pataki won every Upstate county save Albany, warren of bureaucrats. In counties surrounding Allegany the governor was lucky to win 20 percent of the vote. Anti-Cuomo margins in rural counties ran as high as four and five to one. While the demise of the detested Cuomo blew away one particularly louring cloud, the thunderheads kept coming. Pataki, whose transition team included such non-Zapatistas as David Rockefeller and Henry Kissinger, governed as a Dewey Republican, as accentless as an Orlando TV newsreader. Governor Pataki stabbed gun owners in the back (where else can they go? he reasoned, as the statewide Democrats can be counted on to nominate candidates who barely bother to conceal their contempt for hunters) and did nothing to introduce Upstate themes into school curricula. (His education commissioner, a Vermont transplant, pressured high schools to drop such supremely inoffensive Indian nicknames as Braves, Raiders, and Chiefs. Some rootless suburbanites complied, but the rooted and the rural fight on, bravely.) Pataki was succeeded in 2007 by the spoiled son of a developer, Democrat Eliot Spitzer, who proudly called himself a "fucking steamroller" and who possessed all the sensitivity to bucolic charm implied in that phrase. When the public humiliation of this sanctimonious bully over his pricey dalliance with a doxy led to his resignation in March 2008, he was replaced by his lieutenant governor, David Paterson, also of . . . New York City.

Upstate has not produced a governor since 1920. He was Republican Nathan Miller of Cortland, who was either a principled fiscal conservative or a tool of Andrew Carnegie, depending on who tells the story. (Please don't try to claim that George Pataki of Westchester County or the cousin-marrier of Hyde Park, Franklin D. Roosevelt, was an "Upstater.") We last had a major-party *candidate* for governor in 1954.

Republican, Democrat: No matter which party runs New York, our subjection is inevitable. And so what, ask some of my landsmen. David Harum, the cracker-barrel Yorker of a nineteenth-century regional novel, philosophized, "A reasonable amount of fleas is good for a dog—they keep him f'm broodin' on bein' a dog."[33]

The problem is, Upstate has become a miserable whipped cur. Estonia had more influence in the Kremlin than we do in Albany. (At least they've let us keep our accents.)

As the republican ideal dims, We are becoming more like Them. Henry W. Clune's fine unknown novel *Six O'Clock Casual* (1960) describes an Upstate hamlet in which the prominent men gleefully loot their patrimony. A native daughter, returned from New York City, discovers nothing but soul-sickness and cupidity in her hometown. At novel's end, she again flees to the City, which at least is frank in its corruption.

For all his pessimism, Henry W. Clune remained in the village of Scottsville until the day he died, four months shy of age 106. He tried

New York City once or twice but opted to cultivate a literary career in hardscrabble local ground. He explained: "I longed for Main Street and the friendly nod, the warm greeting, the buttonholing by this, that, and the other passer-by. I wanted to be where I knew the folks . . . Rochester becomes, not the small center around which the world revolves, but almost the world itself."[34] (Rochester, the third largest city in New York, has never produced a governor.)

Clune was sadly unlaureled, but he lived a life richer than a thousand PEN benefits. We are a "culturally undernourished hinterland," according to Norman Mailer, and while Upstaters do exhibit a deplorable ignorance of their heritage, I'll gladly pit Edmund Wilson against Alfred Kazin, John Gardner against Philip Roth, Joyce Carol Oates against any Shawn-era *New Yorker* miniaturist, and, in the historical novelist category, Walter D. Edmonds against Arthur Schlesinger Jr.[35]

Face it: New York City has hit its cultural nadir. The magnet that once drew William Dean Howells now repels us with the agit-prop juvenilia of performance artists and a built landscape of modernist atrocities. Free spirits, Jack Kerouacs cruising jazz clubs, are long gone. The underground has a factitious, sham quality. New York City's two punk celebrities of my day were typical: David Byrne was a RISDE brat and Joey Ramone had a rich psychiatrist mother. Buffalo's best punk band, the Enemies, was led by a swimming-pool cleaner and a cabbie.

So where do we turn, O Lord, where do we turn? To Norman Mailer, of course, whose 1969 mayoral campaign is a fulgurant fugging star in our pitch-black night.

The Brooklyn novelist Mailer ran in the Democratic primary against a quartet of machine hacks and standard-brand liberals. He lost, of course—the good guys always do, don't they?—but I don't believe that any municipal campaign of the last century has been packed with such radical spirit and reactionary sense.

Mailer averred that he was a "left conservative," to the left of the liberals and to the right of the conservatives: wisdom's place! He got clobbered, but not before diagnosing the modern malady: "The style of New York life has shifted since the Second World War (along with the rest of American cities) from a scene of local neighborhoods and personalities to a large dull impersonal style of life which deadens us with its architecture, its highways, its abstract welfare, and its bureaucratic reflex to look for government solutions which come into the city from without (and do not work) . . . Our authority has been handed over to the federal power. We expect our economic solutions, our habitats, yes, even our entertainments, to derive from that remote abstract power, remote as the other end of a television tube. We are like wards in an orphan asylum. The shaping of the style of our lives is removed from us—we pay for huge military adventures and social experiments so separated from our direct control that we do not even know where to begin to look to criticize the lack of our power to criticize . . . Our condition is spiritless. We wait for abstract impersonal powers to save us, we despise the abstractness of those powers, we loathe ourselves for our own apathy."[36] Has any candidate in postwar America been as eloquent? If NYC had listened to Mailer, Paul Goodman, and Dorothy Day instead of John Lindsay, Ed Koch, and Rudy Giuliani, perhaps we'd be friends.

The centerpiece of his campaign was his contention that "our city must become a state." The hour was late. "New York City is today a legislative pail of dismembered organs strewn from Washington to Albany," he wrote, viscerally, and the only way to sew up and reanimate the corpse was through radical devolution of power.[37] Seeking a "hip coalition of the left and right," and understanding that his promises to free Black Panther co-founder Huey Newton and to end fluoridation might not be glue enough, he proposed to make New York City the fifty-first state of the union.[38] As campaign manager Joe Flaherty wrote in his hilarious account of this electoral knight errantry, *Managing Mailer* (1970), the novelist eschewed the trivial and tedious financial arguments and emphasized instead that "by going through the process of acquiring statehood, [New Yorkers] would have a rebirth, a rediscovery of the soul."[39]

There would be no inane happy-talk about the "family of New York" from Norman Mailer. He realized that "the connection of New York City to New York State is a marriage of misery, incompatibility, and abominable old quarrels." His concern was properly with his own brawling grounds, but he did see a favorable fallout for we hicks as well, for going it alone could spark "the development of what has been hitherto a . . . typically colorless national tract."[40] Yes, Niagara Falls, Cooperstown, Lake Placid, Susan B. Anthony, Grover Cleveland, Washington Irving, John Brown's North Elba—we are cultural and scenic starvelings for sure.

"Power to the Neighborhoods!" was Mailer's secondary slogan. (Newspaper reporter Jimmy Breslin, Mailer's running mate as candidate for president of city council, suggested that it be changed to "wisdom of the neighborhoods" lest the word *power* scare off the middle class.)[41] Stormin' Norman wanted to abolish the city government and permit blocks, tracts, and sections to manage their own affairs. Soho, Harlem, Bensonhurst: Each neighborhood would be responsible for its own welfare, trash pickup, fire protection, parks, education, policing, and other municipal offerings.

Out of the hard work of self-governance would come cultural renewal. "I am running on everything from Black Power to Irish Self-Righteousness," Mailer told an Irish Club in Park Slope. (His published speeches, with such interlarded remarks as "Shut up and fuck you! Let me talk" will never be confused with those of Hillary Clinton.)[42] The possibilities for true diversity were dizzying: Mailer suggested that Harlem might declare a holiday for Malcolm X, while Staten Island honored John Birch. One neighborhood might require church attendance, while another mandated serial sex. As he told an audience at Union Theological Seminary in a precocious rebuke to political correctness, "People are healthier if they live out their prejudices rather than suppressing them in uniformity."

"I'm running against urban renewal!" he exclaimed, which is to say he was on the side of beauty, poetry, sentiment, history, and, in a city that destroys everything it does not commodify, losers.[43] His secondary planks—for instance, the Flaherty-inspired call for a world series of stickball to be played in the lanes of Wall Street—shone with a luster that the *Times* editorialists could not appreciate. Even his running mate didn't get it: After a chaotic Village Gate rally, Jimmy Breslin said, "I found out I was running with Ezra Pound."[44] Since decentralism is the diametrical opposite of fascism—a centralized state and economy—Breslin's Mailer–Pound comparison is on the order of linking cantos and cantaloupes. (Credit Breslin for one excellent postrace line: "I am mortified to have taken part in a process that required bars to be closed.")[45]

Mailer won 5 percent of the Democratic primary vote, or about six times less than the winner, machine politico Mario A. Procaccino, who would go on to lose to Liberal incumbent John Lindsay. But je souviens, Norman, je souviens.

Two years after Mailer's campaign, Bella Abzug picked up the statehood baton. Declaring that the city was "in bondage" to Albany, the liberal feminist congresswoman launched a petition drive to put secession on the November 1971 city ballot. The state government, Bella bellowed, was dominated by "farmers and fishermen and political opportunists," a description best characterized as two hopeless strikeouts and a home run.[46]

Abzug kvetched over the alleged shortchanging of New York City by the state. City taxpayers, she claimed, sent $3.55 billion to Albany and received back, in various forms, just $2.907 billion.[47] This balance of payments can be and was interpreted variously, but Abzug was unquestionably right when she complained that the city's rent laws and public employee contracts, among other things, were subject to state approval, an affront to home rule.

Curiously, most of the pro-statehood liberals of 1971, including Abzug, had opposed the high-testosterone Mailer candidacy of 1969. They had raised the specter of Governor Rockefeller sending in the troops, Lincoln-like, to crush a city secession. Mailer predicted that the invading army would never make it past Harlem.[48]

The floppy-hatted Abzug raged against Upstate "appleknockers" who did not understand the historical inevitability of a centralized welfare state run by Manhattan social workers. "The people of New York have hopes and aspirations that cannot be denied by a bunch of backwoods politicians in Albany," she spat.[49] This was a first: a putatively "populist" campaign based on the disparagement and ridicule of rural people and farmers. And you wonder why liberalism got such a bad name.

Abzug's plan was poorly designed: She wanted an urban state, without the buffers of Long Island and Westchester County. (We don't want 'em, either!) Still, it would have had a larger population than forty-two of its sister states. Governor Nelson Rockefeller's Division of the Budget issued a report denouncing the proposal as "fraudulent" and "a hoax" and reminding New Yawkas where their water came from.[50]

Yet Abzug struck a nerve. Ambitious pols who thought they were too urban, too Jewish, or too black to win statewide elections hopped on the statehood train. The secession ranks included five members of Congress, more than forty state legislators, and three borough presidents—including Brooklyn's Sebastian Leone, who took Bella one step farther and called for an independent Brooklyn, asserting, "We've lived too long in the shadow of Manhattan . . . We're being slowly devoured."[51] (As Norman Mailer said, the good folk of Brooklyn were "real people" and far superior to the "fuckin' phony liberals in Manhattan.")[52] The Buffalo City Council passed a "good riddance" resolution.[53]

Ninety percent of respondents to a poll conducted by *New York* magazine answered yes to the question "Should New York City become a separate state?"[54] Petitions were circulated to force a citywide referendum to authorize the drafting of a new constitution, the first step toward statehood. A can-do spirit was in the air. As a full-page ad in the *New York Times* by the Committee to Make New York City a State exhorted, "Sure, it won't be easy. But with the whole city pulling together (for maybe the first time), we could pull it off in as little as a year-and-a-half."[55] Liberal activists were reinvigorating the torpid American ideal of self-rule, and they were, justly, proud of themselves. It was modern urban liberalism's finest hour.

The city establishment and its tedious mouthpiece, the *New York Times*, disapproved. "Demographically," the paper editorialized, "this [new] state would have a disproportionately large black and Puerto Rican population, plus one-seventh of its residents on welfare."[56] (Translation: Those people are fine to pick up our trash and wash our dishes, but we don't want them running things!) The *Times* dismissed the possibility that the city might gain financially from self-rule, citing no less an authority than City Comptroller Abe Beame—the dim bulb who would, as mayor, soon drive the city to the verge of insolvency.

An odd twist to the debate: The anti-secession forces were fortified by a Citizens Union report authored by an obscure professor who argued that decentralism was "reactionary" and unworkable. Her name was Donna Shalala, later President Clinton's secretary of health and human services. On the other side, an executive assistant to Mayor Lindsay produced "City

Statehood—A Time for Serious Study," a report detailing the manifold benefits of the idea and asserting that it "may well be the only sensible approach to governing New York City": He was Leon Panetta, later Clinton's chief of staff and Obama's director of the CIA.

The Shalala paper, huffily titled "New York City-Statehood: An Idea Whose Time Has Passed," is a window upon the liberal technocrat mind. Conceding that New York City may pay into state coffers slightly more than it receives, Shalala nevertheless scoffs at this "crude argument." Of course government transfers wealth from one interest group to another, she says; otherwise, why pay taxes to distant governments? You may as well just keep the money home and spend it on local needs. Well, yes, the reader might think, but Shalala shuts off *that* avenue with the peremptory statement that "the proponents of statehood use a faulty and even reactionary concept—that you should get back what you pay in."

In any event, there are just too damn many little governments around, complains Shalala, and the incredible hulk keeps stubbing his toes on them. "One of the curses of metropolitan America is governmental fragmentation," she declares. We need to abolish those niggling local governments and permit the big boys to extort tribute from everyone: A "completely redesigned governmental system for the entire metropolitan area" would give enlightened Manhattan politicians access to the pocketbooks of the people of Suffolk, Nassau, Westchester, Rockland, and other counties. We don't need to decentralize—instead, Professor Shalala asserts, we must *centralize* power in the hands of those who know best.[57] As her ally Albert Shanker, the longtime president of the United Federation of Teachers, wrote in his weekly *New York Times* adverto-column, "The desire for 'community control' for New York as a city [is] a desire which, if fulfilled, would leave New York economically worse off and which would inevitably lead to similar demands for community control for each *part* of the city. [Yes, yes, Mailer nods his head vigorously.] The end can only be a complete governmental breakdown." Shanker, who had fought bitterly with black parents who had the temerity to insist that their children be taught by black teachers from the neighborhood instead of his union members, concluded that "the 'community control' of cities and parts of cities will lead to the same deterioration as we have seen in the community control of schools."[58] Strip away the circumlocution and what he is saying is that blacks are incapable of self-government. They cannot run their own schools and they sure as hell can't run their own neighborhoods. They need liberal whites to do it for them.

For all the surface sophistication of Gotham's 51st Staters, they were also naive. The city clerk rejected 20,000 of the 55,398 signatures they had collected.[59] (The requisite total was 45,000.) There would be no referendum on whether to authorize a city commission to draw up a constitution for a new state. Governor Rockefeller and the *New York Times*, which had consistently deprecated Abzug's effort as "demagoguery" (translation: a popular idea disliked by liberals), proclaimed it a great triumph for unity, and secession fizzled.

Mailer and Abzug performed the splendidly valuable service of making other politicians think. Former mayor Robert Wagner, as dull a functionary as has dozed in Gracie Mansion, responded to the 51st State movement by recommending that if push came to shove the suburbs should be pulled into the new state, and Mayor John Lindsay went so far as to request the Panetta-penned report on the subject.[60] Why not self-rule? Once thought, the idea is hard to un-think.

And Now a Fugue in Which I Don't Quite Hum "New York, New York" but I Do Go Soft on the City of Allen Ginsberg and Babe Ruth and the Saintly Miss Day . . .

New York City: If you can break it there, you can break it anywhere. Not much of a bridge, eh? Then let's consider the real thing and the confounding matter of bridges, which always seem to stretch too far.

The enduring cinematic visage of New York City belongs not to King Kong or Woody Allen but rather to John Travolta, who in *Saturday Night Fever* (1977) forsook his family and home in Brooklyn's Bay Ridge to cross the bridge to Manhattan. On one side was clan, faith, family; on the other was the promise of wealth, glamour, and sex with girls who don't go to church and don't feel at all guilty about it. Most of us cross that bridge before we even come to it.

Travolta's desertion of Brooklyn is presented as a graduation we are supposed to applaud. After all, a Manhattan transfer is the beginning of enlightenment—just ask those who manufacture so much of America's image of itself from the high-rises of Manhattan.

Because the Bronx is the only one of New York's five boroughs that is on the American mainland, bridges are all that really connect our country, and the rest of New York, to its most atypical city. New York City has always been the antithesis of inland America, and Upstate New York. It is a port, with all that entails: prosperity, a transient and polyglot population, vice and depravity, a sense of action and bustle and excitement. New York was "like a munificent dung hill, where every thing finds kindly nourishment, and soon shoots up and expands to greatness," wrote Washington Irving, who created Diedrich Knickerbocker, the Dutchman who was the city's emblem for so many years—and whose nomenclatorial legacy is the NBA team of highly paid underachievers.[61]

In the weeks after September 11, 2001, the bridge between New York City and America was reinforced. So great was the outpouring of sympathy for the mourning city that even inveterate Yankee-haters found themselves pulling for George Steinbrenner's mercenaries in the fall 2001 World Series. At my village's crossroads, volunteer firefighters collected donations for NYC in their fluorescent hats. I threw in a tenspot every time, remembering, churlishly, how in our time of need New York City had done nothing of the kind for us. Thirty years earlier, nearby Attica State Prison was bloodied by a revolt, which directly touched a far higher percentage of local people than the 9/11 terrorism did in New York. The widows and orphans of the slain guards were not showered with flowers and quilts and charitable millions by the touched hearts of Manhattan; their gift was scorn and mockery, encapsulated in Al Pacino's chant "Attica! Attica!" in the transvestite bank robbery classic *Dog Day Afternoon* (1975). Whatever kindnesses we in the hinterlands extended to Manhattan in the wake of that black day in September were emphatically *not* in return for past favors.

The visitor who enters New York via train is disgorged into the magnificently restored Grand Central Station, with its ceiling depicting the constellations, pinpricks of light that must substitute for the night sky that Manhattanites cannot see through the light-haze and the skyscrapers.

In the 1880s Manhattan was the site of the first serious debates over height limits on buildings. Critics argued that skyscrapers were unhealthy in two ways. In case of disaster, the upper floors were charnel houses, as we relearned on September 11, 2001. And even absent fire or explosion, the towering structures blocked sunlight, contributing to a general urban sickliness.

New York being New York, the builders won, and out of Irving's munificent dung hill arose an urban cordillera whose peaks ranged from the truly impressive (Chrysler Building) to the pointless (Empire State Building) to the assertively ugly government boondoggle that was the Twin Towers, also known as "the largest aluminum siding job in the history of the world."[62]

The outsider is still overwhelmed by the din and anomie of New York: the jackhammers and honking cabs and people who don't look you in the eye. For every valorous fireman or Caribbean immigrant entrepreneur there is a neurotic hypochondriac straight from *Seinfeld* badgering her doctor for Lyme disease treatment should a mosquito alight on her arm. For all the "we're in this together" spirit kindled by the September 2001 attack, New York remains a city of strangers in which even the most genial apartment dwellers do not know their neighbors. Civic attachments are nigh impossible when you and the fellow down the hall do not even speak the same language; the government, perforce, will be the arbiter of your disputes.

The famed New York incivility, as many civil New Yorkers have told me, is a natural response to the environment. The urban dweller must shut down his senses lest he suffer an overload. So he has perfected the art of ignoring the disconsolate failures listlessly passing out "20% Off Hair Styling" flyers to indifferent passersby in front of every sun-blocking skyscraper. Catholic Worker founder Dorothy Day saw the face of Christ in each of these men and women, as well as in sisters and brothers a lot worse off, but Dorothy was a saint. Nevertheless, as I remind myself whene'er I find myself lost in the manswarm, life on an inhuman scale does not make one any less human.

And as one whose perverse literary tastes run to antebellum Northern poesy, the statuary of New York is a delight, recalling a day when poets were read by someone besides other poets. In Central Park, Fitz-Greene Halleck sits amid the elms, fastidiously fenced off from the hoi polloi.

Behind the New York Public Library stretches Bryant Park, once known as Needle Park in the title of another Al Pacino movie. Granitic William Cullen Bryant sits overlooking the greensward, not hearing the sotto voce dope offerings, while just off to his left a bronzed Gertrude Stein squats, as if over Alice B. Toklas's face. (Do I stray? I merely channel John Randolph of Roanoke, of whom Gamaliel Bradford wrote, "He could not stick to the subject, did not try to, did not wish to.")[63]

For fifty-one years William Cullen Bryant, the wunderkind poet of the Berkshires, edited the *New York Evening Post*, urging upon New Yorkers the policies of "free commerce, free speech, free soil."[64] Remarkable as it now seems, nineteenth-century New York was the hotbed of American libertarianism. It was the cradle of the most radically anti-government faction of any major party in our country's history, the Loco Focos of the 1830s. These Jacksonian Democrats—who even opposed government regulation of weights and measures—also denounced the "soulless, cadaverous, unmanly aristocracy of Wall Street," a jarring reminder that the early American free-marketeers loathed corporations as the artificial spawn of the state.[65]

Wall Street won. The Loco Focos disappeared. But then, as Thomas Janvier wrote in his chatty history *In Old New York* (1894), "there was no element of permanence in the settlement of New York."[66] The city has always been mutable, early to raze and eager to rise, and appalling to those of a traditionalist bent.

Manhattan was "characterized by an unparalleled fierceness in money-chasing," wrote a Brooklyn newsman named Walt Whitman.[67] Henry David Thoreau felt claustrophobic—walled-in, one might say. He wrote of New York: "The pigs in the street are the most respectable part of the population." Edgar Allan Poe, on the other hand, positively burbled: "The city is brimful of all kinds of *legitimate* liveliness—the life of money-making, and the life of pleasure."

By *city*, Poe meant Manhattan. The island was New York City. Until 1898.

The bridge that carried John Travolta away from Brooklyn made New York—huge, imperial New York—inevitable.

Across the East River from Manhattan grew beautiful Brooklyn, the city of homes and churches. Brooklyn had affordable homes, healthy air, and an Anglo-Protestant character not unlike that of New England. Manhattan's tenements and jerry-built towers were eyesores to sophisticated Brooklynites. (Edgar Allan Poe, bless his contrarian heart, despised Brooklyn's architecture: "I know few towns which inspire me with so great disgust and contempt. It puts me often in mind of a city of silvered-gingerbread," he wrote. "In point of downright iniquity—of absolute atrocity . . . I really can see little difference between the putting up of such a house as this, and blowing up a House of Parliament, or cutting the throat of one's grandfather.")[68]

But Brooklyn's men on the make were not satisfied with their pretty and insular city. They saw dollar signs on the far shores of the East River. And so, with the aid of a $65,000 bribe to Manhattan's Boss Tweed, was born that extraordinary feat of engineering known as the Brooklyn Bridge. David McCullough, in his history of *The Great Bridge* (1972), summarized its promises: "Property values would soar . . . Merchants could expect untold numbers of new customers as disaffected New Yorkers flocked across the river to make Brooklyn their home. Manufacturers would have closer ties with New York markets. Long Island farmers and Brooklyn brewers could get their wares over the river more readily. The mail would move faster."[69]

By 1890 a quarter of a million people were passing over the Brooklyn Bridge every day. The pokey "Brooklyn Ferry" memorialized by Walt Whitman was all but sunk.

German-born John Augustus Roebling, who fathered both the bridge and the man who would supervise its construction, said that it would "allow people of leisure, the old and young invalids, to promenade over the Bridge on fine days, in order to enjoy the beautiful views and the pure air."[70] The promenade still inspires awe, even if the exhaust-stinking air is impure. But the bridge that was going to put Brooklyn on the map ended up putting it out of existence.

You see, too many young people had taken Horace Greeley's advice and gone west. Chicago was swelling like President Cleveland's waistline; if it kept annexing suburbs, it might soon replace New York as America's largest city.

New York needed more people. Brooklyn needed access to New York's plentiful water supply. Queens, the Bronx, and Staten Island needed New York's municipal services. Combination was in the air.

A New York lawyer named Andrew Haswell Green lobbied tirelessly for the cities and villages of the region to merge into one enormous city of Greater New York. "Cities are the crowns . . . of empire," declared Green.

Brooklyn patriots, gathered in the League of Loyal Citizens, argued that their home should remain "a New England and American city."[71] They spoke of local self-rule and community pride, while the consolidators thrummed their siren song of "Progre$$ Progre$$ Progre$$."

Andrew Haswell Green had the classic progressive's contempt for any value not reducible to charts or tax tables. He dismissed Brooklyn patriotism as "senile sentimentalism . . . which vainly strives to stay the wheels of beneficent progress by a display of flags and banners, the din of brass bands and other claptrap."[72]

In the pivotal 1894 referendum, what became the five boroughs of New York voted for union. Only in Brooklyn was the debate fierce; by the narrowest of margins, 64,744–64,467, Brooklynites voted to dissolve their proud city. Desperate resistance delayed consummation of this marriage made in hell, or at least in the fever dreams of real estate speculators, until January 1, 1898. On that day Brooklyn, the fourth largest city in the country, was swallowed whole. Andrew Haswell Green's "wheels of progress" have rolled over Brooklyn ever since.

Bird Coler, the first comptroller of the imperial New York City, chirped his vision of what consolidation meant in a language that can only be called ravenous. Bird foresaw a day when "all divisional lines have been forever obliterated, and there is no Manhattan, no Brooklyn, no village by the sea, no localized settlement upon the Sound, no isolated community upon the hills of the Hudson, but one grand and glorious New York."[73] On such visions are tyrannies built.

Dreamy sons of Brooklyn have since tried to divorce their beloved mother from that foul old lech across the river, testing Daniel Webster's dictum, "Because a thing has been wrongly done, it does not follow that it can be undone."[74] Columnist Pete Hamill still decries the "Mistake of '98." He laments, "An independent Brooklyn would never have mutilated those amazing beaches by putting in high-rise public housing projects as far as possible from any kind of job . . . An independent Brooklyn probably would have built a new stadium for the Dodgers, so today there might be not just baseball but also the only football team on this side of the Hudson."[75]

Regrets came even quicker on Staten Island, by far the smallest and least urban of New York's boroughs, and the place where Dorothy Day found her faith and was laid to her rest. Staten Island has trees, Republicans, and no subways. It joined Greater New York in 1898 by a vote of about four to one and almost immediately had second thoughts. By 1900 patriots had formed the Staten Island Separation League, whose secretary announced: "During the past few months, many hundreds have declared themselves in favor of the Jeffersonian principle of decentralization and have become convinced that Staten Island can only become truly great when divorced from New York and incorporated as an independent city."[76] When in 1916 New York City's sanitation department assigned a garbage dump to the piquantly named area of Fresh Kills, a Staten Island Vigilance Committee and City Separation League fought the law—and though the dump was closed, in the long run the law won, as Fresh Kills eventually held 80 percent of the city's garbage.

Robert Moses's 1964 Verrazano-Narrows Bridge, which wreaked eminent domain on Brooklyn's Bay Ridge, brought not John Travolta but grime, exhaust, crowding, and other blessings of urban life to Staten Island. Discontent spread. "What we ought to do is tear down the Verrazano-Narrows Bridge and get back to the way it used to be," said sixty-eight-year-old retiree Katharine Winter several years ago.[77] Heeding Winter, Staten Island tried to repeal imperial New York—though not the bridge, alas—in one glorious swoop during the 1990s.

Staten Island's demographic profile cuts a sharp contrast with the other boroughs. Where they are heterogeneous, Staten Island's mien is Italian American. Staten Island accounts for less than 1 percent of New York's prisoner population; its percentage of citizens on public assistance is about one-third the city average. And it has far and away the largest percentage (61) of owner-occupied housing.

Despite its relatively sparse population (now 475,000), Staten Island found a voice within NYC's Board of Estimate and Appointment (later just Board of Estimate), which consisted of the five borough presidents, the mayor, the comptroller, and the president of the board of aldermen (later city council). The weighting of their votes varied over the years, but by 1983 each borough president had one vote, while the three citywide officials each cast two votes. It wasn't exactly the US Senate, but Staten Island, as the smallest borough, had a place at the table.

The board, which began life as a budget-making body, ceded power over the years to the city council, but it remained responsible for real property, capital projects, and land development in imperial New York. In other words, the Board of Estimate could stop the other four boroughs from such assaults as ramming liquefied natural gas tank "farms" into Staten Island soil.

The board had survived previous legal challenges on "one-man, one-vote" grounds because it was not a "general governing body" possessing a "legislative role." Its luck ran out in May 1983, when the US Court of Appeals for the Second Circuit ruled that the board did in fact "perfor[m] general governmental functions." The case wended its way up the judicial channel, but the writing was on the subway wall. If the Board of Estimate were abolished, then the city council, on which Staten Island held but three of fifty-one seats, would be unchecked by a countervailing power. As borough president Ralph J. Lamberti told the *Washington Post*, "I see Staten Island being the new dumping ground for all the unwanted projects, all the not-in-my-backyard problems."[78]

If anyone on Staten Island could read the ominous signs it was Republican state senator John J. Marchi, a classicist, Staten Island native, proud Son of Italy, and fixture in the state senate who had been elected to that body in 1956 and did not leave until fifty years later.

Marchi, chairman of the Senate Finance Committee, commissioned a 1983 report that bore the poetic title "Remedies of a Proud Outcast: The Legal Probability and Implications of Restructuring the Government and Boundaries of the City of New York." In his stirring foreword to this document, Senator Marchi wrote, "I am now prepared to say that secession is not only feasible, but that it is also legally and politically viable . . . We will not abide passively, the semi-colonialization of upwards to [*sic*] 400,000 men, women and children in a society that professes to condemn colonialization."[79]

The report forecast a grim future for a Staten Island unprotected by the Board of Estimate: An "unwelcome power plant" or "unwelcome physical installations" would be forced upon the borough in its "totally emasculated political position."[80] Yet an escape hatch was within reach: cityhood for Staten Island. A new city "would have no problem surviving as an independent financial entity," the Senate Finance Committee declared.[81] The proud outcast, standing on its own, would become the second largest city in New York. All that was necessary was a series of nimble leaps through successive legislative and electoral hoops.

Marchi issued a warning: "Staten Island should throw off its step-child status and separate from New York City if the federal courts take away its voice in the city government."[82] Six years later, the US Supreme Court did just that, upholding lower court rulings that the Board of Estimate violated the US Constitution. (This would have been news to those who drew up that Constitution, but then who cared about dead white men in 1989?) A new city charter scrapped the Board of Estimate.

Marchi replied by drafting legislation that would give Staten Islanders a vote on the question "Shall a charter commission to provide for the separation of the Borough of Staten Island be created?" The Republican-dominated state senate approved by a vote of 34–1, the sole vote against allowing Staten Island to determine its fate coming from Manhattan liberal Democrat Franz Leichter, who apparently figured why even bother with the pretense of choice. The bill went over to the Democratic assembly for its mercy killing. But miscalculation came to the rescue. The island's two Democratic assembly members begged the leadership to pass the bill, else their electoral fates would be sealed. The leaders acquiesced, confident that the hypercentralist Governor Cuomo would veto so radically decentralist a measure. The assembly voted yea, 117–21, and then Senator Marchi received an unexpected phone call from the governor in December 1989: "John, I have a Christmas present for you."[83] The Democratic governor had yielded to democratic impulses.

Staten Islanders, "misled by their own passions," in the condescending phrase of the passionless *New York Times*, approved the charter commission by a margin of 83–17 percent in 1990.[84] The commission proceeded to hold fifty-three public hearings before drawing up a charter whose preamble was penned by the Sophocles-quoting Senator Marchi ("the city is the people").

City officials explored ways to propitiate Staten Island, but Senator Marchi was not bribable. "It wouldn't matter if they gave a chauffeured limousine to every resident," he told reporter Chip Brown. "We're not stepping into a golden cage. No inducements can be extended that are co-extensive with personal freedom and democracy."[85] The nonbinding referendum in November 1993 to establish a city of Staten Island passed by a two-to-one margin, as citizens ignored a sententious editorial in the *New York Times* warning that secession, which was—yawn—"based on emotion and unsubstantiated fears"—would "tear the social and political fabric of the metropolis."[86] Times change, but the *Times* never does: Count on it always to stand for centralization of power and to disparage as crypto-hate-crimes the yearnings of small places for self-rule.

Having been ratified by the people who count—Staten Islanders—secession stalled in the state legislature, which is dominated by the other four boroughs. After all, why liberate your best garbage can? Republicans understand that without the white enclave of Staten Island there would have been no Mayor Giuliani and perhaps no Mayor Bloomberg. Seventeen years later, neither party will let Staten Island go, at least not as long as it contains a single unused inch of landfill or Republican vote.

State senator Serphin R. Maltese (R-Queens), a founder of the state's once-potent but now lickspittle Conservative Party, took a hint from Staten Island and proposed that a commission be established to study cityhood for Queens. His assembly co-sponsor, Democrat Anthony S. Seminerio, said, "I think the whole city has just gotten too big. I'd love to see us become an entity within ourselves."[87]

As the great Jane Jacobs said in 1997, "Brooklyn and other boroughs would all be better off on their own . . . Big bureaucracies can't allow for the diversity and experimentation that are essential to cities."[88] Who but the most obdurate imperialist can take issue with that? A city in pieces is a city at peace. The closer one is to the seat of authority, the more responsive that authority will be. Don't believe me? Then take two actions and call me in the morning. First, attend a meeting of your town board or city council and complain about tardy trash pickup or the lack of police patrols. See if anything is done about it. Then write your congressman or senator or the president himself and urge an end to a war or repeal of an objectionable law. Let me know when you get results.

The novelist Thomas Wolfe, a displaced North Carolinian, once wrote in the borough's famed dialect, "It'd take a guy a lifetime to know Brooklyn t'roo an' t'roo. An' even den, yuh wouldn't know it all."[89] Wise New Yorkers value their little green patches of the city for just this reason. They'd rather live on a block than spend their days crossing bridges.

The Fugue Over, I Re-Rusticate, and Walk the Grounds of Divorce

Upstate independence bills began reappearing in the legislature toward the end of the Cuomo years, and even the ousting of the despised Cuomo did not pacify the most fissiparously inclined. For the imbalance of power is not correctable under the current dispensation. The one-man one-vote Supreme Court rulings that decimated rural representation in the fifty states worked their wickedness on New York as well; long gone are the days in which each county (save Hamilton and Fulton) was guaranteed a seat in the state assembly.

New York's jerry-built equipoise between rural and urban interests was shattered by the US Supreme Court's iniquitous *Baker v. Carr* (1962), which forced states to allocate all legislative seats by population, thus eviscerating rural counties and placing the citizens of wide-open places and sleepy Elm Street burgs at the not-so-tender mercies of the horde.

Our shield, our palladium, was gone. But in the 1990s, Republican assemblyman Donald Davidsen, a veterinarian from rural Upstate Steuben County, led an effort to restore our voice by dividing New York into halves. Specifically, Davidsen would have bundled New York City, Long Island, and the suburban spillover of Westchester and Rockland Counties, let them keep the name New York, and declared the remainder of the state "West New York." (The precise border of Upstate has never been defined. Samuel Hopkins Adams, author of the classic *Grandfather Stories* [Random House, 1955], said that it was "west of Albany," a statement to which Hudson Valleyites would strongly object.[90] The *Daily Star* of

Oneonta in Central New York opined that the state line should be drawn as far up the Hudson as Newburgh in Orange County.[91] We will argue such matters in the sweet by-and-by.)

"Ever since I was a little kid," Davidsen told me when I interviewed him in December 1994, "when Upstaters get together you'd hear 'we oughta just cut that off and let it float away.'"[92] I heard much the same over Genesee County way. Yet Davidsen's bill was dismissed as "so absurd that it doesn't even merit a comment" by the mouthpiece of then-assembly-speaker Saul Weprin of Queens, who shortly thereafter passed on to the great deliberative chamber in the sky.[93] Weprin was replaced by Sheldon Silver, another standard-issue New York Democratic liberal from the same cookie cutter. A speaker of the assembly could keel over and die every month for a thousand years and the assembly would still be run by the same New York City drones. Is it really fair, as the writer G. Scott Thomas asked in the *Buffalo News*, that in a 47,377-square-mile state all our state elected officials hail from either the 301 square miles of New York City or its adjacent suburban counties?[94] What a diverse lot they are: spanning the length and breadth of the New York metropolis, from the syringe-washed shores of Rock Rock Rockaway Beach to the smoldering rubble of the South Bronx. What does a Downstate pol think when she gazes out the window of her chartered airplane as it hopscotches from Albany to Syracuse to Buffalo for a series of brief press conferences on airport tarmacs? Perhaps her meditations go something like this: "Hmmm, do people really *live* on farms? All that green, just sitting there doing nothing. Gee, what a great place for a nuclear waste dump! Or a maximum-security prison! I hope the rednecks don't shoot me!"

Governor Cuomo called Davidsen's bill "divisive"—"which of course it is," chuckled Davidsen. Division tends to be divisive. But it need not be rancorous. Assemblyman Davidsen was given to conciliation—"New York City certainly is a cultural gem," he allowed—for he understood that "people in New York City are unhappy" with Albany, too, and maybe, just maybe, their discontent could ripen into Mailerism. "The state doesn't represent either place very well," said Assemblyman Davidsen. "Upstate we have too many regulations, too many mandates, too many taxes; downstate they don't have enough services, enough gun control." Either the central authority imposes a one-size-fits-all solution on this diverse state, forcing the minority into a procrustean bed, or we separate, peaceably, and make our own laws, fitting them to our own circumstances. What, one wonders, could be the objection to that?

Republican state senator (later congressman) Randy Kuhl, like Davidsen a citizen of Steuben County, sponsored the companion bill in the Senate as well as legislation that would have permitted counties to place on the ballot the question "Do you support the division of New York into two separate states?" Kuhl was mocked by collaborationists in the chain press for saying, "My constituents don't ride subways, live in fear of drive-by shootings and send their children out to play in crack-infested neighborhoods."[95] A faux pas, to be sure: Gotham snobs can belittle the hicks all they want, but woe betide the uppity hick who gives it back, good and hard. Upstaters, said Senator Kuhl, preferred that their tax dollars "be used to preserve farmland and open space, keep lakes clean, improve rural highways"—matters of no demonstrable interest to straphangers and urban ballers.[96]

Newspaper polls showed support for a split of New York into two states running at close to 90 percent in many rural counties. County legislators in Wyoming, Steuben, Cayuga, Columbia, Broome, and Essex endorsed the legislation. A Coalition for Two New Yorks appeared at the state's western end. Opposition came, predictably, from absentee-owned chain dailies, especially the Gannett papers that pimple the region like whiteheads on a teenager's nose. What does vapidity taste like? The *Star-Gazette* of Elmira, a Gannett paper, editorialized: "Consider the Statue of Liberty, for example. All Americans take pride in that awesome symbol of freedom. But New Yorkers hold the statue in special esteem. If [Assemblyman] Davidsen and [Senator] Kuhl had their way, the statue would no longer be a part of Western New York's annals. Neither would the Empire State Building, Central Park, the United Nations . . . And what about what we share in common with downstaters? What would happen to the state flag; the state bluebird; the state flower, the rose; or the state tree, the sugar maple?"[97]

Tell you what, *Star-Gazette*: We'll keep the bluebirds, roses, and sugar maples, and they can have the United Nations and the Empire State Building. Fair enough?

Collaborators lectured we benighted plebs about our good fortune in being subsidized by the philanthropists of Manhattan, who put in more than they take out. (To which Senator Kuhl replied, "In West New York, we'd be able to cut so [many] government regulations that we'd save money immediately.")[98] Syracuse liberals, the *Post-Standard* (owned by the Newhouse chain) of the Salt City informed us, would be "less than thrilled at being stuck in the rump state of New York." (I'll take their word that being "stuck in the rump" is unpleasant.)[99] We were also informed by a doughty Upstate newspaper that "people in high rises, offices, barns and cabins are linked by sophisticated communications networks" and "watch the same television programs."[100] Through *Dancing with the Stars* we are made one.

Davidsen reintroduced his bill in the Pataki era, along with a companion measure permitting the counties to hold nonbinding referenda on the question of a split. But the moment had passed. Sighing their relief at being rid of a despised Governor Cuomo who viewed our region with undisguised contempt, regarding it as fit for little more than radioactive waste dumps and prisons in which to warehouse the killers and yeggs of Gotham, Upstaters exhaled too much. They relaxed their vigilance. They—we—snored back into listlessness.

Yet certain truths are unmalleable: for instance, that a state so large and diverse is not governable except by tyranny. And since Upstate, even by the most liberal definition, constitutes less than 40 percent of New York's population, the tyrant's rod ain't ever gonna be wielded by us.

My friend Steve Hawley, the devilishly charming Republican assemblyman from Batavia, relit the fuse in early 2009, co-sponsoring a bill that would permit counties to place on the ballot the question "Do you support the division of New York into two separate states?" A cognate bill was introduced in the Senate, also by Upstate GOPers. I wish the renascent campaign hadn't such a Republican cast, but the Democratic sweep of 2008 put assembly, senate, and the governorship under the thumb of Downstate Democrats.

In the brutal winter of 2009, when secession bills brightened gray Albany and, mirabile dictu, an Upstater became—however temporarily—a US Senator, I thought on these matters at the intersection of guns and football, which was not, as you might suspect, a University of Miami team party.

For the Super Bowl is a mere anticlimax to the February edition of the triannual Alexander Gun Show, held the morning of the big (bloated and gaudy) game in a volunteer firemen's hall a mile south of the home of the late Barber Conable, the statesman who represented us in Congress for twenty years. Conable was a poetry-reciting antiquarian Iwo Jima vet who used to scour the show looking for Indian arrowheads to add to a collection he had begun in boyhood. Now, *that* was an American.

The phrase *gun show* reduces Ellen Goodman readers to enuresis. Yet Alexander is basically a rural swap meet, as friendships are renewed and shotguns and ammo vended or traded on a Sunday morning. (The attendees have all gone to seven o'clock mass, I'm sure.) Alexander Cockburn once wrote in *The Nation* that the populist left ought to talk to the folks at gun shows; genuine democrats would come away refreshed by an encounter with working and rural citizens who are pro–Bill of Rights, anti-corporatist, and open to radical alternatives. Gene Debs and Huey Long and Norman Mailer would dig Alexander; a Democratic Party financed by Wall Street and choreographed by upper-middle-class hall monitors barely countenances these peoples' existence, though the lackbeards navigating the crowded aisles looking for a good cheap hunting rifle will make perfectly suitable corpses in whatever wars the think-tank commanders are drawing up in their tax-exempt covens. I don't hunt, but my dad is NRA, and I grew up in a gun culture whose rate of violent crime is equal to the number of farmers in Mr. Obama's cabinet. Contrary to the lurid imaginings of Beltway advocates of gun control—recently euphemized to "gun safety"—in Alexander I saw nary Crip nor Blood nor sullen stringy-haired school sniper in a Slipknot T-shirt stocking his armory.

I stop to chat—*chat*: what an epicene verb in this context!—with Mark Shephard and his parents, Barb and Ken, at their customary table. Shep has been my friend since I was five years old. We laugh about a previous Gun Show/Super Bowl Sunday, when, glutted on chicken wings and Genny Cream Ale, we watched Scott Norwood's forty-seven-yard field goal sail wide right in the 1991 game, which carved out a regional slough of despond later visited by the right-wing Calvin Klein model Vincent Gallo's film *Buffalo '66*.

Shep and I spent every other fall day of 1972 visiting McGovern headquarters in Batavia and stuffing our pockets full of REMEMBER OCTOBER 9 buttons. He never stopped collecting. So at Shep's table I buy a button for Charles Goodell, the last US senator from Upstate New York, who was appointed in 1968 to succeed the assassinated Senator Robert F. Kennedy. (Goodell's son, Roger, commissioner of the NFL, will hand out the Super Bowl trophy that night.)

Charles Goodell was a native of Jamestown, which also produced Roger Tory Peterson, 10,000 Maniacs, and Lucille Ball—not bad. In the humanely flighty tradition of his hometown, Goodell joined the quasi-pacifist Oregon senator Mark Hatfield as one of the loudest anti–Vietnam War voices in the Republican Party.

The last Upstater actually elected to the US Senate was Rochester Republican Kenneth Keating in 1958. Keating was bumped off in 1964 by the carpetbagger Kennedy, who cared as much about Genesee County as I care about who slew Marilyn Monroe.

RFK's successor Goodell, an Upstater *and* an appointee, was too low-caste to ever win a statewide race. He proved to be a seatwarmer between carpetbaggers, as he lost a three-way race in 1970 to Connecticut's own James Buckley, who enjoyed birds quite as much as Roger Tory Peterson had but thought the Vietnam War just ducky.

Buckley fell in 1976 to an actual New Yorker, Pat Moynihan, for whom I toiled in magnificent ambivalence, but DPM gave way to yet another carpetbagger, the militaristic schoolmarm herself, Senator Hillary Clinton, who resigned the seat to exercise her diplomatic muscle as Obama's belli-cose secretary of state.

To his great credit, accidental governor David Paterson, in replacing Hillary, passed over heirheadess Caroline Kennedy and Andrew Cuomo (Mario without the wit, just the meanness) to choose Kirsten Gillibrand, a pro-gun, anti-bailout Hudson Valley Democrat. Senator Gillibrand's devotion to the Second Amendment will be sorely tested—her colleague, the beyond egregious Chuck Schumer, has undertaken to educate her on the matter—but if she sticks to her guns, so to speak, the free men and women of Alexander will have the odd sensation of Senate representation by someone who not only has been north of Yonkers but has seen, up close, such rural exotica as a maple tree, a cider press, and a Methodist church.

I drive home from the gun show under the heatless midwinter sun singing along with the car radio to the touched Scott Walker's tristful "The Sun Ain't Gonna Shine Anymore." I don't know; maybe it will.

Senator Gillibrand was more than a scrap tossed from the banquet table but we scurvy mutts can't be bought off that easily, especially since all indications are that she is learning to curtsy to the New York City liberals and like it. But I am pleased to note that Downstaters are also relearning the virtues of state secession. Peter Vallone Jr., a Queens councilman whose father was a former New York City Council speaker and the drubbed underfunded Democratic nominee for governor against Pataki in 1998, launched 51st State efforts in 2003 and 2008. In standard New York City fashion, Vallone spoke the language not of liberty and culture but of dollars and cents.

"If not secession," he told the *New York Sun*, "somebody please tell me what other options we have if the state is going to continue to take billions from us and give us back pennies . . . Not only is it about self-determination and self-rule, but it's about fairness. It's something we see every year in the budget. They take $11 billion from us and give us back a mere pittance and they make it seem like they're doing us a favor to give that pittance back. Somehow they missed the point that it is New York City's own tax money and we deserve it."

Okay, eloquent Vallone is not. He couldn't sharpen Stormin' Norman's pencil, and the "pittance" is closer to 90-some cents on the dollar, but still, give the man credit for knowing a populist cause when he sees one. The balance-of-payments question has been studied intermittently over the last half century, and each snapshot is different. When times are flush, New York City sends more into Albany than it receives; when the market sags, the imbalance is corrected. It is a slim reed on which to secede—culture and justice are far superior—but it's better than nothing.

Councilman Simcha Felder, chairman of the Governmental Operations Committee, expressed support for Vallone's bill, asking, "Why in the world should New York City be held hostage to the state?" He doubted, however, that the avaricious appleknockers—the flannel-shirted members of the nefarious Rural Cabal that secretly runs Wall Street and pulls the strings in Albany—would assent to a divorce. "The people outside New York City in New York State who have been eating the fruits of our labor for all this time . . . aren't going to be ready to just say forget about it."

Wanna bet, Simcha? You eat your fruits, we'll eat ours.

Henry Stern, superannuated office-filler and former parks commissioner, urged Councilman Vallone to consider what he'd be throwing away. "The city needs upstate—it's where the city gets its water. It dumps its prisoners upstate."[101] Stern is right: New York City swipes its drinking water from six reservoirs north of the city, and it supplies 70 percent of New York's prison population. (As anti-statehood New York Democratic congressman Emmanuel Celler admitted in 1971, "The rest of New York is a safety valve for New York City.")[102]

Kick-ass journalist Christopher Ketcham sized up Vallone's plan as "bullshit grandstanding" in the *New York Press*. "First, offers Vallone, we establish a committee to set up a vote on a referendum to set up a committee to look into the idea. Then the committee meets for six months and Vallone and his committeemen draw paychecks while nothing happens."[103] And so it goes.

Strip the anti-rural bigotry from the 51st State cause and you're left with the nigh-irrefutable assertion of Councilman Vallone: "It would be much, much simpler to be able to govern 8.5 million people without having to ask legislators who represent villages on the Canadian border for permission before we do anything."[104]

Vallone's is only the latest, if least poetic, manifestation of the perfectly healthy desire for self-government in the city. The council has walked this path before: In 1959 it created by a vote of 23–1 a committee to consider secession. The thing has been considered to death; can't we just do it?

For who can gainsay Stanley Walker's 1935 observation that "the man who lives in the City may love Broadway, or Fifth Avenue, or Canarsie, or the Flushing Meadows, but he has no affection whatever for Albany, Buffalo, or Hoosick Falls."[105] True, true, as is the vice versa. I love with all my heart a sandlot baseball field in Batavia but I give not a rat's ass for Rockefeller Center, Times Square, or MOMA.

As a matter of practical politics, Republican-leaning West New York would be a logical companion to the Democratic District of Columbia should the Congress ever decide to admit the federal city as a state. So to GOP/Dem rooters, it would be a wash.

I suppose there is no reason for anyone outside of New York to care about our plight, but I'll take a stab at manufacturing "relevance." Division of New York is in the national interest because it would permit a new generation of Upstatesmen to take the stage. We did, after all, give America Martin Van Buren and Grover Cleveland. (With FDR we'll take our mulligan.) Barber Conable would have made a fine president. Democrats from Rochester and Syracuse are colorless, but the rural Democracy is populist, anti-bureaucracy, and green. (In many cow counties the Democrats are the anti-tax, anti-spending party.) Give us our own state and we just might give America another Bob Taft or William Jennings Bryan. I guarantee we won't dump another Chuck Schumer on you.

Yet secession is a cultural, not a partisan, issue. The leadership of the state Republicans is as secession-averse as the aforementioned Democrat Schumer, who is as remote from the land of Henry W. Clune and Frederick Douglass as he is from Neptune's outermost moon.

Upstaters and Downstaters are no more fit for cohabitation under the same governmental roof than are citizens of Kentucky and Norway. State Senator Kuhl simply asked that "you settle your problems your way. We'll settle our problems our way." We'll take care of our farms and lakes and villages and our not-so-big cities, the Buffalos and Rochesters and Syracuses. You take care of your 301 square miles. On what possible grounds can anyone object?

Secession may seem to be motivated by anger or frustration or asperity. Fact is, it flows from love. Love of one's region, of one's neighbors, of one's ancestors and history and land and people. And love, of a different but palpable sort, for folks distant: for a man on Wall Street, a child in Harlem, a tree grower in Brooklyn. Love for these people demands that we let them live their lives as they see fit. That we stop meddling in their business. Secession insists on autonomy, on self-government. Secession is part and parcel of the American faith. What are we waiting for?

❧

If severing New York was about nothing more than trading with slavers, the idea would have deservedly died at Appomattox. But it did not. Indeed, it is New York City more than anywhere else in America that has kept most vividly alive the dream of secession in the century and a half since the Civil War. This Gothamophobe salutes the localist patriotism of New Yorkers. You go, Brooklyn.

On a mid-September day some years ago, Batavians honored Major Philemon Tracy of the Sixth Georgia Infantry, the only Confederate officer buried in Northern soil during the war. Tracy was a Macon, Georgia, boy who spent his summers in Batavia with his uncle, Judge Phineas Tracy. When Major Tracy was felled at Antietam, his uncle had the body smuggled north and interred without fanfare in our founders' cemetery. A century and a quarter later local Civil War buffs, led by the late Don Burkel—an insurance man whose printed cards described his occupation as "Controversial Person"—decided to give Major Tracy a proper memorial.

Fifty or so Batavians paid their respects on a brisk Sunday morning. Reenactment soldiers, blue and gray, planted the rebel flag and the stars and stripes in Tracy's dirt. A Jefferson Davis impersonator made a brief speech. An adorable elementary schoolgirl read Mary Ashley Townsend's poem, "A Georgia Volunteer." The soldiers fired a volley. A bugler played "Taps." Philemon Tracy's grave, its Confederate flag rippling in the September breeze, sent a loud and sure admonition to any romantic fools who might still entertain secessionist dreams: Don't!

And yet . . .

As we left the cemetery, my dad and I talked about the Kauffmans in the Union army, humble privates, farm kids who marched off to war. I felt proud of them even as I doubted the wisdom of choosing bloodbath over negotiation. When I got home I performed an etiolated act of localism worthy of our age: I opened a beer, flopped on the couch, and watched the Buffalo Bills game on television.

The Bills were in the midst of losing four consecutive Super Bowls, and in so doing they set a standard for either futility or perseverance. Upstatehood faces even greater odds, and they grow longer every time another Walmart opens, another dreamer comes in from the front porch and turns on the television, another native son or daughter leaves town on the upwardly mobile expressway to Nowhere. To be worthy of our ancestors, we must first know something of them. We must read their books and learn of their deeds. We must transmit this knowledge to our children. Then, and only then, will we be worthy of a state of our own. Hasten the day.

California Sunset—and What About West Kansas, Jefferson, the Texas Republic, and the Yoopers?

*W*illiam Allen White, a badly underrated novelist, editor of the *Emporia (KS) Gazette*, and for the first half of the twentieth century the plump, self-satisfied embodiment of the Main Street temperament, declared his Sunflower State "the low barometer of the nation. When anything is going to happen in this country, it happens first in Kansas."[1]

As John Brown portended Father Abraham's Holy War, and Carrie Nation prefigured Prohibition, and Dodge City's Dennis Hopper augured . . . well, something, so did West Kansas of the early 1990s give us a foretaste of the coming splintering of overlarge states into polities of more manageable size, closer to the human scale. I'm not talking here about fanciful dreams of independence, of slipping the bonds of the union. Rather, these are the secessions closest to my heart: little states born of big states, new stars for an old flag.

An ex-Kansan once wrote that "anybody who will drive a covered wagon from Boston to Topeka for the sole purpose of finding a fight has a lot of energy and determination."[2] Kansas was not born in lethargy or acquiescence.

This plains pugnacity characterized Don Concannon, a descendant of nineteenth-century homesteaders, who in the early 1990s instigated the most unlikely statehood movement of recent times—the cause of West Kansas. Concannon was a lawyer from Hugoton, an erstwhile state Republican Party chairman (1968–70), and a two-fisted maverick. His home was—is—Stevens County, whose nine hundred square miles are brimful with natural gas and sparsely populated by fewer than six thousand people.

In January 1992 Concannon was infuriated by then-governor Joan Finney's proposal (soon enacted into law as the School Finance Act) to grant Topeka the power to set a statewide uniform property tax levy and to dictate per-pupil expenditures to every school district in the state. Finney's proposal emerged from that most sinister of swamps, that eternal begetter of the devil's spawn: a "bipartisan commission."

Not only did this usurp the traditional right of localities to fund schools according to local preferences, it walloped counties such as Stevens, with its high property values generated by natural gas reserves. Taxes in Stevens County would sharply increase under Finney's plan—and yet at the same time its generous school budgets would be cut by state mandate. "So we pay $8 million for a $1 million budget cut, and it goes to the east . . . It's absolutely asinine," fumed Concannon. King Numbers ruled. As Concannon lamented, "All we hear from Topeka is how to raise taxes on rural Kansas, which does not have the votes to overcome the political machines."[3] As in New York and so many other states, one-man one-vote jurisprudence devitalized rural political strength. It "destroyed the fairness factor," said Concannon, "and created an atmosphere of urban domination that does not help the growth of rural Kansas."[4]

On January 27, 1992, Concannon fired off a letter to the Stevens County Board of Commissioners requesting that it submit to the voters the question of whether to "pursue the steps necessary to immediately disassociate Stevens County from the authority of the state of Kansas for the purpose of establishing a new state or other independent republic."[5]

"They laughed at me," recalled Concannon when I interviewed him three years later. "Then the people started carrying petitions," which in two weeks contained eight hundred signatures.[6] The commissioners authorized a vote. And that April the good people of Stevens County voted 1,469–73 to divorce from Kansas. The rebellion spread rapidly, as Concannon predicted that "rural areas will unite and demand statehood as the only means available to protect their children's future education and their property from confiscation."[7]

Statehood seized the popular imagination; as with the early days of the Ross Perot insurgency (with which it was coeval) it was spontaneous, rambunctious, and invigorating. As one Moscow, Kansas, seventh grader told the county commissioners: "I think we should secede from the state because Joan Finney is running us like a Communist Government . . . Don Concannon may be an old man, but he knows what he is talking about."[8]

Eight other western counties soon voted overwhelmingly to join Stevens. In September 1992, a convention of breakaway West Kansans was held in Ulysses, and the sweet gunpowder smell of 1775 was in the air. "We really believed that if we could keep our own money we'd be better off," said Morton County commissioner Bob Boaldin, whose voice over the phone fair cauterized the cable. "We really don't need Wichita. We really don't need Topeka. We trade with Texas and Oklahoma. All Wichita and Topeka want is our money."[9]

As elsewhere, once broached, the unthinkable became . . . thinkable. Concannon adverted hopefully to the fractured totalitarian giant across the ocean: "When the people of the Soviet Union voted to establish their own republics," he told the Kansas House Education Committee, "they opened the door for Stevens County. Surely our Legislature will not attempt to keep us part of Kansas by force."[10] If the legislature did balk, Concannon speculated, West Kansas might appeal to the United Nations for recognition as an independent country.

Activists in nearby Eastern Colorado, Northwest Texas, and the Oklahoma Panhandle lit fires of independence that blazed with varying intensity. Some even spoke of coalescence, for "the way of life which we have and which we prefer is mutually shared by people in these areas," Concannon noted.[11] So much for borders!

What, you say—you never heard of any of this? Just because CNN and NPR aren't listening doesn't mean that trees aren't falling in the forest.

An independent West Kansas strikes many of us as absurd, conditioned as we are to assume that a placid equability blankets the Plains States. The corporate media from which most (if a happily declining most) of America gets its "news" feeds us occasional images of Moscow across the sea but not a one from Moscow, Kansas, or Moscow, Idaho. All we know of Kansas comes from an entertainment industry that fears and loathes Kansas, *pace* Sunflower State natives Hopper, Don Johnson, Louise Brooks, and Gordon Parks. There may have been no place like home in *The Wizard of Oz*, albeit a drab drear hog-slopping tornado-riven home, but when Hollywood revisited the state in *Kansas* (1988) it was an anonymous wheatscape against which languorous male model Matt Dillon committed petty thuggeries.

In the old America, "Kansas was not just an address, it was something of what you are—a Kansan," says Robert Smith Bader, author of the delightful *Hayseeds, Moralizers, and Methodists: The Twentieth-Century Image of Kansas* (1988). "The nationalization of commerce and the press, mobility, just washed that out." Regional pride survives in pockets, however, particularly in country districts, which have anchorage if not affluence. Although Bader scoffed in our interview at the prospect of a free West Kansas, he also saw it as a redoubt of the "distinctiveness and uniqueness" that once marked our nation of villages.[12]

The West Kansans put secession on hold as they shelled Topeka with the musket balls of contemporary American defiance—lawsuits, filed by seventeen school districts. On December 2, 1994, the Kansas Supreme Court upheld the constitutionality of the 1992 act. Concannon predicted that the discontent "is going to keep building and smoldering, then it's going to erupt."[13]

It didn't. As Concannon wrote in 2001, "We allowed the secession movement to fade away as the legislature responded favorably to our suggestion that all wealth should bear the burden of education."[14] Governor Finney's hated levy was halved; Stevens County remained in Kansas. The fires went out. But they had blazed awfully bright in the early '90s, just as they had a century earlier when Populists like Mary Ellen ("raise less corn and more hell") Lease and Senator Sockless Jerry Simpson (who introduced William Allen White to Thackeray) provoked the question, "What's the matter with Kansas?"

The answer, of course, is nothing—unless the query is posed in the suburbs of Kansas City, in which case the proper response is "It's not Kansan enough." A state of West Kansas would have been, in a sense, more Kansan than that which remained. Sure, its founders proposed replacing the sunflower with the yucca as the state flower, and a popular T-shirt depicted a tornado with the message TOTO WE'RE NOT IN KANSAS ANYMORE!!! 51ST STATE, but in reviving the rebel spirit of John Brown and

Mary Ellen Lease, West Kansans were redeeming their birthright—and good, glorious good, for them.

꙳

The alienation of the outlanders is even more acute in California, where Thomas Jefferson's dictum that citizens must be capable of "transacting in person a great portion of [their] rights and duties" is a nullity on the order of the Sixth Commandment in Las Vegas.[15] The civic responsibility of the average Californian has shriveled to the obligation "to watch television and go out and buy stuff," as once and future governor Jerry Brown has said. [16] The vastness of the Golden State leads to unspeakably vapid campaigns conducted via television, in which the likes of Arnold Schwarzenegger and Dianne Feinstein are no more real to the citizen of Weed or Ukiah than Megan Fox is to the serial masturbater in Edina, Minnesota.

California really ought to have divided long ago. Under Spanish hegemony in the eighteenth century, the Catholic Church had assigned California south of the Tehachapi Mountains ("Baja") to the Dominicans and California north of the Tehachapis ("Alta") to the Franciscans. This bisection has proved remarkably durable.

California might even have come into the union in 1850 as two states but for the suspicion that the "'disaffected' Mexican element" might form "an irredentist movement" to reconnect with the motherland, as Carey McWilliams wrote in *California: The Great Exception* (1949).[17] At the September 1849 constitutional convention that created the political infrastructure of California, a Santa Barbara delegate, Jose Carrillo, argued that the south, with its modest population of Spanish landowners, ought to be a federal territory, while the north, rapidly filling with gold-hunting immigrants from points east, was better suited to statehood. Carrillo was defeated, 28–8, though the six delegates from the south all voted against the state constitution. Kevin Starr, the eminent historian of California, explains that "Old Californians (read: Latino-Californians) were in the vanguard of [the Two Californias movement]. Free from the domination of the Yankee North, the Latino-Californians wanted breathing space to achieve something that would be theirs and, at the same time, part of the Union."[18]

From the beginning, then, Californians "showed a strange distrust of the motives of each other from various sections," according to William M. Gwin, a Mississippi physician turned gold-mine owner who represented California in the antebellum US Senate.[19] The South was agricultural, settled, Spanish; the North was wild, transient, money-mad.

California was admitted to the union as a single state in 1850, though US senator Henry Stuart Foote (D-MS) offered a version of the Carrillo proposal that would have admitted the north and severed the south, renaming it the Territory of Colorado. Foote lost by a vote of 33–23.

Throughout the 1850s, legislators from all parts of the new state suggested fission and the creation of such smaller states as Colorado, Shasta, Columbia, El Dorado, Alta California, and Southern California. The reasons adduced were the incompatibility of interests between north and south, the great distance from Southern California to the capital of Sacramento, and the impossibility of fair taxation when wealth in the south was based in land and northern riches were auric. As an 1851 gathering in San Diego resolved, it is "an utter impossibility for any Legislature of the State, however wise and patriotic, to enact laws adapted to the wants and necessities of a people, so widely differing in their circumstances and pursuits." An assemblage that same year in Los Angeles found, "Experience has demonstrated that the political connection, which exists between the North and the South of California, is beneficial to neither and prejudicial to both."[20] Besides, should vast California be limited to just two senators, the same as Rhode Island?

The die was cast, really, at Sutter's Mill. John Sutter, called by one biographer "the very embodiment of early California," was the gregarious German-Swiss empire-builder at whose Sacramento Valley mill gold was discovered in 1848, setting off a continent-wide case of California dreamin' and a veritable flood of the greedy, the enterprising, and the footloose.[21] Overnight, Californication had been consummated. In mid-1848 California consisted of approximately seventy-five hundred Hispano-Californians and sixty-five hundred Americans. Eighteen months later the population had zoomed to one hundred thousand, with almost all the influx being gold-crazy Americans in the north. Sutter-bricked California was top-heavy.

Even before the discovery, John Sutter had dreamed a different destiny for Alta California. "Jointly with Oregon a great 'Pacific Republic' could be formed with unquestionable success," Sutter wrote in 1845 in a German-language Missouri newspaper.[22] That republic would not have answered to Washington.

Meanwhile, the Mexican south—the "Old Californians," prosperous agriculturalists—desired to form the territory of "Colorado" to avoid domination by the arriviste northerners, gold-panners and railroad barons and other parvenu Anglos. A California split seemed inevitable: In 1853 the *Sacramento Union* editorialized, "A division of the state into two or more states is a political necessity which will be recognized by all parties sooner or later."[23] Sooner, yes; later, oddly, no.

California had not been in the union for a decade when it appeared on the verge of mitosis. In 1859 Assemblyman Andres Pico of Los Angeles, a rancher who just a dozen years earlier had fought the Americans in the Mexican War, proposed to separate the state at the Tehachapi Mountains "just south of Bakersfield," as the Okie Sound saying goes, but the terrible swift sword of the Civil War intervened, and California, unlike so many young men of the day, was not severed. It came close, though. Pico's bill called for a referendum on the split to be held in the south, which was to be denominated the Territory of Colorado. The state assembly (34–25) and senate (15–12) approved the bill by narrow margins, the governor signed it, and the citizens of embryonic Colorado voted overwhelmingly (2,457–828, or 75 percent yea) to go their own way.

Governor John Weller thereupon advised the US Congress of the state's action. The matter was referred to the House Committee on Federal Relations, wherein debate centered not on the merits of division—California was obviously too large and diverse to remain intact—but over whether or not the consent of Northern Californians was necessary. A majority of the House committee (37–26) voted to approve the request for two Californias, and a companion bill was reported out of committee in the Senate. Alas, the war came, and Colorado was lost in the shuffle. Yet the modern California Assembly notes, "Technically, the Pico request of 1859 is still before the Congress."[24]

The Civil War got some Californians to asking what was so great anyhow about union with a strife-riven nation across the mountains, thousands of miles away. As war loomed, Democratic governor Weller made bold to suggest that "California should not go with the South or the North but here upon the shores of the Pacific found a mighty republic which may in the end prove the greatest of all." He was echoed by the Bay Area Democratic congressman John C. Burch, who proposed joining with Oregon, Washington, Utah, and New Mexico to create "the youthful but vigorous Caesarian Republic of the Pacific."[25]

In pre-automobile California, the south cried loudest for independence; Sacramento was awfully remote. Southern Californians "are an agricultural people, thinly scattered over a large extent of country," explained Governor Milton Lathan (who served in that office only five days, before appointing himself a US senator) to President James Buchanan in 1860. "They complain that the taxes upon their land and cattle are ruinous—entirely disproportionate to the taxes collected in the mining regions . . . and that there is no remedy, save in a separation from the other portion of the State."[26]

War crushes devolutionist tendencies; its feeds the monster of centralism. Yet postbellum, the bills to detach one-half or one-third of the state from the rest kept on coming—and went nowhere. In 1907 state senator Robert N. Bulla launched a campaign to revive the Pico proposal, though he would have renamed Pico's Colorado "Los Angeles."[27] In 1909, eight counties of Northern California and seven in Southern Oregon explored the possibility of combining to create the state of Siskiyou.

The banner of separation was now upheld by the north, as you didn't need a demographer to know which way the population boomed. The south teemed with prohibitionist newcomers hostile to the mining industry and its seamy overbelly. In 1918 one San Franciscan warned that "the people of the sanitary southland are preparing another slaughter of real Californians . . . Give 'em a separate state and let them call it Puritangeles."[28] (A moniker rather less appropriate today.)

Which leads us to a would-be state of far nobler name, which almost arose on the eve of the Second World War, when several Northern California counties joined with a county in Southern Oregon in what was to be the felicitously styled State of Jefferson. The poor condition of roads was the prosaic rationale, but the grievances went much deeper than rutted turnpikes.

Last time I visited my sister-in-law and brother-in-law in Lewis and Clark territory, I was amused by the DON'T CALIFORNICATE OREGON bumper stickers on pickups and Lexi and everything in between. Many of these likely were driven by ex-Californians, but never mind that—in best Booker T. Washington fashion, these good folk were casting down their buckets where they were.

Californication is a sin both venereal and venial, but let us not similarly damn conjugation—in particular, the joining of far Northern California with Southern Oregon. That is a match made in . . . well, in Yreka, California, 1941.

The kinship of Southern Oregon and the northern cap of California has long been as obvious as a John Denver lyric. In January 1854 the *Mountain Herald* of Yreka announced a meeting of citizens of Siskiyou County "for the purpose of taking measures to secure the formation, at an early date, of a new Territory out of certain portions of Northern California and Southern Oregon."[29] That early date never did arrive, but legislative hoppers were filled to bursting throughout the 1850s with proposals to create such states as Shasta, Klamath, Jackson, and Jefferson out of that magnificent land of mountains and forests and wild rivers. Nothing came of these, or of the later proposal to create a state of Siskiyou.

Until 1941, that is, when the ought-to-be State of Jefferson was born of high spirits and sweet rebellion.

So what was the beef that fed Jefferson: Confiscatory taxes? Onerous regulations? Curtailed liberties? Nah—just bad roads, "oiled dirt lanes," impassable in bad weather, that impeded efforts to transport minerals and timber from mountain to market.[30] Chromium and copper laced the hills, as did ponderosa pines and oak trees, but it was a hard slog getting them down. The people of the counties of Jefferson "shared the ironic circumstance of a flagging economy amid an embarrassment of natural riches," write Michael Di Leo and Eleanor Smith, authors of the useful survey *Two Californias* (1983).[31] Locals were tired of begging Sacramento and Salem for better roads. They would have to do it themselves. Thus Jefferson was born under a strange sign indeed: It was a secession based on the *failure* of the central authorities to intervene in local life.

The dynamo behind Jefferson was Port Orford, Oregon, mayor Gilbert

Gable, a hustling public relations man from back east (Philadelphia) who called himself the "hick mayor of the westernmost city of the United States."[32] He'd only been in Port Orford, a fishing and lumber port on the Oregon coast, since 1935, but that was long enough to have absorbed the local attitude toward the bloodsucking leeches and malefactors of great wealth in Salem. Gable was an engaging mix of huckster, booster, and dreamer—he was, among other things, a "hunter of dinosaur eggs"—and he envisioned Port Orford as a bustling harbor connected to the treasures of the mountains by a system of good interior roads.[33]

On October 2, 1941, Mayor Gable and his band of brothers requested that the Curry County Court take steps to transfer their forgotten slice of Southwestern Oregon to California, which might better appreciate—or at least pave the roads in—Curry County. The court appointed a commission to consider the matter, which it did, moving with a most un-commission-like alacrity to break from Oregon.

Gable and a delegation traveled to Sacramento to ask California governor Culbert Olson for help. The governor was flattered, telling the petitioners that he was "glad to know they think enough of California to want to join it," but he really wasn't up for starting a border war.[34] The renegades needed to look closer to the ground for allies. So Gable took his campaign to Del Norte County in California, where his grievances sounded much like those of Northern Californians. The capital ignored them, distant interests exploited them, and city slickers ridiculed them. (Interestingly, there was a parallel, if less clamorous and successful, movement on the plains. In 1939 parts of Wyoming, South Dakota, and Montana explored the possibility of accreting to form Absaroka—Crow for "children of the large beaked bird"—whose people were characterized by the *New York Times* as "conservative, self-sufficient and wanting mostly to be left alone."[35] Despite electing a Miss Absaroka, the state sputtered and died.)

As Western historian Richard Reinhardt wrote, "It was in Yreka"—the Siskiyou County seat "which had suffered for close to a century from a cruel and widespread slander to the effect that the place did not really exist but was just a way of misspelling Eureka"—that Gilbert Gable struck gold. The Yreka Chamber of Commerce suggested linking adjacent Oregon and California counties in a new state of Mittelwestcoastia. Good idea, rotten name. The Yreka-based *Siskiyou Daily News* sponsored a contest to find a better tag and wound up with a grab bag of some of the most infelicitous monikers this side of the [Fill in Name of the Butt of Your Local Jokes] maternity ward. Many of them, wrote Reinhardt, were "equally repulsive" as Mittelwestcoastia—Del Curiskiyou, Siscurdelmo, Bonanza, Discontent, Orofino.[36] The winner was Jefferson; its minter, J. E. Mundell of Eureka, who received a prize of $2, wished to honor the author of the Declaration of Independence, "the great instrument that states that the people have a right to govern themselves."[37]

Mayor Gable, jumping the gun on his anticipated governorship of the new state—but then what did you expect: that he'd be satisfied being Clerk Gable?—declared that Jefferson would impose no income, sales, or liquor taxes. Its modest bureaucracy would be funded by a royalty—don't dare call it a tax!—on the mining and timber industries. Lest this sound like a laissez-faire paradise, he also pronounced a pox on slot machines (a protectionist measure to shore up the vital stud poker sector) and a ban on strikes.

Jefferson, editorialized the *Siskiyou Daily News*, was composed of "people who are wearied of governmental pap, demagoguery, waste and excessive taxation." Yes, they protested the "lack of roads," but this was an ephemeral complaint, hardly the basis of a vigorous statehood movement. Jeffersonians were "tired of being regarded as a hill-billy group who are not of sufficient importance to be given considerate treatment."[38] The two essential ingredients of any successful secession movement—love of place and resentment of the capital—were present. The state seal consisted of two crosses—a double cross, get it?—on the bottom of a mining pan.

On November 27, 1941, hell-bent members of the Yreka 20–30 Club ("a group of guys in their twenties and thirties with a sense of humor and nothing to do," explains Brian Petersen, current keeper of the Jefferson flame[39]) set up roadblocks on Highway 99. Cradling deer rifles, warmed by bonfires of revolution, they stopped traffic and posed for ineffably cool photographs in which all the men look like Robert Mitchum and the women either Jane Greer or Jane Darwell.

This was a far cry from Checkpoint Charlie. Motorists were handed I HAVE VISITED JEFFERSON, THE 49TH STATE windshield decals and a copy of the state's Proclamation of Independence, which read, in its entirety:

You are now entering Jefferson, the 49th State of the Union.

Jefferson is now in patriotic rebellion against the States of California and Oregon.

This State has seceded from California and Oregon this Thursday, November 27, 1941.

Patriotic Jeffersonians intend to secede each Thursday until further notice.

For the next hundred miles as you drive along Highway 99, you are travelling parallel to the greatest copper belt in the Far West, seventy-five miles west of here.

The United States government needs this vital mineral. But gross neglect by California and Oregon deprives us of necessary roads to bring out the copper ore.

If you don't believe this, drive down the Klamath River highway and see for yourself. Take your chains, shovel and dynamite.

Until California and Oregon build a road into the copper country, Jefferson, as a defense-minded State, will be forced to rebel each Thursday and act as a separate State.

(Please carry this proclamation with you and pass them out on your way.)

STATE OF JEFFERSON CITIZENS COMMITTEE
TEMPORARY STATE CAPITOL, YREKA[40]

Stories bearing a Jefferson byline appeared far and wide, thanks to Stanton Delaplane, a *San Francisco Chronicle* reporter whose romantic dispatches from the forty-ninth-state front earned him a Pulitzer Prize. Delaplane, who in later years was credited with introducing Irish coffee to America, described the secessionists as "partly mad, partly in fun, partly earnest about the new state."[41] In other words, they were hale, healthy, red-bloodedly insubordinate Americans who blended poetry, patriotism, good-natured humor, and orneriness.

Jefferson comprised four counties: Curry in Oregon, and the California counties of Siskiyou, Del Norte, and Trinity. Others—Modoc, Lassen, Shasta—were in and out, or interested but not willing to take the leap of faith. When the solons of Shasta County, California, haughtily informed the Jeffersonians that they might throw in, too, if Redding were made the state capital, the rebels mailed 'em a bottle of castor oil with the message, "Start your own movement."[42] (After Modoc's hasty withdrawal from Jefferson, Democratic state senator Randolph Collier of Siskiyou County, whose ardor for asphalt led him to be dubbed "Father of the Highways," said, "I'd like to know who put the pressure on who over there.")[43]

The four-county new state would be "larger than the combined areas of Delaware, Rhode Island, and Connecticut," boasted its backers.[44] Admittedly, the contemplated State of Jefferson was shaped like a clumsily gerrymandered congressional district. California's elongated Trinity County dipped and dangled into the Golden State like a man clinging desperately to a window ledge. (Current Jeffersonians favor a model that looks more like a quadrilateral state and takes in all the border counties and more.)

Jefferson was on the verge of . . . something. Imaginations fired, her partisans had gone beyond pranks and into the dizzying realm of "hey—who knows?"

But as the luckless protagonist in the classic noir B-movie *Detour* (1945) explained, "Whichever way you turn, fate sticks out a foot to trip you." On December 2, 1941, fifty-five-year-old Mayor Gable dropped dead of a heart attack. Flags dipped to half-mast, but the show—in this case a "Provisional Territorial Assembly" scheduled in Yreka on December 4—must go on.

Fortunately for Jefferson, the very able Judge John Childs of Crescent City, California, was the obvious choice for governor. The Yreka assembly tapped Childs for the position, and also filled the offices of lieutenant governor, attorney general, secretary of state, and US senator and representative. Jefferson was ready.

(Governor Childs was my friend June Chamberlain's great-great-uncle's brother by marriage—okay, it's tenuous, but it fits under the six degrees of separation rules. Judge Childs had proposed secession back in 1935, when Jefferson wasn't yet a gleam in Gilbert Gable's eye. Judge/Governor Childs grew up in my neck of the woods, Genesee County, New York, specifically Indian Falls. He studied at Batavia's high school and taught in nearby Basom. Pneumonia drove him westward, to Crescent City, where in rapid succession he bought a newspaper and was elected clerk, district attorney, and then superior court judge of Del Norte County. He was an associate of that scourge of the corporations Hiram Johnson, the antiwar Republican US senator from California. Politics was in his bloodstream and there warn't no cure: He would serve as district attorney until he was eighty-seven years old. Till the end of his long life he strolled the streets of Crescent City, hobbling about on a cane, smoking a big cigar, and walking his dog. Now, there was a Governor.)[45]

Governor Childs explained in his inaugural address of December 4, 1941—which, unlike most inaugural addresses, the governor wrote on his own, without the purpling of hired inkslingers—"The State of Jefferson is a natural division geographically, topographically, and emotionally. In many ways, a world unto itself: self-sufficient with enough water, fish, wildlife, farm, orchard land, mineral resources, and gumption to exist on its own."[46]

Inauguration Day featured a torchlight parade through Yreka led by brother bears named Itchy and Scratchy. Marchers carried signs reading OUR ROADS ARE NOT YET PASSABLE, HARDLY JACKASSABLE; IF OUR ROADS YOU WOULD TRAVEL, BRING YOUR OWN GRAVEL; and THE PROMISED LAND—OUR ROADS ARE PAVED WITH PROMISES. Well, look—Mayor Gable had been a flack for the phone company, so don't expect poetry on the order of "Winston tastes good like a cigarette should." But what a pity that Gable the PR pro had not lived to see this rally and the gaggle of newsreel photographers from Paramount, Pathe, News of the Week, and other genuine Hollywood articles. *Time* and *Life* were there, too. "Please wear western clothes if they are available," the *Siskiyou Daily News* advised its readers.[47] Local color sells.

Of course Jefferson had its collaborators, too, loyalists who modified an old Oregon war cry to "Forty-eight States or Fight!" But the fight was called off.

Three days after Governor Childs's inauguration, the Japanese attacked Pearl Harbor. The governor announced that "the acting officers of the provisional territory of Jefferson here and now discontinue any and all activities."[48] A grim and bland unity replaced hell-raising and knee-slapping and neighborly anarchy. The war came, and state identities (not to mention Thomas Jefferson) lost a relevance they have not since regained. Rallying to the national cause, the Jeffersonians put their movement in abeyance. The roads did get built, though—there was manganese up in them thar hills.

A California split, however, remained more than just the title of one of Robert Altman's few good movies.

As in New York, the dream never really died.

Under the "Federal" Plan, ratified by voters in 1926 and modeled in a way on the US Senate, the California state senate had apportioned its seats by county: each senator represented from one to three counties. Thus the County of Los Angeles, whose population in 1949 was more than 3.5 million, had as many state senators—one—as the did the counties of Mono and Inyo, whose combined district as of 1949 had 12,270 people. Unfair, or guarantor of the rights of the rural north? You make the call. As Di Leo and Smith note in *Two Californias*, the Federal Plan took effect just before the 1930 census would have resulted in a drastic redrawing of legislative borders to reflect the south's population boom. Because seats in the lower house were still apportioned by population, "the Southland established a hammerlock on the California Assembly that it has never relinquished."[49]

Political advancement deranges a man, or perhaps it is fairer to say that in substituting a different set of incentives it reangles his point of view. When governor of California, Earl Warren had defended the Federal Plan, but as Chief Justice of the Supreme Court he scoffed, "Legislators represent people, not trees."[50] The Warren Court's *Baker v. Carr* demolished the Federal Plan and put the Southland's hammerlock on the California state senate as well.

Northern senators introduced secession bills in response to *Baker v. Carr*, but nothing came of them. Randolph Collier, a veteran of the Jefferson movement of 1941, proposed an unusual east–west division, bifurcating the state between urban and coastal California and the woods and mountains and deserts of the inland. Rural California was seething, but urban California, out there havin' fun in the warm California sun, cared not.

State senator Richard J. Dolwig (R–San Mateo County) proposed to divide the state at the Tehachapis. Incredibly, his bill was sponsored by twenty-five of the forty members of the state senate and passed that body easily before dying in the assembly, snuffed by Southern Californians unwilling to set free the resource-rich north. You never can tell when you might need to steal water, after all.

Governor Edmund G. "Pat" Brown, father of Jerry, victor in 1962 over Richard "You won't have Nixon to kick around anymore" but loser to Ronald Reagan in 1966, confessed in his querulous book *Reagan and Reality* (1970) that as governor he had been "inclined to support a bill in the legislature to split California into two" but held off in the interests of "conciliation."[51] His tongue loosened by forced retirement, Governor Brown unloaded on Southern California, blaming it for everything from Ronald Reagan to, well, Ronald Reagan, and declaring, "I have reluctantly concluded that California should be divided legally into two states, north and south." As newcomers poured into the south, further diminishing the political influence of progressive San Francisco, Brown expected secession sentiment to swell. Division was "at least ten years off," he wrote in 1970, but he foresaw the "ultimate establishment of two states."[52]

In the early 1990s, when populist passions sent forth gushers (Ross Perot, Jerry Brown, Pat Buchanan, term limits, the militia movement) and spurts (Free Staten Island! Free West Kansas!), California went fission once more. In 1992 voters in twenty-seven of thirty-one mostly northern counties approved an advisory ballot question asking if they wished to divide California into two states.

Spearhead of the movement was Assemblyman Stan Statham of Shasta County, which was memorialized by Joaquin Miller as:

> *That great graveyard of hopes! of men*
> *Who sought for hidden veins of gold;*
> *Of young men suddenly grown old—*
> . . .
> *Where one gray miner still sits down!*
> *'Twixt Redding and sweet Shasta town!*[53]

Shasta had held the State of Jefferson at arm's length, but fifty years later it was if not volcanic then at least volatile. And in Stan Statham, a former radio disk jockey and TV anchorman, it had a fluent spokesman. It is ridiculous, argued Assemblyman Statham, "that LA should tell us how to manage and harvest our timber and I get to decide whether the LA school district should be broken up."[54]

Like the New Yorkers, Statham began with a lovingly provincial vision of two Californias: the north country, the sylvan and grapy land above San Francisco and Sacramento (except for hedonic Marin County), and everything else. "I started with two Californias because I'm a rural legislator," Statham told me in an interview. "I wanted to pull rural California away from metropolitan California."

But in the course of leading his people out of California, this Moses discovered that "there are not ten commandments but twelve. The eleventh is that San Francisco and Los Angeles don't really want to be in the same state. The twelfth is that rural California doesn't want to be in a state with either of them."[55]

So Statham amended his proposal to include three Californias: the rural north, with its redwoods and lumberjacks and pot growers (and 2.3 million residents at the time); the sprawlingly urban-suburban south (17.5 million people), a spicy hash of the Spanish-surnamed—old California grandees and illegal busboys alike—and beach blondes and sybaritic movie stars; and paradisiacal Central California (10.5 million strong), from the San Joaquin Valley to San Francisco, from Silicon Valley to Santa Barbara, with plenty of other sibilant sites in between. "Logland, smogland, and fogland," went one jest.[56] Proud northerners suggested that their new state be called Superior California, while superior San Franciscans recommended Baja Oregon. Hurrah for local rivalries!

The triune plan recognized the reality, stated its backers, that "the economies, life-styles and interests of South, Central and Northern California are markedly different. The cost of this excessive diversity is frustration, overregulation and gridlock. Each part of California desperately needs to focus on solving their [*sic*] own unique problems. Political boundaries can easily be redrawn to benefit our citizens, not enslave them."[57]

Striking while the iron was hot, Statham next introduced a bill requiring a 1994 statewide advisory vote on whether the California legislature "shall send a plan . . . to the Congress of the United States by November 8, 1995, requesting the division of California into 3 states."

Statham's bill passed the assembly 48–27 in June 1993 (those forty-eight yeas were divided proportionately among the three Californias) but was buried in the Senate.

Statham and his allies, including then-speaker Willie Brown (who was perhaps attracted by an escape from impending term limits), were unfailingly placatory. They guaranteed the parched south that its contractual rights to northern water would be inviolate; skittish students and parents were assured that no public college or university could charge out-of-state tuition for a resident of any of the Californias; licenses and suchlike were to be valid throughout the tristate. The legislation authorizing the scission even guaranteed that "taxes may not be raised in any of the three states as a result of the division."[58] If residents of a county were unhappy with the new state to which they had been assigned, they would have the right to vote themselves into the adjoining state.

As Staten Island's Senator Marchi had done in 1983 with "Remedies of a Proud Outcast," the California splitters commissioned a report chockablock with pie-divvying graphs. The Assembly Office of Research's March 1992 study "Two New Californias: An Equal Division" noted that "California has become too large and too complex to be managed efficiently as a single unit."[59] The choices, really, were three: inefficiency, tyranny, or decentralization of power via scission.

The assembly researchers recommended two states, divided at the Tehachapi Mountains, à la the Pico Plan of 1859, though they admitted the feasibility of Statham's preferred tripartite California. (Others have puckishly suggested that Hearst Castle in San Simeon be the dividing line, as it is the "legacy of a northern publisher run amuck, Southern California style.")[60]

This assembly report was the high-water mark of modern multi-Californians. The California State Assembly Office of Research had examined, in some depth, the matter of division and pronounced it doable. Decentralization of political power could "revitalize California," offered the researchers, who also determined that in a division of assets and resources neither of the new states would get the short end of the statehood stick, as revenues in each would be sufficient to meet expenditures under then-current policies. As for the three-state plan, "We also conclude that a new state encompassing the 27 northernmost counties (mostly north of Sacramento) would be financially viable," they noted, although this was not the case for hypothetical states consisting only of the southernmost counties.[61]

How thirty-two (now thirty-eight) million people can be governed from an isolated city four hundred miles from the state's population base is a puzzle that admits of no solution. The small size of the state's lower house (eighty members, about half the size of New York's assembly) means that California assemblymen represent districts of 475,000 people—eight times more than the average American state legislator, and not far from the typical size of a congressional district. The forty state senators serve districts of about nine hundred thousand people—a ratio so lopsided as to make effective representation impossible.

The sense of powerlessness at the local level is exaggerated by a tangle of mandates, so that as much as 90 percent of a California county's budget is effectively written in Sacramento. When Bigness is made God you get the "same educational system in Los Molinos [population 1,952] as in Los Angeles," groused Statham.[62] Legislators from populous Los Angeles dictate the curriculum and services of the public school in Los Molinos. Does that accord with anyone's idea of fairness?

At an 1851 secession meeting in Santa Barbara, Southern Californians declared that the unwieldy cobbled superstate was "in contradiction to the eternal ordinances of nature, who herself had marked with an unerring hand the natural bounds between" the gold of the north and the fertile valleys of the south.[63] The Field opinion poll taken during the debate over the Statham bill indicated growing support for division in all parts of the state, as Californians slowly wised up to the eternal ordinances of nature. And while regional enmities are sometimes bitter, the gall and wormwood on which Upstate and Downstate New Yorkers breakfast is rarer in California cuisine. There are clashes, of course, especially over environmental issues. As Lassen County supervisor Jim Chapman told the *New York Times*, "The urbanites think we're chainsaw fanatics. But restoration of the forests has happened because we do it, not some guy sitting in a swivel chair in Santa Monica."[64] Good shot, Chapman! Yet the guys in swivel chairs call the shots: Stan Statham represented nine counties, while the County of Los Angeles sends twenty-six legislators to the assembly.

While advocates of Three Californias scrupulously avoid any hint of racialism, the prospect of minority status within an increasingly Mexicanized state is not widely considered desirable in the north. Hispanics are now the largest single ethnic group in the southern part of the state, and their numbers are ever ascending. Yet at the same time, historian Kevin Starr sees support growing for a "Latino-dominated state of Southern California, in which they would hold clear-cut advantages of historical heritage, geographic propinquity to Mexico and the Spanish Southwest, and demographic dominance."[65] Fair is fair. Among the fruits of statehood for Southern California would be, sooner rather than later, a Mexican American governor and US senator(s). The Assembly Office of Research noted that "the 22 smallest states have the same population as California, but they have 44 U.S. Senators compared with California's two."[66] And both of them are Jewish ladies from the Bay Area, Dianne Feinstein and Barbara Boxer. Diversity, anyone?

The twenty-seven- or twenty-eight-county north would be, by far, the whitest, poorest, and greenest of the Cali-states: a redneck marijuana-growing redoubt of pickups, logging, fishing, and hunting, and a live-and-let-live conservative libertarian ethos. "We don't need as much government, regulation, or taxation," said Statham, who in a Gilbert Gable way was the presumptive governor of Superior California. "We don't need a full-time Legislature." Central California would be a rich mélange of agriculture (or agribusiness, less romantically), Silicon Valley, and self-consciously chi-chi cities such as San Francisco all the way south to Santa Barbara. Sacramento might despair; as S. J. Diamond wrote in the *Los Angeles Times*, "Winds would whistle through the corridors of power," though the erstwhile capital could be converted to "a housing complex, a mega-mall, a theme park."[67] The minority–majority south would have both the highest average household income and the greatest concentration of illegal immigrants in America. Pat Brown to the contrary, it would be among the most liberal states, though unlike, for instance, the District of Columbia, whose path to statehood or a simulacrum thereof is perpetually blocked by the simple fact that it would send two very liberal Democrats to the Senate, Southern California would come into the union balanced, politically, by the conservative Northern and the moderately liberal Central California. Even the most crazed Caliphobe will concede that California is under-represented in today's US Senate; something like the Statham plan would treble its voice in the world's greatest deliberative body.

"If the Russians can do it, what makes you think we can't do it?" asked Lassen County supervisor Chapman.[68] Massive bureaucracies are not only expensive and inefficient, but they sap the life from those they rule; they dispirit and discourage a people. "We have lost our sense of who we are as Californians," said Kevin Starr. "It's almost scary." In a statewide opinion poll of September 1993, almost half—43 percent—of Northern Californians favored two Californias, as did 26 percent of those in the south.[69] Not bad for a radical idea that had yet to be discussed in any depth in the popular media. (The regional difference is most often explained as such: The north has the water, the south has the people. And the people of the south fear nothing so much as a hostile and detached north turning off the spigot, blowing up the dam, shutting down the aqueduct, letting rust the pipes. San Francisco attorney Steve Pitcher remarked in 1982, "The legislature is blocked by the Southerners. There's no way they're going to voluntarily split the state . . . It would be like killing the goose that lays the golden egg. The South is a resourceless area; they don't have our timber, our water, our natural resources. They get too much from us, in the way of taxes and natural resources.")[70]

Division suffered a setback in 1994, when after eighteen years in the assembly Stan Staham ran a spirited but losing campaign for the Republican nomination for lieutenant governor. He declared that "a vote for Stan Statham . . . will be a vote for three Californias, plain and simple," but he plainly and simply lost to a suburban Southern Californian, another sign of the impuissance of the thinly peopled north. With Statham subtracted from the legislature, the Three Californias plan, too, vanished without a trace.

For a time, that is. No good idea ever really dies. The next decade saw the citizens of Southern California discover the virtues of secession, as middle-class San Fernando Valley, with its 1.4 million residents spread over 222 square miles, attempted in 2002 to break from the elephantine City of Los Angeles and thereby become the nation's sixth largest city.

Race was not an issue: "Hispanics have rapidly become the dominant ethnic group" in the Valley.[71] The real grievance was and is size. The 3.8 million people of Los Angeles are represented by a city council of just 15 members, for a ratio of about 250,000 to 1. Under such an arrangement the individual citizen is a cipher, a nothing: His voice is a whisper in a hurricane.

Moreover, the Valley, which was annexed by the city in 1915, has been milked and mulcted for years by a downtown establishment deaf to its concerns. The San Fernando Valley sends to the city treasury 6.3 percent more in taxes than it receives in services.[72]

Assemblyman Tom McClintock (R-CA), who in 2008 was elected as a carpetbagging congressman from a Northern California district, cast city secession as the wave of the future: "Large, centralized command-and-control structures were very much a 20th-century phenomenon, actually a throwback to medieval governing modalities. We have been relearning the lessons of the Enlightenment, that human institutions produce far more satisfactory results when powers are decentralized and dispersed."[73]

Contemporaneously, the working-class harbor communities of San Pedro and Wilmington, which are twenty-seven miles distant from downtown LA and "connected to the city by a mere 'shoestring' of land," banded together to propose a long-overdue secession from the colossus to the north. Harbor VOTE, the primary secessionist organization, was, according to Julie-Anne Boudreau and Roger Keil writing in the journal *Urban Studies* (2001), "accentuated by a language of family values, building on the sense of community, and trying to be good people, good citizens, caring for their 'own' disadvantaged people."[74]

Boudreau and Keil dismissed most secessionists as "largely conservative middle-class movements . . . attempting to 'secede from responsibility,'" thus defining *responsibility* as the willingness to subsidize indefinitely interests with greater political power than you have.[75] But servility is not responsibility, any more than smugness is wisdom.

Los Angeles remains intact—for now. A 2002 referendum in which the Valley voted for independence was blocked by a citywide No vote, and the harbor communities have been stymied by the city's refusal to give up the Port of Los Angeles. The aquapolis rules—for in the arid south the fear of decentralization is always based in water.

The grotesqueries of the Bush administration sparked talk of secession statewide as well, though with a twist: Rather than adding a fifty-first and fifty-second state to the flag, Californians began to wonder if they oughtn't to leave the union and go it alone. The 2004 reelection of a man accurately labeled a war criminal birthed multiple Web sites devoted to nationhood for California, since, as the founder of the Committee to Explore California Secession explained, "citizens on the West Coast are finding themselves increasingly disenfranchised from the conservative cultural domination of the large middle and southern sections of the country, dubbed by some pundits as 'Jesusland.'"[76]

The sneeringly anti-Christian tone, and the implied moral superiority of the author, are distasteful, to be sure. And does CaliforniaMan, to use the alias he applies to himself, really think that the Iraq War was planned, declared, and executed by working-class evangelical Christians in Tennessee?

More plausibly, the political economist Gar Alperovitz wrote in the *New York Times* in February 2007 that "regional devolution," if not outright independence, is "all but inevitable." The only question is when the fuse will be lit.

Even mainstream figures wondered aloud about an independent California, which would be the eighth largest economy in the world. "We are the modern equivalent of the ancient city-states of Athens and Sparta," boasted Governor Arnold Schwarzenegger. "We have the economic strength, we have the population and technological force of a nation-state. We are a good and global commonwealth."[77] (That California's twentieth-century boom was fueled, in part, by federal subsidies to transportation, housing, and defense that rained disproportionately on the Golden State, Arnold did not mention. And as state coffers blushed a deeply indebted red in 2009, and the governor took tin cup in hand to Washington, the Kindergarten Cop toned down the Los Athens and San Sparta talk. Mighty California was now a humbled mendicant.)

Okay, so the nation of California is deader than Zohra Lampert's career.

But the dream of Three Californias lives, based as it is in simple justice and respect for place and self-rule.

Michael Di Leo and Eleanor Smith muse on the lessons Jefferson holds for California today: "What could happen, one wonders, with an issue more profound than road maintenance—say, water use and water rights. It is not hard to envision a broad secessionist coalition forming under these circumstances."[78]

How can a unitary state govern, under one suffocating umbrella, Yreka and East Los Angeles, or Fresno and Barstow? And it's only going to get worse. "Fifty million people by 2050 is just too much for one state," writes Jim Gogek of the *San Diego Union-Tribune*. "The time to split up the Golden State may not be upon us now. But as our population continues to swell, the idea will look better and better."[79]

∼◦∽

Contemporary patriots of the State of Jefferson emphasize cultural awareness before lobbying, for songs and stories offer a more promising route to statehood than wearying political agitation.

State of Jefferson signs adorn the region, most spectacularly in ten-foot-high letters painted by the late Jefferson advocate Brian Helsaple and his nephew atop a hay barn near Yreka. (An attempt to "rebrand" the northern tier of counties "Upstate California" was launched by local business leaders on September 10, 2001—an ill-fated eve. As with Jefferson in 1941, nothing could be heard above the death-din of war.)[80]

The NPR affiliate in Ashland, Oregon, KSOR, calls itself Jefferson Public Radio; there is a State of Jefferson Community Band based in Yreka, a State of Jefferson Mathematics Congress organized by Humboldt State in California and Southern Oregon State University, and—aptly, one supposes, given the grievances of November '41—a 108-mile State of Jefferson National Scenic Byway authorized by Uncle Sam himself, in the guise of the Forest Service. There are locksmiths, plumbers, pest exterminators, and other businesses proud to embed Jefferson in their names. In fact, business tags are a strong indicator of regional self-awareness. The great sociologist John Shelton Reed, in trying to answer the question "Where is the South?" opted for defining it as that territory wherein the percentage of "Southern" business entries in telephone books was at least 35 percent of the number of "American" listings. "This one statistic," writes Reed, "indicates the presence of the sort of regional institutions . . . [and] regional enthusiasm" that underlie a healthy self-identity.[81]

There is even a musical, *State of Jefferson*, a delightful work by the Oregon composer Jason Heald based on the 1941 uprising.

"I had just completed a musical, *National Insecurity*, about Ethel and Julius Rosenberg," Heald tells me, "and was looking for a lighter historical subject for a musical drama. The 'mythical state of Jefferson' is a frequent reference in this region, and I was very pleased to discover that the State of Jefferson was not mythical at all!"[82] *State of Jefferson* ran on the Centerstage Theater in Roseburg, Oregon, for eighteen performances in May 2006; long may it run!

I am reminded of the Puerto Rican Independence Party, which holds that the development of a national theater is more critical to the island's health than any gross national product. The road to self-determination, or statehood, is paved with poetry, not asphalt.

More prosaically, the frustrations expressed today by politically active Jeffersonians tend to be based on property rights and perceived violations thereof by federal regulators. "Up here it's a completely different world," Gary Hulsey, owner of the Forest Lodge Motel in the cheerfully named Happy Camp, California, told Sandy Kleffman of the *Contra Costa Times*, "and the laws that they make down there don't work here."[83] Restrictions on logging, fish and game protections, disputes over water rights: These have fed the secessionist fire, and while it may be tempting for environmentalists to dismiss these as the whinging plaints of exploiters and extractors, every time a lumber mill closes those are real lives that are shut down, cut off, shoved into the humiliating queue of the unemployment line. Moreover, Jeffersonian Californians, as outvoted rural folk in an urban state, must live under gun-control laws that are drawn up and ratified by citified legislators who wouldn't know a cougar from a cow.

Brian Petersen, head of Jefferson Enterprises, is a jack-of-all-trades: stump-grinder, T-shirt silkscreener, car washer, grape grower, and interim governor of the State of Jefferson. He is of Yreka, historic home of Jefferson, and he vends hats, keychains, and other Jeffersoniana whilst keeping the movement's archives and bearing its torch. (Not too close to the archives, I hope.)

Petersen got involved in the movement in 1998, "when the timber industry was coming under attack by radical environmentalism," he told me. Petersen took his stand with his neighbors, the loggers. "My own politics are conservative," he says, but the Republican rejection of limited government in the early twenty-first century has convinced him that "basic freedom and liberty is at stake and everyone is affected." So a movement that a decade or so ago was "90 percent tied to . . . property rights" today welcomes "greens, liberals, and centrists."[84] Bloom, thousand flowers, bloom.

The empire's collapse has fueled this latest effort. Yreka hardware store owner Richard Mitchell told the *San Francisco Chronicle*, "If there was a vote today to form a new state, it would pass in a heartbeat."[85] To the south, Bill Maze, an ex-assemblyman from Visalia in agricultural Tulare County, is pushing a plan to banish thirteen coastal counties from the "new revitalized California."[86] The train keeps a-rollin', though when it arrives at a station—and which station that is—only God can say.

The Pacific Northwest's other active secession movement, Cascadia, would establish an eco-republic of Oregon, Washington, and British Columbia. It has reached its fullest flower in popular fiction.

Ernest Callenbach's novel *Ecotopia* (1975), like Edward Bellamy's horrific and unintentionally dystopian *Looking Backward*, features a traveler from our world who ventures into the author's eidolon, in Callenbach's case the land of Ecotopia, an isolated country of the Pacific Northwest (Washington, Oregon, Northern California) that has seceded from the "hated" Americans.[87] Ecotopia has banned or vanquished internal combustion engines, garish signs, sugar, baseball and football and basketball, fat people, nuclear families, credentialed experts, pets, and microwave ovens. Ecotopians smoke marijuana, screw freely, ride bicycles and magnetic trains, work twenty-hour weeks, use the metric system, and have turned recycling into a kind of state religion. Ecotopia's governance is decentralized; its defense is entrusted to the militia, à la the early American republic; and its schools are, happily, divorced from the state, but the self-satisfaction of its citizens is unendurable. Ecotopians lecture visitors on the evils of synthetic fibers and not sharing your feelings and give off such smug vibes that as sympathetic as I am to Callenbach's decentralism, give me a few sticks of dynamite and I'd blow the fucking place up myself.

Interestingly, Callenbach's American visitor finds Japanese, black, and Hispanic ethnic enclaves. These offend his liberal sensibilities; he writes, "The way propounded by Ecotopian ideologues leads away from the former greatness of America, unified in spirit 'from sea to shining sea,' toward a balkanized continent—a welter of small, second-class nations, each with its own petty cultural differences."[88] Maybe national greatness, planted as it is in soil bloodied by war and paved over by concrete for gargantuan monuments to the almighty state, isn't all it's cracked up to be. Maybe Ernest Callenbach's dream, potted as it may be, is the stuff that humane societies are made of.

"I think Northern California would be a reasonable-size state—about 9 million people," said Callenbach in the early 1980s. "It would be a comfortable-size country or a comfortable state, if we're still a state. It's small enough to have some sense of direct contact between the government and the citizenry. It's small enough that you can travel all over it without greatly exerting yourself and get to know the place. It is a compact entity geographically because of the particular way it's situated, with the drainage all going out through the San Francisco Bay. It makes a whole, gives you a sense that you belong here. You can say, 'This is my place.' It makes some sense."[89]

So do a lot of other American places, each cherished beyond measure for singular and holy (or joyously profane!) and altogether unduplicatable reasons. As Wendell Berry has written:

> *There are no unsacred places*
> *there are only sacred places*
> *and desecrated places*[90]

Consider the Upper Peninsula of Michigan, which sits atop Wisconsin like a feisty terrier barking into three Great Lakes. The UP, which wasn't even connected to Lower Michigan until the completion in 1957 of the five-mile-long Mackinac Bridge ("which men made to join what God had put asunder," as the Michigan writer Jason Peters has it[91]), is home to less than 5 percent of Michigan's population. "Yoopers," as its proud residents are called—those who live below the Mackinac Bridge are "trolls"—have dreamed of statehood since the late nineteenth century, when a proposed State of Superior was to include the Upper Peninsula and Northern Wisconsin. The idea of an independent UP was revived in 1962 by the Upper Peninsula Independence Association, and it found a political champion in Democratic state representative Dominic Jacobetti, a miner and union leader who would represent his native dirt in the Michigan House of Representatives for a record forty-nine years, from 1955 to 1994. Petitions were even passed in the early 1980s to put secession on the ballot, though the campaigns fell short of the signature threshold.

Ah, but here sterile documentary must bow before the more reliable history of anecdote and hearsay. Greg Kaza, who served as a libertarian Republican in the Michigan House, recalls: "It would be a serious error to characterize supporters of Superior statehood as advocates of secession or independence. The movement to establish Superior as the 51st state was a political strategy advanced by the late state Rep. Dominic Jacobetti, D-Negaunee, to obtain more adequate funding and representation for the Upper Peninsula. Rep. Jacobetti['s] . . . last term in the Michigan House was my first. Privately, he told me that when he first served in Lansing in the mid-1950s the Republicans would 'nickel-and-dime' him over his legislative office expenses, including 'my phone calls back home to my constituents.'"[92] Jacobetti used the threat of secession to secure better treatment. Up my phone allowance or the UP splits.

The Upper Peninsula has, in spades, the essential precondition for any vital independence movement: cultural self-awareness. It has its own idiom, its accent, its house band (Da Yoopers), and its own writers, most notably Robert Traver, pen name of John D. Voelker, author of books on fishing as well as the UP-based novel *Anatomy of a Murder* (1957). Voelker was the longtime prosecuting attorney in Marquette County and later a justice of the Michigan Supreme Court. He was also a UP patriot who opposed construction of the Mackinac Bridge.

The elements are there for a UP statehood movement. It awaits a new political champion.

So does the Texas Panhandle.

In 1915 representatives of the Panhandle put in a bill to secede from the Lone Star State and establish a State of Jefferson—that name is ever-inspiriting, ain't it? Texas had entered the union in 1845 with a guarantee of fission: "New states, of convenient size, not exceeding four in number, in addition to the said State of Texas, and having sufficient population, may hereafter, by the consent of said State, be formed out of the territory thereof, which shall be entitled to admission under the provisions of the federal constitution." Imagine five little Texases!

In 1930 Representative John Nance Garner (D-TX), House minority leader, threatened Republicans with that very prospect if they didn't lay off the Smoot-Hawley protectionism.[93] They did. Republican state legislator David Swinford called for freeing the Panhandle during the secessionist flurry of the early 1990s. Not enough Texans rallied to the colors.

If fairness and democratic self-rule ever intruded into political calculations, our union would be graced with multiple Texases. But Texans, bless their prideful hearts, historically have taken pride in their size—contra Chesterton's dictum that a patriot boasts of the smallness, not the largeness, of his country. So the perfectly sensible case for dividing Texas has all the appeal of a lutefisk vendor on the streets of Laredo. Instead, the cause that refreshes is that of an independent Texas: a Lone Star Republic.

Several small groups promote the secession of Texas from the United States, but, well, how can I put this? Although its twenty-five million people, distinctive culture, abundant resources, long coastline, and sharing of a border with a friendly country give Texas independence a pragmatic and intellectual force, its most vocal advocates rustle in the fringes.

The cause has been taken up occasionally by loons, though what would American history be without its loose kites, whether holy fools or unhinged obsessives or just plain wackos? In 1996–97 a band of secessionists led by an organic winemaker declared a Republic of Texas, its capital, fittingly, in Jeff Davis County. They issued millions of dollars of "worthless but official-looking Republic of Texas checks" and clogged the courts with hundreds of frivolous liens. Schism and even kidnapping cleaved this Republic of Texas.[94]

Then in the 2008 GOP US Senate primary, an advocate of Texas independence named Larry Kilgore attracted more than 225,000 votes, or 18.5 percent of the total cast. Besides freeing Texas, he called for a US withdrawal from Iraq and the enactment of "biblical law," which seemed to involve the releasing of all prisoners and the enforcement of the Ten Commandments. Hey, it beats the Texas of LBJ and the Bushes.

Next door, Professor Charles Truxillo of the University of New Mexico dreams of a Republica del Norte, a "Hispanic homeland" reconquered, he says with a certain vainglory, "by any means necessary." The porousness of the border is leading to a fusion, Truxillo believes, of "Southwest Chicanos and Norteno Mexicans," who "are becoming one people again."[95] As with Hawaii, the question arises: What to do with the whites and blacks and Asians who have migrated thereto over the last century and a half? That, I suppose, would be the work of subsequent secessions.

From the Eastern Shore of Maryland to the woods of Northern Maine, neglected hinterlands and poor-relation backwaters have found legislative champions for fifty-first statehood in recent years. So do blocks and neighborhoods and redheaded stepchildren of the boondocks dream of breaking away.

Staten Island does not host the only municipal secession movement. The good folk of Roxbury, the twelve-mile-square African American quarter of Boston, tried and failed on multiple occasions in the 1980s to secede from the city. Residents, perhaps concerned that the property-tax base was insufficient to support an energetic Roxbury government, defeated the measure. On the east end of Long Island, environmentalists who wanted to "save what's left of the Long Island I knew as a child," as schlockmeister Billy Joel said—or were they snobs appalled by the tackiness of their adenoidal middle-class neighbors to the west?—fought to break away from Suffolk County to form Peconoic County.[96] Coincidentally, the fishing community of Long Island, Maine, broke free from the city slickers of Portland. The potentates of the desert city of Needles, California, known to Southwestern travelers as the get-out-to-piss-and-grab-a-burger stop on Route 40, debated defecting to Arizona or Nevada.

In 2007 citizens of the whilom Milton County, a suburb of Atlanta that was absorbed into gigantic Fulton County in 1932, tried to form anew their own county. As the once and future Milton County is much whiter than the rest of Fulton County, the usual squawks of "racism" were heard. Democratic state senator Vincent Fort warned that if the secession measure "gets to the floor [of the state legislature], there will be blood on the walls." Now there's a solon who learned his lessons from Father Lincoln!

The state representative who sponsored the Milton County secession said that the real issue was not race but size. Fulton County, with almost one million people, is "too large, and certainly too dysfunctional, to truly be considered local government."[97] Unquestionably true. Nevertheless, the walls of the state capital remain bloodless, and Milton County is yet unreborn.

How fitting 'twould be if the first Americans could show us the way. In the spirit of Crazy Horse, a delegation of Lakota Indians, led by former American Indian Movement firebrand Russell Means, announced in December 2007, "We are no longer citizens of the United States of America and all those who live in the five-state area that encompasses our country [Nebraska, South Dakota, North Dakota, Montana, Wyoming] are free to join us."[98] American expats were welcome in Lakota Country, which set up shop by distributing the petty accoutrements of a sovereign nation: driver's licenses and passports. Whether Means & Co. mean business or not will only become clear as the years pass: Means is a bright and angry man with a surly charisma but he changes tack as often as he changes wives.

Independence from the Great White Father in Washington has been a central demand of the modern American Indian rights movement. On November 20, 1969, about ninety mostly urban Bay Area "Indians of All Tribes" motorboated over to Alcatraz Island, cursed home of the famed Rock.[99] The empty prison complex had been deemed surplus property by the government; the Indians were to occupy it for the next nineteen months. They came to the island afire with dreams and grievances. Alcatraz was to be the site of schools and a spiritual center and a museum; it was to be, in the words of activist Adam Fortunate Eagle, "a showcase of Indian virtues and Indian greatness." If it eventually fell victim to "alcohol, drugs, and factionalism," it was, for a golden year, a symbol of Indian resistance and Red Pride, and a working example of pan-Indian community-building.[100]

These truths come in colors white and black as well as red.

Howard Husock, writing in the *City Journal* of pro-capitalist think tank the Manhattan Institute, explains that the "long-standing American preference for localism makes sense" because "we don't all want the same thing from our local jurisdictions. Those with small children may care most about education, unmarried joggers may want to spend public money on parks, and the tidy-minded may want the streets cleaned three times a week."[101] Small, homogeneous political units can deliver something close to these preferences; large bureaucratic clots cannot.

Nevertheless, the hurdles are formidable. Most American newspapers today suffer under absentee ownership and are edited by deracinated careerists whose first loyalty is to their corporate paymasters, not the communities in which they live. They are wont to ridicule any authentic expression of indigenous radicalism. These papers, owned by Gannett and Knight-Ridder and other octopi, tut-tut the "divisiveness" of the secessionists, who are advised to shut up, pay their taxes, and pull a lever for Tweedledee or Tweedledum. A newspaper's "function is to serve the established by moulding public opinion," as Jack London wrote in *The Iron Heel* (1908).[102] They fustigate, they objurgate, they shoot the poison darts of -isms and -phobias at dissenters. The *Wichita Eagle*, a cog in the Knight-Ridder machine, was anti–West Kansas secession, and the Gannett papers that blotch Upstate New York were just as unfriendly to the localist cause. Still, family-owned weeklies have championed provincial self-rule, and some California dailies have given the state split respectful attention. I am skeptical about the likelihood of online newspapers being any more welcoming of dissent—I have a flylike aversion to webs—but can they be any worse than the party-line print-wasters in newsboxes today?

Jerry Brown, as mayor of Oakland, was ridiculed by the Gannett newspaper chain for saying, "I want to emphasize place. Re-inhabit, going back, learning what was before, what is, what isn't, what could be because of its physical location, its place in the economy, its fauna, its flora, its racial, ethnic, and cultural diversity."[103] Another errant ray from the moonbeam, sneered the corporate caption writers, but in fact Brown was displaying a rare sentience for a political man. Would that Browns dappled the countryside.

"Sooner or later other states take up these things," said William Allen White of Kansas's avant-garde enthusiasms.[104] If a fifty-first star on Old Glory for West Kansas seems fanciful, a whimsy straight out of *The Mouse That Roared*, the prospect of three Californias or two New Yorks is less so. And why not states for the Upper Peninsula and the Texas Panhandle while we're at it?

We are a nation born in secession, consecrated to the right of a free people to rule themselves, and our inherited radicalism has never quite been extinguished. In 1933 the North Dakota Senate took up a resolution introduced by eighty-three-year-old "Wild Bill" Martin of Morton County calling for Middle America to break away from the nine New England and Middle Atlantic states, which were said to view Middle Western farms as colonies and its boys as cannon fodder. By a vote of 28–20, the North Dakotans, resolving that "whereas, there has grown up in the Eastern States a financial oligarchy, with Wall Street as the center of the Union," proposed that "we, the remaining thirty-nine states secede from the above named states, carrying with us the Star Spangled Banner, and leaving them the stripes, which they so richly deserve; let them continue to prey upon their own people; give them a free hand but they must keep off us."[105] That's the spirit, Dakota!

Seven and a half decades, several wars, and trillions of dollars later, the antipathy of the outland for Wall Street and Washington grows fiercer by the day. Independence for the provinces may strike cosmopolitan ears as an airily capricious notion, the delusion of romantics who obdurately cling to verities long ago immured in the foundation of empire, but the foundation has cracks that no mortar can fill.

The Center cannot hold—or so the cowlick Jeffersonians hope and pray. It took a Civil War to stanch Bleeding Kansas. Cleaving Kansas (and California and New York and maybe even Michigan) will be ignored for as long as possible, then disparaged and mocked, but when in the course of human events it becomes necessary for one People to dissolve the Political Bands that have connected them with another, self-evident truths have a funny way of asserting themselves.

CHAPTER FOUR

Why Is This a State? Or, Will Walrussia Give Its Star Back?

*F*ive decades of statehood for Alaska and Hawaii, and what do we have to show for it? The Iditarod, countless bad puns about getting lei'd, and a sweatshop Betsy Ross stitching a fifty-first star for Puerto Rico. We can't say we weren't warned.

A chorus of reactionaries and wise liberals, from Senator William Fulbright (D-AR) to Columbia University president Nicholas Murray Butler, cautioned that admitting noncontiguous states—abandoning the "united" part of the United States—would be venturing down "the road of empire" and "the road to colonialism," as Senator James Eastland (D-MS) said. "We must not take it. If we go down this road . . . there will be no turning back."[1] To President Butler, writing in 1947, bringing in Alaska or Hawaii "would be the beginning of the end of our historic United States of America . . . We now have a solid and compact territorial Nation bounded by two great oceans, by Canada, and by Mexico. This should remain so for all time."[2]

It was "folly," said North Carolina representative Woodrow Jones of the Hawaiians, "to believe that these people some 5,000 miles from Washington and 2,100 miles from the mainland of America" can possibly "be imbued with the national spirit."[3] Congressman William Wheeler (D-GA) predicted that "in a few years, if we follow the precedent we seem to establish here," the House would teem with "the gentleman from Guam, the gentleman from the Virgin Islands, the gentleman from Liberia, the gentleman from Israel . . . I have grown up thinking that this is the United States of America, not the United States of the entire globe."[4]

Mississippi Democratic senator John Stennis, the principal foe of statehood for Alaska, wondered "whether we shall take a disconnected area, whether it be in the Pacific, in South America, in Africa, or anywhere else ... in the bosom of our nation? We are changing the pattern of our Union once we launch out on this program."[5]

Now, you may write off Stennis as a segregationist apparition, but if you are going to discount the considered opinions of every man and woman of the past who fails to meet your elevated moral standards, then you have cut yourself off from all that has come before. You're navigating blind, man—blindly and arrogantly. I hope you've brought a life jacket. The River Styx is mighty deep.

The rest of us, sinners to be sure, might listen to Senator Stennis. (Who was a courtly gentleman, by the way—yes, he was a servant of the military-industrial complex, but he escorted my grandmother and great-aunt onto the Senators Only elevator and sent them on their way to visit me in Senator Moynihan's office with kindness and good directions. That counts for something.)

A handful of Southern Democrats, Taft Republicans, and independent liberals could not save the flag from its forty-ninth and fiftieth stars. They foresaw another constellation's worth down the road. That old South Carolina horndog Strom Thurmond, then a segregationist Democrat, declared: "Once these two Territories are admitted to the Union, the precedent will have been set for the admission of offshore Territories which are totally different in their social, cultural, political, and ethnic makeup from any part of the present area of the United States. Would we then be in a position to deny admission to Puerto Rico, Guam, American Samoa, the Marshall Islands, or Okinawa?"[6]

Probably not. Though whether or not Puerto Rico—or the native populations of Hawaii and Alaska—wanted in was an open question.

Statehood for Alaska and Hawaii, grafted onto the union largely for dubious "national security" reasons and in egregious violation of the contiguous integrity of the forty-eight United States, is being reexamined by a surging native Hawaiian movement and by a feisty if still fringe band of Alaska secessionists. Why not do jigsaw-puzzle makers a favor and grant these two remote colonies their independence? Let us give their stars to worthier places—say, West New York and Superior California.

❧

"The central paradox of Alaska," wrote John McPhee in *Coming into the Country* (1977), "is that it is as small as it is large—an immense landscape with so few people in it that language is stretched to call it a frontier."[7]

Even more is language stretched to call it *American* in any but the continental—which is to say, with a nod to McPheean paradox, the least significant—sense.

For most of its existence, to all but the intrepid, the hearty, the fugitive, and the romantically misanthropic, Alaska has seemed a nice place to exploit but you wouldn't want to live there. The Danish seaman in Russian employ Vitus Bering landed on Kayak Island in 1741; he and his crew were the first non-native explorers on Alaskan soil. Fur was the lure that kept Russia and later Spain and Great Britain coming into the country, and out of the greed and barbarism of the fur trade grew Russian America. "Through the savages of the new world they had cut a path of blood," as Jack London wrote in "Lost Face."[8]

The Russian American Company (RAC), a private trading firm chartered in 1799, ran Russian America, or an exploitable slice of it, with the Russian imperial navy. Sitka was its cultural center, but since there were never more than 823 Russians in Alaska, they left little residue.

The Russians concluded that the cost of developing Russian America was prohibitive, especially given the presence on the same continent of a young and confident nation with expansionist tendencies. Wary of the possibility of a British-French seizure of Sitka during the Crimean War, the RAC let it be known that a sale to the United States might be arranged.

Here we pick up the textbook version: Secretary of State William Seward bought it for two cents an acre, shortsighted editorialists mocked "Seward's Folly," but Alaska would become the northern jewel in the American crown—a breathtakingly beautiful expanse of caribou and oil and defense installations. In reality, the path to statehood was a little more rutted than all that.

As early as 1846, William Seward had envisioned the US flag flying over "icy barriers of the north."[9] But if Republicans, the party of freedom for the slave, were at times also the party of the land grab, the first abortive effort at purchasing Alaska was a Democrat project.

Robert J. Walker, energetic filler of the offices of US senator from Mississippi, secretary of the Treasury under the diarrhea-ridden President Polk, and the Buchanan-appointed governor of the Kansas Territory, was a leading expansionist Democrat who had been slavering over Alaska since 1845. Walker had wanted to take all of Mexico, and after the Civil War he would agitate for annexing Alaska, Canada, Greenland, Iceland, the Virgin Islands . . . He would not be satisfied until the American flag flew over every patch of land on the globe, and even then he would gaze covetously upon the moon. Call him the first neocon.

Walker was a five-foot-two Mississippian with a massive head, a homunculus topped by piles of curls dyed black, a rash runt given to issuing duel challenges, a pygmy popinjay eager to rule the world.

In an 1847 letter he announced that he was "quite certain" that an American–English empire would one day extend "over nearly the balance of North America, much of Europe & large portions of Asia." He proposed to Britain, in all seriousness, that its constituent parts become states of the USA, leading to "a perfect cosmopolitan state of fusion, a unity of thought and action on all the great questions."[10] A century and a half later Robert Walker would have been a voice in the globalist chorus.

Leaving Mississippi behind, Walker became a resident of Washington, DC, whence the shrimp under the chevelure prophesied "the onward march of the American people over the North American continent."[11] As a leading War Democrat, he hated secession with a passion, as it denied the inevitability of enlargement: After all, "disunion is opposed to the physical laws of this continent." He was a frank racist, believing that "the negro, altho to be regarded as a man, and treated with humanity, belongs to an inferior race, communion or association with whom is not desired by the whites"—but since slavery posed an obstacle to expansionist unity, it must be abolished.[12]

He wrote his brother-in-expansionist-arms Seward in 1868: "The theatre of our greatest triumph is to be the Pacific where we will soon have no formidable European rivals—The consequences are *ultimately*, the political and commercial control of the world."[13]

This is megalomania. This is madness. But this is the vision that came to dominate American politics.

To Walker's disappointment, Russian America would remain Russian during the presidencies of Zachary Taylor and the handsome pacific Millard Fillmore, but the alcoholic Democrat Franklin Pierce, in whom Nathaniel Hawthorne saw intimations of greatness, was open to negotiation. Russia, purse-pinched and casting a chary eye at the swelling United States, saw the writing on the igloo. The only question left was how many rubles she could get for the real estate.

The Russians realized that Russian America was not defendable and besides, the ever-westering Americans would eventually make their way toward the northern lights. Having seen President Polk at work robbing Mexico in the Southwest, the "owners" of this sea of land thought it wiser to sell than be dispossessed. (The native population was not consulted.) Action was imminent. Rumor even had it that Brigham Young might lead the Mormons to a gelid refuge.

Secretary of State William Marcy and California Democrat senator William M. Gwin told the Russian minister to the United States, Baron Edouard de Stoeckl, "that if Russia wanted to sell Alaska, the United States would buy."[14] Senator Gwin suggested a price of $5 million in 1859. The Russians thought that too little, but before haggling could bring the parties together the war came.

Russia was a friend to the union; her stock in American eyes jumped. Yet the Russian American Co. underwent "rapid financial decline," with its stock dropping from 500 rubles per share in 1857 to 75 in 1866.[15] The fur trade and lumber and mining industries were ailing. The company, in best monopoly fashion, asked the Russian government for a bailout, but the government opted to sell this white elephant. (We interrupt this narrative for a question by Alaskan Independence Party leaders Dexter and Lynette Clark: "By what principles were [the Russians] in a position to sell? The right of discovery overlooks the indigenous population . . . It is safe to say that 99% of Alaska's aboriginal Indians and Eskimos never saw a Russian, let alone somehow lost their birthright to one.")[16]

The secretary of state under President Andrew Johnson was William Seward, and no more ardent expansionist than Seward has ever set heel to American soil. Seward foresaw in the 1850s that "our population is destined to roll its resistless waves to the icy barriers of the North, and to encounter Oriental civilization on the shores of the Pacific."[17] To his credit, I suppose, the hawk-nosed Seward preferred to take land by the checkbook, not the rifle. He coveted possessions for their commercial and military uses and imagined the United States someday bestriding the globe, or at least one of its hemispheres. We would need coaling stations, foreign ports, naval bases, all the hideous apparatus of empire.

In 1852 Seward had come out for acquiring Hawaii, but as Seward biographer Glyndon G. Van Deusen writes, "President Fillmore was not interested."[18] Mild Millard would pass. Seward waited for a tribune—himself?—with broader vision. In a speech at St. Paul, Minnesota, on September 18, 1860, he speculated on "the ultimate central seat of power of the North American people." He once supposed it "in the valley of Mexico; that the glories of the Aztec capital would be renewed, and that city would become ultimately the capital of the United States of America." But he had since turned his gaze northward, to the Arctic, and he imagines himself telling Russia: "Go on, and build up your outposts all along the coast up even to the Arctic ocean—they will yet become the outposts of my own country—monuments of the civilization of the United States in the northwest." From the Hudson Bay to the "Spanish American republics," all are in "the preparatory stage for their reorganization in free, equal and self-governing members of the United States of America."[19]

This "megalomania," as the diplomatic historian Victor J. Farrar called it, reached its peak—its nadir?—in Seward's raving to a Boston audience on June 24, 1867: "Give me only this assurance, that there never be an unlawful resistance by an armed force to the President bearing the authority of the United States, and give me fifty, forty, thirty more years of life, and I will engage to give you the possession of the American continent and the control of the world."[20]

What if we don't want it, Auburn Bill?

Why did Seward covet Alaska? Historian Thomas A. Bailey asserts that "Seward acted to satisfy his own insatiable passion for territorial expansion, to improve the strategic position of the United States in the Pacific, and at the same time to revive the decaying popularity of the State Department, which was sharing the opprobrium being heaped upon the head of Johnson." He was emphatically not responding to public pressure, for "there was no popular demand whatsoever for more territory, let alone this inhospitable region."[21]

Let's deal, Seward told Russian minister Stoeckl. Haggling commenced, and the bargainers came up with a price of $7.2 million, or two cents per acre. Seward and Stoeckl drew up a treaty the evening of March 29, 1867, and signed it at 4 AM on the 30th, and the administration presented it to the Senate the next day, asking for immediate ratification.

Senator Charles Sumner, chairman of the Senate Foreign Relations Committee and no friend of President Andrew Johnson, played the party man, shepherding the treaty though his committee by a vote of 4–2. The nays were cast by William Pitt Fessenden (R-ME) and James Patterson (R-NH). Fessenden joked, "I'll go for it with an extra condition that the secretary of state be compelled to live there and the Russian government be required to keep him there."[22]

Sumner introduced the treaty to the full Senate, expatiating for three interminable hours on Alaska in all its geographical and mineralogical glory. Sumner's virtuoso oration praised the treaty as "a visible step on the occupation of the whole North American continent."[23] The United States would splay across the continent, smothering the most distant Eskimo and Mexican with her institutions, whether the heathens wanted them or not. Sumner even ventured into nomenclature: "As these extensive possessions, constituting a corner of the continent, pass from the imperial government of Russia, they will naturally receive a new name. They will be no longer Russian America. How shall they be called? . . . The name should come from the country itself. It should be indigenous, aboriginal, one of the autochthons of the soil. Happily such a name exists"—that which the Aleutian Islanders called the continent: Alaska.[24] (As George R. Stewart writes in his classic *Names on the Land: A Historical Account of Place-Naming in the United States* (1945/1958), "The name itself began to appear shortly after 1760, in various spellings, as Alaeksu, Alachschak, Alaschka, and Alaxa."[25] Thankfully the mushmouthed *ch*s were dropped, and the prescription-drug-sounding Alaxa was flushed.)

Radical Republicans such as Sumner, who had been zealous for crushing the Confederacy, were among the leading expansionists. ("His sympathies were for race—too lofty to descend to persons," a wag remarked of the

Massachusetts senator, one of those lovers of mankind who never seems to find time for individual men.)[26] Pennsylvania representative Thaddeus Stevens, the vindictive and embittered hater of all things Southern, was also an ardent expansionist and, despite his dislike of Seward, gung-ho for taking Alaska.

The Senate rejected by 29–12 a motion by Senator Fessenden to delay the vote. Final passage came on April 9, 1867, or less than two weeks after this massive land transfer had been presented to the Senate, by a vote of 37–2. The nays were cast by Fessenden, who "objected to the cost of the territory," and the noble old Vermont Republican Justin Morrill, who "opposed foreign entanglements."[27]

The heroic Fessenden of Maine had served the last few months of Lincoln's term as his secretary of the Treasury. He later broke with the vengeance-crazed Radical Republicans and voted for Andrew Johnson's acquittal. Unlike the Radicals, who harbored seemingly limitless notions of governmental power, Fessenden had an intelligent conservative's sense of limits. He had stood manfully against Democratic doughface presidents Pierce and Buchanan when they desired Cuba, and as a member of Sumner's Foreign Relations Committee he stood against Seward's folly. Fessenden was no changeable hack: He was consistently anti-imperialist, in the best (if so often ignored) Republican tradition.[28]

All hail Maine! She has given us superb writers (Sarah Orne Jewett, Carolyn Chute) and painters (Marsden Hartley) and musicians (David Mallett) and premier anti-imperialists. She may be an extremity but I think of her as America's heart.

The Maine-born Wisconsin Republican congressman Cadwallader "Caddy" Colden Washburn, the very model of a major general in the Civil War, was part of a legislative dynasty, as three of C. C.'s siblings also served in Congress. Unlike Senator Fessenden, Washburn was a thoroughgoing Radical Republican, but unlike radicals such as Stevens and Sumner he was quite satisfied, thank you, with the size of the United States. He called Alaska "utterly worthless and God-forsaken" and told Congress that he'd gladly vote to give Alaska to anyone who had a spare $7 million lying around.[29]

Washburn could have taught the dithering Democrats of Iraq II a lesson: If you object to a policy, zip the damn purse! On November 25, 1867, he put forth a resolution that "in the present financial condition of the country any further purchases of territory are inexpedient, and this House will hold itself under no obligation to vote money to pay" for them. Make all the treaties you like, Secretary Seward, and you august senators may ratify them like waistcoated robots, but the House, guardian of the peoples' purse, was giving no lines of credit.

"I do not intend that resolution to apply to the purchase of Walrussia," snickered Washburn. That ice floe was under the bridge. But "it is rumored," he said, that Secretary Seward "has been making another purchase without consulting any one, in the absence of any public sentiment requiring it, or of any demand from any quarter." The rumor had a grain of truth, as we shall see, and Washburn wanted to "serve notice upon the kingdom of Denmark that the House will not pay for that purchase; and I mean to serve notice upon the world that we will pay for no purchase that the Secretary of State, on his own motion, may see proper to make."[30]

His colleagues approved Representative Washburn's resolution by a vote of 93–43. The anti-expansionists were in the House! Seward had been served notice. Washburn & Co. would not stand for a United States of "states dissevered, discordant, belligerent."[31]

American skeptics called it Icebergia, Walrussia, Frigidia, and Johnson's polar bear garden, though it is not true that many Americans mocked it as "Seward's Folly," as Richard E. Welch Jr. demonstrates in his study of newspaper opinion. Most Americans didn't give a damn either way. This is the usual attitude of Americans toward foreign affairs, which is why the hyperinterested minorities call the shots. Most of us could not care less about Cuba, Israel, and Ireland, so the Cuban, Israeli, and Irish lobbies shape US foreign policy toward those nations.

Welch writes that "a majority of the American press seems either to have favored the treaty or at least not to have been opposed to it."[32] The *New York Times* was all for it, but the *New York Sun* lectured that "territorial expansion has always been the bane of nations."[33] The most significant anti-Alaska voice was Horace Greeley's *New York Tribune*, which explained, "We have more territory than we want." (Robert J. Walker and William Seward would reply that a nation can *never* have enough territory.) Moreover, a successful occupation of Russian America "will require an enormous outlay to maintain a warlike establishment."[34] Empire costs money; why bother?

On October 18, 1867, at the Russian barracks in Sitka, the flag of Russia was lowered and Old Glory raised. The presiding officer of the US Army was the pan-Americanly named General Jefferson Columbus Davis. Alaska was ours—but the House of Representatives had yet to pay for it. A mere formality, it was thought, until the recusants opened their mouths. Some objected that Seward hadn't the constitutional right to make the treaty and take the territory without an appropriating act of the House. Others, such as Samuel Shellabarger (R-OH), denounced a "system of foreign colonial possessions."[35] An anti-expansion minority of "anti-Johnson Republicans and a few House Constitutionalists" balked at paying for "Walrussia."[36]

Representative Orange Ferriss (R-NY) of Upstate's Glens Falls, no stranger to the niveous, called Alaska "a barren, unproductive region covered with ice and snow" that "will never be populated by an enterprising people." Representative Benjamin F. Loan (R-MO) said that "the acquisition of this inhospitable and barren waste will never add a dollar to the wealth of our country or furnish any homes to our people. It is utterly worthless."[37] Besides, it wasn't even adjacent to another state.

Bah! retorted the Alaska men. Acquiring this barren waste was but the first step! Representative Rufus Paine Spalding (R-OH) scoffed at the contiguity argument. "Sir," he declaimed in debate on July 7, 1868, "as an American citizen, and a republican at that, I deny that any territory upon this western continent is to be deemed foreign to the Government of the United States when it seeks to extend its limits. I believe that if anything under the heavens be fated, it is that the American flag shall wave over every foot of this American continent in course of time. This proud Republic will not culminate until she rules the whole American continent, and all the isles contiguous thereto . . . Including South America, by all means."[38]

By all means or by any means? Representative Spalding's colleague, the stomach-crampingly named Green Berry Raum (R-IL), added, "I am ready to see all of North America, from the North pole down to the Isthmus of Darien [Panama], under the sway of the United States of America."[39]

The House finally did approve the appropriation for Alaska on July 14, 1868, by a vote of 113–43.

Having swallowed Alaska, Seward set his sights on Santo Domingo and on the Danish West Indies, where, confirming Representative Washburn's suspicions, he sought to buy two islands (St. Thomas and St. John) in 1867 for $7.5 million. The purchase foundered on domestic indifference and criticism by the likes of Charles Francis Adams—there's that family again—who feared that such expansion would be deadly "to the permanency of our Institutions."[40] The indefatigable *New York Tribune*, bless Horace Greeley's eccentric soul, weighed in, "We cannot have colonies, dependencies, subjects, without renouncing the essential conception of democratic institutions."[41]

Meanwhile, the tireless Robert J. Walker recommended to Secretary Seward that he obtain Greenland and Iceland from Denmark. Seward requested a report on "the condition and resources of Iceland and Greenland," and Walker obliged, with a seventy-two-page chamber-of-commerce-worthy rhapsody over "superb" fisheries, "vast beds of lignite," and other goodies begging to be plucked from the Danes. The fix seemed to be in. But Seward had reached too far. Congressman Ben Butler (R-MA) ripped anyone "insane enough to buy the earthquakes of St. Thomas and the ice fields in Greenland."[42] Before we add Butler to the Little American Hall of Fame, however, consider that he, like Seward, had favored annexing Canada. A coeval attempt to make the Dominican Republic a territory was also failing, and so Seward's Danish dreams "were entombed in the Senate Committee on Foreign Relations without hope of resurrection," in the sepulchral words of historian Donald Marquand Dozer.[43] The Little Americans had won a couple of rounds.

Still, we would always have Alaska.

⌒◎⌒

Once purchased, Alaska was put under military jurisdiction. For its first seventeen years 'neath the American flag, Alaska had no civil government: no land claims, no property transfers, no wills, no criminal prosecutions, no legal marriages—only a general at Sitka until 1877, when the military was called southward to take care of the Nez Percé. Fewer than three thousand Americans moved to Alaska in its first fifteen years, a trickle that seemed to validate the mockeries of "Walrussia." The Organic Act of 1884 finally brought civil governance, or at least an appointed governor, to Alaska, which was now a "district" of the United States.

Having taken Alaska without much forethought, the rulers of the United States were not quite sure what to do with it. Except, of course, for one man. William Seward's August 12, 1869, address at Sitka concluded: "Nor do I doubt that the political society to be constituted here, first as a Territory, and ultimately as a State or many States, will prove a worthy constituency of the Republic."[44] He saw the star in Alaska's future.

Nonetheless, few Americans trekked north until 1896, when George Carmack and his Indian friends Skookum Jim and Tagish Charley discovered a gold nugget in the Yukon, and the Klondike gold rush was on. The gold was in Canada, but the best route thereto went through Alaska. By 1900, thirty thousand non-natives were resident, if not planted, in the polar bear garden.

In 1906 Alaska attained the splendid irrelevance of a nonvoting delegate to the US House. It gained territorial status and an elected, if relatively impotent, bicameral legislature in 1912, though it was the merest silhouette of self-rule. The governor was appointed, the courts were federal, and all laws were subject to congressional veto. Step out of line and the Man would come and put you back in your place.

Alaska's delegate to the US House, James Wickersham, introduced the first statehood bill on March 30, 1916. It was a forlorn hope, a showing of the flag without any real chance of success, but Alaska, its economy now based on salmon & gold, salmon & gold—can't you hear the Burl Ives snowman crooning it?—had transmogrified, in the American imagination, from lonely frozen wasteland to romantic land of the midnight sun. Barrett Willoughby, popular novelist of the 1930s, wrote adventures with an Alaska setting, stories of sourdoughs and salmon fishermen. Bred (but not raised) in Alaska, she was no travel-writing poseur. With Jack London, Willoughby wrote Alaska for those Outside. And the Walter Mittys to the south were captivated.[45]

Yet Alaska differed from the United States in ways that cast doubt upon its fitness for statehood. With the large absentee ownership of such key Alaskan industries as salmon canning, gold mining, lumber, and oil, territorial governor Ernest Gruening, an old Harvard-*Nation* New Deal liberal who went north and went native, denounced its relationship to the American economy as "colonialism."[46] The place was in no way self-sufficient: as geographer James R. Shortridge writes, despite efforts to introduce "the cow and the plow in interior Alaska," inclement weather and inhospitable soil dashed agrarian dreams. Efforts to promote wheat and cattle came a cropper, though the elongated summer days did produce strawberries fat enough to choke an elk. High transportation and marketing costs foiled commercial agriculture development.[47]

E. L. Godkin, founding editor of *The Nation* and a consistent anti-expansionist, derisively termed Alaska "a frozen desert of a colony."[48] It might have remained so—but then war worked its demonic sorcery.

General Billy Mitchell told Congress in 1935: "Alaska is the most central place in the world for aircraft, and that is true of Europe, Asia or North America. I believe in the future he who holds Alaska will hold the world, and I think it is the most important strategic place in the world."[49] Hyperbole, perhaps, but air bases followed, and with them generous infusions of federal money.

World War II, writes Stephen Haycox in *Alaska: An American Colony* (2002), militarized Alaska, blotting it with defense installations: "The war transformed Alaska, as it had transformed the American West, through massive federal expenditures for bases, three hundred thousand personnel who served in the territory . . . Then, astonishingly, the level of spending continued after 1945 as the United States entered the Cold War, and Alaska played a critical role in global strategic defense."[50] Alaska was now a federal dependent, tethered to Washington even as it resented distant bureaucrats.

Mary Childers Mangusso and Stephen Haycox, editors of *Interpreting Alaska's History: An Anthology* (1989), write that "World War II changed Alaska even more drastically than had the gold rushes. People flooded into the territory—soldiers, contractors, construction workers, support personnel."[51] Some stayed; but even those who did not left the mark of Mars. (One such soldier was young Gore Vidal, leader of the antiwar America First group when a student at Phillips Exeter Academy. Gore enlisted in the army and in 1945 found himself first mate aboard a freight-supply ship in the Aleutian Islands. Vidal's first novel, *Williwaw* (1946), paints an Alaska whose harbor towns are congeries of horny drunken pissing sailors manically pursuing weary whores.)[52]

By 1943 Alaska's military population hit an incredible 152,000. "The United States spent about $3 billion in the territory over the entire course of the war," writes Haycox. A military infrastructure of airfields and roads was overlaid, and it survived. Just as the Interstate Highway System was conceived during the Second World War, so was the Alaska Highway, fifteen hundred miles long, a war baby of 1942. "Alaska would never return to the quiet and isolated days of the prewar period."[53]

The population almost doubled from 1940 (72,000) to 1950 (130,000), and the newcomers were not crusty old sourdoughs who wanted to be left the hell alone. Observes economist George Rogers: "The people who came with military Alaska were not independent, self-sufficient agricultural pioneers of past centuries . . . They required and expected the same standards of community living and services available elsewhere."[54] They grooved to Julie London, not Jack London.

John S. Whitehead, historian of Alaska statehood, concludes that "World War II did not so much transform and change an old Alaska as it created a new modern Alaska with very few remnants from the past."[55]

A pastless place, filled rapidly with transients under the press of war and mobilization, is not the ideal soil in which small-scale democracy might grow.

Alaska's proximity to the Soviet Union gave it an even larger role in the Cold War that followed World War II just as surely as putrefaction follows death. Alaska was now a linchpin of US defense, broadly defined. It was, writes Haycox, "a free world military bastion," every bit the welfare dependent that other military bastions are, for "federal spending became the most substantial element in the Alaskan economy after World War II, replacing salmon as the most important sector."[56]

President Truman endorsed statehood for Alaska and Hawaii in his 1946 State of the Union address, thirty years after Delegate Wickersham's bill and fourscore minus one years after Seward's purchase of Walrussia. It was the least Uncle Sam could do for this brick in the Cold War wall.

❧

Any state worthy of the union needs a song, a poem, a founding myth. Alaska, Star 49, might have taken a lesson from the forty-eighth star on the flag, Arizona, and her poetical queen.

Born in 1870 to a Kansas buffalo hunter and his Bohemian pioneer wife, young Sharlot M. Hall kept buffalo calves for pets and recalled watching her mother "wash the heads of men who had been scalped by the Indians."[57] At age eleven, Sharlot rode "a long-legged, dapple gray mare" along the Santa Fe Trail to her family's new ranch and its hopefully named but far from immaculate "Virgin Mary" gold mine near Prescott in the Arizona Territory.[58]

The ranch girl's poems and articles, many published in the California magazine *Out West*, helped interpret the Southwest for the dudes and armchair tourists back east. Hall was contemptuous of eastern cities, whose denizens "grow small in the huddled crowd."[59] Only in the wide-open West could one stand with "his feet on the earth." Her regional pride flared to a white-hot intensity when in 1905 President Theodore Roosevelt endorsed Senator Albert Beveridge's (R-IN) proposal to grant statehood to Arizona and New Mexico only if they merged into a single state with the ridiculous and bumptious name of Arizona the Great. (Arizona was too Democratic, and New Mexico too Catholic, for Protestant Republican tastes.)

Hall learned of Roosevelt's action while she was on assignment in Northern Arizona for an *Out West* issue promoting statehood for her territory. She grew "more and more indignant" as she pondered the slight. Upon arriving home, she recalled, "I asked my mother, who thought I was coming down with pneumonia, to let me have a fire in the sitting room and have the family go to bed and let me alone."

By the time the fire went out, she had composed the poem "Arizona," a defiant assertion of Arizona's claim to statehood:

> *No beggar she in the mighty hall where her bay-crowned sisters wait;*
> *No empty-handed pleader for the right of a freeborn state;*
> *No child, with a child's insistence, demanding a gilded toy;*
> *But a fair-browed, queenly woman, strong to create or destroy.*

If the United States didn't want Arizona in their company, then to hell with them! "Bar your doors instead," she snarled, "and seal them fast forever!" You'll be sorry, Uncle Sam.

Perhaps, she mused, Arizona was too good for the rest of the country. After all, she conceded:

> *Cities we lack—and gutters where children snatch for bread.*
> *Numbers—and hordes of starvelings, toiling but never fed.*

If Arizona was judged unfit to enter the nation, then it would just sit tight. Time was on its side.

> *We will wait outside your sullen door till the stars that ye wear grow dim*
> *As the pale-dawn stars that swim and fade o'er our mighty Canyon's rim;*
> *We will lift no hand for the bays ye wear, nor covet your robes of state—*
> *But Ah! By the skies above us we will shame ye while we wait!*[60]

The poem, capturing so well the hurt pride of Arizona, was a sensation. Territorial governor Joseph H. Kibbey printed "Arizona" as a broadside and had it placed on the desk of every US senator and representative. Reciting the poem on the House floor, Arizona delegate Marcus Aurelius Smith—great name!—persuaded Congress to permit the two territories to hold referenda on the shotgun marriage. New Mexicans approved the merger, but Arizonans, preferring their own humble state to Arizona the Great, voted it down.

Thus, fair-browed, queenly Arizona finally entered the union on her own on Valentine's Day, 1912, the last—for now—of the forty-eight contiguous United States.

Sharlot M. Hall went on to build a museum of Arizona history in Prescott. Her pet cause was placing gravestones over the interred bodies of forgotten pioneers. And though her verse, too, is forgotten, Arizonans may thank her that their state, while perhaps great, is not Great.

Alaska was too big for Hall, but it did have a propagandist of its own: Edna Ferber, the novelist best known for *Giant* (1952), whose best seller

Ice Palace (1958) was called by the *Chicago Sunday Tribune* "the *Uncle Tom's Cabin* of Alaska statehood."[61]

In Ferber's creaky novel, boorish outsiders ask dumb questions and receive enlightenment in matters Alaskan, including its second-class territorial status. As the dazzling Christine Storm lectures, "Would you like to pay government taxes if you couldn't have a voice in the state you live in, and couldn't vote for President of the United States? Would you like taxation without representation? . . . Don't you know Alaska has no Congressman or Senator in Washington! We're a Territory. Everything we do, and everything the Territory yields, goes out. Outside. Everything goes out and nothing stays in. Gold. Copper. Timber. Fish. Millions and millions and millions a year. Outside. We're slaves."[62]

Okay, so it's not exactly Eliza crossing the ice, but it encapsulated the postwar arguments that Alaska deserved a place at the adults' table.

That case was made most publicly by Ernest Gruening, the territorial governor appointed by President Franklin D. Roosevelt over the objections of that loathsome symbol of evil, Interior Secretary Harold Ickes. Gruening was in the progressive anti-imperialist tradition, a liberal civil libertarian, while Ickes hated liberty as much as any man who has ever drawn a breath. They were bound to be enemies.

Throughout FDR's reign, Secretary of the Interior Ickes possessed "czar-like powers over Alaskan affairs and enjoyed using them," explained Robert B. Atwood, editor and publisher of the *Anchorage Daily Times* and chairman of the Alaska Statehood Committee. Ickes, to give the devil his due, had ideas. For instance: "He proposed colonization schemes involving the introduction of large foreign populations in Alaska. He proposed making the Rat Islands in the Aleutian chain a penal colony. He forbade the issuance of patents to homesteaders because he disapproved of the separation of any more land from the public domain."[63] He was detested by his subjects, who redoubled their efforts toward statehood in order to escape Ickes. (Independence from the United States would have done the trick even better.)

Tired of government from afar, on October 8, 1946, Alaskans answered yes to the question "Are you in favor of statehood for Alaska?" by an unimpressive margin of 9,630–6;822. Three years later, the Alaska Statehood

Committee was created by the territorial legislature to act as a clearing-house and lobby for unionist activities.

In May 1948 Harry S. Truman, the most icily determined of the Cold War presidents, sent to the Congress a *Message on Statehood for Alaska* in which he urged statehood "at the earliest possible date." This would bring to Alaska the blessings of local self-government, said Truman, which is surely something to be desired, but also federal highway aid and a "sound, modern tax structure"—that last an ominous phrase indeed.[64]

Anti-statehood forces, John S. Whitehead writes, were plagued by a "general lack of public organization."[65] The Seattle-based salmon-canning and -packing industry was a consistent foe of statehood and steps there-toward, since it feared taxation and the abolition of fish traps by a more potent state government. (Alaskans voted overwhelmingly to prohibit these traps in 1948, but the federal government refused to act.)

Others, speaking in voices tinged with a premature awareness of loss, feared that statehood would bring more people and more development and erode Alaskan identity. Some preferred a Puerto Rico–style common-wealth arrangement, as Senator Mike Monroney (D-OK) had proposed in a *Collier's* article titled "Let's Keep It 48." Monroney complained that his colleagues "have been much too casual about statehood," not much caring one way or the other and satisfied by the simplest of math equations: that is, $2 = 2$. Democratic Alaska and Republican Hawaii would cancel each other out in the Senate.[66] (Half a century later the party affiliations are reversed.)

Commonwealth status would have exempted Alaskans from paying federal taxes—no little attraction in the libertarian North.

John S. Whitehead, noting the presence of such rooted patriots as territorial legislator Mrs. Alaska Linck of Fairbanks in the Anti crowd, remarks that foes of statehood "did appear to represent the older, pioneer segment of the population who had established an acceptable pattern of life, who legitimately feared that they might lose what they had, and who to some extent resented newcomers. Some thought statehood would lead to an overall increase in the scope of government resulting in the loss of personal freedom they had sought in coming to Alaska."[67]

They were right, of course, and they were crushed. And though commonwealth was part of the discussion of the 1950s, independence talk was as rare as golf courses in Nome.

The territorial legislature called a convention to write a state constitution, even though admission to the union was no sure thing. The fifty-five elected delegates (the same number as gathered in Philadelphia in 1787 in a somewhat warmer clime) met from November 1955 until February 1956 at the University of Alaska in Fairbanks, where temperatures dipped that winter to thirty below. Native Alaskans took little part in the deliberations, though the fifty-five delegates did include Tlingit Indian Frank Peratrovich—ah, the legacy of Russia![68]

The convention was hardly an orgy of rugged individualism. Alaska and Hawaii produced the "two great managerialist constitutions" of the union, according to political scientist Daniel J. Elazar.[69] They were very much artifacts of the postwar bureaucratic age, with a strong executive who mirrors the imperial president.

The convention determined upon the "Tennessee Plan," so named because Tennessee, rather than sit back and wait for statehood in the late eighteenth century, had elected and then sent to Washington a congressional delegation to lobby for its admission. It worked then, as it did later for Michigan, Iowa, California, Minnesota, Oregon, and Kansas. The idea was to act like a state and in the acting become so.

On April 23, 1956, Alaskans approved both the constitution (17,447–8,180) and the Tennessee Plan (15,011–9,556) and sent a three-member phantom delegation to DC, where they lobbied to be made real.

An Alaska statehood bill had passed the US House of Representatives back in 1950 by 186–146 but died in the Senate, where Southern senators were in no hurry to admit two new anti-segregation members. Eight years later, on May 28, 1958, the Alaska statehood bill again passed the House, this time by 208–166—not exactly a landslide—but it was approved easily in the Senate on June 30 by 64–20. President Eisenhower signed the bill into law, and on August 26, 1958, Alaskans voted in plebiscite, 40,452–8,010, to join the union as of January 3, 1959.

Among those eight thousand or so Antis was a bush pilot and commercial fisherman named Jay S. Hammond, who would serve two terms as governor from 1974 to 1982. "Hammond's background," writes Whitehead, "was a curious one for an anti-statehooder," for the Upstate New York native "was neither a sourdough nor an agent of the Seattle interests." In a 1987 interview Hammond said that he had viewed the statehooders as "advocates of aggressive, no holds barred growth." Hammond had come north to flee the "environmental degradation" of the states. Now it was following him. Statehood, says Whitehead, "seemed to spell the end of Alaska's differentness. It would make Alaska just like the rest of the US." (Ironically, Walter Hickel, a longtime pro-statehood and pro-development Hammond rival, later was elected governor on the Alaskan Independence Party ticket—more anon.)

Jay S. Hammond suspected that the state would subsidize developers. His preferred policy was "Development must pay the price of admission."[70] No free rides for the extractors and exploiters. In 1958, when there seemed no limits to growth, of either the economy or the economy's government, that was not a winning message.

Ernest Gruening liked to quote Dwight Eisenhower: "Quick admission of Alaska and Hawaii to statehood will show the world that America practices what it preaches."[71] This was the best argument for statehood: equity, an end to colonialism. Who but the most arrant serf *wouldn't* support statehood if the alternative was the continuation of territorial status, a kind of subordinate citizenry? Commonwealth was discussed at the margins, but the unspoken option—full independence—was not in the cards drawn from a Cold War deck.

Since independence was off the table, statehood seemed the best option for Alaska patriots. As the pro-statehood editor explodes in Ferber's *Ice Palace*, "Slaves! Worms! Second class citizens of the greatest democracy in the world! Voteless tax-paying men and women of Alaska, and your fathers and mothers before you for sixty years."[72]

And yet as Senator Strom Thurmond pointed out, "a State which is almost wholly owned by the Federal Government cannot exercise any significant degree of sovereignty. It has no opportunity for any real independence of action. Such a State is merely a puppet State."[73]

Reading through the *Congressional Record* of the 1950s, one is struck by the persistence of two strains of the anti-statehood argument: noncontiguity and precedent. Yes, anti-communist blowhards red-baited the Hawaiian unions, and the relatively scant population of Alaska was adduced as evidence that it was not star-worthy, but the most forceful if underutilized case for the old forty-eight was the same as it ever was. Hark:

- "I believe we overlook the physical structure of our great Nation, the compelling factor in our strength, our unified and contiguous land mass of cohesive States all jointed with common borders to other States of similar makeup, having the same history, the same background of ideas and ideals, economies which are closely related to each other and transportation and communication which closely knit together the cultural, business and social lives of 160 million Americans living in the ideal neighborhood of free States in an indissoluble union."[74] —Senator Monroney (D-OK), 1954 (how states can be "free" in an "indissoluble" union is a question for metaphysicians)
- "We are a great Nation. We are a great people. At least so we say, and presumably so we think. But my reading of history tells me that from the very beginning of time right down to the Great Britain of today that the nations that have gone down, that have faded out as world powers, have been the nations that have kept reaching out and reaching out for more territory, and which overextended themselves until they found that they had destroyed their foundation at home. The ambition of the politicians of Rome, Greece, and many others led them to grow too large, take in too many people of different ways and ideas. The result was the loss of their existence as nations. That is what I am afraid we are doing."[75] —Representative Clare Hoffman (R-MI), 1953
- "Alaskan statehood would establish a most embarrassing precedent for the admission of Hawaii, Guam, and the Virgin Islands."[76] —Representative John Pillion (R-NY), 1958
- "Breaking the line of contiguity in one place makes it easier to breach it in another."[77] —Senator Willis Robertson (D-VA), 1959

- "Once Alaska becomes a State, the doors will be wide open for Hawaiian statehood. And with the admission of Hawaii, out goes any rule about North-American-continent-only. Then will come the deluge: Guam and Samoa, Puerto Rico, Okinawa, the Marshalls. The next logical step in the process would be . . . the incorporation in the American Union of politically threatened or economically demoralized nations in southeast Asia, the Caribbean, and Africa."[78] —Senator Strom Thurmond (D-SC), 1958

- "This is a proposal to extend the shoreline not simply by leaping over Canada, but by leaping clear to the middle of the Pacific Ocean."[79] —Senator John Stennis (D-MS), 1958

- "And when we have set this precedent, where will we stop? Will we deny statehood to Puerto Rico, upon request? To Panama? To Guam? To the Virgin Islands? And if to any or all of these, why not San Marino, or Ghana, or Cyprus? Panama is in a way more 'American' than Hawaii. Puerto Rico, and Guam, and the Virgin Islands, are just as 'American' as Hawaii is. And if we are to go outside the American Continent for new States, why stop with the Pacific Ocean or any segment of it?"[80] —Senator James Eastland (D-MS), 1959

Good questions. Too bad no one ever bothered to answer them.

We live in an age when hall monitors patrol the dank corridors of American political discourse, and tattletales squeal if ever a candidate has exchanged friendly words with someone who misfits the ideological straitjackets of Fox News and the *New York Times*. Thus the final six weeks of another depressingly inane presidential race in 2008 was punctuated by shrieks of horror that Barack Obama knew a former Weatherman and Todd Palin was for several years a member of the Alaskan Independence Party, to whose 2008 convention Governor Sarah sent a taped greeting. Come quick! Come quick! I feel faint!

As it happens, I have at various times exchanged cordialities, even drained cordials, with New Left militants *and* Alaska secessionists, not one of whom has done nearly as much harm to this country as have, say, the Presidents Bush. But inhale those smelling salts, faint hearts, for we are about to meet the godfather of Alaskan secession.

Alaska came into the union with 170,000 people and the lowest population density of any state. In exchange for the privilege of paying federal taxes and enmeshing itself even deeper into the federal regulatory state, Alaska gained a real live countable vote in the US House of Representatives, giving it 1/435th of a voice in the people's house, as well as an admittedly better 2 percent of a say in the Senate. Then again, its territory is one-fifth the size of the forty-eight truly United States.

The sheer size of Alaska—586,400 square miles, with 26,000 miles of coastline; the second (Texas), third (California), and fourth (Montana) largest states would all fit inside her—boggles the mind. Alaska itself is larger than any country ought to be, let alone a state. Juneau, Nome, Fairbanks, Prudhoe Bay: In what way, beyond a certain boreal brotherhood, are their residents bound? Why should the people of any one of those places make the laws under which those of the others live? And why should Alaskans obey outsiders who know nothing of life in Walrussia?

The force of one man's personality injected the i-word—independence—into Alaskan politics. He was Joe Vogler, who conceived Alaskans for Independence in 1973 over lunch with members of the informal "Cuss and Discuss Club" in his mining-equipment repair shop. A handsome craggy sourdough in a "ruffled gray fedora," Joe Vogler was something of a nut, but then I suppose a cautious burgher would have said the same thing about Sam Adams in 1775.[81]

John McPhee included a warm profile of Vogler in *Coming into the Country*, though he did not whitewash what must have been one cantankerous old coot. "He is a roamer, a garrulous companion," wrote McPhee, as well as "a sort of cartoon Alaskan, self-drawn," a fuck-you-I'll-do-it-my-way gold prospector who carried a derringer .22 magnum in his pocket just in case a weaselly bureaucrat should try to block him from bulldozing a trail across federal land. Vogler was not a let's-split-the-difference kinda guy. He once told the mayor of Fairbanks: "You son of a bitch, get ready to look at this town for the last time, because I'm going to close your left eye with one fist and your right eye with the other."[82] Man and cartoon eventually merged into symbol.

Joe Vogler considered himself an exile from an America that was no longer worth loving. A Kansas farm boy who studied law at the University of Kansas, he was working at Dow Chemical in Texas when, in his view, FDR—"a dirty rotten sonofabitch communist traitor"—maneuvered us into the Second World War by provoking Japan. Vogler, a man not given to keeping his impolitic opinions private, unburdened himself of this contention at work, which led, in his account, to a tap on the shoulder from a representative of J. Edna Hoover's FBI and an invitation to leave the patriotic premises of Dow Chemical. Ad hominem remarks had no place in a corporation dedicated to improving the quality of life through napalm.

Vogler went north to Alaska. First to Kodiak in 1942, then a couple of years later to Fairbanks. He began mining for gold in 1951.

"It was a different world," he told a University of Alaska interlocutor in an engaging oral history taped in 1991. "You could do anything that you were big enough to try." Vogler rhapsodized over the Fairbanks of the 1940s: its hotels, its twenty-four-hour cafés, its sense of freedom and possibility. It was the "friendliest, most lovable place," he said, and after half a century of wrangling with the Power he loved it still. "The best people on earth live right here," he said two years before he died. "And I manage to fight with most of 'em."

Vogler was a Tundra Rebel who followed fearlessly the logic of his position. Washington, he charged, had "deliberately impeded development" in Alaska. Mining, oil extraction and refining, dams: The industries and infrastructure necessary to capitalist prosperity in the forty-ninth state had been banned or crippled by faraway regulators who wanted Alaska as "a market and a playground."[83] He fumed, Alaska writer Mike Coppock recalled, over federal regulations that "brought an end to time honored Sourdough customs such as building temporary cabins on public lands."[84] He refused to acknowledge federal ownership of anything Alaskan and took a contumacious pleasure in flouting roads bans and the like. He was a bad boy, a raiser of hell and maker of mischief, and he couldn't understand how a country that had been built on Joe Voglers could now condemn him.

Vogler denounced "colonialism," and instead of demanding the transfer of land-use decisions from the national to the state government, he opted to remove state from nation altogether. Vogler pointed back with pride to the Alaska Tea Party of May 4, 1911, when about three hundred Cordovans, pissed off that coal was locked in reserves, dumped "several hundred tons of imported British Columbia coal into Orca Bay."[85] This was direct action taken in broad daylight, as Alaskans like to boast, not under darksome cover of night, as at Boston Harbor.

"Land to the people!" Vogler cried. "The government is not a good landlord." Yet he was a tertium quid: neither a leftist anti-colonialist nor a lackey of the developers. Joe Vogler demanded that *all* land in Alaska be privatized, even the parks, but he wanted a substantial allotment to native tribes and a prohibition on the ownership of land by corporations. He criticized corporate personhood and its legal immortality, sounding rather like one of the more radical greens, and in the next breath he denounced environmentalist bureaucrats who "couldn't design and build a path to an outhouse." He dug gold but he was not a gold-digger.

Vogler is such a crotchety old American sort that the country would have missed him even if he wouldn't have missed the country. "Why is Alaska the only place that a white man can't own a reindeer?" he asked his oral history interviewer. I like to think of him lovingly grooming Dancer and Prancer and Comet and Vixen but I think he meant to eat them. No matter. "These are the things you get mulling around in your head," he said. "And you get to see the injustice of the way America is treating Alaska."

At times, especially in his writings, Vogler committed the fatiguing sin of the autodidact—chapter and verse, or article and number, recitations—but where would we be without our obsessive eccentrics?

"America is a long, long way off course," he said. "I don't think we can ever be pulled back on. I'm very pessimistic." The train of abuses that "finally destroyed my allegiance to America" included run-ins with assorted federal agents who must have thanked the Northern Star that irascible Joe didn't wing 'em with a black-powder shotgun.[86]

His goal: "ultimate independence by peaceful means under a limited government fully responsive to the people."[87]

If a few eggs had to be cracked to make this northern omelet . . . well, Joe would crack 'em. "God, I hate those sons of bitches," he said of the men who rule the United States and its Alaskan satellite. "If I ever get a revolution going, I'm going to import a bunch of guillotines and lop off their lying heads."[88]

Yet his appeal transcended the fringe. In 1974, as historian Terrence Cole notes, Vogler wrote to eminence grise Ernest Gruening with an unusual half proposition: "If I did not feel that it would be a gross imposition upon your energies, I would ask you to seriously consider stepping up to lead our Independence Movement. We are seeking the same thing that you were—the right to determine our destiny."

Gruening—the grand old man of the Alaska Democracy—replied that he "was not ready to join YET"—unless federal obduracy continued and convinced him that "total secession was the only answer."[89] After only fifteen years in the union the optimism of statehood had curdled, even in Ernest Gruening.

Joe Vogler seized whatever part of the moment he could. He ran for governor on a platform of Alaskan independence in 1974, when he won 4,770 votes, or 5 percent of the popular vote in a race that was decided (for the old anti-statehood Republican environmentalist Jay Hammond) by only 287 votes. He won less than 2 percent in 1982 and then in 1986, as standard-bearer of what was now officially known as the Alaskan Independence Party, he scored his personal best of 5.6 percent with more than ten thousand votes.

In the next quadrennium the AIP actually won the statehouse—sort of. The party endorsed Walter Hickel, former governor and Nixon's secretary of the interior, who campaigned on making Alaska an "owner state" rather than a colony. "I ask only that you run Alaska as an Alaskan," Vogler told Hickel, who won with 39 percent in a three-way race.[90] Hickel was a developer who wished to leave no natural resource unexploited, and while his emphasis on Alaska First was sweet music to localist ears, Vogler came to consider him a typical Republican servitor of big business.

If the Vermont *independentistas* are green, the Alaskans tend to be pro-development—at least if that development has an Alaskan stamp. Governor Hickel proposed to open the Arctic National Wildlife Refuge

(ANWR) to oil and gas extractors, and nothing nettled Joe Vogler quite so much as federal restrictions on land use. Yet the party detests Big Oil, and with its Alaska First philosophy it decries the "international mega corporations" such as British Petroleum that batten on Alaska's resources.

It was inevitable that two men as quarrelsome as Joe Vogler and Wally Hickel would come to blows. According to Lynette and Dexter Clark of the AIP, a face-to-face meeting "ended with the Governor chasing Joe Vogler out of his office brandishing the office stapler like a club."[91] In this sense only was Joe Vogler clubbable.

The legalistic gold miner and his party denied the legitimacy of the 1958 plebiscite by which Alaskans voted to join the union. Somewhat amusingly for a go-it-aloner, Vogler appealed to the United Nations, arguing that the United States had violated international law relating to decolonization. He spoke of the "human right of self-determination" and noted that the UN charter required that "non-self-governing" lands, of which Alaska was one, were entitled to vote on independence.

"Why weren't we given the same rights as Puerto Rico?" asked Vogler, by which he meant a plebiscite in which citizens choose among statehood, commonwealth, territorial status, and independence.[92] This choice is what the AIP sought and seeks still.

Vogler drew up a petition to the UN asking "that Alaska be restored to the list of non-self-governing territories so that we may exercise the options, by democratic process, which we should have been afforded on August 26, 1958." He further requested that military personnel "be not allowed to vote" and, in a nice poke in Uncle Sam's inspecting eye, that observers from the United Nations or Switzerland monitor the election.[93] (Mark Chryson, a former AIP chairman, says that when Latvia and Lithuania voted to secede from the USSR, "they followed international law and the [Soviet] occupational forces were not allowed to vote."[94] What's sauce for the imperialist goose is sauce for the imperialist gander.)

"We were a simple, naive people, and they kept us uninformed and ill advised," wrote Vogler, playing the ingenue card.[95] But the game was up, the scam was exposed, and now it was time for an honest vote.

Vogler and the AIP claim that not only were aboriginal Alaskans disfranchised by English-only ballots, but that army brass pressured the troops into casting yea votes in 1958. John Whitehead is skeptical. His research found "no particular difference in voting patterns in Anchorage and Fairbanks, where military presence was heavy, than in Juneau and Ketchikan, where the military was not present."

Whitehead is frank on the subject of the AIP's founder. "Joe Vogler, whom I knew, was quite charming in many ways," he tells me. "He was extremely articulate. Once I chaired a panel for governor candidates and Joe stole the show and was quite the crowd pleaser. Of course, people who did business with him came to despise him. He called birch trees 'arboreal weeds.' He required that people who bought property from him must clear-cut the land. This caused mudslides in the hills on other people's property. So Joe was always in court—which he loved."[96]

Okay, he was a bastard, but a lovable bastard. He did not, as an old man, grow conciliatory. "The fires of hell are frozen glaciers compared to my hatred for the American government," he liked to say.[97]

Eighty-year-old Joe Vogler disappeared in May 1993, shortly before he was to address the United Nations General Assembly on the colonial status of Alaska. His sponsor for the talk: Iran.

Vogler was found dead in a shallow grave near Fairbanks in the fall of 1994—secessionists await their Oliver Stone. A lowlife was convicted of the crime; the motive, it was said, was burglary, but AIP members have other theories. "Everyone knows we've got to genuflect to the powers that be," said Lynette Clark at the time of Joe's disappearance. "But Joe refused to bow and scrape. And for that he was labeled Public Enemy No. 1."[98]

"I am an Alaskan," Vogler declared, and his oft-announced refusal to be buried under the American flag was honored when his body was interred in Dawson City, Yukon. "When Alaska is an independent nation they can bring my bones home to my country," said Vogler.[99] Someday. Maybe someday.

~❧~

Today's Alaskan independents and the anti-statehood forces of the '50s hail from different valleys. "The anti-statehood people were most concerned that Alaska did not have an economic base to support itself," John Whitehead tells me. "So independence would have been an even more expensive option than statehood." He adds, "Though once an elementary student told me he would have declared independence and then asked the US for foreign aid."[100]

Rest assured that the economic base part has been taken care of. Worries that Alaska could not afford a state government ended with Atlantic Richfield's 1968 discovery of "North America's largest single petroleum deposit" at Prudhoe Bay—on state-owned property. After Congress permitted a massive pipeline to be built from Prudhoe Bay to Valdez, the oil flowed, and the lucre gushed back into state coffers, from which it—or a portion thereof—was distributed to taxpayers via the Alaska Permanent Fund.

Oil money brought people and it brought development. It enriched the Alaskan treasury as it eroded the Alaskan self-image, however exaggerated it may have been, of hardy sons and daughters of the midnight sun. "It transformed a modest, somewhat remote outpost of civilization into a thoroughly modern late-twentieth-century, technologically oriented, and literate society," writes Stephen Haycox.[101]

It also taught Alaskans that federalism is dead. In 1978 the US Supreme Court struck down Alaska's local-hire law for work on the pipeline. Why shouldn't Alaskans give preference to citizens over outside mercenaries? Because in postrepublic America to prefer one place over another is place-ism, a xenophobic thought crime. In 1980, in *Zobel v. Alaska*, the Court ruled that the Permanent Fund could not distribute oilfare checks based on length of Alaskan residence—again, Big Brother several thousand miles away overrode a perfectly legitimate local preference law. Moreover, federal law dictates that Alaskan exports must be carried on American ships, which greatly increases costs.

"Alaska's political culture before the petroleum boom of the 1970s and 1980s could be called small-town, populist, and parochial," write Gerald A. McBeath and Thomas A. Morehouse in *Alaska Politics and Government* (1994).[102] Music to my ears! After the stormy petrol years, however, "non-Native Alaskans are virtually indistinguishable from people in the rest of the country in their experiences and attitudes," assert Mangusso and Haycox.[103] It's not all oil-based, of course: The communications revolution that brings Internet porn and Oprah within sight of every American is largely to blame.

Its isolated outposts are *really* isolated, but for the most part Alaska is, counterintuitively, an urban state, as 70 percent of Alaskans live in urban areas. The transiency rate is very high, which militates against cultural self-awareness and certainly secession. Federal employees do their time in Alaska and go south as soon as they are able. There are just too many *cheechakos*—Alaskan for "newcomers"—though paradoxically it is also the state with the highest native population (Eskimos, Aleuts, Indians). On the credit side of the ledger, Alaska "has the lowest percentage of lawyers among its lawmakers of any state legislature," but, appallingly, the state does not have an Alaska history requirement for high school graduation.[104] Oh, Alaska, turn in and find yourself!

By the late 1970s the "Tundra Rebellion" echoed the Sagebrush Rebellion of the West, as Alaskans asserted control, or the desire for control, over their lands.

Even though the feds conveyed 103.4 million acres to the state when it entered the union, more than 60 percent of Alaska is still owned by Washington. No one likes an absentee landlord, least of all one who taxes and regulates and wages war with impunity.

And so in August 1980, by a popular vote of 46,705–45,598, the citizens of the forty-ninth state created an Alaska Statehood Commission. Its job: to "study the status of the people of Alaska within the United States and to consider and recommend appropriate changes in the relationship of Alaska to the United States." It was, the commission later stated, "the first time since the Civil War that citizens of a state have by their vote indicated their unease with the federal union."[105] Symbolically, the ASC's chairman was Jack Coghill, who had served in the convention that had written the state constitution a quarter century earlier.

"Though the commission breathed fire," writes Whitehead, "it backed away from independence."[106] Its report, issued in 1983, endorsed statehood as preferable to independence or a reversion to territorial status or commonwealth. But notice had been served. Sort of. Alaskans were not averse to thinking the unthinkable.

On a parallel track to the AIP and ASC arose the strongest Libertarian Party in the sweet land of liberty.

"Independence and individualism are outstanding characteristics of

Alaskans and the Alaska political process," write political scientists McBeath and Morehouse.[107] A minority of Alaskans state a party preference when registering; it is a state of independents, if not advocates of independence. Beginning in 1978 Libertarians, those consistent advocates of a minimal state and maximum personal freedom, were elected to the Alaska House of Representatives. In 1980 Libertarian nominee Ed Clark polled 12 percent in Alaska, the party's best showing ever, anywhere, in a presidential race. In 1982 Libertarian Dick Randolph, an insurance agent from Fairbanks, won 15 percent in the race for governor.

In 1986 I spent a week in Juneau working on a profile for *Reason* magazine of Andre Marrou, a Libertarian state legislator from Homer, the end of the road, where the highway really does stop. Marrou, who went on to run as the Libertarian candidate for president in 1992, told me, "Alaskans generally came up here to get away from whatever they didn't like in the Lower 48. By and large, when you ask them it turns out they didn't like the oppressiveness of government in the Lower 48, so they came up here to get more *freedom*. Things go fine for a year or two until it finally dawns on them that Alaska is a very socialist state."[108] And that's how Libertarians are born. (Think Andre was the giant hyperbolist? When we spoke, the percentage of Alaskan land that was privately owned was less than the percentage of land in the Soviet Union that was devoted to private plots. As Milton Friedman said, in Alaska the "government owns almost everything.")[109]

The leave-us-the-hell-alone spirit of the Libertarians fits Alaska, no matter what the "Alaskan individualism is a myth" revisionists may say. An Internet connection is a thin wire on which to balance a transcontinental bond. Alaska is isolated, unavoidably, no matter how many channels the satellite dishes bring in. Joe Vogler observed that one effect of noncontiguity was the lack of natural allies based on common conditions. "We've got a problem, we're all by ourselves," he said.[110] Wheat-growing states have neighbors in the same field, but who else but Alaska has permafrost?

The *New York Times*, which notices Alaska (or Idaho or Montana or North Dakota) only on those occasions when five skinheads and a psychopath burn a cross, attacked Anchorage for "isolationism and racism" when in 1987 its voters rejected, by a three-to-one margin, a proposal to name what eventually became the Alaska Center for the Performing Arts for the

Reverend Martin Luther King Jr. As a former Democratic state senator patiently explained to the clueless reporter, the vote was due to "the feeling that King was not part of Alaska, not part of Anchorage."[111] He noted that the state legislature had, earlier in the decade, rejected a proposal to name a street for President Eisenhower on much the same grounds. Why in hell should Alaska name its streets and buildings and public spaces for people from outside? Would it be "racism" if the New York City Council refused to rename Fifth Avenue for a prominent Eskimo?

The *Times* is astonished that people even live in Alaska, let alone that some of those people would object to being under the thumb of a nation whose most influential newspaper is the *New York Times*. Had the *Times* bothered to notice, it would have been shocked when in 2008 Republican governor Sarah Palin, former Miss Wasilla and then something of an Internet sensation as the nation's foxiest chief executive, addressed the Alaskan Independence Party convention with a short video greeting. She told the attendees that she shared their vision of a "self-sufficient" Alaska based on liberty, and while she did not endorse secession, is it even remotely conceivable that any other governor in the land would welcome a secessionist convention?

Governor Palin—soon to become a household name when the rootless John McCain selected her as his running mate in the 2008 presidential race—is widely heralded as the best-looking politician in America by those who do not know my wife, Lucine, supervisor of the Town of Elba, New York. The governor's husband, Todd, multitime winner of Alaska's Iron Dog snowmobile race, was once an AIP member, and before her overnight elevation (or lowering) into the celebrity class Sarah Palin was rumored to be sympathetic. Upon her headfirst tumble into fame, Vermont's Thomas Naylor wondered if she might be a "closet Alaska secessionist," a "radical Alaskan populist disguised as a neocon," or "just a coldblooded technofascist."[112]

None of the above, it turns out. Come fall 2008, Governor Palin married the recitation of neocon talking points to an aw-shucks deportment, to disastrous effect. She sounded no more secessionist on the stump than Hillary Clinton, though as Dexter Clark points out, "she slept with an AIP member for seven years," and surely something, ahem, rubbed off.[113]

Thomas Naylor admired Sarah from afar, saying that "she would make one helluva president of the independent Republic of Alaska."[114] She might at that. It's hard to rattle sabers in Juneau, and the prospect of a nuclear exchange with Russia is easier to contemplate in the Heritage Foundation's mausoleum in DC than it is on an ice floe in the Kotzebue Sound.

By canine coincidence, Governor Palin has a puppy named Independence (or Indy, for short). Alas, it's a Pomeranian-poodle mix and not, as it should be, an Alaskan husky.

"Speaking of puppies, I'm a pretty happy one, too," Lynette Clark, chairwoman of the AIP, told me after the party's 2008 convention in Fairbanks. The party has almost fourteen thousand registered voters, or 2.9 percent of the state total.

The AIP gave its 2008 ballot line to Chuck Baldwin of the Constitution Party—an imperfect fit, to be sure, given the CP's theocratic tincture. The Clarks had been "Ron Paul fans," and Alaska had been one of the best states (17 percent) for the libertarian Paul, the mild-mannered revolutionary obstetrician-congressman from Texas, in his bid for the 2008 GOP presidential nomination.[115]

But an Alaskan was on the national ballot for the first time, and a little home-state pride was a natural feeling. After the election, Lynette Clark told me that the "national media absolutely misrepresented Sarah." The governor has "her people's needs in her heart and is ethical in her conduct," said Lynette. "The United States should be so lucky as to have her as a president. I, however, would rather she be president of the independent nation/republic of Alaska."[116]

Schoolteacher and baseball broadcaster Bob Bird, the AIP's candidate for US Senate in 2008, adds that the DC-NYC demonizers of the party "would have been horselaffed off the street by Alaskans, who do not fear the AIP, even if they do not understand its history or platform. Many Alaskans are with the AIP in heart, if not in hand." Bird, who drew more than 4 percent of the vote with his pro-life, antiwar, and Alaska First platform, sees an untapped constituency of "independents or conservative Republicans who understand that when the federal government refuses to abide by the rules, all obligations from the states are negotiable."[117]

Work within the system, radicals are told, rather as the spider advises the fly to rest for just a moment on a silken rung of web. The AIP tries. But the system is rigged. In both 2003 and 2007, the state denied certification of petitions that would have presented Alaskans with the chance to vote on an initiative to authorize Alaskan independence. In the words of the Alaska Supreme Court in *Kohlhass v. State, Office of the Lieutenant Governor* (2006), "When the forty-nine star flag was first raised at Juneau, we Alaskans committed ourselves to that indestructible Union, for good or ill, in perpetuity. To suggest otherwise would disparage the republican character of the National Government." Announced the office of the state attorney general, "Secession is clearly unconstitutional and to seek changes in the law to allow a state to secede from the indestructible Union is also unconstitutional."[118]

Indestructible Union: Sounds ominous, doesn't it? Inflexible, unfeeling, adamantine. Inhuman. Brutal. Unworthy of a free people.

The ghost of William Seward reproves the Alaskan Independence Party. In 1850 Seward told the Senate, "The Union was not founded in voluntary choice, nor does it exist in voluntary consent." Once in, never out. He continued, in language that would strike dead Alaskan independents, "The Union, then, *is*, not because merely that men choose that it shall be, but because some Government must exist here, and no other Government than this can."[119]

If we are to be held captive to such abstruse theoretical gush, then God help us. It is time, I say with a twinge of regret as a landsman and sometime admirer of my Whig-Republican neighbor to the east in Auburn, to flush Seward. Stand on your hind legs, Alaska, and walk away.

CHAPTER FIVE

And Why Is This a State? Aloha, Hawaii

*H*awaiian statehood is even more inexplicable than Alaskan. At least Alaska is on the same continent as the Lower 48. The Hawaiian islands are almost five thousand miles from my Genesee County. In what way, other than in the profound but, in practice, attenuated sense that "we are all brothers under the skin," are a Hawaiian (of whatever ethnic background) and I countrymen? Why, pray tell, should I have even a whisper of a say in how he lives his life or how his government is organized? And vice versa.

Though the Hawaii islands were settled by Polynesians around AD 750—the date is of course only barely approximate, and native activists sometimes assert that settlement predated the birth of Christ—they were "discovered" for the West in 1778 by Captain James Cook, who sycophantically named them the Sandwich Islands after one of his patrons. On a return trip to the archipelago the next year, Cook fell afoul of the natives and was killed. His flesh may or may not have been consumed, though probably not between slices of bread, as his onomastic contribution would have suggested.

In the years following Cook's demise, Kamehameha the Great, ruler of the Island of Hawaii, attacked and took Maui and Oahu and effected, by military force, consolidation of the islands into the Kingdom of Hawaii, which from the 1790s on served as a trading partner and port for American ships. Those ships carried away sugar and coffee but they brought missionaries and misunderstanding.

The land use, ownership, and sexual practices of Hawaiians were vastly different from those of Americans—plural marriage, communal property, and native gods and goddesses were the rule. New England missionaries to Hawaii disapproved. Of these "bloodsuckers of the community," the US consular agent said that they had "much better be in their native country gaining their living by the sweat of their brow, than living like lords in this luxurious land, disturbing the minds of these children of Nature with the idea that they are to be eternally damned unless they think and act as they do."[1]

The natives' sexual practices appalled, and perhaps titillated, New England missionaries, who with Yankee shrewdness bought heavily in the real estate market, yet the missionaries' record is not without distinction. They developed a Hawaiian alphabet, opened schools (and compelled attendance), and ministered to the Hawaiian population, which was ravaged by smallpox and venereal diseases and alcoholism.

And give the missionaries their due for "their remarkable preservation of the nomenclature." As toponymist extraordinaire George R. Stewart writes, "The Protestants not only did not replace the names, but also did much to preserve them by transliterating them into the roman alphabet and recording them. No important name [in Hawaii] seems to have originated under the missionary influence."[2] The Sandwich Islands never stood a chance.

As Hawaii is halfway between the West Coast and the China Sea, the trading and warmaking nations of the world took notice. Britain and France had designs on the islands, but Hawaii gravitated into the orbit of the United States. The US and the Kingdom of Hawaii negotiated a series of reciprocity agreements in the second half of the nineteenth century: Their sugar came in duty-free, and the US Navy gained eventual control of Pearl Harbor.

Sugar, however, was souring the flavor of the islands. For sugar is a plantation—which is to say slave—crop, cultivated on vast landholdings, inconsistent with the Jeffersonian vision of a nation of small freeholders. As Lawrence H. Fuchs wrote in his classic *Hawaii Pono* (1961), "The success of sugar depended on two things: a market on the mainland with no tariff and cheap servile labor to work in the fields."[3] The sugar barons got both, though the cheap labor had to be imported since Hawaiians had no desire to fall into peonage on their own islands. Asian laborers—Chinese and Japanese mostly—were shipped in by the thousands to work sugar plantations along with the Portuguese, who though European were dark-skinned, largely illiterate, and not considered *haole*, or white.

By 1893 *haoles* owned 80 percent of property on the islands, but they made up less than 10 percent of the population. I do not intend to slide into cheap and easy anti-white racism of the sort one sometimes finds in the anti-imperialist work of academic leftists. The *haoles* were not monsters— they were often paternalistic, charitable, and genuinely devoted, in their way, to the islands. But they were invaders, displacing the people to whom these islands belonged. They delivered Hawaii to the Americans.

The expansionist Democratic administration of President Franklin Pierce and the jittery King Kamehameha III, who feared revolution or invasion by Californians, combined in 1853 to produce a draft treaty that provided, among other things, that the islands be "incorporated into the American Union as a State." The king, the queen, and limitless "other persons whom the King may wish to compensate or reward" would receive annuities of $300,000.[4] Secretary of State Marcy demurred, the king died in 1854, and the treaty, if not the dream, perished, too.

Statehood for the islands had been proposed as early as 1849 by a Lowville, New York, newspaper, although the only visible enthusiasm for acquisition was in the South, where the islands were seen as conducive to slavery. Hawaii, at first viewed as an entrepôt, a link to Far East trade, was by steps absorbed—as a coaling and refitting station, a reciprocal trade partner—into the aborning commercial empire of the United States. These steps were not uncontested. In 1884 President Arthur's secretary of state, former senator Frederick Frelinghuysen (R-NJ), cautioned that "even as simple coaling stations . . . territorial acquisitions would involve responsibility beyond their utility. The United States has never deemed it needful to their national life to maintain impregnable fortresses along the world's highways of commerce."[5] But by the reign of Queen Liliuokalani, American expansionists, appetites long whetted by the thought of gobbling the Sandwich Islands, took a bite. The queen was overthrown in January 1893 by an American-dominated cabal with the assistance of US minister John L. Stevens and a military force disgorged by the USS *Boston* in Honolulu Harbor.

The fate of the Hawaiian Islands was to be determined in Washington,

DC, where discussants included the queen's cinematically named attorney, Paul Neumann. A treaty to annex Hawaii to the United States was hastily drafted by American diplomats, but time, for once, was on the side of the angels. President Benjamin Harrison, who would leave office in March 1893, favored annexing Hawaii, though he did concede that its people should vote on the matter in a plebiscite. (Which provision his secretary of state John W. Foster dropped from the treaty. No use cluttering it with democratic trivia.)

President Harrison's treaty had but one foe in the Senate Foreign Relations Committee, Senator George Gray (D-DE), but the incoming president, Grover Cleveland, was an anti-imperialist and a gentleman who thought the queen had been shafted. Upon taking office he scuttled the treaty. I have elsewhere (*Ain't My America*, 2008) feted the great Cleveland. Just another three-hundred-pound Buffalo lardass sitting on a barstool and cursing the Bills? I don't think so. Here I wish to praise his secretary of state, Walter Q. Gresham, quite possibly the most anti-imperialist diplomat of that or any other era, almost certainly the greatest of all secretaries of state. As his biographer Charles W. Calhoun writes, "Gresham, in the spirit of the Founders' warnings, worked to limit the country's overseas entanglements, with the result that nearly all his acts and policies encountered bitter denunciation."[6] No good republican deed goes unpunished.

Walter Q. Gresham was an Indiana politician whose Diogenes-like search for honesty led him through the Republicans, Democrats, and Populists until he capped his career as the voice of the better America. He abstained from patronage politics, crossed party lines when conscience impelled him, and otherwise ran afoul of Republican dogma. He defended his conspicuous probity by saying that the "sentiment that to the victors belongs the spoils is preposterous. When it comes to that, sir, your government will be rottenness, and there will be no more hope for the patriot."

Gresham, while an Indiana state legislator, wrote his wife in January 1861: "My opinion is that the sooner the North & South have a peaceable separation the better."[7] But war came. He enlisted in the Thirty-eighth Indiana Volunteer Infantry and was later appointed lieutenant colonel and then brigadier general. Gresham took a minie ball in the leg in the summer of 1864 and was goin' back to Indiana with a permanent limp. He was no saint of peace or tolerance: Though he fought for the Union, he held the typical Southern Indiana view of African Americans. Upon returning he resumed his law practice and was appointed by President Grant as a district judge for Indiana.

Gresham was a generally anti-states'-rights and anti-labor-union nationalist until late in his career, but he was always scrupulously honest. President Arthur appointed him to the position of postmaster general, as close to a political mausoleum as one can sleep in. By the late 1880s, however, "he grew increasingly alarmed that the Republican party was becoming the tool of corporate interests."[8] Okay, we all learn at different speeds. But by 1892 his independent stance and criticism of plutocracy led to a flirtation with the Populist Party, in whose ranks there was substantial support for a Gresham presidential candidacy. He withdrew his name from consideration by the Populists and endorsed Grover Cleveland, who shared his low-tariff good-government views. Cleveland, recognizing a kindred spirit, offered Gresham the secretaryship of state. The nomination was lamented by Princeton professor Woodrow Wilson, who, as American doughboys were later to discover, did not share Gresham's reluctance to send men off to die in foreign wars.

Gresham and Cleveland, stubborn rectitudinous men who abhorred imperialism, became fast friends. Gresham said bluntly that "a free government cannot pursue an imperial policy," so he opposed the annexation of Hawaii and sought, vainly, to remove the United States from the joint protectorate it had established with Germany and Great Britain over the islands of Samoa. Gresham denied that America had any legitimate interest in managing the affairs of Pago Pago. He declared that "the only safeguard against *all* the evils of interference in affairs that do not specially concern us is to abstain from such interference altogether."[9]

He similarly was "opposed to a large army and navy."[10] These were at best a waste of money, and more probably an invitation to aggressive expansionist policies. Such views, so heretical today that they would push Gresham off the main stage of politics, were perfectly respectable in 1893. (Memo to self: A Gresham statue shall adorn the State Department after the revolution.)

The first order of business at State was doing right by Hawaii. Secretary

Gresham denied, in an 1893 letter, that the queen had been "overthrown by a revolution of the people on the Islands. On the contrary, the Queen was overawed by the American Minister and the presence of a body of armed troops landed from one of our warships. Her submission was thus coerced. The affair was discreditable to all who engaged in it, including, I fear, some men at this capital. It would lower our national character to endorse a selfish and dishonest scheme of a lot of adventurers."[11]

What to do about the coup? Gresham counseled action. "Should not this great wrong be undone? 'Yes,' I say decidedly."[12] President Cleveland concurred, telling Congress on December 4, 1893, that the "honorable course" was to undo the mischief done by Minister John L. Stevens and restore the queen to the throne of her independent constitutional monarchy.[13]

Some anti-imperialists applauded; others doubted the wisdom of what could become a messy intervention. The new Hawaiian government was not going to give up power without a fight, and the anti-interventionist Cleveland administration was not about to send troops to reinstall the monarch. Efforts at negotiating Liliuokalani's peaceful return to the throne foundered on her insistence that the plotters receive not amnesty but a swift beheading.

Attorney General Richard Olney reminded the cabinet that without an explicit congressional declaration of war any intervention in Hawaii would be unconstitutional, and since such a declaration was not forthcoming a restoration was not in the cards. Dig the anachronism: cabinet officials taking seriously the Constitution! When last did *that* happen?

July 4, 1894, was the ironic date chosen for the unveiling of the sham Republic of Hawaii, which, as constitutional law professor John W. Burgess urged, was "placed in the hands of the Teutons."[14] Gresham opposed US recognition, though that was granted. Annexation was out of the question—at least until Cleveland left office in March 1897.

As for Walter Q. Gresham, he died May 28, 1895. Shortly before his death he had written attorney Thomas G. Shearman: "I cannot escape the belief that if our Government, departing from the sound, honest and patriotic teachings and warnings of its founders and earlier statesmen, enters upon a career of foreign acquisition and colonization, the results will be disastrous. Such a policy is essentially an imperial one . . . This is the first time it has been seriously maintained that we should leave our continent and annex remote regions. Popular government will not long survive under such a policy."[15] Upon his expiry, *Literary Digest* noted that Gresham's "foreign policy has been denounced as un-American, unpatriotic, and treacherous." Plus ça change. This noblest of State secretaries left us a warning: If Americans did not "stay at home and attend to their own business," then "they would go to hell as fast as possible."[16] We didn't, and we did.

The anti-imperialists sensed that annexing Hawaii was, as Senator Stephen M. White (D-CA) said, "the entering wedge for an imperialistic policy." Their congressional ranks included Populists (Sockless Jerry Simpson of Kansas, Tom Watson of Georgia); Republicans (Richard F. Pettigrew of South Dakota; House Speaker Thomas B. Reed of New York, who famously said in 1897 that "Empire can wait"); and such Democrats as the sound-money New York City Irishman Bourke Cockran and Ohio congressman Joseph H. Outhwaite.[17]

They focused, as is proper, on the domestic consequences of expansion. "I contend that the area of this country is great enough," said Senator Pettigrew. To pursue a policy of "imperialism and conquest" would require the "centralization" of power and a concomitant shrinkage of liberty.[18]

Many in the Give Hawaii Back caucus would soon fill the ranks of opponents of US acquisition of the Philippines and Puerto Rico. For as the *Albany (NY) Times* predicted: "To annex Hawaii would be to enter upon a new policy of foreign acquisition for which the American people are hardly prepared. Once entered upon, where would it end?"[19] In body bags and Patriot Acts, and it hasn't ended yet.

The anti-annexationists were, for the most part, anti-militarists. They did not object to trade with Hawaii, or to using the islands for refueling, but they did not believe that the defense umbrella of the United States stretched halfway over the Pacific Ocean. Explains historian Thomas J. Osborne: "The peaceful American Republic, they feared, would be transformed into a militant empire, burdened with the high costs of a large standing army and a powerful navy to defend the colonies and to suppress the natives."[20]

Mugwump George Ticknor Curtis endeavored to show the readers of the *North American Review* that annexation of noncontiguous territory was unconstitutional and was "never a favorite with considerate people." Why, he harrumphed, if Hawaii should be acquired illegally "we shall then have Manifest Destiny substituted for the Constitution."[21] Plundering blackguards masquerading as Americans would sail the seven seas, searching for outposts to seize and peoples to vanquish.

Some anti-imperialists feared the erasure of Hawaiian culture; others fretted about the adulteration of American stock. Of Hawaii's 109,000 residents, almost 40,000 were of Hawaiian ancestry, 25,000-plus were Japanese, more than 20,000 were Chinese, and barely 20,000 were of European or American background, the vast majority of those being Portuguese. Racial concerns, both liberal *and* unhealthy, were at work in both camps. "No evidence has been found to indicate that xenophobic considerations significantly influenced the shaping of Cleveland's Hawaiian policy," writes Thomas J. Osborne, though anti-annexationist Representative Josiah Patterson (D-TN) was not speaking only for himself when he spurned "leprous colonies 2,000 miles from our western shores."[22]

Hawaiian sugar interests were actually cool toward annexation because US law would interfere with their system of Chinese contract labor. Much of American organized labor, including Samuel Gompers, opposed annexation for fear of competition with Chinese Hawaiian workers who, they suspected, would flood the mainland. In Gompers's words, "The annexation of Hawaii would, with one stroke of the pen . . . open wide our gates, which would threaten an inundation of Mongolians to overwhelm the free laborers of our country."[23] I don't suppose the AFL-CIO today is eager to disinter *that* quote.

The Republican platform of 1896 had declared: "The Hawaiian Islands should be controlled by the United States."[24] The new Republican administration of President William McKinley kept that promise. What the GOP did not promise was to consult the native population on this question—who needs consent of the governed and all that Jeffersonian rot? In late 1897 approximately thirty thousand Hawaiians—the number is in question because some signatures were doubtless fraudulent—signed the so-called monster petition, which read: "We, the undersigned, native

Hawaiian citizens and residents who are members of the Hawaiian Patriotic League of the Hawaiian Islands, and others who are in sympathy with the said League, earnestly protest against the annexation of the said Hawaiian Islands to the said United States of America in any form or shape."[25] Into the circular file that petition went.

The imperialists did not have the necessary two-thirds vote to approve an annexation treaty in the Senate, so Hawaii was annexed by joint resolution, which requires a simple majority. On July 7, 1898, President McKinley signed the joint resolution—not treaty—of annexation. The request of the anti-imperialists that the forty thousand native Hawaiians have a say via plebiscite was ignored. Some Hawaiians maintain to this day that annexation by joint resolution was unconstitutional, although given the general disregard of that document the point seems moot. How many acts of the federal government today are authorized by that feckless charter, as neglected and irrelevant as a toothless old man wearing a DON'T FORGET MY SENIOR DISCOUNT hat at a singles bar?

These arguments had been rehearsed in the 1870 debate over the annexation of Dominica. "Congress have no power by joint resolution to annex territory to the United States," declared Senator Thomas F. Bayard, who in the last half of the nineteenth century never seemed to be far from the Old Republic's barricades. "By treaty stipulation alone can we become possessed of territory."[26] Fernando Wood, former mayor of the would-be Free City of New York and then a Democratic congressman, agreed. Yes, Texas came in via joint resolution instead of treaty, Wood conceded, but it was part of the North American continent and headed for statehood. Dominica—"The population is of a most degraded character," hissed Wood—would never gain statehood and was in no way eligible to follow the Texas model.[27] (Wood ought to have argued, as many did in the 1840s, that Texas had been annexed illegally. But he was too much the big-d Democrat to do so.)

Senator Bayard did not want to "embark the Government of the United States upon the vast and trackless sea of imperialism, to change it into an Imperial Government of outlying and distant dependencies with a foreign population, strangers to us in race, in blood, in customs, in all their systems, political, social, moral, and religious." Senator Bayard was no ebony-and-ivory the-world-is-black-the-world-is-white racial harmonist, but he disdained "the unscrupulous course of empire" and asked of those who wished to pocket a few more islands: "At the cost of what losses by war, at what cost of death by climate, of public treasure, of demoralization to our people, who shall say?"[28]

A quarter century later, Bayard, by then President Cleveland's ambassador to Great Britain, wrote Walter Q. Gresham: "I fully agree with you— that our great Republic will perish if we embark upon an Imperial system of acquisition of outlying dependencies—and that the methods employed under the late administration in the Hawaiian Kingdom were disgraceful to our Country, and will not be sustained by the American people when they are fairly comprehended."[29] What charming and naive faith Bayard had in the American people! Today they—we—barely object when our government sends armies to invade and kill by the tens of thousands citizens of countries that have never done a lick of harm to us. If we sit quiescently in front of the television as Iraqis and Afghans are slaughtered, would we have even bothered to lift our fat asses from the couch to object to the theft of Hawaii?

The outmanned dissenters left us prophecies. South Dakota's Senator Pettigrew said, "If we set this example, regardless of honor, of acquiring title to a territory from puppets that we have set up, what will we not do? . . . Tramp the course that has caused the death of every republic in the past, and see our flag go down in misery and in shame. The glory of this Republic has been that we have offered an asylum to the oppressed and a hope to mankind which has been followed wherever freedom has burst into bloom throughout the world. Shall we stain that record?"[30] *Stain* doesn't begin to describe it.

The Hawaii Organic Act gave Hawaii the gift of territorial government, with Sanford Dole, president of the provisional government that overthrew the queen, installed as governor of the Territory of Hawaii on June 19, 1900. In the Sovietish words of a 1955 Department of Defense publication, "Hawaii came into the Union proudly and voluntarily, preferring the American democratic way of life to the many other forms of government she experienced and was offered."[31] Sure she did. Just like Estonia joined gladly and of its own free will in the glorious Union of Soviet Socialist Republics.

⎯⎯∾⊚∾⎯⎯

Hawaiian nationalism in the colonial era found its expression through the Home Rule Party, led by Robert Wilcox, a part-Hawaiian royalist supporter of Queen Liliuokalani. The party was for native suffrage, land reform, and Hawaiian language usage. Its motto: "Hawaii for the Hawaiians."[32]

Wilcox, who had taken up arms in the fin de siècle in defense of Hawaiian sovereignty, was elected territorial delegate but then defeated in 1902 by Prince Jonah Kūhiō Kalaniana'ole. The prince had once been jailed for trying to restore the queen, but as a delegate in Washington he was a popular bon vivant who understood well—too well—the limits of dissent.

His people, the native Hawaiians, were fast receding in the political calculus of Hawaii's territorial government, which wielded centralized power largely immune from public pressure. The prince was a jovial public face for Hawaii, but as Royal M. Mead of the Hawaiian Sugar Planters' Association told a US House subcommittee in 1920: "I do not think that there is any contest as to who shall dominate; the white race, the white people, the Americans in Hawaii are going to dominate and will continue to dominate—there is no question about it."[33]

The natives were racked by booze, disease, and an inability to conform their lives to *haole* rhythms, rather like mainland Indians. They made bad field laborers, intransigent sugar slaves. "The haole civilization emphasized competition, individual planning, and material success; Hawaiian culture stressed co-operation and day-to-day living," wrote the sociologist Fuchs.[34] It made for an uneasy mix.

Sugar powered the Hawaiian economy, whose business elite, known as the Big Five, comprised a quintet of mercantile firms dating back to the nineteenth century. Oligarchy it may have been, but give the Big Five this: Its roots were in Hawaii, not Wall Street. Not that the economy of the islands was autarkic. "Don't be deceived by the twenty-five hundred miles of water between Hawaii and California," John Whitehead tells me. "The two were totally intertwined in the sugar industry. The sugar growers in Hawaii even owned a huge sugar refinery outside of Berkeley. Hawaii had much stronger ties to the American mainland economy than did Alaska."[35]

Still, as a nonstate it took its lumps. The Jones-Costigan Act of 1934 dumped Hawaii in with Puerto Rico and the Philippines as "non-domestic" sugar producers, thus decimating (literally a 10 percent cut) Hawaii's sugar quota. Statehood would put the Hawaiian sugar industry on equal footing within the union. Not having a vote in Congress was one thing, but discriminatory treatment of Hawaiian sugar? This was too much. The sugar industry, not theretofore sweet on statehood (for fear of local regulation), reconsidered. But how to attach an exotic archipelago to the good old USA?

War. Assay unnatural political connections and the germ of origin is almost always war.

World War II "put both territories [Alaska and Hawaii] on center stage of the American national consciousness and served as the catalyst that would eventually propel the two toward statehood," wrote Whitehead.[36] Prewar Hawaii was at the fringes of that consciousness. A Roper poll of January 1940 found that 55 percent of Americans favored defending Hawaii if it were attacked, as opposed to 74 percent who would have our military defend Canada.[37] Hawaii was just 25 percent *haole* in 1940, a factor surely in American indifference, but the biggest reason was propinquity: Canada was our neighbor, an adjacent country with which we shared a three-thousand-mile border. Hawaii was far, far, far away.

Till Tora, Tora, Tora.

The Japanese bombing of Pearl Harbor melded the islands to America just as it also emphasized the differentness of Hawaii. Martial law was invoked in the islands on December 7, 1941. This entailed censorship of the mails and telephone, curfews, spying, forced labor—hell, absenteeism was *criminalized*—and it was not revoked until October 1944, despite the manifold demonstrations of loyalty by Japanese Hawaiians. Habeas corpus? The Roosevelt administration treated it in Hawaii as so much toilet paper, rather as the Bush administration did anytime the bogey word *terrorism* was spoken.

About a thousand mostly first-generation Japanese were interned in FDR's concentration camps. This was not widely lamented by non-Japanese Hawaiians. As Jonah Kūhiō had said in 1919: "The Japanese think and act, not as members of an American community, but collectively as Japanese."[38] The prince would later be echoed by Kamokila Campbell, who was either the dying grandmother of the old Hawaiian nationalism or the founding mother of the new.

The war brought America to the islands. In 1944, 406,811 soldiers and sailors and military personnel occupied Hawaii, as well as upward of 75,000 civilian workers from the mainland. Hawaii had been militarized, and when World War II ended a Cold War took its place. Mars joined the pantheon of island gods.

By 1959, writes Lawrence H. Fuchs, military expenditures "exceeded the total value of all exports from the Islands." Almost 25 percent of "Hawaii's people depended directly on defense spending for a living." Virtually all of this spending was on the island of Oahu; this resulted in a "significant shift in population and wealth from the outer islands to Oahu."[39] It also forged the last critical link in the long chain that led to statehood.

Governor Sanford Dole had envisioned statehood from Hawaii's birth as a territory. The first statehood bill was introduced into Congress in 1919 by delegate Prince Jonah Kūhiō Kalaniana'ole. It sank quickly, but by midcentury the issue had its sea legs. Between 1935 and 1958, twenty congressional hearings were held to discuss Hawaiian statehood. The House approved statehood several times—1947, 1950, 1953—but the Senate demurred. As with Alaska, segregationist Southerners were in no hurry to admit a pair of anti-seg senators—and of mixed race, no less.

Hawaii, I admit, vexes me. Yes, its mainland advocates tended to a fathomless expansionism. The most indefatigable champion of statehood, Louisiana appliance dealer and freelance lobbyist George Lehleitner, was a votary of Clarence Streit's *Union Now* (1939), a plea for world government. Hawaii was, to Lehleitner, merely another stitch in the single flag that would one day shroud, like the cerecloth on a corpse, the entire world. Representative Jim Wright (D-TX), who in later years was to make it to the summit—House speakership—only to be pulled down by his own corruption and remorseless hounding by a future speaker, Newt Gingrich (R-GA), spoke in Gingrichian terms: "What is to be our destiny? Is the United States finished with growing? Are we still young and vibrant and vital with a message and a mission and a future to the world?"[40]

Such men are easy for a localist to loathe. But the Antis on the mainland—oy vey! What a doltish and incult crew.

Most congressional opposition to Hawaiian statehood was based in grubby politics (the dread of two more Republican senators) or anti-communist hysteria directed at the May Day red longshoremen's union (ILWU) or just plain anti-Asian or anti-Polynesian prejudice. The really potent weapon in the Anti arsenal—the noncontiguity argument, which figured so prominently in the sophisticated and patriotic resistance to Hawaiian annexation in the 1890s—went mostly unfired.

Consider the major congressional critics: Representative John Pillion (R-NY) asserted that the communist influence was so strong in Hawaiian unions that the United States would be permitting "four Soviet agents to take seats in our Congress."[41]

Senator Hugh Butler (R-NE), chairman of the Senate Committee on Public Lands, proposed that Alaska and Hawaii be made counties of Montana and California, respectively.[42] To such men, *home rule* and *decolonization* were code words for the red harvest.

I mean, who wants dunces like this for allies? It is embarrassing to read the red-baiting anti-statehood arguments and realize that *these* are the folks with whom I, as a Little American anti-imperialist, would be standing.

So what do you do when you find that the men with whom you have linked arms, historically speaking, are either nitwit Republicans who care more about Moscow, Russia, than Moscow, Idaho, or Southern Democrat segregationists fearful of two new pro-nigra senators? Look homeward, my boy. Seek not defenders of Hawaii in Washington; rather, seek and ye shall find them in Hawaii.

I bring you Kamokila Campbell.

Kamokila Campbell was, John S. Whitehead writes, "a cultural phenomenon understandable only within the unique social context of Hawaii."[43] Her mother was Hawaiian royalty, her father a Scots-Irish financier. Her bequest was the second largest private estate in the islands and a charming aristocratic candor that she displayed in a lacerating critique of statehood on January 17, 1946, in Honolulu, before a hearing conducted by the Subcommittee of the Committee on Territories of the US House of Representatives.

The thrice-married Kamokila was a socialite as well as a Democratic territorial senator and national committeewoman. She had hosted hundreds of thousands of US servicemen at her Lanikuhonua estate, which the soldiers and sailors dubbed "Camp Bell." After years abroad in

San Francisco, she had repatriated as the compleat Hawaiian, dedicated wholly to the preservation of native culture and the restoration of self-government. To Kamokila, sovereignty harmonized with the old songs, the old teachings.

Resplendent in "black satin dress and bedecked with red and yellow leis,"[44] Campbell bluntly told the House subcommittee, "I am definitely against statehood for Hawaii in any form and at any time." She had voted against it in the legislature—hers was the sole nay on the matter in 1945—but she was speaking now "from the heart and soul of all Hawaii."[45]

The overthrow of the queen had been a "profitable business transaction for the Federal Government," but man does not live by cash alone, and dollars and cents are "not sufficient grounds on which we of Hawaii should forego [sic] our individual identity." She deplored the depredations of the Big Five and the "numerical superiority of the Japanese," for whom she had a special scunner.[46] In the course of Kamokila's two-hour testimony she made an unfortunate detour into anti-Asian polemics directed at those Japanese Hawaiians "with Shintoism still deeply impregnated into their very blood stream." The Japanese, she said—and recall, her islands had just emerged from a war in which they were a prime target of Tojo—had abused aloha, the Hawaiian spirit of tolerance, and constituted "a serious menace." She had supported "100 percent" martial law and the incarceration of the Japanese in FDR's concentration camps during the war; now she seemed to call for their expulsion and the expropriation of what she regarded as excessive Japanese Hawaiian wealth. I wish she hadn't said this, but she did. If you want flawless heroes go read Parson Weems. Campbell's "most precious" Hawaii needed, she said, to guard against "the selfish aspirations of strangers to her shores." To be overwhelmed by foreigners and outside capital would be "national suicide."[47]

She insisted that "we should not forfeit the traditional rights and privileges of the natives of our islands for a mere thimbleful of votes in Congress." Nor should "we, the lovers of Hawaii from a long association with it . . . sacrifice our birthright for the greed of alien desires to remain on our shores" or to "satisfy the thirst for power and control of some inflated industrialists and politicians who hide under the guise of friends of Hawaii" yet keep "an eagle eye on the financial and political pressure button of subjugation [caution: word pileup on prolixity avenue] over the people in general of these islands."[48]

She concluded with a simple entreaty: "Please take this message back to Congress: Hawaii and Kamokila ask nothing else but to be left alone."[49]

Joseph Farrington, Hawaii's delegate to Congress, pointed out to Kamokila that in 1940 she had spoken, if equivocally, *for* statehood. She had even observed that King Kamehameha III, and not the demonic *haoles*, had first proposed attaching Hawaii to the United States.

Kamokila, unflappable—I doubt that anything flapped her—reminded Farrington that people do change their minds, and that in the intervening six years a world war had been fought, and Hawaii had emerged the worse for it. Farrington pressed her, but no one pressed Kamokila, either, and after calling for "an independent form of government" for Hawaii, albeit one with a "slight" connection to the United States—"so that we could not go absolutely haywire"—she took her leave, presenting Farrington with a kiss and a lei.[50] (The spelling here is important.) Of Kamokila, Whitehead writes that "her eyes had the mist from the smoke of both a distant and a future fire."[51] And no, she never played ukulele with the Sanford (Dole)-Townsend Band.

Kamokila had style but not votes. The induction of Hawaii became more a question of when than if. In 1950 Hawaiian statehood forces called a convention to draw up a constitution in anticipation of catasterization. In Cold War fashion, the conventioneers created a powerful executive. Unlike Alaska, however, Hawaii did not adopt the Tennessee Plan and send a shadow delegation to Washington. Nor did the two hopeful territories twine themselves into a single legislative package, for fear that the foes of one or the other would combine to defeat an omnibus bill. Better to go in one at a time.

Congressional debate steadfastly refused to rise to the Webster-Hayne level, though occasionally a sensible voice rang out. "Hawaii is about 3,000 miles from here," said Representative Clare Hoffman (R-MI). "I have never been there and probably never will go there. I am not much of a world-government man, and I do not like to see us stepping out in that direction . . . I am perfectly satisfied for the term 'United States of America' to stand. I have no ambition to make it any type of world union."[52]

If Hawaii came in, who would be next? When would the land hunger be sated? Would the country even be recognizable?

Senator Stennis vainly suggested commonwealth for Hawaii, but it was too late. He knew the score. He threw up his hands. "I do not see how we can simply turn a deaf ear to Guam, the Virgin Islands, and Puerto Rico."[53]

Well, we have, in a fashion, anyway.

It was funny how little men cared about states forty-nine and fifty. Edward R. Murrow devoted a March 1958 episode of *See It Now* to the issue. "There has been no great debate on the matter of bringing these two territories into the union," he intoned. Murrow sought to fill the void. CBS aired the show; it received almost no response.[54] People just did not give a damn.

Even Hawaiians weren't all that hot for union. Polling in 1958 found that 43 percent of islanders were pro-statehood and 24 percent were opposed—hardly landslide numbers. Japanese were the most pro-statehood ethnic group and natives the least; 27 percent of native Hawaiians "strongly opposed statehood."[55] Yet no prominent Hawaiian political figure stood with the Antis, so their allies in Washington could not easily call upon island voices to oppugn the unionists.

The US Senate approved statehood for Hawaii on March 11, 1959, by a vote of 76–15; the House followed suit the next day by 323–89. By robust majorities, both houses of Congress invited into the union a military-dependent archipelago with no obvious American features. It was far smaller than Alaska, composing but two-tenths of 1 percent of the area of the United States, but it would have the same say in Senate affairs as New York, Virginia, and Massachusetts.

Statehood was approved by Hawaiians in a June 1959 plebiscite by a margin of 17–1. As with Alaska, the vote was up or down on statehood, with a no being a vote for continued territorial status. Commonwealth and independence were unchoices.

Privately owned Nihau, with 107 voters, all either native or part native, was the only island to vote no. In fact, it was the only one of Hawaii's 240 precincts to register a negative. As Fuchs wrote, "On that little island, invariably overwhelmingly Republican, Hawaiians, still trying to recapture the past, registered their protest to the final act of the absorption of Hawaii into the American Union."[56]

Nihau's nay can be seen as a last gasp. Or perhaps it was a portent. A daughter of Hawaiian royalty lamented in the 1950s, "Every Hawaiian holds in his bosom a longing for the monarchy and a deep distrust of the haoles, but our cause is hopeless. What can we do?"[57] A resurgent native movement, part of the worldwide anti-colonial uprising but also unmistakably Hawaiian, would answer that question over the coming decades.

As for Kamokila Campbell, she was only half reconciled to becoming a full-fledged American. "I have always been opposed to statehood," she said, "but now it is here and many of my friends like it. I shall try to like it too."[58] In devoting herself to the preservation and invigoration of native music and legends, though, she eventually subverted statehood in a way that no political speech ever could. Resenting Asian-Hawaiian economic success was a dead end, not to mention a soul-deadener. Kamokila best served the cause of her precious Hawaii with ukulele and Pele, not ukase and melee.

There is a paradox in the final two statehood movements. John S. Whitehead writes, "Statehooders were by their very nature states' rightsers and even secessionists. They wanted to sever their existing territorial connection to the nation. Both Alaska and Hawaii demanded statehood because they objected to the way they were being treated by the same United States they wanted to join."[59] So to favor statehood was not the act of a cringing toady; it was, rather, a form of patriotism, even if ultimately misguided.

Once in, however, the way out recedes. The American Empire needs, or thinks it needs, Alaska and Hawaii. Alaskan Independence Party officials say that an independent Alaska would lease military bases back to the United States, assuming residents approved. Somehow I doubt that would mollify Washington. Even less would the archons of the War Party dig the independence lays of Hawaii.

The state of Hawaii developed a quadruped economy of sugar, pineapple, tourism, and defense, though the agricultural legs have buckled of late, leaving the military as the primary support. Visitors flooded the islands; aloha was diminished to an advertising slogan.

The rapidity of change left many older Hawaiians disconcerted. "Before statehood, people were nicer," retired Honolulu firefighter Richard Ishida told the Associated Press in 1999. "In those days, everybody was closer. Not today."[60]

The changes have also sparked a reaction, or maybe it's a revolution. The sons and daughters of Liliuokalani and Robert Wilcox and Kamokila Campbell have rediscovered their cultural legacy, and its logical political expression, which is independence. The Hawaiian Movement, born in the 1970s, was about marches and démarches, yes, but more important it rescued from linguistic oblivion the lost language of the people of Hawaii. The movement was born "in rural areas," writes one of its partisans, for its most basic grievance is the displacement of native Hawaiians from the land.[61] From protesting development and tourism projects that would dispossess natives and despoil the land, the movement evolved into a comprehensive—if fragmented—cultural-political force that is both meliorist (trying to improve the condition of native Hawaiians, who lag in every socioeconomic index) and radically restorationist.

Its most widely read author, Haunani-Kay Trask, is the daughter of a prominent Hawaiian family, a professor at the University of Hawaii, an admirer of Frantz Fanon and Malcolm X and Angela Davis, and a polemicist who is alternately trenchant and irritating.

I recall the punk band the Angry Samoans. Trask is a bandful of righteous fury herself, an angry Hawaiian with none of Kamokila Campbell's socialite charm but a similarly desperate resolve to fight for a battered and forlorn people because—noble reason—*they are her people*. At her worst, she descends into leftist thought-substitution (the tiresomely promiscuous use of the charge "racism"), but at her best, as is fitfully on display in *From a Native Daughter* (1993), hers is a stirring voice for genuine diversity, as she celebrates the Hawaiian Movement as a "counter to the New World Order." We need, she says, "not more uniformity, more conformity but more autonomy, more localized control of resources and the cultures they can maintain."[62] She is unreconstructed, that's for sure: "No matter what Americans believe, most of us in the colonies do not feel grateful that our country was stolen, along with our citizenship, our lands, and our independent place among the family of nations. We are not happy Natives."[63]

Whitehead hears echoes of Campbell in Trask. In their own ways, these native women defended an endangered culture against absorption by powerful outsiders who, as aliens, could not possibly grok Hawaii. Trask denies that outsiders can understand, let alone share, *aloha*, which means "love" in a specific, not universal, sense. "It is nearly impossible to feel or practice *aloha* for something that is not familial," writes Trask.[64]

Throughout 1993, the centenary of the overthrow of the queen, a newly invigorated Hawaiian sovereignty movement protested, sang, even entreated the fire goddess Pele to bless its cause. The year began with almost twenty thousand Hawaiians marching on the Iolani Palace, residence of the queen, and ended, or nearly so (in November 1993), with Congress and President Clinton formally apologizing for the role played by the US government in the queen's deposal—though it was not about to undo the wrong that had been done.

That formidable task is left to such groups as Ka Lahui Hawai'i (the Hawaiian Nation), formed in 1987 and led by the formidable Trask sisters, Haunani-Kay and attorney Milalani. The several-thousand-member-strong Ka Lahui Hawai'i has set up a kind of shadow government, with three branches similar to the US system supplemented by an advisory council of High Chiefs. Milalani Trask was the first Kia'aina, or governor, of this government-in-exile. There is no one-man, one-vote nonsense to deprive smaller islands of influence: Each of the eight islands elects representatives to the Ka Lahui legislature, so that "urban O'ahu does not overwhelm the neighbor islands as it does in the state legislature."[65] Ka Lahui demands land and nation-within-a-nation sovereignty, not unlike the arrangement the US has with American Indian tribes.

As for *haoles*...Ka Lahui Hawai'i prefers that you go home.

Ka Lahui Hawai'i has a sound strategy for sovereignty. It looks not to politicking, or sloganeering, or tromping through the streets singin' songs and carryin' signs. Rather, it lays out five preconditions for independence. They are: (1) "A strong and abiding faith in the *akua*" (Hawaiian gods); (2) A "common culture, language and tradition"; (3) "A land base on which to live and practice . . . cultural traditions"; (4) "A government structure to enable the people to be self-determining"; and (5) "An economic base that will enable the people to become self-sufficient."[66] A welter of self-interested and anomic individuals is incapable of achieving independence, as Ka Lahui Hawai'i envisions it; a people, sharing an organic culture and distinctive tongue, just may pull it off.

Ka Pakaukau (the Table) is a coalition of smaller groups demanding full independence. Professor and activist Lilikala Kame'eleihiwa notes, archly, "Ka Pakaukau has not articulated the means by which America could be persuaded to relinquish its control over Hawai'i, which has one of the highest densities of US military installations per square mile of any state in the Union."[67] Yes, that is a problem. Full independence may seem less achievable than "nation within a nation" status, as the American Indians enjoy, if that is the right word. But you see how well it has worked for them.

Another group, the Hawaiian Kingdom Government (HKG), occupied the palace (now a museum) of Queen Liliuokalani in the spring of 2008, briefly but symbolically. Her Majesty Mahealani Kahau, of royal Hawaiian lineage, held court in a tent pitched outside the Iolani Palace. "We're here to assume and resume what is already ours and what has always been ours," Her Majesty bravely told reporters, though by late spring another claimant to the throne, King Akahi Nui, who asserts descent from the kings Kamehameha, occupied the palace for a couple of hours after two dozen protesters stormed the grounds.[68] The king and his court were unceremoniously arrested.

The HKG is an uneasy mix of admirable filiopietism and unrealistic legalism. It hopes to reestablish the kingdom by appeals to international law and the laws of the whilom kingdom, which it asserts are still in effect. In 2007 the Hawaiian Kingdom Government fined the current Hawaiian government $7 trillion. Lotsa luck in collecting that. More promising are the quotidian acts of the restorationists: using "Kingdom of Hawaii" license plates, reciting the poetry of their ancestors, and, perhaps most meaningfully, relearning the Hawaiian language, which for so many years the government schools tried to extirpate.

Hawaiian-language immersion schools are filling their classrooms today, reanimating a tongue that the imperialists never could quite silence. As Pila Wilson of the University of Hawaii at Hilo explains, "The language permeates the life and culture, connects you to past and future. It creates a connection with people throughout time."[69] It infuses the speaker with the spirit of those who have gone before; it works subtle alterations even in the way that she sees the world around her. Who knows what fruit delicious the seeds of these immersion classes will bear? In time, friends, in time. Meanwhile, the dream of independence concretizes, it assumes form in waking hours, and though sovereignty is not secession, insists Jon Olsen, a Maine-bred Hawaiian activist who lived in the fiftieth state for thirty-five years before recently repatriating, the two concepts move "on parallel tracks but they do not merge."[70]

The men and women of the movement are not blind to political hurdles or demographic realities. "After 100 years of American rule," says Lilikala Kameʻeleihiwa, "Hawaiians are a minority in the land of their ancestors."[71]

Kameʻeleihiwa contributed to the work of the International Tribunal on the Rights of Indigenous Hawaiians, which in August of the centennial year of 1993 held hearings throughout the archipelago on the historic crimes committed against the native peoples of Hawaii.

The tribunal had such a leftist cast that its influence was nil, though ten years later it produced a useful compilation of material on indigenous Hawaiian nationalism. The tribunal called upon the United States and the United Nations to "acknowledge the right of Kanaka Maoli [native Hawaiians] to decolonize," a fine idea that, because it was backed by the force of ideas, not the force of the state, was inoperative.[72]

I can't stand cant, whether leftist PC-speak or right-wing jingoism, so patches of the tribunal's output are verbigeration to me. But it did good work, too, especially in listening to and then amplifying the voices of Hawaiian dissent, and in its recommendation that the "United States and the world should immediately recognize the sovereignty and right to self-determination of Lahui Kanaka Maoli."[73]

Fixing on the US apology, University of Illinois law professor Francis Boyle has said that "the only appropriate remedy" under international law is "restitution"—that is, restoration of the pre-overthrow kingdom.[74] Liberal Democrats hear talk like that and reach for their wallets, or rather the wallets of taxpayers. There's nothing, it seems, that a welfare check can't cure. Yet sovereignty groups fear co-optation if they accept the feeble half measures of the establishment, and can you blame them? Would you trust the apologizer Bill Clinton or the decider George W. Bush or even the rootless "Hawaiian" Barack Obama, who as far as I can tell has never listed a single island poet or novelist or singer as a favorite, with your liberties? "Left to their own devices, the various Hawaiian groups in the sovereignty movement would coalesce and resolve any residual differences," claims Lilikala Kame'eleihiwa, optimistically. "However, the greatest threat to the process of decolonization and self-determination for the Native Hawaiian is cooptation by the Democratic Party machine that controls the State of Hawaii."[75]

The movement will make inevitable gains in the form of grants of money and land, perhaps even reparations. What it must arrest, even reverse, however, is the process by which Hawaii has been made "less Hawaiian culturally, ecologically, and politically," as Haunani-Kay Trask writes.[76] Cultural self-awareness is a precondition for political self-determination, as Kamokila Campbell knew, so Hawaiians are learning to sing the old songs (and I don't mean "Tiny Bubbles"). Expelling the US military, or at least minimizing its presence, is essential, though as for how to do that . . . well, the people of Puerto Rico have an idea or two.

Then there is that unappeasable enemy of independence-yearning minorities everywhere: King Numbers. As John Whitehead pointed out to me, "The Hawaiian sovereignty crowd today seems to forget that half the population of the islands is Asian American, who have little if no link to the Hawaiian native culture and who weren't really a part of the Hawaiian v. American clash in the 1893 revolution. Today they fly under the radar and quietly control the state both politically and economically."[77]

Intermarriage is "vast," says Whitehead. "The older the family the more likely the intermarriage. Many Hawaiians are married to Chinese." In response to my question of whether or not the native radicals are anti-Asian, he says, "Difficult to say since they are probably related."[78] Asians are neither *haole* nor *kanaka* (native); they are, perhaps, whatever the Hawaiian word is for "resented." Movement speakers do not sound anywhere near as blatantly anti-Japanese as was Kamokila Campbell. Instead, they reserve their venom for whites. (There are, of course, many exceptions. The genial independence advocate Ku Ching tells me that "a real Hawaiian may be Hawaiian by blood or not.")[79]

Haunani-Kay Trask, however, evidently despises *haoles*. "Non-Natives," she says with what is at least a refreshing frankness, "no matter how long their residence in Hawai'i, should acknowledge their status as settlers, that is, uninvited guests in our Native country." As for those wanting to fly the friendly skies and be greeted by a pretty girl offering a lei—forget it. "If you are thinking of visiting my homeland," says Trask, "please do not. We do not want or need any more tourists, and we certainly do not like them."[80] This message is *not* approved by the Oahu Chamber of Commerce, but since tourists outnumber natives by thirty to one, according to some estimates, the mainlanders are not getting the message.

Even if Hawaii were given its immediate and unconditional independence, the natives, who make up maybe 15 percent of the population, would be out of the driver's seat. Unless, that is, to continue the inapt vehicular metaphor, there was not one car in which every citizen of Hawaii had to be stuffed but a multitude of autos, going at their own speeds and wending down roads of their own choosing. That is the viatic and viable path to harmony.

The granting of statehood to noncontiguous entities opened a door through which no other has yet marched but that no one quite seems to know how—or if—to close. Puerto Rico seems to be closest to the threshold, though as we will see in the next chapter she is of several minds about statehood. The scattered island territories of the empire—the US Virgin Islands, American Samoa, Guam—are useful possessions, but no one outside the terminally naive thinks they will ever be admitted as states. Ditto the commonwealth of the Northern Mariana Islands. Farther afield, a "51 Club" in Taipei promotes Taiwan as the next member of the union, but the 51 Club missed the Cold War boat by about four decades.[81] The $5 billion annual subsidy from American taxpayers to Israel would seem to betoken potential statehood, but joining the union would mean a pay cut for the Israelis. So for now, Alaska and Hawaii are the only interlopers in the interlocked union.

"A noncontiguous state cannot be fairly represented or protected in the American political system," said Alaska's Joe Vogler.[82] Kamokila Campbell—oh, she and Joe would have been a match for each other!—told Congress, "We are too far away to be intimately connected with you."[83] Can we finally listen to them?

Abraham Lincoln, no lover of statehood for Texas (or, as it turned out, secession), explained that he "did not believe in enlarging our field, but in keeping our fences where they are and cultivating our present possessions, making it a garden."[84] My, how that garden has grown. Tundra here, sugarcane there . . . and maybe even a little patch of corn and pumpkins, just for old times' sake. Shall we prune?

CHAPTER SIX

Viva Puerto Rico!—Or, An Island Interlude Masquerading as a Chapter

O n the matter of statehood, Puerto Rico's outstanding novelist has written . . . actually, I have no idea what he or she has written, because I do not read Spanish, nor do I plan to learn. Should our flag be defaced by a fifty-first star for Puerto Rico—which is, admittedly, more deserving of stellification than the ersatz states Alaska and Hawaii—most of us will be incapable of reading its writers or understanding its songs. Doesn't it seem the least bit odd that we will be unable to read the novelists and poets and polemicists of another of our *United* States? Even Mississippi's Faulkner is, theoretically, readable. (Hawaii is the exception—and the precedent—*pace* Don Ho.)

A century ago, the Yale sociologist William Graham Sumner warned that overseas expansion carried within it the germ of destruction, for "all extension puts a new strain on the internal cohesion of the pre-existing mass, threatening a new cleavage within."[1] The anti-imperialists—Brahmins and hardscrabble Populists, the James Gang (Henry and William) and ferocious ole Tom Watson—fought courageously against the absorption of the rotten spoils of the Spanish-American War and lost, and the Old Republic was never quite the same. As one anti-imperialist wag had it, "Dewey took Manila with the loss of one man—and all our institutions."[2] And so we are left to count the blessings we have derived from our colonial possessions: Pearl Harbor, once-pacific islands that target practice has bombed to rubble, and the unspellable Samoan football players of the Western Athletic Conference.

The acquisition of far-flung territories was, as Senator George Frisbie Hoar (R-MA) announced in 1899, "the greatest question that has ever been or ever will be put to [Senators] in their lives, the question, not of a year or of a Congress, but . . . the great eternity of national life." Hoar predicted that imperialism "will make of our beloved country a cheap-jack country, raking after the cart for the leavings of European tyranny." The abhorred standing army would become a permanent feature whose expense was "sure to make our national taxgatherer the most familiar visi-tant to every American home."

Hoar, an authentic profile in courage, had been the most conventional of Gilded Age Republicans, a man for whom party loyalty was next to godliness, but he would not stand by and watch his nation stray from "the ancient path of republican liberty which the fathers trod down into this modern swamp and cesspool of imperialism." Even today, at this late date, when the game is over and the box scores have been printed, who but an editor of the *New Republic* can fail to be moved by the hoary patriot's pathetic cry: "Is there to be no place on the face of the earth hereafter where a man can stand up by virtue of his manhood and say, 'I am a man'?"[3]

Puerto Rico's acquisition was not an afterthought to the Spanish-American War's ostensible purpose of liberating Cuba from Spain. The island was not a lagniappe given the United States, or a mistake ("Puerto Rico? Jeez, we're sorry, we thought it was Cuba"). Teddy Roosevelt, whom Gore Vidal memorably dubbed the sissy of Kettle Hill, panicked at the swiftness of the Spanish-American War. "You must prevent any talk of peace until we get Porto Rico and the Philippines," TR wrote Henry Cabot Lodge on June 12, 1898.[4] Major General Nelson A. Miles, whose grim résumé included Antietam, the successful pursuit of Geronimo, and the suppression of the Pullman strike, commanded the military government established over Puerto Rico following the US invasion. He promised to "bestow upon" its people "the immunities and blessings of the liberal institutions of our government . . . [and] the advantages and blessings of enlightened civilization."[5] Cue images of carnage from Wounded Knee, Chancellorsville, and General Miles's other campaigns for enlightenment. By comparison, benightedness doesn't look so bad.

Statehood for Puerto Rico, like its acquisition 110 years ago, is largely a Republican project borne of the same ghastly mixture of expansionism and Great White Father benevolence. The opposition, we are told, consists of a few grizzled graybeard Spaniards, some wild-eyed Puerto Rican communists mixing Molotov cocktails, and stateside racists who will admit, after a beer or two, that their real fear is putting "four million spics on welfare."

This is a serviceable lie that has crowded out a lambent truth: that Puerto Rican *independentistas* are patriots, and that Americans who wish to grant the island her long-overdue freedom are acting in the best interests of *both* countries. "Independence," says Senator Ruben Berrios Martinez, long-time leader of the Puerto Rican Independence Party (PIP), "would end Puerto Rico's lifeless imitation of the colonizer, typical of colonies."[6] The Uncle Tomases of statehood offer Disney and food stamps; the poets and patriots of the independence movement dream of the cultural flourishing of their enchanted isle. The dream has lasted decades.

The classic exposition of the debilitating effects of US colonialism in Puerto Rico was provided by the brilliant young patriot and aristocratic bon vivant Luis Munoz Marin in the pages of the *American Mercury* in 1929. Inflammatory, mordant, spiked with enough punches at the Elks and Odd Fellows and Rotary to suggest that either Marin flavored his rum with Mencken or the Sage of Baltimore was an overactive editor, "The Sad Case of Porto Rico" explains that "the American flag found Porto Rico penniless and content. It now flies over a prosperous factory worked by slaves who have lost their land and may soon lose their guitars and their songs."[7]

Republican trade policies transformed an island of small landholdings and independent coffee growers into a virtual sugarcane forest. Coffee, the crop of human-scale farming, was not protected by the US-imposed tariff; sugar was, and so, writes Senator Berrios, an economy of "small and medium-sized farms producing primarily for local consumption . . . became under the stimulus of US tariff laws a large sugar plantation dominated by absentee landlords in the United States and tilled by a pauperized peasantry."[8]

Munoz Marin, in his 1929 essay, achieved the kind of threnodic savagery that is only possible when the writer is witnessing the murder of something he loves. He panned the Protestant do-goodism that was assaulting the island, though he ventured, "I doubt that such implied notions as Christ's disapproval of cigarettes gets much serious attention from the local young men." He deplored the depressing effect of the uplifters, as "charity becomes slightly organized, evangelical preachers thunder in the villages . . . three or four prominent citizens become Protestants and are considered funny, women are beginning to be feared as the rolling-pin follows the flag, virginity still abounds and often attains to old age, but is perceptibly on the wane."[9]

To which Puerto Rican collaborators rejoined: GDP is rising! Exports are swelling! Disposable income is . . . being disposed of!

But something far greater than the Yankee dollar was at stake. To Munoz Marin, "saving a culture, even an inferior one, from becoming the monkey of another, even a superior one, is a good in itself." At all costs a Puerto-American hybrid must be avoided; yet he feared, "Perhaps we are destined to be neither Porto Ricans nor Americans, but merely puppets of a mongrel state of mind, susceptible to American thinking and proud of Latin thought, subservient to American living and worshipful of the ancestral way of life. Perhaps we are to discuss Cervantes and eat pork and beans . . . Perhaps we are going to a singularly fantastic and painless hell in our own sweet way. Perhaps all this is nothing but a foretaste of Pan-Americanism."[10]

Munoz Marin was to fall in with a bad crowd—FDR, Rexford Guy Tugwell—and find, to the disgust of his erstwhile compatriots, that Old Scratch rewards his administrators handsomely. He would become the island's first elected governor and the chief architect of the peculiar commonwealth status it achieved in 1952.

As Munoz Marin delivered his people into the gilded cage of colonialism, patriot leadership was assumed by the fiery Harvard-educated Pedro Albizu Campos, whose uncompromising Nationalist Party took up the gun and created the official pretext for a half century of vengeful and brutal repression of independence activities.

The "culturally conservative" Albizu Campos believed in La Raza and the Catholic Church and took inspiration from his co-religionists in Ireland; his movement opposed canned goods, US-sponsored birth-control programs, and any hint of collaboration with the colonial power. He feared that his land was "crushed by the materialism of the Protestant barbarians," historian Raymond Carr has written.[11] Nationalists despised the New Deal and refused to accept government employment. Albizu Campos called young Puerto Ricans who disdained independence "sissies."

Modern Latin American historians of the Left are not quite comfortable with Campos and the Nationalists. Yes, they battled the colossus across the water, but they also were "particularly concerned with the idea of promoting the Puerto Rican bourgeoisie and turning workers into small landholders."[12] Most were devout Catholics.

The Nationalists marched, fought, illegally flew the Puerto Rican flag, and used such proscribed terms as *nacion* and *patria*. They rejected the ballot box; for the *nacionalistas*, culture and the gun were enough. As Senator Berrios notes, from the 1930s through the 1950s advocates of a free Puerto Rico "were arrested and imprisoned for almost any reason, including reciting patriotic poetry, making speeches, and unfurling the Puerto Rican flag."[13] Pedro Albizu Campos was to spend most of these years in prison for inciting violence; he stubbornly refused to beg for a pardon or renounce revolution. No scraping vassal was he.

World War II and its Cold War sequel turned Puerto Rico into an alleged strategic asset. The Roosevelt-Truman administrations lavished federal moneys on the island while jailing and silencing patriots. Commonwealth—a travesty of self-government, plausible only to those who believe that junior high school student councils actually run the schools—was hatched. Under commonwealth, the island was given home rule, of a sort—that is, its elected officials make laws under the watchful eye of Big Brother to the north. Although they became citizens of the United States under the Jones-Shafroth Act of 1917, Puerto Ricans in the commonwealth are exempt from federal taxes. They are eligible for federal subvention (and the eleemosynary flows; more than half of Puerto Rico's population is below the government-defined poverty line), but they cast no votes in federal elections—though they do send voting delegations to the Democratic and Republican conventions, those widely unpopular quadrennial summer replacement series.

Commonwealth, as Yale's Jose Cabranes, later a federal judge, assessed it in *Foreign Policy* (1978–79), "was an authentic expression of the postwar American liberal worldview: a poor and racially mixed Third World community undergoing modernization as a result of the inventive application of American capital and American liberal ideology." It brought a measure of prosperity, as American manufacturers were attracted by the island's cheap labor, but in time Puerto Rico was less the exemplar of post-war liberal dynamism than it was a dependent of the welfare state. As the youthful Munoz Marin had foreseen, it was becoming spiritless, sequacious, a pathetic distant cousin to whom one grudgingly tosses scraps of charity. By the mid-'70s, writes Cabranes, Puerto Rico was "a veritable welfare state."[14]

Despairing Nationalists cursed Munoz Marin for forsaking independence in favor of commonwealth. Hotheads and homicides among them responded with mad assassination attempts against President Truman, Munoz Marin, and members of the US House of Representatives. And that was all she wrote: The resultant crackdown, on both the gun-toting Nationalists and the nonviolent middle-class Puerto Rican Independence Party, destroyed political manifestations of Puerto Rican patriotism for a generation or more.

Los derrotados, or *The Vanquished* (1956), is Cesar Andreu Iglesias's novel about Puerto Rican Nationalists fighting for "independence the way Don Pedro Albizu Campos wanted it: without a single Yankee soldier left to trample upon the holy soil of Puerto Rico!"[15] If it is not the great Puerto Rican novel, it is not far back in the pack. Andreu, who had been president of Partido Communista, the Puerto Rican Communist Party, presents these men as honorable anachronisms, men out of time, doomed paladins of the *patria* whose plot to assassinate an American general hasn't even the juice to distract the targeted myrmidon from forethoughts of golf. The mass of Puerto Ricans have forgotten their past; they are "rootless beings, coming and going, a rudderless crowd."[16] The *nacionalistas*, by contrast, disdain imported beer, imported coffee, and imported furniture, not so much dreaming as remembering a Puerto Rico that was Puerto Rican: built of native woods, native foods, and *jibaro* (peasant) music and dress. "Today's so-called progress is simply the embezzlement of our heritage," says one character, unimpressed by the bounty of washing machines and televisions washing upon Puerto Rican shores, and if the novel ends on a note of hope we are also given to understand that it's gonna be a long walk home.[17]

If ever one needs evidence of the devitalizing, emasculatory effects of colonialism, look no farther than the paltry vote totals tallied by today's *independentistas*. In 1952, barely one-eighth of Puerto Rican voters supported pro-statehood parties, while almost one-fifth favored the independence-minded parties. Today, almost half support statehood, and barely 5 percent cast their votes for a free Puerto Rico.

Writing in *The Nation*, Antonio M. Stevens-Arroyo asserts that "the abundance of consumer goods that has resulted from the US presence has limited the appeal of the *independentistas*."[18] The Puerto Rican Independence Party is asking people bred in political serfdom to choose liberty and dignity over welfare checks and hip-hop CDs. It may be a lot to ask.

Since the Cold War, US policy makers have assured us that *independentistas* are "left of red," to borrow Animals lead singer Eric Burdon's felicitous phrase. While it shouldn't much interest Americans what kind of economic system other peoples may choose, the messy fact is that Puerto Rican statehood is advertised by its proponents as a pass on the gravy train, a free tray at the welfare-state buffet, while independence leader Senator Berrios is given to such commie observations as "the founding fathers did not intend statehood as a ticket for a poor nation to a cornucopia of federal welfare benefits" and "the basic economic problem of Puerto Rico is . . . dependence on US subsidies."[19]

Moreover, Berrios, like Albizu, has been condemned by communists as "fascist" for purging the PIP of its relative handful of Marxist-Leninists and Castro admirers and for ignoring class struggle in favor of a cultural-nationalist vision of a free Puerto Rico.[20]

Statehooders—the "good Puerto Ricans," in the view of the Democrats and Republicans—base their case almost exclusively on welfarist grounds. (The title of fervent statehood advocate Carlos Romero-Barcelo's 1978 book is *Statehood Is for the Poor*.)[21] It is the *independentistas* who reject the statehood utopia of one big happy alms-fattened bilingual Puerto Rican state. While the Republican National Hispanic Assembly gushes that statehood would turn welfare into a "right rather than a charity," the "leftist" Stevens-Arroyo argues that "the statehood myth carries the seduction of dependency. Like a hospital patient on a life-support system, Puerto Rico's economy has become dependent on subsidies."[22]

Independentistas assert that cultural regeneration must precede economic prosperity. This is why the typical university-entombed activist who uses words like *transgressive* is unsympathetic to the Partido Independentista Puertorriqueno: The party tends to "attribute many social ills to the excessive dependency on government handouts." Party leaders also believe that independence will instill "a new work ethic" and allow Puerto Ricans "to regain their dignity and pride."[23]

An indigenous creation, the PIP is not easily translated into terms intelligible to Barack Obama and Mitt Romney. It has attacked government waste and politicians who travel abroad and called for an emphasis on "manly sports." Historian Raymond Carr, in a study for the Twentieth Century Fund, noted that, to the PIP, "a national theater is . . . as important as a national economy." Television is loathed for its "violence, cultural assimilation, individualism and the excess of consumerism."[24] These are the principles of *Los derrotados*—except today's *independentistas* are not vanquished, and unlike the *nacionalistas* they spurn the gun, for as Emma Goldman said, he who picks up the sword hands it to his enemies.

The PIP is also absolutist—extremist!—when it comes to Puerto Rico maintaining her language. The island's English-speaking masters have discouraged the use of Spanish off and on over the last hundred-plus years, and Puerto Rico is unlikely to achieve statehood without some requirement, however ineffectual, that her people learn a Spanglish macaronic. (More than 60 percent now speak no English at all.)

Unlike Hawaii, where the natives were "overwhelmed by an immigration process," as Fernando Martin, executive president of the Puerto Rican Independence Party, told a House subcommittee, Puerto Rico remains a Spanish land.[25]

I understand completely why many Americans think that speaking English is an essential component of citizenship, but "English only" laws are sticks and stones of petty tyranny. Statehooders who press bilingualism on Puerto Rico seek to remove her heart and accept the corpse into our union. (Imperialists care about "the cage, not the birds," according to Albizu Campos.)[26]

Independentistas are right: Puerto Ricans who advocate statehood are not merely misguided; like the Americans who sat on metric-conversion boards or worked for the CIA, they are collaborators in the destruction of their nation. They gutlessly eschew the seemingly unobjectionable phrase

Puerto Rican people and instead describe themselves as "US citizens resident in Puerto Rico." What bloodless wretch would deny the primacy of his home? Senator Berrios is easier to understand, with his pronouncement that "Puerto Rico's heart is not American. It is Puerto Rican. The national sentiment of Puerto Ricans is entirely devoted to our patria, as we call our homeland in Spanish. We are Puerto Ricans in the same way that Mexicans are Mexicans and Japanese are Japanese. For us, 'we the people' means we Puerto Ricans."[27]

The bombing of Vieques, an island-municipality of ten thousand people lying eight miles to the east and under Puerto Rican jurisdiction, emphasized the colonial status and un-Americannness of "we Puerto Ricans." Since 1941, the US Navy had used Vieques as a bombing range. The military had at first purchased and then seized via eminent domain two-thirds of Vieques. For the next sixty years residents of the island would never quite grow inured to the sounds of warplanes and artillery and exploding missiles. As with any occupied colony (or American town with a military base), social rot set in. Puerto Rican journalist Carmelo Ruiz explained in 1999, "Military personnel have brought along with them drug addiction, prostitution and street violence, which were virtually unheard of on the island in the pre-Navy years." Ruiz noted also that the "Navy has destroyed coral reefs, lagoons, mangroves, coconut groves and beaches."[28]

It is not in the nature of an imperial power to apologize for trampling the flowers when it exits the cathouse—the Spaniards, who colonized the island for five hundred years, sure didn't—but PIP-led protests, which took on amplification and urgency when David Sanes Rodriguez was killed by errant bombs dropped from a US Marine F-18 jet during a 1999 training mission, achieved their goal. Senator Berrios and a band of squatters held the beaches in a months-long "big triumph in the struggle for decolonization," in the senator's words.[29] This was a far cry from 1971, when Berrios had launched a similar campaign of civil disobedience to reclaim Vieques that was crushed in a matter of days, and left Berrios in prison for three months.

In 2003 the navy withdrew, leaving an estimated twenty-two million pounds of industrial waste and military detritus on Vieques. A cleanup was promised, though in scope it would make sweeping the Augean stables look like removing a piece of lint from an old maid's navel. Besides, the United States has other spending priorities, most of them having to do with the projection of military might on the other side of the globe. The people of Vieques are shell-shocked on their pockmarked island, but the bombing has ceased. Uncle Sam left. Hope appears in flinders and orts.

So where do we go from here? Shall Puerto Rico join Hawaii and Alaska? (Fittingly, the seemingly permanent Alaska congressman Don Young has been the leading advocate of statehood in the House, but the other side finally has representation in high—which is to say low—places: In her Princeton senior thesis on the life of Munoz Marin, Supreme Court Justice Sonia Sotomayor identified herself as pro-independence . . . a youthful indiscretion, no doubt.)[30]

Periodic referenda as well as opinion polls on the island's status indicate a rough split between advocates of statehood and those of commonwealth, with a 5 percent remnant standing on its own two feet for independence. Statehood tallied 39 percent in a 1967 plebiscite and 46 percent in both a 1993 plebiscite and a 1998 referendum.

"There seems to be a feeling in the United States against permitting others to be responsible for their own welfare," wrote Munoz Marin eighty years ago.[31] That feeling seldom extends beyond Wall Street, Hollywood, and the District of Columbia—do any of *your* neighbors give a damn about Puerto Rico one way or another?—but it has earned us the hatred of people against whom Main Street Americans harbor no ill will. Kidnapping Puerto Rico and jamming her into the union would enrage the best of her people—why on earth would we want to do that?

That statehood talk is in the air suggests just how thoroughly Puerto Rico has been routed. The loss of one's culture, which is the pretty poison of statehood, is "insidious," wrote Munoz Marin. "It works while you sleep. It changes the expression of your eyes, the form of your paunch, the tone of your voice, your hopes of Heaven, what your neighbors and your women expect of you—all without giving you a chance to fight back, without even presenting to you the dilemma of fighting back or not."[32]

Puerto Rico, he predicted, "will never be incorporated into the Union as a State save through the operation of cultural forces: that is, not unless, and until, our manner of life and thought has been respectably Americanized" (or until Americans have been Puerto Ricanized).[33] A fantastic and pain-less hell, Munoz Marin called it, with a grinning newt standing at the gate. The price of admission is the loss of Puerto Rico's soul. What kind of monster regards this as a bargain?

Under Puerto Rican statehood, the Democrats will keep Maria's welfare checks coming, and the Republicans will force her children to speak English and scorn their mother's tongue, as well as the mother tongue. Maria's great-grandchildren may become fanatical nationalists, but by then it will be too late. They'll need Berlitz tapes to relearn the language.

Young Munoz Marin wanted "Porto Rico to be Porto Rico, not a lame replica of Ohio or Arizona."[34] It is just as likely today that Ohio will become a lame replica of Puerto Rico, for the children of Akron and Ponce snooze through the same federally mandated history lessons and follow the same Fox spoor on TV and learn everything about Lindsay Lohan but nothing about Sherwood Anderson or Pedro Albizu Campos.

The *independentistas* appeal to what G. K. Chesterton called "the democracy of the dead." They share an inheritance with both ancestry and posterity. Senator Berrios quotes Edmund Burke: "A nation is not an idea only of individual momentary aggregation. It is a deliberate election of the ages and generations, a partnership not only between those who are living, but between those who are dead, and those who are to be born."[35]

America, says Senator Berrios, "cannot live with a remnant of 19th-century empire like Puerto Rico. It's not being true to its history nor its future."[36] If we intercalate "the best part of" before "its history" then he is correct. The United States of America, the forty-eight contiguous states of the North American continent, cannot absorb Puerto Rico without dishonoring our ancestors and adulterating the cultures of both countries. *Vivan los independentistas!* For Puerto Rico's sake, yes—but for ours, too.

CHAPTER SEVEN

To Live and Die (and Live Again) in Dixie

*Y*orker bred, libertarian bent, I despair of writing the South. Like Bob
Seger, "everytime I been there, it's been great," but *it is another country*, and I have a hard enough time understanding my own.

Cant, blind resentment, cheap moralizing, and bilious outrage still
corrupt so much intersectional discourse—or shouting past each other. I
wonder if we will ever really listen to the heartsongs and midnight stories
that render Brother Jonathan and Johnny Reb, or Robert Johnson and
Robert Gould Shaw, or Johnny Cash and Emily Dickinson, complex,
contradictory . . . human.

Let us take the angle less measured—though you might not like that
you like what you find.

❧

Mark Royden Winchell, the late Clemson University professor of English
and biographer of the Southern agrarian poet Donald Davidson, told me
that on the eve of Iraq War II, he and a few League of the South comrades
were flying the South Carolina flag at an antiwar rally on the Clemson
campus.

"Why are y'all against the war?" asked a passing student.

To which the South Carolina LOS chairman replied, "This is the same
Yankee empire that invaded us in 1861!"[1]

Winchell died in May 2008 of cancer. I had just gotten to know him
over the previous year as I edited his fine survey of reactionary cinema *God,
Man, and Hollywood* (2008). Ours was one of those friendships nipped in
the bud. Ah, time and the river.

Mark Royden Winchell was to be my guide through the League of the
South, a cultural-political entity that is defiant, controversial, and, much
like the native Hawaiian independence movement, hard for an outsider

to fit into a labeled pouch ("safely liberal"! "conservative nationalist"! "romantic nostalgist!"). Mark was an Ohioan who had moved South and embraced the literary heritage of his adopted place. Its political heritage, too, though he was careful to call himself a "Copperhead"—the ophidian epithet applied by unionists to antiwar Northerners in the War Between the States. Mark's wife, Donna, is a professor of African American literature at Clemson, and unlike many of the league's leading lights, Mark was never, to my knowledge, called a racist.

But he died, leaving a rich body of work on subjects ranging from Leslie Fielder to Joan Didion to Cleanth Brooks. Like any good shortstop, he had range; he could go to his left or his right. If necessary, he could flip the ball with his off hand. The poet Davidson, in his essay "Still Rebels, Still Yankees" from his marvelous book *Attack on Leviathan* (1938), quotes the playwright-screenwriter Laurence Stallings: "What I like about Charleston is that it has resisted Abraham Lincoln's attempts to put the country into Arrow Collars. If the South had won the war, the country would have had lots more color."[2]

Winchell would have agreed.

"If the South would have won, we'd have had it made," boasted Hank Williams Jr. of football preparedness fame. What do you mean *we*, kemosabe?, a skeptical descendant of slaves might answer. Not that the question isn't worth asking.

John Tierney, the *New York Times* writer who must have, like R. P. McMurphy, avoided swallowing the soma they pass out to the likes of Gail Collins and Thomas Friedman, wondered on July 4, 2006, what might have been had the South become independent. Two professors gave the answer demanded by the commissars of CorrectThink: slavery extended into the later part of the nineteenth century, followed by apartheid of a sort. The half-a-million-plus Americans who would not have died in the Civil War go unmentioned. But then Tierney interviewed Jeffrey Rogers Hummel, historian and the author of *Emancipating Slaves, Enslaving Free Men* (1996), a learned and provocative reconsideration of the war.[3] Look, we all have biases, and discourse would be much healthier and freer if we were franker about them. Hummel is a libertarian. His heroes of the age are the abolitionists, à la William Lloyd Garrison, who demanded immediate freedom for the African bondsmen and, if necessary, breaking the constitutional link to the southern slavocracy.

One of Hummel's central insights is the unrealized potential of personal liberty laws to undermine slavery. Garrison's cry of "No Union with Slaveholders" posed "a danger to the peculiar institution," writes Hummel. "Northern secession represented an effective way to eliminate this subsidy [that is, retrieval of runaway slaves] to slaveholders. The abolitionists realized that this would help make the North an asylum for runaways."[4]

So you see, secession cuts both ways, even in 1861. An independent South has as its concomitant an independent North. In that spirit, let's pretend that we are independents living in a free country. Are we so cowed by the marksmen in their towers, shooting at (if usually missing) heretics in the land of the quavering and the home of the discrete, that we cannot consider the implications of an independent South without an attack of the vapors?

Fuck the Thought Police. Let's go. First stop: the League of the South.

The LOS was founded at a conference of scholars and activists in Tuscaloosa, Alabama, in June 1994 as the Southern League, in a conscious echo of the Northern League, or Lega Nord, the federalist party of Northern Italy whose principal American explicator was Thomas Fleming of *Chronicles*. The Southern League—which later redubbed itself the League of the South due to a copyright conflict with the Class AA baseball circuit of the same name—is dedicated to "the independence and well-being of the Southern People." It was not born singing "The Bonnie Blue Flag," but early on it put Washington on notice that "if the current regime continues its tyranny, we shall not hesitate to advocate secession and self-rule for the Southern states."[5]

The early to mid-'90s were a fecund age in the decentralist garden. As league co-founder and University of South Carolina history professor Clyde Wilson recalls to me, "Dissatisfaction with an over-centralised [*sic*—we'll get to that shortly] and unresponsive federal government and disillusion with the two-party system was becoming widespread." Think Ross Perot, Jerry Brown, Pat Buchanan, the rise of talk radio, Parti Quebecois, Lega Nord, Scottish National Party. "It seemed possible," continues Wilson, "that there might be a historic opportunity to push for devolution in the United States." Moreover, "attacks on the historic South were many and vicious and were arousing an active response in otherwise apolitical people."[6]

Clyde Wilson is the descendant of North Carolina dirt farmers, a former textile mill worker and crime reporter who earned his PhD in history at Chapel Hill and spent the better part of his long academic career at the University of South Carolina editing the papers of John C. Calhoun. Clyde is the league's best-known academic partisan. He is also not what you expect. For instance, Clyde wrote admiringly of Jesse Jackson's presidential campaigns as from-the-heart expressions of Southern populism; he defended the Dixie Chicks, the pop-country band whose lead singer ran afoul of the Clear Channel radio hydra when she told an English audience that she was "ashamed" that George W. Bush hailed from her home state of Texas. "Any real Texan, as opposed to the carpetbaggers (like Bush) and foreigners who now reside there, would have to agree," wrote Wilson, who praised the Chicks for their unabashed use of *Dixie* and added that "a genuine Southern 'redneck' had much rather defend a lady than a politician. A real redneck thinks for himself and is not the kind of big city trash that participates in screaming demonstrations and tirades."[7]

At first, the league seemed Jeffersonian; it spoke of decentralizing (I am a Yorker and I'll keep my *z*, thank you) power and preserving agrarian values, and it claimed to be animated by Christian love. Its national coming-out party, as it were, was hosted by the *Washington Post*, wherein Fleming and Southern League president Michael Hill laid out "The New Dixie Manifesto." They called for a return of power from Washington to the states, and then from the states to localities, but the meat of their argument was cultural. Fleming and Hill asked, "What would American literature be without Mark Twain, Edgar Allan Poe, William Faulkner, Walker Percy and Eudora Welty? What sort of political system would our ancestors have given us, if George Washington, Thomas Jefferson and James Madison had decided to remain British? What kind of popular music could we listen to, if white 'crackers' like Hank Williams and Merle Haggard and Southern blacks like Louis Armstrong and Ray Charles had been content with the bland commercial music churned out by Tin Pan Alley?"[8]

The literary references were not rote or forced. In its infancy, the league was a beguiling blend of redneck and intellectual. Southern novelists who have been associated with the league or its activities include Madison Jones, Tito Perdue, and James Kibler. The title character of Perdue's funny 1991 novel *Lee*—a name obviously not chosen randomly from a phone book—returns to his Alabama hometown dreaming of a smaller world with many books and fewer people. He calmly announces to the librarian who will not give him a library card unless Lee provides references: "I'm thinking of beating the shit out of you."[9] Lee has not been reconstructed.

The league's early mission was as poetical as it was political. Its Montgomery Declaration of Southern Cultural Independence on March 4, 2000, announced: "Looking ahead to the time when political self-determination is a reality, we hereby pledge ourselves to the preservation of our culture in preparation for, and in the fervent hope of, the coming of that day." Rejecting corporate culture as "violent and profane, coarse and rude, cynical and deviant"—do you disagree?—the league called for a kind of secession from "this alien, national culture." Screw *Sex and the City*; read Faulkner! Madonna is a trull; listen to June Carter Cash! The alternative is desiccation, then death. Music, literature, manners, speech, cuisine: "Cut off from these permanent things, the South will become only a point on the compass."[10]

The Montgomery Declaration was an elegant and moving statement of cultural particularism. It applies with equal force and cogency—though it differs in the all-important specifics—to patriots in Puerto Rico, Hawaii, Upstate New York, Vermont, the Upper Peninsula, Southern Oregon, and your hometown, too.

But of course we all know, from lifetimes spent in catatonic communion with the television, that a white Southern accent means trouble. It signifies a racist redneck shit-kickin' moron, sometimes pinned to a sheriff deputy's badge. Intellectuals who speak in such accents and refuse to disavow their people or history are even more dangerous; they are not to be lampooned but slimed.

And so the snitches and enforcers who try to control political debate in America libeled the league as racist on the basis of a primeval fear of white Southern men. Right off the bat, says Clyde Wilson, he and his confreres were vilified as the "Ku Klux Klan in suits."[11] In fact, its founders were neither windbag Ku Kluxers or Tara-choked sentimentalists; rather, they were an impressive set of Southern intellectuals and businessmen. But this is *not* to say that the league is without faults, warts, and assorted maladies—some of them quite serious, and possibly fatal.

A Southern writer whom I admire very much told me of the LOS: "They started out talking a good game about trans-racial Southernness, but seem to have taken a harder turn somewhere along the line . . . I always said I'd join as soon as they had a half-dozen black members. As far as I know, they still don't, and it doesn't seem to be a high priority, to put it no more strongly."[12]

I ask Clyde Wilson about this. How many blacks are among the league's several thousand loyalists? He replies that the league will not recruit blacks actively—"that would smack of affirmative action"—but adds that "we recognise that blacks are and always have been a part of the South and that we cannot achieve our goals without them."[13]

The founder and president of the League of the South, Michael Hill, is sick and tired of addressing this question, I'm sure. I met Michael early in the league's existence when I spoke on decentralism at a conference of the Old Right John Randolph Club. Hill was a bearded, soft-spoken, forty-ish son of Winfield, Alabama, who had driven a truck before earning his doctorate in history. We talked of Lynyrd Skynyrd and Crimson Tide football. I asked him, point-blank, if the league's vision of the South encompassed blacks. (For rumor had it that a couple of racist assholes whom the Randolph Club president had barred entry to had sought dialogue with the Southern League, as it was then styled.)

Hill was emphatic that the Southern League was biracial. He was a Southern rocker, after all, a huge fan of the Allman Brothers, that black and white blend of country and jazz and blues.[14] Michael was also a professor at Stillman College, whose student body was 98 percent black. No time-server, Hill had been president of the faculty association; Stillman president emeritus Cordell Wynn called him "one of the finest young Christian family men I'd ever met." (Wynn later expressed rue over Hill's league involvement.)

"We get calls from people who think we're some kind of racial thing or a militia group," Hill told the *Atlanta Journal-Constitution* in 1998. "I've had to kick out some former Klansmen. Any movement is going to get bad apples."

As for civil rights, "if blacks and whites in the South had been allowed to work it out for themselves, it might have taken a little more time, but the outcome would have been better."[15] A little more time, unfortunately, can mean ten minutes or one hundred years.

Hill has fallen somewhat quiet in recent years, passed by in the movement for whatever reason. He remains league president, however, as well as a guitarist in tune with his home region, the Shoals of northwest Alabama, rock 'n' blues cradle of the Muscle Shoals Sound, the Drive-By Truckers, and Sam Peckinpah ensemble legend Donnie Fritts. You can't get much more righteously Southern American than that. And just as Edward Abbey insisted that he had become more radical with age, wishing as a sexagenarian that he might lead a revolt against Tucson City Hall, neither has Michael Hill mellowed. In the latter part of 2009, Hill published a furiously eloquent assault on modern education that most leftist critics of the megaschool would applaud. He concluded, "Should the current educational trend away from a humane regionalism and toward a soulless nationalism continue, then perhaps in this new millennium all men will have equal destinies in American society. They will be destined to live as deracinated 'human resources' cut loose from their unique cultural and historical moorings and fit only to be producers and consumers of trinkets in the global marketplace."[16]

Quarrels over the display of the Confederate flag in public places and atop civic buildings drained much of the league's energy in the early years. Hill saw the extirpation of these symbols as prelude to the extirpation of Southerners themselves, while others—myself included—wonder what good is a state flag to which a substantial portion of a state's citizens object. Fleming and Hill wrote, exasperatedly, "If the Confederate flags are tainted by the abuses of slavery, so are the flags of the United States, Great Britain, France and Spain—all countries that engaged in the trading of human beings. We do not claim that all our ancestors were infallible or even honorable in all their actions, but we utterly repudiate the one-sided and hypocritical movement to demonize Southerners and their symbols."[17]

As the years went by and the flags came down, the rhetoric heated. "The timid and vacillating man's day is past," said Hill in March 2000. "Defeat for us is not an option. Threats shall not cow us; filthy Yankee money shall not buy us; nor shall the Establishment's guile and duplicity deter us from our noble cause of Southern independence."[18] He invoked not only Washington and Davis and Lee but also Nathan Bedford Forrest, the Memphis slave trader, daring cavalry officer, and, after the war, co-founder of the Ku Klux Klan. (Forrest later requested that the Klan disband—it did not.)

The pro-flag rallies, often in a losing cause, did provide striking tableaux: At one gathering in Montgomery, ninety-three-year-old Alberta Martin, the last surviving Confederate widow, sat next to an African American Confederate reenactor bearing a HERITAGE NOT HATE sign. Ebony and ivory in a Confederate key?[19]

In 2005 the league's board of directors issued a Statement on Racism. Like mission statements, such avowals are usually bullshit, but this one read:

> The League of the South has never before issued a statement denying that it is "racist" because racism is a wax nose charge. Those who resort to this charge can never be satisfied. The more we deny it, the more we will be forced to deny it, until at last all that we will have time to do is to repel the latest charge of "racism." However, we make this one statement, to satisfy strangers of good will, that we bear no ill will or hatred to any racial, ethnic, or religious group.
>
> We believe that Christianity and social order require that all people, regardless of race, must be equal before the law. We do not believe that the law should be used to persecute, oppress, or favour any race or class.
>
> We believe that the only harmony possible between the races, as between all natural differences among human beings, begins in submitting to Jesus Christ's commandment to "love our neighbours as ourselves." That is the world we envision and work for.
>
> We believe that the politics of race—baiting whites against

blacks and blacks against whites—has been profitable for politicians but catastrophic for the South and Southerners.

We believe that black Southerners want and need what we
want and need: a safe country for their families, liberty, and the
Gospel of Jesus Christ.

We believe that the last thing the South's enemies want is to
see black and white Southerners sitting down together to determine their common destiny and work for authentic harmony,
a just social and economic order, and an independent South.
We can't foretell precisely what that order will look like, but
certainly it will not make room for diversity police and political
correctness. Rather, we hope it will bring the greatest freedom
for the greatest number of all races, and good will among them
all.[20]

If sincere, the statement puts the league beyond reproach where charges
of racism are concerned. But the league will never be credited with sincer-
ity, for among its members are surely some die-hard segregationists of
the sort who made several folks I spoke with feel uncomfortable at LOS
meetings. What is the acceptable percentage of kooks in an organization?
Five percent? Ten? One in three? Even one is too many, in the sanctimonious phrase of the publicly holy, and so long as one unregenerate
Faubus-Maddox seg sends in his $50 annual dues, the league will always
be suspected of darkheartedness.

The League of the South sure is brambly. Kirk Sale, the left-anarchist
founder of the Middlebury Institute, and the gently rambunctious hippies
of the Second Vermont Republic wandered into an ambuscade when they
invited the league to secessionist gatherings and even, in the case of the
institute, co-sponsored events with the Southrons. For this is twenty-first-
century America, don't you know, and cowardice is the better part of valor
for those who remain politically engaged. Talk to the wrong people and
you'll be crushed between neo-Hooverian snoops and neo-McCarthyite
dissent hunters.

In response to the guilt-by-association smears, Sale, who in writing
SDS (1973), the definitive history of that student radical group, learned a

thing or two about the limits of American dissent in a corporate-military age, produced a graceful document titled "On Collegiality." It is disconcerting to think that any freeborn American, let alone the distinguished anarchist historian Sale, must defend his decision to engage in discussion with other freeborn Americans, but that's post-9/11 life. Sale patiently explained that diversity—not to sound like a college administrator—is a strength, and that "the whole point of secession" is that "different people in different places will have different ideas, desires, goals, and strategies." Aiming squarely at the Thought Police, he wrote that "the kind of people who insist on telling others how to live and think so as to have one unanimous right-minded uniformity are dangerous people and precisely the kind that establish national governments and pass laws applicable to entire populations." They are, to use a word so hopelessly overused as to have been drained of all meaning, operationally fascist.

"As to the League of the South," Sale writes, and here I quote at length because this is one of the best defenses of the big tent I have read, "it is demonstrable that as an organization it is not racist and would not establish a racist state if they were successful in secession." The league, he says, is "an honorable and legitimate—and non-racist—organization sincerely and intelligently devoted to peaceful secession from the empire."

> We accept the fact that there may be people in the LOS who have expressed intemperate and intolerant opinions—but of what group, we ask, could that not be said? (And the scaremongering charges along these lines by the Southern Poverty Law Center have much more to do with its desire to squeeze money out of people made to be afraid of hobgoblins than by any genuine exposure of misbehavior.) Moreover, even if there are, as individuals, LOS people we could from our point of view deem racist, that would matter not one whit as to whether they were legitimate colleagues in the secessionist movement. It is irrelevant.
>
> People turn to secession because they want their own form of government, on their own terms, and hope to create a state that will live out their beliefs, principles, ideals. It is no more

justifiable for one organization to question or criticize or casti-
gate those goals if they work toward a Christian-directed
government that outlaws abortion and adultery than if they
work for a secular democracy favoring gun-control and same-
sex marriages. The beauty of secession is that it looks toward
having a world where those and many other kinds of states can
exist, free and independent, and not impose its ideas on others
or have others' ideas imposed on it.[21]

I would dispute that last paragraph. What of the adulterous atheist in
the former state, or the Christian hunter (*not* Christian-hunter) in the
latter? Those states that do not protect minority rights—whether the
minority is black or white or yellow, Christian or Jew or Muslim—deserve
to be rebuked. Not invaded, or bombed, or hectored by Tartuffes and
shrews, but a rebuke—why not? And in fact in a March 2007 Middlebury
Institute paper Sale drew up a list of "minimal rights and freedoms of individuals" deserving of protection; these paralleled the Bill of Rights (with
the important exception of the right to bear arms) and also included an
explicit right of "secession by any coherent unit."[22]

An understandable secondary charge against the league, based on its
Christian diction, is that it is "theocratic." This criticism is a stretch. True,
the LOS would not bar communities from instituting prayer in public
schools and public celebrations of Christianity. But the Southern intellectuals associated with the league often speak proudly of the tolerance the
South has traditionally shown Jews: The first Jewish cabinet member, they
will remind you, was Judah P. Benjamin, secretary of war in the Confederacy.
Clyde Wilson, who has tussled with some LOS Orthodox Presbyterians
under the influence of the pro-slavery theologian Robert Lewis Dabney,
says, "Southerners are too individualistic to ever come under a theocracy."[23]
So if recitation of the Lord's Prayer at civic events spells theocracy to you,
then yes, a league-flavored South would be a theocracy. But Deuteronomy
would not supplant the legal code. Nor would a chicken-fried sharia. Iran
under the mullahs it ain't.

Cards on the table once more, faceup. I am a sentimental liberal on
matters racial, very much of the Rodney King "can't we all just get along?"

school, but 'neath the sentiment there is still a hard integrationist fact: Black and white, we share this beautiful and heart-scarred country, whose soil is watered and made fertile by the blood and toil and dreams of our ancestors. I detest as much as anyone the suffocating blanket of political correctness, the thought-control regime that would anathematize frank talk and honesty and criminalize dissent. But our loathing of the Little Hitlers and "You can't say that!" heretic-hunters must not obscure the truth that we are all brothers and sisters under the skin, and that to love each other is the main and invigorating task of our threescore and ten.

◦◦◦

The South *is* different. Richard Weaver said in 1957 that "being a Southerner is definitely a spiritual condition, like being a Catholic or a Jew," and in his cold exile at the University of Chicago, Weaver was at least warmed by the knowledge that Southerners, like Catholics and Jews, "can recognize one another by signs which are eloquent to them, though too small to be noticed by an outsider."[24] (If you believe Hollywood, those Southron signifiers include grammatical imprecision, poor dentition, and a fondness for the noose. Hollywood wouldn't lie, would it?)

I spoke in Chapel Hill with John Shelton Reed, who has been called "beyond doubt the most accomplished and influential living sociologist of the US South."[25] Born in Manhattan (Manhattan? don't worry; he repatriated to ancestral ground in infancy), raised in East Tennessee, and for thirty-one years a professor at the University of North Carolina, Reed is the irreverent explainer of the South—to itself and the rest of America. Author of more than a dozen books, Reed has one of the most unusual résumés in academe: He is also a barbecue judge and a country songwriter (Tommy Edwards recorded his tune "My Tears Spoiled My Aim"), and he has even appeared in a music video—the Reverend Billy C. Wirtz's "Teenie Weenie Meanie," a tasteful vignette about a "midget lady wrestler." He is not a member of the league, nor is he terribly sympathetic. His South is written in black and white and many shades of gray.

"Religiosity and religious affiliation," responds Reed when I ask how Southerners still differ from non-Southerners. "The South is the one part of the world where most people identify with evangelical Protestant churches. You've got differences in attitudes toward violence and use of force: Southerners are half again as likely as households in most other parts of the country to have weapons." And "the South is more conservative in political attitudes and values."[26]

This "culture of violence" is not necessarily to be deplored. "The kinds of homicides we've got more of are culturally understood, excused, and in some cases approved," says Reed. "They have to do with private redress of grievances. We have more homicides involving romantic triangles, more homicides that grow out of arguments and disputes. If you listen to country music, this is the kind of violence that is sometimes celebrated or at least presented sympathetically. Someone's got a grievance and is working it out."

Working it out: I like that understatement.

"Please don't misunderstand me," adds Reed. "I'm not saying that high homicide rates are a good thing. But I am saying that this is an extreme instance of the individualism and self-reliance that used to be American traits, and still are in some parts of the country, including this one."

I ask Reed if Southerners are right to feel ill served by the national media-political colossus.

"If you ask people what their grievances are as Southerners," he explains, "you used to hear complaints about economic conditions and political power—that Southerners never get elected president. These days hardly anybody else does. But people do complain that television and movies look down on Southerners. The thing is, *Deliverance* was written by a Southerner. *Tobacco Road* was written by a Southerner.

"Television representations of Southerners have been either amusing hillbillies or vicious rednecks. The *Gone with the Wind* strain of elegant aristocrats has run out of steam. Not all media designations of Southerners have been unflattering. *Designing Women* put classic Southern social types in a New South Atlanta. And there's a great movie called *Mississippi Masala* (1991) about an East Indian family that runs a motel in the Mississippi Delta. All over the South there are Patels running motels, you know. This is a Romeo and Juliet story with the Indian girl and Denzel Washington falling in love. That's not your father's South."

I ascend toward the peak of high culture. What about the *Dukes of Hazzard*?

"The *Dukes of Hazzard* was set in Georgia, filmed in California, and showed a pan-Southern South that doesn't exist anywhere. One week Bo and Luke are wrestling gators in the Hazzard County swamp, and the next they're running moonshine through the Hazzard County mountains. There's no county in the South that has both alligators and mountains. But that's people's image of the South, so they put it all in one Georgia county and let these two Yankee actors work it out."

Do most blacks in the South think of themselves as Southerners?

"They do now," replies Reed. "If you asked what *Southerner* meant a hundred years ago to most Southerners, it meant an ex-Confederate who stood up for 'Dixie' and venerated Robert E. Lee. That means a lot of people living in the South, including black folks, aren't Southerners. Years ago *Southerner* almost invariably meant a white Southerner. One exception was Booker T. Washington, who made a point of talking about himself as a Southerner."

That changed in the '60s, says Reed. "The University of Michigan does something called a 'feeling thermometer' where they measure how warmly people feel toward politically significant groups. In 1964 blacks in both North and South were much cooler toward Southerners than whites in the same regions. By 1976 there's no difference. Blacks in the South were, if anything, warmer than white Southerners toward 'Southerners.' What happened in those twelve years? The civil rights movement made fundamental changes. White Southerners' image had changed: the most prominent white Southern politician in '64 was George Wallace. In '76 it's Jimmy Carter. The meaning of *Southerner* changed so that by 1976 blacks understood it included them. You get more and more Southern black politicians—Andy Young, Harvey Gantt, Doug Wilder—referring to 'we Southerners.'"

Reed points out that two-thirds of all black officeholders in the country are in the South, and that Mississippi has more than any other state in the union. Devolving political power from Washington to Mississippi would empower—to use the shibboleth of the day—Mississippi's African Americans.

John Shelton Reed is justly proud of the South—an intellectual homeboy, a man who loves his place for reasons of the heart and the head—but he irritated some old friends in the 1990s by calling for the removal of the Confederate flag from public places.

"I've got absolutely no problem with folks that want to fly the flag, put it on their license plates, tattoo it on their foreheads," he says. "They're entitled to under the First Amendment. But when it comes to putting it on the state flag as they did in Georgia and Mississippi and flying it over the statehouse as they did in South Carolina and Alabama, that's a recipe for conflict. The state flag ought to be a symbol of unity, and the Confederate flag does not evoke warm feelings on the part of a substantial fraction of the population."

Not that he's against a Southern flag. Far from it. He has suggested the dancing pig as the perfect emblem of the region.

"Barbecue joints are one of the few places in the South where you get all kinds of people: black and white, bikers and lawyers, Christians and cowboys. All kinds of folks appreciate good smoked pork. So dancing pigs, which you see on barbecue joint signs, would make a great flag."[27]

Look: I realize that a lot of folks just are not going to give the League of the South the benefit of any doubt, especially when the doubt is wrapped in White Citizens Councils and praise of Klan founder Nathan Bedford Forrest. But if moonlight and magnolias are a myth and paternalistic Southern conservatism was blind to the reality and deaf to the aspirations of black Southerners, the canard that all whites in the pre-civil-rights era South were racist serpents or fire-hose-spraying oafs is just as mendacious. Walk a mile in the shoes of William Faulkner, shall we?

In a Halloween 1948 interview with John K. Hutchens in the *New York Herald Tribune*, Faulkner said, "I'd be a Dixiecrat myself if they hadn't hollered 'nigger.' I'm a States' Rights man. Hodding Carter's a good man, and he's right when he says the solution of the Negro problem belongs to the South."[28] He was not counseling benign, or malign, neglect. Faulkner told Russell Howe of *The Reporter* in 1956: "The Negroes are right—make sure you've got that—they're right . . . I've always been on their side, but if there's no middle ground, if people like me have got to choose, then I'm on the side of Mississippi.

"I will go on saying that the Southerners are wrong and that their position is untenable, but if I have to make the same choice Robert E. Lee made then I'll make it. My grandfather had slaves and he must have known that it was wrong, but he fought in one of the first regiments raised by the Confederate Army, not in defense of his ethical position but to protect his native land from being invaded."[29]

Faulkner was a Mississippi patriot with a profound understanding of the historic injustices done black Americans but he was not a self-hater, not a quisling willing to sell out his people for head-pats by the East Coast media. Blacks were right, Faulkner said. But a deliverance from the South's predicament that would come via tanks and writs from Washington was, to him, no deliverance at all. If Mississippi has not the right—and the will—to guarantee equal treatment under the law for each of its citizens then not only the state but the republic is doomed.

In *Harper's* (June 1956), Faulkner laid out the problem: "Now the Constitution guarantees the Negro equal right to equality, and the states' rights which the Mississippi voices are talking about do not exist anymore. We—Mississippi—sold our states' rights back to the Federal Government when we accepted the first cotton price-support subsidy twenty years ago. Our economy is not agricultural any longer. Our economy is the Federal Government. We no longer farm in Mississippi cotton-fields. We farm now in Washington corridors and Congressional committee-rooms."[30]

Mississippi had become a colony. An alms-beggar. The states' rights that it wanted to assert were shadows of a long-gone past.

In Faulkner's *Intruder in the Dust* (1948), Uncle Gavin, defending the wrongly accused black man Lucas Beauchamp against a charge of murder, tells his nephew Chick that black Southerners have as much to fear from virtue-wielding Northerners as from Southern lynch mobs: "I'm defending Sambo from the North and East and West—the outlanders who will fling him decades back not merely into injustice but into grief and agony and violence too by forcing on us laws based on the idea that man's injustice to man can be abolished overnight by police. Sambo will suffer it of course; there are not enough of him yet to do anything else. And he will endure it, absorb it and survive because he is Sambo and has that capacity; he will even beat us there because he has the capacity to endure and survive but he will be thrown back decades and what he survives to may not be worth having because by that time divided we may have lost America."[31]

Faulkner is *not*, I think, saying to the black Southerner: Endure. Turn the other cheek. Offer up your welted back to the lash. Rather, he (or Uncle Gavin speaking for the author in this most didactic of Faulkner novels) is begging Southerners, white *and* black, to make their own peace, their own long-overdue readjustments—else General Sherman rides again. Faulkner loved and respected Lucas Beauchamp; snot-nosed twenty-one-year-olds come down from Princeton to liberate Mississippi from Mississippians he did not.

Why do you think Gram Parsons flew the Confederate flag and wrote his loveliest song ("Hickory Wind") about South Carolina? Why did Levon Helm labor to "make General Robert E. Lee come out with all due respect" in the Band's "The Night They Drove Old Dixie Down"?[32] Why did the New Left Southern Student Organizing Committee choose as its symbol a Confederate flag across which white and black hands are joined? The qualities that individuate Southern small towns are and have been under attack by Washington, Wall Street, and Hollywood for decades now, and to stand up for Southern distinctiveness is to defend diversity against stifling conformity. Harper Lee, whose novel *To Kill a Mockingbird* (1960) is perhaps the best-loved and most-read book ever written about the little towns of the Deep South, told the story of Atticus Finch and Tom Robinson not to damn her people but to commemorate them. Lee spoke of her desire to "chronicle something that seems to be very quickly going down the drain. This is small-town middle-class southern life as opposed to the Gothic, as opposed to *Tobacco Road*, as opposed to plantation life.

"As you know," Lee said, "the South is still made up of thousands of tiny towns. There is a very definite social pattern in these towns that fascinates me. I think it is a rich social pattern. I would simply like to put down all I know about this because I believe that there is something universal in this little world, something decent to be said for it, and something to lament in its passing."[33]

This is the South that no man possessed of a soul would wish to obliterate.

Poet! if on a lasting fame be bent
Thy unperturbing hopes, thou wilt not roam
Too far from thine own happy heart and home;
Cling to the lowly earth, and be content[34]
—HENRY TIMROD

Timrod, Bob Dylan's favorite verse maker, was the poet laureate of the Confederacy, though it must be conceded that the 1860s, as with all war-scarred decades, was literarily thin. (I am partial to John W. DeForest's *Miss Ravenel's Conversion from Secession to Loyalty*, 1867. DeForest coined the phrase *the great American novel* and damned if he didn't make a creditable effort at writing it.)

The contemporary Southern secessionists have their own literary men, one of whom is the best friend the letter *u* has had in many an American year. He is James Everett Kibler, professor of English at the University of Georgia, novelist, agrarian, and spelling reformer—or, rather, restorationist. Kibler has been the primary advocate within the LOS of rejecting the Yankee Noah Webster's orthography and using British spellings such as *honour* and *organise*. This gives LOS documents a studiedly quaint feel, fusty and bachelorish. Kibler, however, asserts his position with great vigor, saying, "*Webster's* codifies and standardises our spelling and removes the colourful ingenuity and personality of alternative regional ways. We can see the white-ruffled, black-garbed, long, grey-faced Puritan with cane of punishment over the heads of so many Southern children labouring over their spellers."[35] How can you have any pudding if you won't have your meat?

Kibler is a Southern romantic in whose fiction honor—excuse me, honour—is extolled, mammon derided, and progress doubted.

"It has long been a fact," he writes in *Child to the Waters* (2003), "that gold in the sun is far brighter than gold in the tomb of a bank's vaulted dark cells, and that stars seen of a winter cold night through bare limbs of the roof tree of home are far brighter than stars on a chart on a digital screen, or the silver of thirty strewn coins, thrown in the pitch-black of night."[36]

Our Fathers' Fields (1998), which was awarded the Fellowship of Southern Writers Award for Non-Fiction, is Kibler's loving and meticulously documented history of the Hardy plantation, the ruined manor he began restoring in 1989 in his native South Carolina county (though the Hardys were not his kin).

He writes of its trees, fauna, flora, soil, and people, both black and white; its garden, its architecture, and the stories embedded in its ledgers and letters. In 1850 the Hardys had forty-six slaves living in ten slave houses, and the best and most controversial chapter of the book, drawing heavily upon WPA oral histories with ex-slaves of the area (but not the Hardy plantation) conducted 1936–38, is about the lives the slaves lived.

"In actual practice," writes Kibler, "slavery was not a monolithic institution," for "it differed from region to region, community to community, and crop to crop."[37] Eugene Genovese told us this in his classic *Roll, Jordan, Roll: The World the Slaves Made* (1974), and it ought to be as apparent as the fact that Ukrainian Catholics differ from Kenyan Catholics, or that Icelandic secondary schools are not identical to those in Bolivia. (Genovese, the great Marxist historian of the American South, also remarked, in defense of Southern pride, that no one should be forced to spit on his ancestors' graves.)

Kibler's slaves work the fields, hunt, fish, and live in a complex interconnected community. But that community has one enormous and, to many readers, including this one, soul-sullying flaw—manowning. Kibler, though, neither apologizes for slavery nor condemns everything it touches. It is in the very warp and weft of the societal fabric. He never goes quite so far as an earlier Southern litterateur, Andrew Lytle, who in his biography of Nathan Bedford Forrest wrote, "The slave understood his relationship, that he owned the master as much as the master owned him."[38] But, like Lytle, Kibler rejects the Manichaean historiography that would assign to the North the role of goodness and to the South the basest evil. In Lytle's view, Lincoln's canny Secretary of State William Seward exploited the slave issue not out of moral indignation but "for strategic reasons. Nobody knew better than he that it was the conflict between a people living almost entirely on the land and a people loyal to a commercial and fast-growing industrialism which demanded that the duty of the citizen must be not life, liberty, and the pursuit of happiness but a willing consumption of the produce of Northern manufacture."[39]

Speaking up for my neighbor down Route 5, this is unfair to Seward, who was genuinely affronted by a system in which men owned other men, and had the legal right to sell them and their families in the marketplace, a fact that never loses its capacity to appall. Seward was an expansionist, alas, whose roving eye coveted land with frightening avidity, but there isn't a pencil sharp enough to write slavery out of the central role in the crisis of 1860–61. There just isn't. The primary cause of the war was slavery. On the great moral question of the day—slavery, not war or secession—Lincoln was right.

Which is not to deny Andrew Lytle the brilliant and humane insights that marked his work. He was one of the few contributors to the landmark Southern agrarian manifesto *I'll Take My Stand* (1930) who stayed loyal to the South by living in the South.

I like, and I believe Lytle would have liked, the inscription on H. P. Lovecraft's headstone: I AM PROVIDENCE. August Derleth, the eldritch Wisconsin regionalist, quoted Lovecraft in his memoir *Walden West* (1961): "A man belongs where he has roots—where the landscape and milieu have some relation to his thoughts and feelings, by virtue of having formed them. A real civilization recognizes this fact—and the circumstance that America is beginning to forget it, does far more than does the mere matter of commonplace thought and bourgeois inhibitions to convince me that the general American fabric is becoming less and less a true civilization and more and more a vast, mechanical, and emotionally immature barbarism de luxe . . . I cannot think of any individual as existing except as part of a pattern—and the pattern's most visible and tangible areas are of course the individual's immediate environment; the soil and culture-stream from which he springs, and the milieu of ideas, impressions, traditions, landscapes, and architecture, through which he must necessarily peer in order to reach the 'outside.'"[40]

You can't get much Yankier than Lovecraft, but his truth applies equally to a South resisting not so much Yankee-fication as the steamroller of homogenization.

∽§∽

So who and what is the League of the South?

The league is not legion—it has a few thousand members at most, although its Web site gets about twenty thousand visitors each month. Scattered public opinion polls indicate that its stance for Southern independence has some support: For instance, an April 2009 Daily Kos/Research 2000 poll found that 18 percent of Georgians (and 32 percent of Georgia Republicans) surveyed would approve "of Georgia leaving the United States."[41] So the league is an outlier, but not a pariah. It represents a distinct, but not negligible, minority of Southerners.

"We're not radical, fringe nuts," protests Donnie Kennedy. "This is an American idea."[42] Yes, and I give them points for Americanness for their consistent loathing of the homicidal imperialism of the Bush-Cheney administration. (They are no kinder to Obama, who has far fewer kills to his credit, though give him time.) The League of the South reviles the GOP—the party, it never forgets, of Lincoln. Michael Hill scorns "the professional 'conservative Christian' leaders—the Pledge-of-Allegiance, hypernationalistic, God-Bless-America, Old-Glory-Waving, John-Ashcroft-loving, let's-bomb-the-bastards-back-into-the-stone-age, neocon-enabling superpatriots."[43]

"We are not conservatives," says Franklin Sanders, for conservatives haven't conserved a damn thing in the last half century. Today's conservatives are castrato cheerleaders for war and empire. Sanders instances the conservative abandonment of the principle of habeas corpus, "the most sacred right of an Englishman and American not to be arrested and held on the whim of tyrants," which post-9/11 Republicans would sacrifice to the Moloch of the War on Terror, whose appetite for our liberties never will be sated.

"We are not libertarians," adds Sanders, lest his defense of personal liberties give you the wrong impression. In Sanders's view, liberty is subject to limits imposed by "the law of God." And His interpreters do get some queer notions now and then.

"We are not the White Folks Liberation front," says Sanders. "We are not the Klan with college degrees." Racial harmony is consistent with—is enjoined by—the teachings of Jesus, no matter what the segregationist ministers of the '50s might have said.

Finally, "We are not constitutionalists," Sanders announces, because that document has failed to stem the tide of tyranny.

What they are, declares Sanders, is Southerners, by God's grace. And "We want out. We want our own nation. We want a new nation, a nation obedient to God. We want liberty, not license. We want our own nation, because we are our own people."[44]

Sanders emphasizes relocalizing the economy. Trading with one's neighbors, patronizing local farmers and businesses, strengthening the humane as opposed to the corporate economy: The Small Is Beautiful song of the greens can be sung in Southern, too. "Economically," reads a LOS statement, "we encourage Southern self-sufficiency, debtlessness, and the purchase of Southern goods and services. We must keep our capital at home."[45]

"Georgia First!" was the slogan of Ray McBerry, a part-Cherokee independent television producer and chairman of the Peach State's chapter of the League of the South, who ran for governor in the Republican primaries of 2006 and 2010. He appealed to state pride and the sense that Georgia was somehow becoming less Georgian. Who, after all, wants to be just another gob in the homogeneous lump of states? McBerry criticized "folks that are not native to Georgia that have chosen to take up residence in Georgia. Many of them have congregated in downtown Atlanta and have a very different set of values than what most of us have that are native Georgians."[46] You may choose to read this as a suspicious parochialism; I do not know McBerry, but I take that as a tenacious defense of the integrity of his place. The rootless cosmopolitans of Atlanta are of a piece with the fadsters and hucksters of the New South who crave the acceptance of non-Southern elites (and the profits they expect to follow that acceptance). They are the people responsible for the atrociously bloodless Atlanta Summer Olympics of 1996, which purged the South from Atlanta's Olympic image. You can read their handiwork in the pathetic anti-localist marketing campaign of North Carolina's biggest city, which blazons the most appallingly "We're not really Southern!" New South slogan I have ever seen: "Charlotte USA."

"North Carolina," it seems, is so redolent of hickdom that it embarrasses the sub-Babbitts of Charlotte's shovel-ready-for-the-global-economy-in-this-shrinking-world class. So NC is gone, ostensibly because Charlotte is no mere city but is instead a sixteen-county two-state blob that absorbs all the little communities within devouring distance, chewing them up into one masticated bolus flavorless enough to be swallowed by savvy global investors put off by states with directional adjectives in their names.

I say "sub-Babbitts" because the fictional George F. Babbitt loved his hometown, just as novelist Sinclair Lewis loved the character he had created, Babbitt, and his home state of Minnesota, whose eighty-seven counties and county seats Lewis memorized. The image-makers who erased North Carolina from Charlotte's identity quite obviously are ashamed of the Tar Heel State. Sure, North Carolina gave us Willie Jones, Michael Jordan, Thomas Wolfe, Fred Chappell, and dancing-pig barbe-cue shacks, but there's that embarrassing Gomer and Goober thing, and besides, what do states matter when all are bathed equally in the bathetic "God Bless the USA"? Richard Weaver of Weaverville, North Carolina (*not* Weaverville, USA), said in the 1950s that "the relative incapacity for business of the Southerner has cost him sadly in this acquisitive world," but them old times sure are forgotten.[47]

Men who dismiss their places are unfit to be citizens of anything but TV Nation. From the comfort of my front porch in the Burned-Over District of New York, I hereby suggest that my patriotic kinsmen in North Carolina—our two states were among the Anti-Federalist strongholds in 1788—beautify (or un-deface) the ubiquitous "Charlotte USA" banners by putting the NC back where it belongs.

The Charlotte slogan does have the virtue of frankness. The states have become administrative units of the empire, political nullities that meekly obey diktats from Washington and wouldn't know the Tenth Amendment if its cremation smoke snaked upward from a medical marijuana pipe.

But let us look on the bright side. Perhaps the financial collapse will refresh our maps. After all, the Great Depression was the last time regional-ism was a really potent force in American cultural, though not political, life.

State pride ought to be based in culture rather than politics anyway. Like anything good, it begins at home. In small acts. In laughter rather than bombast. In whimsy, not rage. Even in dreams.

When our daughter was young we had great fun exaggerating the differences between states. (Maybe truth-stretching leaves behind a fuller truth?) We told her that Pennsylvanians subsisted on a diet of pretzels and spoke in an indecipherable Keystone language, so as we passed over the border into Lawrenceville we would shout loudly from our opened car windows, stressing each syllable, "We are from New York. Can you un-der-stand us?"

Each state we would endow with unusual properties and bizarre customs. We once saw a van driver with Michigan plates picking his nose so that became, and has remained, the "Michigan hello." Vermont is the tie-dye state, and Maine was embodied by our friends Carolyn and Michael Chute: wise country people with guns and dogs, homegrown radicals of the forest.

"Love the state, and let the nation save itself," said Senator Silas Wright, the New York Jacksonian.[48] How can one love the United States if one does not first love a single state? Can one love the sum and be indifferent to its factors? If the states are blandly indistinguishable morsels, then what good is the union?

Ahem . . . as I was saying when Georgia was on my mind: Ray McBerry promised to "govern based upon the Christian principles embodied in the Bible." He was pro-life, pro-gun-rights, pro-privacy, and he said that "good Christian Georgians have more in common with each other, no matter the race, than either of us have with outsiders who wish to destroy our valuable way of life."[49] McBerry picked up about 12 percent of the vote in 2006; as this book went to press he was looking to improve upon that showing in 2010, although a "states' rights Republican," as he styled himself, is something of an oxymoron in an age when the national GOP is devoted to militarism, empire, and the surveillance state and, with a few isolated libertarian exceptions, scorns such petty concerns as personal liberty and cultural diversity. A campaign professing loyalty to Georgia above loyalty to the United States may be quaint, anachronistic, or prophetic—but not, we may be sure, winning. At least not yet.

Novelist James Kibler stresses the South's distinctiveness in everything from music to gardening to architecture to cooking. Southern nationhood, or at least the radical devolution of political power, has an "inevitability" about it, he argues, pointing to the "growth of secession movements around the world" as evidence of the league's foresightedness. "I expect the League is about as up-to-date and current (even prophetic) an organisation as you might have encountered in the last 15 years," he tells me. For the lesson of the early twenty-first century is that "empires are simply not life affirming and sustainable." A self-governing South would be sustainable and even liberating, he says, and based on a "live and let live" philosophy.[50]

Live and let live? The South? Why, that runs counter to every Stanley Kramer movie I've ever seen. Hollywood wouldn't lie about such things, would it?

Well, yes—and no. For there are League of the South activists who wade in cesspools. When a member kindly gave me a few LOS names to check out, one or two, I found, had trafficked regularly with some pretty cankerous sores on the body politic. Their anti-black spume ought not to be taken as representative of the group or its cause. But it's there—and as long as it is, many Southerners who feel a rightful pride in their cultural heritage will shy from the League of the South.

Just what a Southern nation might look like is delineated in *The Grey Book: Blueprint for Southern Independence* (2004), which posits that the United States is "beyond reform" and that a Southern nation, its Constitution blending the best of the US and Confederate Constitutions, waits to be born.[51]

(The Confederate Constitution, modeled upon the charter of 1787 that it proposed to supplant, often borrowing from it verbatim, both improved upon the original—as for instance in having no general-welfare clause and a one-term presidency—and was also in some respects inferior: The one-term president served an elongated six-year term and possessed an imperial line-item veto. Of course it countenanced slavery, though not the importation of slaves, for all eternity.)

The Southern Republic contemplated by *The Grey Book*, consisting of the eleven states of the erstwhile CSA, would have a population of eighty million, making it one of the twenty largest countries in the world. (Add in the border states, says Franklin Sanders, and the South would be the twelfth most populous country, just behind Mexico and ahead of the Philippines.) Its GDP would make it the third richest, behind only the United States and Japan.

This new Southern Republic, according to *The Grey Book*, would be based on "private property, free association, fair trade, sound money, low taxes, equal justice before the law, secure borders, and armed and vigilant neutrality."[52] This is conservative-populist boilerplate, offensive only to a painfully sensitive soul that has been marinated in decades of political correctness. "Free association" does mean the repeal—or rather, the non-enactment—of civil rights legislation pertaining to private property, but this cuts both ways: Black-owned businesses would be entitled to the exact same protections as white-owned. And really, now, are there all that many Lester Maddoxes out there itching to chase African American patrons from their stores with axes? *The Grey Book*'s collective authors assert that reform is impossible: Federal judges tyrannize the states, third parties are kept off the ballot by onerous laws, and the country has grown so large that real representation no longer exists at the national level. The War on Terror has tightened the vise: "The USA PATRIOT Act and the Department of Homeland Security have undermined the Bill of Rights in the name of national security and provide the blueprint for a police state in the US."[53] Peruse the Democratic Party platform on civil liberties for a statement one-tenth as forthright.

Remarking that "the business of government is to mind its own business and keep its nose out of the citizens' business," the league calls for the repeal of corporate subsidies, crony capitalism, gun control, and extensive absentee ownership of land. And yes—the league "insists on the legitimacy of the right of secession," although its Web site states "we realise that secession is not a practicable alternative at present."[54] Its practicability, asserts the league, will be realized when the corruption and unreformability of the current system are too obvious to ignore.

Law enforcement would be locally centered—excuse, me, centred—around the office of the sheriff. National paramilitary organizations—the FBI, BATF, and the like—would not be replicated. The Southern Republic of *The Grey Book* would pursue alternatives to prison for nonviolent offenders; judges would be elected for finite terms, not appointed for life. Significant transfers of land would be made to Indian tribes in the South, who would be self-governing and not subject to a Bureau of Indian Affairs.

Does this sound like a restoration of the Bourbon South, or a pitchfork party for Kleagles? Hell, I agree with most of the above, and I've voted twice for Jesse Jackson and twice for Ralph Nader in presidential elections. Yet the South, if not its intellectuals, has also been the most hawkish section of the country in all of America's wars since 1898. Had we listened to New England, we'd have had no Spanish-American War; if the Midwest had a voice commensurate with its population, we'd have stayed out of the Second World War. And if the Pacific Northwest predominated in councils of war and peace today, Americans and Iraqis would not be killing each other. So the South has some 'splainin to do.

Moreover, as frustrated liberals have noted, the South has become something of a welfare dependent, mooching tax dollars from the rest of the country. Thomas Fleming, a friend of Dixie, says that "the states of the Old Confederacy are too busy collecting their share of federal funds to worry too much about their rights."[55]

Writing in *The Southern Partisan*, William Cawthon of Eufaula, Alabama, a founding member of the league, broke down congressional votes by section and found that Southerners, had they been the only members of Congress, would have banned abortion, restricted immigration, permitted school prayer, and kept the Panama Canal.[56] Some of that you might like and some you might not like, but what is most troubling is that the South would have given George W. Bush the keys to the White House via landslide victories—reason enough, I expect, for the rest of us, Garrison-like, to expel the South. Begone, you mongers of war!

Is the South to be bleached out of existence, its hollers and hamlets as devoid of personality as Orlando? Clyde Wilson thinks not. Yes, "many parts of the South have received vast Yankee and foreign immigration in recent years. The Carolinas are demographically starting to resemble Florida—a haven for rich Yankees and a fast-growing Hispanic population. The South has always been able to absorb newcomers and make them its own, because the South, unlike 'America,' is a real thing. Every Northerner and foreigner who had lived in the South for any length of time before The War was a loyal Confederate. The question [today] is whether the amount of immigration is too great to be civilised [when in Rome, Georgia . . . I defer to Clyde's Southron orthography] and absorbed. That is one of the reasons that we need to get control of our own fate. I am not afraid that the South will disappear because I have seen too many earnest and talented young people who still identify themselves with it. What I fear is that the whole of this American enterprise is sinking into a decadent consolidated empire in which there is no possibility of reform, where no part of the people will ever be able to reassert self-government."

I bring up race—again—which, when writing about the South, no one ever seems to be able to let down.

"White and black Southerners are both Christian and have good manners and do not relate to people as abstract classes, unlike Yankees," says Clyde, who, post-comma, commits the very sin he decries. No matter. I let it slide.

The dangers to racial harmony are two, says Wilson: first, Hispanic immigration, which introduces into the South an ethnic group without roots in the region; and second, "the great Northern in-migration bringing in Northern attitudes and behaviour—proclaiming brotherhood while fleeing to the suburbs."

Southern secession, adds Wilson, is "anathema to white supremacists," who are nationalists nursing their "imaginary 'white nationalism'"—a hateful brew for which Wilson has contempt.

I ask Clyde if the feds would be any more lenient toward a breakaway South today than in 1861.

"The feds would nuke South Carolina but they will not nuke Vermont," says Clyde, and at that one I have to demur. Cynical as I am, I still cannot believe that the US government would drop bombs from the sky on an American state. Yet I also suspect that Vermont, should she break free of Uncle Sam's chokehold, would not be permitted to skip daintily away. Some casus belli would be invented: Thomas Naylor would be accused of manufacturing methamphetamine in his basement, or the Second Vermont Republic would be run through the media blackwash and come out the other side a grizzled band of Mormon polygamists who marry girls on the shy side of menses. *Something—anything—*to whip up the requisite hatred of the outcast.

Clyde sticks to his sectional guns, however: "There is great precedent for invading the South and coercing Southerners. Racism would be alleged, and the politicians, media, and public would bathe themselves in righteousness in suppressing us."

I like and respect Clyde Wilson. He has brains and he has guts and he is loyal to his people. He lays on the anti-Yankeeism too thickly for my taste, never missing an opportunity to make his point that the South is the region of tolerance, the North of fanatical intolerance. ("It was the Yankees who burned down convents," he says, tweaking me that "Growing up as a Southern Methodist, the only anti-Catholic remarks I ever heard were from a visiting preacher from your neck of the woods.")[57]

We are, North and South—the real North and South, that is, not Myrtle Beach and the *Today* show—separate peoples, speakers of different languages. We might shake hands and enjoy drink and conversation late into the night, but when we wake we are no less separate. And so in June 2008, Thomas Naylor, concluding that the League of the South would never be rid of the taint of suspected racism, sent from Vermont a memo to the league's "foremost strategic thinkers" urging them to give up the gray ghost and pursue Southern independence under other auspices.

"First and foremost, the League is simply carrying too much racial baggage from the past," wrote Naylor. "For whatever reason, there is the widespread perception that the LOS is a racist organization. I don't believe there is anything you can do to turn this around short of dissolution."

Naylor had other criticisms—the LOS is unfocused, it lacks media savvy, it has no viable secession strategy—but the seemingly inexpungable stain of racism was his gravamen. He encouraged the league to fold its most "important strategic resources"—the Franklin Sanders–edited *Free Magnolia* newspaper and North Carolinian Mike Tuggle's greenish "Agenda for Bioregional Economies"—into Thomas Moore's Southern National Congress, an explicitly biracial—at least in profession, if not membership—convention of Southerners and members of the Southern diaspora tasked with considering What Is to Be Done?[58]

Naylor followed this up with an open letter calling upon the league to discard "the albatross of racism" through a series of steps including an "unconditional denunciation of all forms of racism," the recruitment of black members and speakers, and a de-emphasis on the Civil War.[59] The Southerners were unmoved.

"The New England secessionists," Clyde Wilson told me, "have treated us as suspected 'racists.' Typically, with their 1 percent black population and their supposed desire for devolution, they still feel entitled to correct and control our race relations in South Carolina with its 40 percent black population."[60] Or as Thomas Fleming cracked in another context, "New England never felt comfortable in a union with slaveowners, cowboys, or students at Big 10 universities."[61]

Thomas Moore, whose Southern National Congress Naylor viewed as the league's promising successor, disavowed any such ambition while making clear his respect for the Vermonter. The Southern National Congress "is much more narrowly focused" than the LOS, says Moore, a league member himself.[62]

Moore, a former Republican Party operative, organized the Southern National Congress upon the proposition that "Southerners are a separate and distinct people, rooted in kinship and soil, and with a common culture and history—in other words, a *nation*."[63] Moore's Southern political inspirations are Patrick Henry, Thomas Jefferson, and John C. Calhoun; the models for the SNC, which he says is based on "non-violent resistance—refusal, civil disobedience, and non-cooperation," are "Mohandas Gandhi, [Sinn Fein founder and Irish patriot] Arthur Griffith, and Martin Luther King."[64] (Michael Hill also instances Sinn Fein as a model, particularly for the way it "developed and nurtured its own parallel institutions to which Irishmen could attach their loyalties.")[65]

When I spoke with him in July 2008, Moore expressed the hope that perhaps 120 to 130 delegates might attend the First Southern National Congress in Hendersonville, North Carolina, in December of that year. In fact, somewhere around a hundred showed up at this first in what are to be annual meetings that will provide, says Moore, "the rationale and impetus for Southerners to withdraw their consent from the Empire." Representing fourteen states—as in the Continental Congress and the Congress under the Articles of Confederation, each state voted as a single unit—the delegates were there, in Moore's words, "to withdraw their consent from this corrupt and criminal Regime" and to create an alternative institution to which they could "transfer our allegiance."[66] The SNC is intended as a kind of shadow Congress of that Southern nation which Moore and Hill and Wilson hope or dream is aborning.

Voting delegates had to be at least eighteen and resident in one of the states of the Confederacy or Kentucky or Missouri, though when a delegation from Maryland showed up the SNC welcomed its members, too. Delegates took this oath: "I believe that I have a duty to my home State. I believe that the Southern people are a distinct people. I believe in the right of voice, the right of preservation, and the right of recognition, for the South and her people." The SNC did not endorse secession—yet. Moore thinks such a move is premature, even presumptuous, given the embryonic nature of the Congress. It must first prove its legitimacy. The inaugural Southern National Congress passed a series of "Remonstrances and Petitions for the Redress of Grievances"—that is, petitions to the federal government requesting it to stop undertaking unnecessary and unconstitutional wars, halt mass immigration, end agribusiness subsidies and policies that discourage small-scale farming, abolish the Federal Reserve and corporate personhood, transfer from Washington to the Southern States control over Southern natural resources, and repeal federal gun-control laws. Washington's response was . . . well, it did not respond. Though I suspect the delegates from the FBI and the Department of Homeland Security sent back subliterate reports on the proceedings.

A second plenary session, held at Cheaha State Park near Anniston, Alabama, in September 2009, produced a "Southern National Covenant" decrying "a godless national culture and a corrupt, despotic federal government that knows no limits to power." The 109 delegates also approved a resolution calling on Southern sheriffs and state and local police not to cooperate with the feds in the event that a "national emergency" licenses Big Brother to disarm citizens, conduct warrantless searches, impose martial law, and otherwise crack down on personal liberties.[67]

The Congress, Moore asserts, "is not play-acting" nor a "comic-opera Confederacy." He spurned "people deluded by a vision of reliving a romantic Southern past." Of what Wendell Berry called "the hidden wound" Moore said: "We seek Delegates with a magnanimous spirit of Christian charity toward all others, including our black brothers and sisters. Black people are a part of the South, have been, and always will be. Black Southerners have contributed immeasurably to the building of our country. Black and white Southerners share a common culture, including a religious faith, sense of manners, and attitudes toward many aspects of life that are part of our distinctiveness. Black Southerners who wish to be Delegates are welcome. If you are unable or unwilling to accept this, or if you nourish a spirit of animosity toward black Southerners, then we invite you not to apply."[68]

It would be hard to find a more forthright repudiation of racists. A Southern Republic that didn't have black Southerners at its heart and soul wouldn't be worth a Confederate shinplaster. "If all we get are white middle-class men I'll be disappointed," Moore told me three weeks before the first congress.[69] He was disappointed. He had expected at least two African Americans; neither showed. It's a long, long road. Kirk Sale, newly resident in South Carolina, told me that he was going to raise the subject of the monochromatic nature of the congress but he "felt like too much of a carpetbagger to do it."[70]

Unlike the league, which views outreach to blacks as affirmative action or pandering, Moore seems determined to extend the hand of brotherhood. "Blacks are part of [the Southern] nation," he says. "We need to show them that we have their interests at heart as well as our own. We need to show them our desire to protect our freedom and our prosperity is not aimed at them, and that it will benefit them as well as Southern whites.

"Some may be suspicious at first," he continues, "but many will listen if we reach out. Of course, the last thing the Enemy wants is for us to 'come reason together.' And this is why we serve the Enemy's cause when we resort to hostility and contempt. In addition to which, it's morally wrong. If we Southerners are truly the Christians we claim to be, then we have a duty to love our black brothers and sisters as we love ourselves."[71]

Moore is an interesting example of the way that many of the keener minds on the right were radicalized by the disaster of Bush-Cheney Republicanism. A Goldwater youth, an activist in his native South Carolina Republican Party, Moore served as a Reagan political appointee in the Department of Defense. He was director of national security studies for the Reaganite Heritage Foundation, which never met a military expenditure or unconstitutional war that it didn't like. And then . . . something happened. Appalled by the Iraq War, Moore walked away. "The neoconservatives are neofascists," he says flatly, who are building a "fascist empire" and police state. Rejecting the Republican Party and the conservative machine, he took his stand with the South.

I ask Moore how the drones back at Heritage took the news. "The last time I saw [longtime Heritage president] Ed Feulner," Moore laughs, "he shook his head, more in pity than anything else, and said it was sad how I had marginalized myself."

To which Moore replied, "In times like these, the margin is the honorable place to be."[72]

I am quite sure that Feulner had no idea what he was talking about. What would such a man know of honor?

Tom Moore thinks we may be approaching the breaking point. Our system "is irredeemably broken," he said in summer 2009, and "can't be fixed because it's fallen totally into the hands of the big corporations and money power." We are headed, he says, for "a crisis . . . unlike any the modern world has seen—a perfect storm of economic meltdown and social and political collapse, darkened by the growing power of a demonic tyranny."[73] Time is running out for the South to skip out of the prison and into the light.

The South may never rise again. If it does, it will have to be suffused, like the old Southern Student Organizing Committee flag of the radical '60s, with biracial harmony. Black and white together, brothers and sisters of the heart. A flailing American empire that relies on Southern boys as its cannon fodder sure isn't going to let the region go without—well, you know.

But give Clyde Wilson the last word: "Southerners are used to bad odds."[74]

CHAPTER EIGHT

Made in Vermont

While many seek the truth by scanning galaxies through powerful telescopes, my eyes have been glued to a microscope—looking down, not up, inward, not outward. America has often seemed transfixed by big. I am captivated by small.[1]

—FRANK BRYAN

*W*e have come back, time and again, to Vermont, our virid little inspiration, the state that is not island or peninsula or archipelago or Francophone or Polynesian and yet it breathes independence like no other of its forty-nine sisters. We will speak more of the Second Vermont Republic, but just as William Carlos Williams said there are no ideas but in things, I believe that there are no ideas but in people, and who better to introduce us to Vermont than its native-son avatar and intellectual and my candidate for its first president?

Frank Bryan is that rare political scientist who can begin one statistics-dappled tome by describing his wife as "the sexiest wench in the galaxy" and enliven another with footnotes recounting his first gun, cows he has milked, getting beat up in a dance hall over a girl, and the abandoned farms of his Vermont boyhood: "The only trace of the old McEachearn place is in a faraway corner of my heart."[2]

He once ran afoul of the town ordinances of Starksboro, where he lives in a converted deer camp on Big Hollow Road, by having twenty junker Chevettes in his yard. (As a communitarian, not a libertarian, he disposed of these parts-cars with only moderate grumbling.) Bryan is a legend-ary character at the University of Vermont, where he teaches political science: He is the horny-handed son of toil who does regression analysis, the regular-guy intellectual who prefers the company of "working-class people . . . the old Vermonters."[3] The irrepressible Bryan made a major contribution to his field (and his country, which is Vermont) with *Real Democracy* (2004), his magnum opus, the most searching and sympathetic book ever written about the town-meeting democracy of New England. The book is a veritable four-leaf clover of academia: a witty work of political science written from a defiantly rural populist point of view. If we are going to conclude this book with a look at the Second Vermont Republic, the sophisticated, down-home, and generously localist secessionist band in the Green Mountain State, we need first to meet the archetypal—the exemplary—Vermonter.

I met Frank Bryan over breakfast at the Oasis Diner on Bank Street, the working-class Democratic eatery in downtown Burlington that for fifty-plus years, until its sale in 2007, was owned and operated by the Lines family, making it an oasis of family ownership in the desert of Applebee's and Olive Gardens.

Former governor Howard Dean may be the best-known living political Vermonter, but Dean, Bryan notes, is a cosmopolitan flatlander who was "raised in an environment as completely estranged from town meetings as one can imagine."[4] Although Dean has displayed spasmodic heterodoxy, notably in his 2004 presidential campaign, he does not embody the "curious mixture of radicalism, populism, and conservatism" that Bryan says has defined Vermont politics since the days when Anti-Masonry and abolition were in vogue.[5] If the Green Mountains had a face, it would be Frank Bryan. He is the real Vermont, the enduring Vermont, not the picture postcard, not the *New York Times* reader in her air-conditioned summer home, but the Vermont of Robert Frost (a Grover Cleveland Democrat who placed his faith in "insubordinate Americans") and craggily iconic Republican senator George Aiken, who explained that "some folks just naturally love the mountains, and like to live up among them where freedom of thought and action is logical and inherent."[6]

"My mother raised me a Democrat. Vermont raised me a democrat. This book springs from a life of fighting the dissonance between the two," writes Bryan in *Real Democracy*.[7] Son of a single mom who worked in the mills, Bryan has that "redneck's chip on my shoulder" essential to a healthy, authentic populism.[8] His Class of '59 at Newbury High totaled seven, which led to his politics: "Keep it small. The basketball isn't good, but everybody gets to play," as he told the *Vermont Quarterly*.[9]

After graduation, "I went off to school and heard about how poor and destitute and dumb people like me were because of the size of my community." One summer he hiked Mount Moosilauke with his brother, who was studying for the priesthood. "I went up that mountain a Kennedy Democrat and came down a Goldwater conservative because my brother convinced me that the Democrats were going to destroy the small towns; they didn't care about small farms or town meeting."[10]

Bryan has since shed his illusions about the commitment of Republicans to any small-town value not reducible to the bottom line on an annual corporate report. The modern GOP is the party of war and Walmart (four of which deface Vermont, the last state to have been infected by the Arkansas Plague). Bryan now calls himself a "decentralist communitarian" whose heart "is with the small is beautiful crowd."[11] Yet he is no dewy-eyed idealizer of The People: "Jefferson said rural people are the chosen people of God—that's a bunch of crap. But forced intimacy is good for society; it makes us tolerant. The reason I'll stop and help you out of a snowbank on Big Hollow Road isn't because I particularly like you. But I might see you tomorrow at the store and have to explain why I didn't. And I expect reciprocity."[12]

Washington–New York conservatives despise Vermont for its "liberalism," though I cannot see how Bernie Sanders is any more destructive of American liberties than, say, Rudy Giuliani. Or perhaps they hate Frank Bryan's state because, lacking any sense of place or local loyalties themselves, they fear communities organized on a human scale. Burlington, Vermont's largest city, has fewer than forty thousand residents, and the state leads the nation in the percentage of its population living in towns of under twenty-five hundred.

Frank Bryan calls himself a "Vermont patriot."[13] One recalls G. K. Chesterton's dictum that a patriot boasts never of the largeness of his country but rather of its littleness. As Bryan and John McClaughry wrote in *The Vermont Papers* (1989), their blueprint for a devolutionary overhaul of state government: "Vermont matters most because it is small, not in spite of it."[14]

୶

The proposals that Vermont secede from the United States and Kingdom County secede from Vermont were moved and passed, as they had been annually since 1791, when the Green Mountain State first joined the Union. These were the only two measures the people of Lost Nation ever agreed upon unanimously.[15]

—HOWARD FRANK MOSHER, *Northern Borders* (1994)

Mosher, Bryan's favorite Vermont novelist, depicts town meeting as a blend of cussedness and community, radicalism and renewal. Elsewhere Mosher has written of Northern Vermont as being "full of fiercely antiauthoritarian, independent-minded individualists" for whom "independence, rooted in local land ownership and local government, seems to have remained the chief objective."[16] *Ecce* Frank Bryan.

Bryan views town meeting as the palladium of this independence. His research into its workings and meaning has been his "life's work," says Harvard's Jane Mansbridge. *Real Democracy* is the result.[17]

Every March since 1969, Professor Bryan has sent his students at St. Michael's College and later the University of Vermont to the school gyms, auditoriums, church cellars, and fire stations of the 236 Vermont towns holding annual meetings at which the citizens present—about 20 percent of a town's population, on average—vote on budgets, elect officials, levy taxes, and otherwise decide whichever governmental business has not been usurped by the central authorities in Montpelier and Washington, DC.

Bryan's sample is enormous: almost fifteen hundred town meetings "encompassing 238,603 acts of participation by 63,140 citizens in 210 towns."[18] This mountain of data is vast and unique, for as Bryan notes incredulously, "No article on town meeting has ever been published in a major political science journal. Never . . . We know much more about the Greek democracy of twenty-five hundred years ago than we do about real democracy in America today."[19]

Why the neglect and nescience among political scientists?

"They don't trust common people," he says of his confreres. "They were trained by professors who were trained by people who were terrified by fascism and the 'tyranny of the majority.'"[20]

Transient suburbanites and hypermobile city dwellers fear nothing so much as the unlettered rural man with a voice and a meaningful vote. They cannot see that the diffusion of power inherent in town meeting is the best defense against tyranny. Bryan quotes Goldwater speechwriter turned Wobbly Karl Hess, who "once said that Adolf Hitler as chancellor of Germany is a horror; Adolf Hitler at a town meeting would be an asshole."[21]

Yes, localized direct democracy is majoritarian, but the citizen unhappy with a law may appeal to her neighbors, who are often kin or lifelong friends. At the national level, however, she is just a single vote in a mass of anonymous millions—not even a brick in the wall. A Vermonter who dislikes his town's junk-car ordinance can remonstrate with his landsmen; a Vermonter who dislikes the Wall Street bailout or the Iraq War can shut up or get drunk, but he can't get within a Free Speech Zone of Barack Obama.

Bryan's central finding is that "real democracy works better in small places—dramatically better." The smaller the town, the higher the percentage of citizens who participate in town meeting. The only other variable with any potency is the presence of controversial items on the agenda. If town meeting is waning, as pulseless technocrats often claim, it is because "Vermont towns have steadily been losing the authority to deal with controversial issues."[22] Voting up or down on the purchase of a snowplow is fine, but for grassroots democracy to thrive we must restore to small places control over education, welfare, and economic regulation.

"Issues are absolutely essential," Bryan stresses. "Liberals think you go to town meeting because you have a civic duty. There's some of that, but no one is damn fool enough to give up a spring day [for that]. But if their kids' education is up for grabs, they'll damn well be there."

Bryan sums up the key to successful direct democracy: "Keep jurisdictions small and give them real things to do."[23]

❦

And where do I live by preference, when I am not teaching? Vermont. Why? Because it is, in most of the ways of freedom and space, more like the West I grew up in than most of the Contemporary West is.[24]

—WALLACE STEGNER, 1971

Since the 1930s Vermont has attracted rusticating intellectuals who "bought abandoned farms and stayed from last frost to first," Bryan jokes.[25] Vermont doughtily gave landslide-loser Alf Landon three of his eight electoral votes in the presidential campaign of 1936, and on Town Meeting Day of that same year her gallant citizens rejected by a vote of 42,318–30,987 the Green Mountain Parkway, a federal proposal to build a freeway through the Green Mountains, despoiling them in the service of faster travel and car-window tourism.

Frank Bryan calls the defeat of the Green Mountain Parkway "the most democratic expression of environmental consciousness in American history."[26] I suppose that today's Beltway conservatives would revile Vermont for spurning national greatness, progress, and the gracious gift of asphalt proffered by that modern conservative hero, FDR. (Bryan later opposed, unsuccessfully, the infliction of the Interstate Highway System upon northern Vermont. The Vermont writer Castle Freeman Jr., as fine a novelist as you'll find anywhere, described I-91 as a "serpent, vast, corrupting worm, fell messenger, incubus—a soul-harlot lewdly lying beside the chaste green hills.")[27]

The rejection of the Green Mountain Parkway, which Frank Bryan sees as mythic in its defiance and radical in its implications, reveals an old Vermont that is green and truculent, little and rebellious. I am reminded of *Where the Rivers Flow North* (1993), Vermont filmmaker Jay Craven's fine adaptation of Howard Frank Mosher's story of a hook-handed Northern Vermont logger and his Indian common-law wife, played con brio by Rip Torn and Tantoo Cardinal. The leased land on which the logger's family has lived and died for generations is bought by the Northern Power Co., which intends to flood it for a dam. The logger, declaring that he will not be "bribed off my land," tries instead to cut down the trees and, not incidentally, ruin the "nature park" the power company has planned. Northern Power would deliver the Vermont desired by many of the newest immigrants: no old Vermonters, but plenty of nature parks.[28]

Frank Bryan describes the two waves of post–World War II immigration to his state: the first salutary, the second malignant. "The first were hippies who came for ideological reasons: They wanted to live small, get a horse or cow. They bought chain saws and wounded themselves. But they've done a lot to preserve town meeting and local government because they were real lefties."

The "post-1980s influx," by contrast, "is much more upscale: Let's go to the cleanest, safest state in America and get a trophy house with a nice view. They want to preserve the ambience of small—no old Chevettes in the yard; cows are okay as long as they don't shit too much—but they want to use the politics of centralized authority. They don't care who's living here or how we make decisions as long as Vermont looks like a theme park. They want to *be* in Vermont but they don't want to *live* in Vermont. We spend tons of money to preserve old farm buildings but there's nothing like that to preserve town meeting or the citizen legislature or the two-year term for governor [which is under bipartisan assault] or the democratic values that created [Vermont] in the first place."

Bryan notes the social gulf between the old Vermont and the new. "The people that had the [anti-gay-civil-unions] TAKE BACK VERMONT signs were the people that created the image that these new guys want: They extol them. When a farmer stands up at a town meeting the flatlanders all go, 'It's a farmer!'—like God is here. But do they invite them over for tea? No. They don't socialize with them." (Civil unions between same-sex couples "didn't have much impact," says Bryan. "The Right thought everything's going to hell, we'll be the haven, but nothing like that happened." The way the unions were achieved, however—by a "court-directed legislative cave-in"—affronted Bryan's democratic sensibilities. "We overturned twenty-five hundred years of Judeo-Christian tradition in three months without an election. The people who backed civil unions were so intolerant of those who didn't; the professional people couldn't understand why the rednecks were all bent out of shape."[29] They were bent further out of shape by Vermont's 2009 enshrinement of gay marriage.)

The Take Back Vermonters were acting in a long Vermont tradition of resistance to centralized tyranny. The state's political genius was a kind of stony Jeffersonianism—without the stain of slavery. Vermont learned early the virtues of states' rights when it defied the Fugitive Slave Act. Vermont would not return a slave without a "Bill of Sale from the Almighty," declared state Supreme Court Justice Theophilus Harrington in 1804.[30]

Vermont remained an independent republic, outside the nascent union, from 1777 to 1791, and imaginative Vermonters are asking why not go out again? In 1990 Bryan traveled the state with State Chief Justice John Dooley debating Vermont's secession from the union. Bryan, who argued the affirmative, is "very sympathetic" to the campaign for a Second Vermont Republic.

"When I put the secession argument to the test intellectually, I can't think of a reason not to, even economically," says Bryan, who nevertheless opposed secession for several years for perhaps the only legitimate reason: sentiment.[31] "I couldn't sit around and let a bunch of crazy Vermonters like me tear down the American flag. My heart would break."[32] But in the intervening years the rest of America broke his heart, and he is with the secessionists today, if reluctantly.

The regionalist who actually lives in the place he loves is often given to alternating fits of lachrymose romanticism and utter despair. Bryan sounds the occasional plangent note, but in the main he radiates optimism: a quondam technophobe, he credits computer technology with making possible "a dramatic decentralization of lifestyle and culture."

"People are living and working in the same place," he says. "They don't have to drive to a centralized workplace, which was the great dislocation of the twentieth century." The divorce of work and home visited upon us horrors ranging from day care to the Interstate Highway System; its reunion may bear fruit delicious, including the revitalization of local democracy.

In any event, Frank Bryan is in Vermont, for better or worse. As a patriot, he stands on what he stands for. With *Real Democracy*, he gave his state, and us outlanders as well, the most detailed and affectionate portrait ever painted of town meeting, which is, says Bryan, "where you learn to be a good citizen." His book is also an act of love. It shows Vermont how to stay Vermont. For as Bryan avers, "The only way to save Vermont is to preserve our democratic institutions."[33]

Bryan likes to quote Jack London, who said, Neil Youngishly: "I would rather my spark should burn out in a brilliant blaze than it should be stifled in dry rot."[34] Those fires you see lighting the Green Mountain sky are Frank Bryan's bonfire, which burns so brilliantly because its kindling is so dear to him, so dear and so wonderfully, life-givingly small.

Having met Mr. Bryan, you may understand why it was not all that startling when organizers billed the Vermont Independence Convention of October 28, 2005, as "the first statewide convention on secession in the United States since North Carolina voted to secede from the Union on May 20, 1861."[35] North Carolina, the final state to join the Confederacy, overcame its unionist scruples with some reluctance, but the 250 or so Vermonters gathered in Montpelier, coziest of state capitals, gloried in the prospect of disunion. Montpelier is the only McDonald's-less state capital in the land, and from its late-October splendor issued a Jeffersonian firebell in the night, ringing a warning to the national capital: The United States deserve a break(up) today.

Only in Vermont, with its town-meeting tradition and tolerance of radical dissent, would the golden-domed State Capitol be given over to a convention exploring the whys and wherefores of splitting from the United States. And all for a rental fee of $35! (It would have been free if the disunionists had knocked off by 4 PM.) It was richly symbolic, messily democratic, and funkily audacious. You can do that in Vermont: Sacramento has as many lobbyists as Montpelier has people.

Thomas Naylor, the Mississippi native and longtime professor of economics at Duke who migrated north in retirement in 1993 to the Green Mountain State, is the founder, theoretician, and chief sticker-of-stamps-on-envelopes for the Second Vermont Republic (SVR), which declares itself "a peaceful, democratic, grassroots, libertarian populist movement committed to the return of Vermont to its status as an independent republic as it once was between 1777 and 1791."

The Second Vermont Republic has a clear, if not simple, mission: "Our primary objective is to extricate Vermont peacefully from the United States as soon as possible."[36] The SVR people are not doing this to "make a point" or to stretch the boundaries of debate. They really want out.

Although SVR members range from hippie greens to gun owners (and among the virtues of Vermont is that the twain do sometimes meet), Naylor describes his group's ideological coloration as "leftish libertarian with an anarchist streak."[37]

The SVR lauds the principles and practices of direct democracy, local control of education and health care, small-scale farming, neighborhood enterprise, and the devolution of political power. The movement is anti-globalist and sees beauty in the small. It detests Walmart, the Interstate Highway System, and a foreign policy that is "immoral, illegal, and unconstitutional."[38] It draws inspiration from, among others, Aleksandr Solzhenitsyn, who in bidding farewell to his neighbors in Cavendish, Vermont, where he had lived in exile for seventeen years, praised "the sensible and sure process of grassroots democracy, in which the local population solves most of its problems on its own, not waiting for the decisions of higher authorities."[39]

Naylor likes to say that Walmart, which is "too big, too powerful, too intrusive, too mean-spirited, too materialistic, too dehumanizing, too undemocratic, too environmentally insensitive, and too unresponsive to the social, cultural, and economic needs of individual citizens and small communities," is the American metaphor in these post-republic days.[40] Perhaps it is. So why not a new metaphor, suggests Naylor: that of Vermont, which is "smaller, more rural, more democratic, less violent, less commercial, more egalitarian, and more independent" than its sister states.[41]

When Naylor laid out the case for independence in *The Vermont Manifesto* (2003), the political air was heavy, sodden, statist. "Even in the best of times secession is a very tough sell in the USA," lamented Naylor in 2002. "Since September 11, it has proven to be an impossible sell."[42] But George and Dick, for whom Vermont was just another inconsequential state full of potential body-bag fillers, came to the rescue, putting a rebarbative face on the empire and opening the door to radical possibilities.

In stepped the Second Vermont Republic, with a blend of whimsicality and seriousness and "eye-catching street theater [that] has proven irresistible to the media," according to Cathy Resmer of the Burlington weekly *Seven Days*.[43]

With polemical wit provided by Vermont's Bread and Puppet Theater, the SVR has staged mock funeral processions (on January 10, anniversary of the 1791 vote of 105–4 by which a Vermont state convention voted to join the union), parades, and Fourth of July floats in which children declared their independence from bedtime, "annoying siblings," and "my floaties."[44] There are US OUT OF VERMONT T-shirts sold at Riverwalk Records in Montpelier and a rousing anthem: "Two Hundred Years Is Long Enough" by Pete Sutherland and the Clayfoot Strutters. (Sample verse: "Why should we feed the bankers, if they won't feed our farms/ Or run and point a gun at folks who ain't done us no harm?/Come all you 'clayfoots,' you 'woodchucks,' you freedom-lovers all/Stand up and cheer to hear secession's call!")[45] The SVR has even achieved a symbolic political success, persuading the legislature to declare January 16 Vermont Independence Day in commemoration of the establishment of the First Vermont Republic in 1777. The SVR's tincture is green, but conservative, too, and although Naylor refuses to kiss up to his state's hack politicians (he calls Democratic senator Patrick Leahy "a world-class prostitute"), the Republican lieutenant governor at the time of the convention praised SVR members for "their energy and their passion."[46]

Secessionist whispers have soughed through Vermont for years. The state's blessed contrariness is an expression of what Frank Bryan and Bill Mares, in *The Vermont Owner's Manual* (2000), call "the anarchy of cussed-ness."[47] Economist David Hale essayed a "modest proposal" for a Vermont republic in 1973. In 1990, when Bryan stumped the state arguing seces-sion with Vermont Chief Justice John Dooley, following each of the seven debates a majority of the audience voted to secede. Bryan and Mares also published *Out! The Vermont Secession Book* (1987), a blend of fantasy and such it-ain't-braggin'-if-you-can-do-it claims as this: "Vermonters can do it better themselves. We are better at education, welfare, building roads, catching crooks, dispensing justice, and helping farmers. We report our own news better. Vermonters know much more about what's happening in Vermont than Americans know about what's happening in America. We're better at democracy, too, much better. We can balance our budget! We've watched as Congress pitters and patters, dillies and dallies, postures, poses, and primps. If that's America's idea of democracy, we want out!"[48]

The presidency of George W. Bush made the fanciful seem a little less fantastic. The SVR-inspired Middlebury Institute, directed by Kirkpatrick Sale, sought to "put secession on the national agenda." Audacious, perhaps, but hardly a forlorn hope, for as Naylor asks, "Do you want to go down with the *Titanic*? No empire has survived the test of time."[49]

The Second Vermont Republic confounds those who would analyze it using the gauge of practical politics. It pursues with humor and dogged optimism a goal that seems manifestly impossible. It speaks radical notions with a conservative diction. It operates at the political fringe yet attracts such eminent establishmentarians as John Kenneth Galbraith, who communicated his "pleasure in, and approval of the Second Vermont Republic."[50]

Or consider the case of George Kennan, to whom *The Vermont Manifesto* and its follow-up, *Secession: How Vermont and All the Other States Can Save Themselves from the Empire* (2008), are dedicated and whom Thomas Naylor calls "the godfather of the movement."[51] Kennan—diplomat, memoirist, the only Wise Man of the 1940s worthy of the sobriquet—had speculated about the United States devolving into "a dozen constituent republics" in his valediction *Around the Cragged Hill* (1993).[52]

Nearing his centenary (he died March 17, 2005, at the age of 101), Kennan became much taken with the idea of an independent Vermont, although he told Naylor that "we are, I fear, a lonely band; until some of the things we have written are discovered by what we may hope will be a more thoughtful and serious generation of critics and reviewers, I am afraid we will remain that way."[53] Kennan's secession letters, dictated from a sickbed, are pointed and poignant. "All power to Vermont in its effort to distinguish itself from the USA as a whole, and to pursue in its own way the cultivation of its own tradition," he wrote in May 2002.[54] This was no deathbed conversion. As a young foreign service officer during the Second World War, Kennan had written a position paper for Undersecretary of State Sumner Welles in which he urged a policy for postwar Germany of a "return to the particularism of the eighteenth century—a return to the small kingdoms, the chocolate soldiers, the picturesque localisms of an earlier day."[55]

In his lengthiest discourse on the subject, Kennan wrote Naylor that in the matter of independence for Vermont and her neighbors, "I see nothing fanciful, and nothing towards the realization of which the efforts of enlightened people might not be usefully directed. Such are at present the dominating trends in the US that I can see no other means of ultimate preservation of cultural and societal values that will not only be endangered but eventually destroyed in an endlessly prolonged association of the northern parts of New England with the remainder of what is now the USA."

Ah, but there is a complication. Kennan was attracted to the Second Vermont Republic partly because he deplored the Hispanicization of the United States.

Instancing Mexican immigration, Kennan saw "unmistakable evidences of a growing differentiation between the cultures, respectively, of large southern and southwestern regions of this country, on the one hand," and those of "some northern regions," including Vermont. In the former, "the very culture of the bulk of the population of these regions will tend to be primarily Latin-American in nature rather than what is inherited from earlier American traditions."[56]

"Could it really be that there was so little of merit" in the American republic, asked Kennan, "that it deserves to be recklessly trashed in favor of [a] poliglot mix-mash?"[57] This wasp never did lose his sting.

It is no small portion of Vermont's charm that the secessionists were given use of the statehouse in Montpelier, which lent a certain sobriety to what might otherwise have been a rambunctiously motley conference. Thomas Naylor fretted the night before the convention that the crowd might overwhelm the two-man Capitol security force, but not to worry: The secessionists behaved splendidly, so that the officers had no duties more pressing than giving directions to the restrooms and transmitting the request, "Will the owner of a black Mercedes please move your vehicle?" Days of Rage these were not.

The Reverend Ben T. Matchstick, a radical puppeteer, called the assembly to irreverent order with a benediction invoking "the flounder, the sunfish, and the holy mackerel." Men in business suits, white-maned Vermont earth mothers, and ponytailed college kids wearing winter skullcaps indoors packed Representatives Hall, sitting at the desks elsetimes occupied by state representatives and filling the room with the fragrance of winsome rebellion and localist patriotism.

Under a portrait of George Washington, Naylor, the founding father of this republic in gestation, charged that the US government has "no moral authority . . . it has no soul," and he denied the salvific properties of the Democratic Party: "It doesn't matter if Hillary Clinton or Condoleezza Rice [or, you may be sure, Barack Obama] is the next president—the results will be equally grim."

Rodomontade was kept to a minimum; the gathered had plenty of "what about?" questions. Asked what would become of abortion rights in a Second Vermont Republic, Naylor shrugged and replied, "Whatever the people decide." The SVR takes no position on abortion, gay rights, gun control, and the like; these are questions to be debated within an independent Vermont. Devolution is the great defuser of explosive issues: Let Utah be Utah, let San Francisco be San Francisco, let Vermont be Vermont.

Naylor grew up in Jackson, Mississippi, but he rocked uneasily in the Confederacy's cradle. He was a liberal who loved the Ole Miss Rebels but never for a second fell for the myth of happy field hands singing under the hot plantation sun. When a delegate asked the inevitable Civil War question, I expected to see Naylor's long frame dance around it nimbly. Instead, he met it head-on. "South Carolina and the Confederate states had a perfect right to secede," he told the assembly, adding that "the bottom line of the Civil War was preserving the Empire." I expected audible gasps and fainting Unitarians but the unsayable, having been said, was not confuted.

Would not the empire treat a seceding Vermont with as little forbearance as Lincoln showed South Carolina in 1861? Naylor scoffed: "Would all of the black and white Holsteins be destroyed or perhaps the entire sugar maple crop be burned?"[58]

Maybe they would, Thomas. Certainly the din and clang of war would belch from the cable-news shows and the serious-miened rent-a-scholars who litter them. When Russell Wheeler of the Brookings Institution was asked about Vermont's secession, he scoffed: "If Vermont had a powerful enough army and said, 'We're leaving the union,' and the national government said, 'No, you're not,' and they fought a war over it and Vermont won, then you could say Vermont proved the point. But that's not going to happen."[59]

Those Brookings boys do play a mean game of Risk. Cross 'em and they'll order the working-class and ghetto and barrio kids of the army to wipe your sorry parochial ass off the map. A Brooklyn boy has the answer to Wheeler: The Marxist historian Eugene Genovese, author of the classic *Roll, Jordan, Roll*, has said that "it is remarkable with what ease so many liberal historians declare that the meaning of the Constitution was settled by the Union victory, for it would be hard to imagine a clearer example of the doctrine that might makes right."[60]

Frank Bryan, introduced by Naylor as "hands down the most interesting person in Vermont . . . since Solzhenitsyn left the state," confessed to being "sad" and "melancholy" because "my nation needs Vermont to secede." Bryan has long been achingly ambivalent about secession. He is, like many decentralists, an American patriot who reveres the crazy old idiosyncratic America and whose heart stirs to patriotic tunes. But something has happened; the country seems to have gotten away from itself. "The reservoirs of citizenship are dried up and that's why we've got to secede," asserted Bryan. (Lest we forget, Bryan reminded us that in many other countries of the world, "we'd be shot for doing what we're doing here today.")[61]

Bryan later expanded on these remarks in the pages of the independence-inclined newspaper *Vermont Commons*. After disposing of the accounting canard that Vermont would come up short if she detached from the federal teat—which isn't really true, and besides, the proper answer is So What?—Bryan cut to the heart. The "best way," he concluded,

> to preserve our capacity to live independently is to maintain a government of human scale, where the need to be controlled is balanced by the ability to do some controlling oneself.
>
> Vermont is such a place.
>
> And the United States is a nation (some say an empire) over which we Vermonters no longer have much, if any, control.
>
> Let us get up on our hind legs, then, and send a message of peaceable secession to the nation from the frost-bound hillsides of the land of the American conscience.

Vermont—the once and future republic—this is where I stand.[62]

Bravo!

The keynote speaker in Montpelier was that scourge of suburbia, James Howard Kunstler, Upstate New York Democrat and slashingly witty Jeremiah, who predicted that "life and politics are going to become profoundly and intensely local" as the age of cheap oil slips away. Kunstler is a novelist and social critic, not a secessionist, though as one ponders his visions and their implications—Walmart will topple like a statue of Lenin; food will be grown for local markets; New England, the Middle Atlantic, and the Upper Midwest will endure while Las Vegas loses its shirt—one might be excused for thinking him a utopian.

Kirk Sale, pointing to the state motto "Freedom and Unity," offered his good-natured anarchist appraisal, remarking that "the more unity you have, the less freedom. It is disunity that allows freedom." (I had driven to Montpelier that morning with my buddy Marty Stucko and Sale, a delightful dinner companion. "Park here! Park here!" Kirk said as we passed spots featuring conspicuous NO PARKING signs. "What are you," I finally asked, "a fucking anarchist?")

After eight hours of small-scale democracy in action, the assembled Vermonters voted to "peacefully and democratically free [themselves] from the United States of America."[63] You may call it a lark, but on the last Friday before Halloween 2005 I thought I saw it grow wings.

∽◎∾

Vermont secession is not an "issue" like entitlement reform or industrial policy. It is an eidolon, a Vermont-specific image of the American Dream (the real dream, not the imperial nightmare) that may not concretize— what an inapt verb for green Vermont!—for many years but that has the power to fire imaginations, to inspirit those in despair, to keep flying a banner to which patriots can rally. An independent Vermont is not a joke, nor is it an ignis fatuus; it is the shape that hope takes in the darkening shadow of a crumbling empire.

John McClaughry, the Vermont Republican who heads the free-market

Ethan Allen Institute, detects "a virulent anti-American leftism" in the SVR, adding that "whether this goes so far as a willingness to forswear the continued receipt of social security checks from the despised US of A the organizers have yet to say."[64] (Naylor responds that expatriates currently receive their Social Security checks without incident. And to the common argument that Vermont receives $1.15 for every dollar it sends to Washington and therefore would shortchange itself by separating from the Union, Frank Bryan has replied, "Would you rather have $10,000 to spend any way you want or $11,500 that you have to spend as I say?")[65]

John McClaughry is a thorny original whose work I have long admired, but unless the defining characteristics of "anti-American leftism" are a loathing of Walmart, the Iraq War, and Big Government and a fondness for organic farming, town meeting, and a Vermont First ethic, the SVR seems to me a wholesomely shaggy band of ur-Americans, not anti-Americans. Yeah, I saw a fistful of nuts at the Montpelier convention. I kept a judicious distance from the man who stood to announce that he had once "stuck a fake knife" through his head. There was a collegiate white Rasta or two and a Montreal pwog who informed us that "the US is based on genocide," but they were the sort of free-floating crazies who show up wherever two or more are gathered in the name of revolution. In the main, in the heart, the Second Vermont Republic is based on love: love of a place, of a culture, of an agriculture.

I heard much talk of the need for libertarian conservatives and anti-globalist leftists to work together. There is a sense that the old categories, the old straitjackets, must be shed. When the Reverend Matchstick preaches that we need decentralism because communities that ban genetically modified food must have the power to enforce those bans, he is speaking a language that pre-imperial conservatives will recognize—the language of local control. When the "Vermont nationalist" CEO of a consulting firm insists that Vermont should have the right to determine where (and where not) its national guard is deployed, I hear an echo of the Old Right. Why should the Vermont National Guard be shipped overseas to fight the empire's wars?

"Long Live the Second Vermont Republic and God Bless the Disunited States of America," concluded Thomas Naylor.[66] You got a better idea?

❧

What happens next is anyone's guess.

The SVR ebbed in early 2009 because . . . well, let Rob Williams tell the joke:

Q: Who was the loneliest person in the United States the day after the Obama election?

A: A Vermont secessionist.[67]

But the body bags keep coming home, filled, and those leftists who can see the world in colors richer than just blue and red are souring on the Nowhere Man. Meanwhile, the empire, mired in unwinnable wars in the Middle East and Asia, sagging at home under debt and military bills no honest man could pay, is collapsing, to the delight of American patriots. The Second Vermont Republic is holding out an alternative to empire that is rooted, green, humane, and vivifyingly small. Its answer to the current crisis—LOVE HOME—is rather more attractive than VOTE DEMOCRAT or MOVE TO MYRTLE BEACH. So we shall see.

Alas, we live in an age in which public discourse is crudely regulated by bullying hall monitors. No independent thought goes unpunished. And so in 2007–08 the SVR was pinged for "racism" by the character assassins of Blog Land. The charges? First, that the SVR linked to the League of the South on its Web site. This was incontrovertibly true, and so what? Naylor responded, "The SVR website has URL links to thirty-five secessionist organizations. Ideologically these groups vary from Hawaii and Puerto Rico on the far left, to Alaska, which is pretty far to the right. Although SVR is in contact with all of them, SVR is in bed with none of them."[68]

The second, and really contemptible, charge was that Thomas Naylor, because he is a son of Dixie, is automatically suspect as a racist. Naylor was floored by this libel. He had been a Southern liberal in the 1960s, a co-founder of the L. Q. C. Lamar Society, whose members included such paragons of the New South as Jimmy Carter, Terry Sanford, and Hodding Carter III. He chaired Bobby Kennedy's 1968 presidential campaign in North Carolina. Naylor was an almost paradigmatic progressive Southerner.

Ah, but you see, Naylor's late father, also Thomas H., was a state education official, an associate of the racist Mississippi governor Ross Barnett, and a member of the Mississippi Sovereignty Commission (MSC), a state agency that defended Jim Crow and spied on and maligned integrationists. The MSC was a nasty tentacle of the segregationist octopus and fully deserved to be hacked to bits.

The senior Naylor may well have been a segregationist. Most Mississippi politicians of the 1950s were. But what is his son supposed to do about it? What kind of man would publicly repudiate his father? "He and I fought nonstop on this," Naylor told me of his father.[69] But Naylor is hardly going to disavow his dad. Only a monster would do so. And only a monster would ask a man to reject his own father.

Though he denounced the attacks as part of a "sophisticated techno-fascist smear campaign," the besieged Naylor did draw back a bit from his League of the South allies.[70] He took a closer look and found the kooks in the margin that had always been there. But he insisted upon common interests between those pursuing independence for Vermont and the South, and he kept open a line of communication. The league, and other Southern independence groups, would continue to be invited to secessionist gatherings, though the days of Naylor or other SVR leaders offering public praise and chummy collegiality to the League of the South are probably over. Vermont and South Carolina are two different countries.

Conference-itis is an occupational plague of think tanks, but Kirk Sale's Middlebury Institute has kept it under control. Its October 2007 Secessionist Convention in Chattanooga had been a qualified success. There was plenty of press coverage, much of it fair and thoughtful. Acquaintances deepened into friendships; e-mail pals became comrades, of a sort. Releasing non-grandiloquent declarations is a fine way to close a convention, and so sixteen delegates produced a Chattanooga Declaration that read, in part: "The deepest questions of human liberty and government facing our time go beyond right and left, and in fact have made the old left–right split meaningless and dead . . . The American Empire is no longer a nation or a republic, but has become a tyrant aggressive abroad and despotic at home . . . The States of the American union are and of right ought to be, free and self-governing."[71] Felicity courtesy of Mr. Sale, I'll bet; sentiments straight from the American marrow.

The Middlebury Institute's next conference, in Manchester, New

Hampshire, in November 2008, held 'neath the slate sky and against the leafless boughs of my favorite bleak month, was something of a mixed bag.

The deep recession—or is it a depression?—of the twenty-oughts had laid low the Dow Jones just a month earlier, and as Naylor told me, "The meltdown is the biggest boon to our movement since Bush was reelected in 2004." Yet he also groused that in the view of many Vermont liberals, then-president-elect "Obama walks on water."

I drove to Manchester via Governor Dewey's New York State Thruway and President Eisenhower's Interstate and Defense Highway System—Republicans were into socialist giantism long before the Bushes burned. In the passenger seat sat Pat Weissend, curator of our local history museum and one of the nation's foremost grave hunters. (I told Pat I was going to report that he sang Air Supply tunes all the way to New Hampshire but I cannot tell a lie. He did hum Bon Jovi—same difference.) En route we detoured to Natick, Massachusetts, to find Henry Wilson, Grant's second vice president, and while I was sitting in a room the next day listening to rambling speeches in the momentarily radicalized Radisson, Pat was getting lost in Boston scouting out dead Unitarians. There are lots of them.

The conference, attended by fifty-five delegates, observers, and Persons of Interest to the Department of Homeland Security, was duller than those of previous years, perhaps because the imminent de-Ovalizing of George W. Bush had produced a collective sigh of relief that, I suspect, will last until Secretary of State Clinton cheerleads the American war machine's bombing of some ragtag Muslim country for its insufficiently feminist domestic policies.

At the convention, I was delighted to visit with my friend Carolyn Chute, the Maine novelist and voice of the rural poor, whose 2008 novel, *The School on Heart's Content Road*, marked her very welcome return. But the whiff of crackpottery trailed a handful of the delegates. They are easily mocked, though I prefer to spray whatever bile I produce at people who do real harm—Masters of War, Defilers of the Republic—rather than at a helium-voiced fifty-one-year-old polyester-encased alien who fancies himself Ambassador from Uranus. Still, the disconnect from the reality-based community was unsettling.

Texan Larry Kilgore boasted of turning his back when the Pledge of

Allegiance is recited. Francis Bellamy's nationalist pledge may be a lemon, but conspicuous displays of disrespect for the Pledge, flag, or other symbols of the United States seem, to this sentimental slob, bullheadedly bad ways to persuade one's neighbors to Consider the Alternative. Anyone who *has* neighbors, and not just contempt for his neighbors, understands this.

Over drinks I asked Kirk Sale if putting the gloriously, whimsically, seriously localist Vermonters on the same program as mad tinfoil hatters doesn't do the Green Mountain Boys a disservice. Kirk, with his roots in the New Left, has an admirable distaste for edict-issuing. He said that purges and excisions smack of right-wing socialism and neoconnery (not to be confused with the Scottish Nationalist Sean Connery). Point taken. Still, the nut quotient this time was too high even for an indulgent sap like myself.

Saturday was my birthday, and Pat and I drizzled it away drinking New Hampshire beer (Smuttynose) in a dive bar while feeding the juke box to keep the Pogues in our ears. Shane was singing about kissing his girl by the factory wall in his dirty old town.

The young drunks at the other end of the bar sang along, in love with their dirty old town on the Merrimack. To each his own.

The Middlebury convention went on hiatus in 2009, but it (and I, God willing) will be back.[72]

Thomas Naylor's "Genteel Revolution," he says, brings together "thoughtful writers, artists, academics, blue collar workers, doctors, farmers, lawyers, merchants, and other rebels committed to helping save America and the rest of the world from the American Empire."[73]

In the early years of this sadsack millennium Naylor flirted with creating a Green Mountain Party, a virescent echo of the admirable Mountain Party of West Virginia. That seed fell on stony ground, as did the 2008 gubernatorial run of thirty-year-old SVR Web site designer Sam Young—who reminded Naylor of "a cross between James Dean and Paul Newman."[74] Calling for a return of the Vermont National Guard from the Middle East and the shutdown of the Vermont Yankee nuclear power plant, he attracted a meager 1 percent of the vote. Young is a real Vermonter; hell, he's justice of the peace in Glover. From small things, baby, big things—or a plenitude of small things—one day come. Or might come. As I write, secessionists are launching a 2010 gubernatorial campaign, and the SVR is minting "50 Clover Silver Tokens," handsome coins that might serve as currency in a free Vermont. The first token bears the image of Scott Nearing, the communist-pacifist and advocate of subsistence living who became the weathered face of the Vermont counterculture. Nearing was a turgid prose stylist but he marched to the beat of his own drummer. Why the hell not put him on a coin?

The group's next goal is "200 towns by 2012." That is, the SVR hopes by 2012 to persuade 200 of Vermont's 237 towns to call for a convention at which Vermonters can debate the merits of independence. Scoff if you will, but by 2012, a decade into a nightmarish "War on Terror" that our rulers have assured us will last our lifetimes, will Americans be content with a status quo of perpetual war and unending empire?

Will Vermont secede next week? No. But when the Center for Rural Studies at the University of Vermont asked residents "Do you think it would be a good idea for Vermont to secede from the United States and become once again an independent republic as it was between 1777 and 1791?" 8 percent answered yes in 2006, 13 percent agreed in 2007, and 11.5 percent concurred in 2008. That's not bad. And when you consider that in 2008, 77.1 percent answered yes to "Has the US government lost its moral authority?" the savory makings of sedition are there.[75]

It goes beyond Vermont. Startlingly, given 1861 and all that, a 2008 Middlebury Institute/Zogby Poll found that 22 percent of Americans surveyed agreed that "any state or region has the right to peaceably secede and become an independent republic." The South (26 percent) and East (24 percent) led the way, and among demographic categories Hispanics (43 percent), African Americans (40 percent), and eighteen- through twenty-four-year-olds (40 percent) gave the most support to the proposition. Liberals (32 percent) were likelier than self-described conservatives (17 percent) to agree.[76] Hope abides.

Decentralization—which in its final course reaches secession—is the political expression of the relocalizing of American economies. Free exchange at the local level, among neighbors, is its lifeblood; citizens of a free Vermont are likely to enjoy economic liberties that would warm the heart of Milton

Friedman, although corporations, especially absentee firms, probably would find the Green Mountain air stifling. Naylor has written, "A free and independent Vermont could also create its own business rules and regulations. If Vermonters grew weary of seeing Wal-Mart drive small, local merchants out of business, they could tell Wal-Mart to pack up and ship out. They could also limit the number of McDonald's and other fast food restaurants allowed to operate in the state. And to Virginia-based Gannett, Vermont could say that it is simply unacceptable for the state's largest newspaper to be owned by a megachain located in the suburbs of Washington, DC."[77] The SVR, as you might guess, is no pet of Gannett's Burlington outlet.

Naylor is seventy-three at this writing, and while with his loping strides and long white tresses he appears ageless, he is not unmindful that with the passage of time torches are passed. They will be carried ably, even brilliantly. The engaging and passionate Rob Williams of *Vermont Commons* is today the state's most media-savvy secessionist. When the *Washington Post* introduced Vermont secession to its readers in April 2007, its guides were *Vermont Commons* publisher Ian Baldwin and Frank Bryan, whose lengthy essay invoked Vermont's principled obstreperousness—its opposition to the War of 1812, its noble anti-slavery stand, its rejection of the Green Mountain Parkway, its defiance of Ronald Reagan's edict to boost its drinking age from eighteen to twenty-one.[78]

For a time, the fires of Vermont independence may dampen. Smitten with Obama, subordinating the virtues of local self-reliance and small-scale community to the Leader Principle, forgetting Bob Dylan's timeless adjuration "Don't follow leaders," some Vermonters may put their trust in princes and principalities, in the celebrity come from afar to save them. But the truest Vermonters understand that salvation never arrives via digital TV or a federal welfare check. They live Walt Whitman's counsel: Resist much, obey little.

Frank Bryan, the soul of Vermont, spoke as the gods of the hills in his 1990 debates with Chief Justice Dooley. His peroration at the First Congregational Church in Bennington rings still:

> Let them speak of us in the future in a way similar to the way
> that Robert Frost, former Vermont poet laureate now buried

near this very church, spoke of himself: "I had a lover's quarrel with the world." Let them say of us, "They had a lover's quarrel with America."

Let our leaving be then an act of deep caring, even of love—a positive affirmation of our dreams for the United States . . .

Let us cry out in peace. We offer not the shot heard round the world, but the *vote* heard round the world. Let it be said of Vermont by the historians of the year 2091: "More than anything else it was the secession of Vermont from the Union one hundred years ago that shook America to its very roots and caused the revolution in federalism that saved the Republic."

I ask you, therefore, to stand and vote for the secession of Vermont from the United States of America.[79]

They did stand and vote for an independent Vermont.

Sooner or later, whether in Vermont or Texas or Hawaii or Alaska, a similar vote will be called, but this time it will be for real. Three hundred million people cannot be ruled from a single city. The center, or rather central authority, cannot hold. Something's gotta rive. Smug liberals and chickenhawk conservatives will mock and threaten, bluster and bluff, but scorn stings only if you let it, and remember: The dipshits sneering and jeering at those citizens who actually believe in self-government are the voice of the empire. You gonna take orders from *them*?

Jim Kibler, the South Carolina novelist and agrarian, tells me, "Free open discussion of devolution and its possibilities would seem to be the American way of getting things out into the light of day, into the fresh air of open free discussion. This was the American way of the old Republic. Shouldn't it be again? The nation was built upon secession, we must never forget."[80]

Some Americans are starting to remember.

From the Green Mountains of Vermont to the redwood forests of California to the waters of Blue Hawaii, agitated patriots have sounded a tocsin to which localist rebels across America are responding. We can see the gathering secessionist movements as a harbinger, a warning—or a blessed sign of hope. I choose hope. What say you, friend?

ENDNOTES

Introduction

1. J. William Fulbright, "The Price of Empire," speech of August 8, 1967, in Haynes Johnson and Bernard M. Gwertzman, *Fulbright the Dissenter* (Garden City, NY: Doubleday, 1968), p. 311.
2. Edmund Wilson, *The Cold War and the Income Tax: A Protest* (New York: Signet, 1964), p. 125.
3. Walt Whitman, "By Blue Ontario's Shore," in *Leaves of Grass* (New York: Doubleday Doran, 1940), pp. 188–189.
4. "In Texas, 31% Say State Has Right to Secede from US, But 75% Opt to Stay," Rasmussen Reports, April 17, 2009.
5. Ron Paul, "Secession an Important Constitutional Principle," April 19, 2009, www.campaignforliberty.com.
6. Gore Vidal, "The Empire Lovers Strike Back," *The Nation*, March 22, 1986, p. 350.
7. Joseph Curl, "Blue States Buzz Over Secession," *Washington Times*, November 9, 2004.
8. Quoted in Bill Kauffman, "Bye, Bye, Miss American Empire," *Orion*, July–August 2007, p. 57. Unless otherwise noted, all quotes from conference participants are taken from this article and/or the author's notes thereof. For another account of the Burlington convention, see Paul Nussbaum, "Coming Together to Ponder Pulling Apart," *Philadelphia Inquirer*, November 6, 2006.
9. The Middlebury Declaration, November 7, 2004, Middlebury Institute.
10. Bruce E. Levine, "Secession and Sanity: An Interview with Kirkpatrick Sale," *Z Magazine* (October 2006), p. 46.
11. Quoted in *Congressional Record*, 86th Congress, 1st session, March 11, 1959, p. 3887.
12. "Newsweek Poll," *Newsweek*, July 10, 1995, p. 26.
13. Katherine Dalton, "Localism with Teeth," www.frontporchrepublic.com, November 5, 2009.
14. John S. Whitehead, *Completing the Union: Alaska, Hawai'i, and the Battle for Statehood* (Albuquerque: University of New Mexico Press, 2004), p. 7.
15. *Congressional Record*, 83rd Congress, 1st session, March 9, 1953, p. 1782.
16. Donald W. Livingston, "What Is Secession?" *Vermont Commons*, November 2005, p. 9.
17. Kenneth M. Stampp, "The Concept of a Perpetual Union," *Journal of American History* 65, no. 1 (June 1978), p. 23. Back to New Hampshire for a sec. No toers of lines or marchers in lockstep, dozens of other Free Staters moved to Wyoming. Cory Matteson, "Freedom on the Frontier: Gun-Toting 'Free Staters' Make Their Move into Wyoming," *Casper Star-Tribune*, July 4, 2007. Meanwhile, former New Hampshire state senator Burt Cohen, a progressive Democrat, has proposed a federation of New Hampshire, Maine, Vermont, and Canada's Maritime Provinces—Nova Scotia, New Brunswick, and Prince Edward Island, as well as the Gaspé Peninsula of Quebec—to be called New Acadia or Novacadia.

"The founding fathers could not have imagined 300 million people," says Cohen. "This country includes a lot of people with disparate points of view, and to have them represented in a single government, you have to ask, 'How realistic is that?'" The asking is under way. Jim Kozubek, "New England Groups Look to Secede," *Manchester Union-Leader*, August 11, 2008.

Chapter One

1. Norman Mailer, "An Instrument for the City," in *Existential Errands* (Boston: Little, Brown, 1972), p. 328.

2. William Appleman Williams, *America Confronts a Revolutionary World: 1776–1976* (New York: William Morrow, 1976), p. 194.

3. Peter Overby, "We're Outta Here," *Common Cause Magazine* (Winter 1992), pp. 23–24.

4. Joint Press Conference of the President and Premier Zhu Rongji, April 8, 1999, Office of the Press Secretary, the White House.

5. Francis Lieber, *Two Lectures on the Constitution of the United States* (New York: Baker & Godwin, 1861), p. 44.

6. Richard Orr Curry, *A House Divided: A Study of Statehood Politics and the Copperhead Movement in West Virginia* (Pittsburgh: University of Pittsburgh Press, 1964), p. 1.

7. Claude G. Bowers, *The Tragic Era* (New York: Riverside Press, 1929), p. 76.

8. James C. McGregor, *The Disruption of Virginia* (New York: Macmillan, 1922), p. 311.

9. Quoted in Curry, *A House Divided*, p. 124.

10. McGregor, *The Disruption of Virginia*, p. 136.

11. *The Jefferson Cyclopedia: A Comprehensive Collection of the Views of Thomas Jefferson*, edited by John P. Foley (New York: Funk & Wagnalls, 1900), p. 940.

12. Paul C. Nagel, *One Nation Indivisible: The Union in American Thought, 1776–1861* (New York: Oxford University Press, 1964), p. 13. New York City attorney John McKesson wrote soon-to-be New York governor (and later arch-Anti-Federalist) George Clinton on June 10, 1775: "We are lately informed that a scheme of setting up two grand Republics in America has been warmly agitated in your Continental Congress . . ." John McKesson to George Clinton, June 10, 1775, in *Public Papers of George Clinton*, vol. 1 (Albany: Wynkoop Hallenbeck Crawford, 1899), p. 200.

13. *Patrick Henry: Life, Correspondence and Speeches*, vol. 3, edited by William Wirt Henry (New York: Scribner's, 1891), p. 503.

14. James Madison, *Notes of Debates in the Federal Convention of 1787*, edited by Adrienne Koch (Athens: Ohio University Press, 1984), pp. 203–204.

15. Ibid., 215–216.

16. Ibid., 230.

17. Richard M. Weaver, "The South and the American Union," in *The Southern Essays of Richard M. Weaver*, edited by George M. Curtis III and James J. Thompson Jr. (Indianapolis: Liberty Press, 1987), p. 233.

18. Madison, *Notes of Debates in the Federal Convention of 1787*, pp. 211, 410.

19. Jonathan Elliot, editor, *The Debates in the Several State Conventions on the Adoption of the Federal Constitution*, vol. 2 (Philadelphia: J. B. Lippincott, 1836), p. 334.

20. Ibid., vol. 3, p. 33.

21. Ibid., vol. 3, p. 594.

22. George R. Stewart, *Names on the Land: A Historical Account of Place-Naming in the United States* (New York: New York Review of Books, 2008/1945), p. 171.

23. Kevin M. Gannon, "Escaping 'Mr. Jefferson's Plan of Destruction': New England Federalists and the Idea of a Northern Confederacy, 1804–1804," *Journal of the Early Republic* 21 (Fall 2001), p. 416.

24. Ibid.

25. Edward Payson Powell, *Nullification and Secession in the United States: A History of the Six Attempts During the First Century of the Republic* (New York: G. P. Putnam's Sons, 1897), p. 62.

26. Aleine Austin, *Matthew Lyon: "New Man" of the Democratic Revolution, 1749–1822* (University Park: Pennsylvania State University Press, 1981), p. 108.

27. For a fresh consideration of the Kentucky and Virginia Resolutions, including their secessionist implications, see William J. Watkins Jr., *Reclaiming the American Revolution: The Kentucky and Virginia Resolutions and Their Legacy* (New York: Palgrave Macmillan, 2004).

28. Daniel Wait Howe, *Political History of Secession: To the Beginning of the American Civil War* (New York: G. P. Putnam's Sons, 1914), p. 15.

29. Thomas Jefferson to John Taylor, June 4, 1798, in *The Papers of Thomas Jefferson*, vol. 30, edited by Barbara B. Oberg (Princeton, NJ: Princeton University Press, 2003), pp. 388–389.

30. Thomas Jefferson to John C. Breckinridge, August 12, 1803, in *Thomas Jefferson: Writings*, edited by Merrill D. Peterson (New York: Library of America, 1984), p. 1138.

31. Gordon Wood, *Revolutionary Characters: What Made the Founders Different* (New York: Penguin, 2006), p. 108.

32. Thomas Jefferson to Joseph Priestley, January 29, 1804, in *Thomas Jefferson: Writings*, p. 1142.

33. Powell, *Nullification and Secession in the United States*, p. 221.

34. *Documents Relating to New England Federalism, 1800–1815*, edited by Henry Adams (Boston: Little, Brown, 1905), p. 338. See also Gannon, "Escaping 'Mr. Jefferson's Plan of Destruction,'" pp. 413–443.

35. Ibid., 339–341.

36. Ibid., 346.

37. Ibid., 345.

38. Ibid., 351–352.

39. William Plumer Jr., *Life of William Plumer* (Boston: Phillips, Sampson, 1856), p. 295.

40. Powell, *Nullification and Secession in the United States*, p. 138.

41. "Brief of Blennerhassett," in William H. Safford, *The Life of Harman Blennerhassett* (Cincinnati: Moore, Anderson, Wilstach & Keys, 1853), p. 229.

42. *Documents Relating to New England Federalism, 1800–1815*, p. 389.

43. Ibid., 391.

44. Ibid., 383.

45. Harold Frederic, *In the Valley* (New York: Scribner's, 1890), p. 123.

46. Samuel G. Bushnell, "On the Aristocracy of Harvard," in *Such Nonsense! An Anthology*, compiled by Carolyn Wells (New York: George H. Doran, 1918), p. 219.

47. Quoted in Ferris Greenslet, *The Lowells and Their Seven Worlds* (Boston: Houghton Mifflin, 1946), p. 118.

48. Ibid., 145–146.

49. Samuel Eliot Morison, "Dissent in the War of 1812," in Morison, Frederick Merk, and Frank Freidel, *Dissent in Three American Wars* (Cambridge, MA: Harvard University Press, 1970), p. 22.

50. A Massachusetts Farmer (John Lowell), "Thoughts in a Series of Letters in Answer to a Question Respecting the Division of the States," 1813, pp. 3–4. Thanks to Katie Papas of Rush Rhees Library, University of Rochester, for her assistance in tracking down this exceedingly rare publication.

51. Ibid., 5.

52. Ibid., 6–8, 15.

53. Ibid., 9.

54. Ibid., 12–13.

55. Ibid., 16, 23.

56. Ibid., 24.

57. Samuel Eliot Morison, *Harrison Gray Otis, 1765–1848: The Urbane Federalist* (Boston: Houghton Mifflin, 1969), p. 364.

58. James M. Banner Jr., *To the Hartford Convention: The Federalists and the Origins of Party Politics in Massachusetts, 1789–1815* (New York: Knopf, 1970), p. 117.

59. Ibid., 110.

60. Jared Sparks, *The Life of Gouverneur Morris*, vol. 3 (Boston: Gray & Bowen, 1832), p. 312.

61. Charles Raymond Brown, *The Northern Confederacy According to the Plans of the "Essex Junto," 1796–1814* (Princeton, NJ: Princeton University Press, 1915), pp. 106–107.

62. Sparks, *The Life of Gouverneur Morris*, vol. 3, pp. 317, 319.

63. Ibid., 325.

64. Morison, "Dissent in the War of 1812," p. 6.

65. *Documents Relating to New England Federalism, 1800–1815*, p. 406.

66. Banner, *To the Hartford Convention*, p. 314.

67. Frank Maloy Anderson, "A Forgotten Phase of the New England Opposition to the War of 1812," *Proceedings of the Mississippi Valley Historical Association* 6 (1912–1913), p. 180. As Anderson wrote, the Hartford men espoused "constitutional doctrines which at a later period would have sounded very strange from the mouths of New Englanders." "A Forgotten Phase of the New England Opposition to the War of 1812," p. 178.

68. *Documents Relating to New England Federalism, 1800–1815*, pp. 410–414.

69. Ibid., 407, 417. Let the last word on the convention's failure be spoken not by a nationalist historian affronted at the insolence of it all—the *nerve* of those New Englanders!—but by Gouverneur Morris, who mocked the mildness of the Hartford men, whom he viewed as no more dangerous than an assemblage of

Shriners. To Congressman Moss Kent (F-NY) he wrote on January 10, 1815: "You will have seen that the Hartford Convention have been prudent. Their doings bring to mind one of La Fontaine's fables. A council of rats being convoked, to devise measures of defence against feline depredations, a sleek young member was much applauded for proposing to tie a bell round puss's neck, which, giving seasonable notice of her approach, would enable every one to take care of himself. Before the question was put, an old rat, (addressing the chair), said, 'I too, Sir, entirely approve of our young friend's proposal, but wish, before I vote, to know who will fasten on the bell.'" Sparks, *The Life of Gouverneur Morris*, vol. 3, p. 326.

70. Banner, *To the Hartford Convention*, p. 117.
71. Morison, *Harrison Gray Otis*, p. 89.
72. Ralph Waldo Emerson, "The Conduct of Life," in *Emerson: Essays & Lectures* (New York: Penguin, 1983), p. 1022.
73. Richard Heath, "Bromley Park, The Origin of the Name," April 14, 2005, www.jphs.org.
74. Morison, *Harrison Gray Otis*, p. 370.
75. Nagel, *One Nation Indivisible*, p. 19.
76. Thomas Jefferson to John Holmes, April 22, 1820, in *Thomas Jefferson: Writings*, p. 1434.
77. *Memoirs of John Quincy Adams, Comprising Portions of His Diary from 1795–1848*, vol. 4, edited by Charles Francis Adams (Philadelphia: Lippincott & Co., 1875), p. 531.
78. Ibid., vol. 5, p. 12.
79. William Rawle, *A View of the Constitution of the United States of America* (1825), www.constitution.org/wr/rawle. On Rawle at West Point, see Stephen E. Ambrose, *Duty, Honor, Country: A History of West Point* (Baltimore: Johns Hopkins, 1999/1966), p. 187.
80. Kenneth M. Stampp, "The Concept of a Perpetual Union," *Journal of American History* 65, no. 1 (June 1978), p. 28.
81. "Calhoun's South Carolina Exposition," in *Constitutional Doctrines of Webster, Hayne, and Calhoun*, edited by Albert Bushnell Hart and Edward Channing (New York: A. Lovell & Company, 1896), pp. 2–7. Calhounian nullification had been anticipated a generation earlier by none other than the rebel Crazy Jack Lowell, who at a rally protesting Madison's suspension of commerce with England at Faneuil Hall on March 31, 1811, offered a resolution to "oppose by peaceable but firm measures the execution of laws, which if persisted in must and will be resisted." Morison, *Harrison Gray Otis*, pp. 313–314.
82. "Hayne's Reply to Webster," in *Constitutional Doctrines of Webster, Hayne, and Calhoun*, p. 9.
83. "Webster's Second Reply to Hayne," in ibid., 22–23.
84. Nagel, *One Nation Indivisible*, p. 253.
85. Stampp, "The Concept of a Perpetual Union," p. 31.
86. Andrew Jackson, "Proclamation to the People of South Carolina," December 10, 1832, in *Documents of American History*, edited by Henry Steele Commager (New York: Appleton-Century-Crofts, 1968; eighth edition), pp. 262–268.

87. Margaret L. Coit, *John C. Calhoun: American Portrait* (Boston: Houghton Mifflin, 1961), pp. 212–213.

88. Nagel, *One Nation Indivisible*, p. 165.

89. Ralph Waldo Emerson, *Journals of Ralph Waldo Emerson*, vol. 8, edited by Edward Waldo Emerson and Waldo Emerson Forbes (Boston: Houghton Mifflin, 1912), pp. 199, 186.

90. Nagel, *One Nation Indivisible*, p. 277.

91. Madison, *Notes of Debates in the Federal Convention of 1787*, p. 502.

92. Howe, *Political History of Secession*, p. 218.

93. John Greenleaf Whittier, "Massachusetts to Virginia," in *John Greenleaf Whittier's Poetical Works* (New York: Crowell, 1902), pp. 79–82.

94. Thomas D. Morris, *Free Men All: The Personal Liberty Laws of the North* (Baltimore: Johns Hopkins, 1974), p. 168.

95. Jefferson Davis, looking back in his *Rise and Fall of the Confederate Government* (1881), criticized the fugitive slave laws: "My own view was, and is, that it was not a proper subject for legislation by the Federal Congress, but that its enforcement should have been left to the respective States, which, as parties to the compact of the union, should have been held accountable for its fulfillment." Jefferson Davis, *Rise and Fall of the Confederate Government*, vol. 1 (New York: Thomas Yoseloff, 1958/1881), p. 81.

96. Morris, *Free Men All*, p. 180.

97. John L . Thomas, *The Liberator: William Lloyd Garrison* (Boston: Little, Brown, 1963), p. 32.

98. Ibid., 329, 348–349.

99. Jeffrey Rogers Hummel, *Emancipating Slaves, Enslaving Free Men: A History of the American Civil War* (Chicago: Open Court, 1996), pp. 55–56.

100. Thomas, *The Liberator*, p. 409.

101. Quoted in ibid., 149.

102. Descendants of the abolitionists throw right back in the Southrons' faces the Free State of Jones, that beguiling mixture of legend and fact brewed up in the Piney Woods of Mississippi. The story, retold and embellished and bowdlerized over the years, concerns the pro-union county of Jones, where gathered Confederate deserters and mixed-race couples. For a sympathetic rendering of the Free State of Jones that pays special attention to interracial relationships and their historical echoes, see Victoria E. Bynum, *The Free State of Jones: Mississippi's Longest Civil War* (2001); Rudy H. Leverett's *Legend of the Free State of Jones* (1984) is a skeptical examination of the story that emphasizes "the brutality and intimidations of the deserters." Believe what you will.

103. Wendell Phillips, "Disunion," in *Speeches, Lectures, and Letters* (Boston: James Redpath, 1863), pp. 350–351.

104. Quoted in Richard Hofstadter, *The American Political Tradition and the Men Who Made It* (New York: Vintage, 1973/1948), p. 176.

105. Phillips, *Speeches, Lectures, and Letters*, pp. 350, 367.

106. Abraham Lincoln, "First Inaugural Address," *Inaugural Addresses of the Presidents of the United States* (Washington, DC: US Government Printing Office, 1961), pp.

121, 123. Donald W. Livingston, resident philosopher of the new secessionists, likes to quote Lincoln's January 12, 1848, oration against the Mexican War: "Any people anywhere being inclined and having the power have the right to rise up and shake off the existing government, and form a new one which suits them better." Abe later changed his mind.

107. Quoted in Howe, *Political History of Secession*, pp. 560–561.

108. Thomas N. Bonner, "Horace Greeley and the Secession Movement, 1860–1861," *Mississippi Valley Historical Review* 38, no. 3 (December 1951), pp. 432, 440.

109. William C. Wright, *The Secession Movement in the Middle Atlantic States* (Rutherford, NJ: Farleigh Dickinson University Press, 1973), pp. 13–14. Wright's book is a rich source.

110. Ibid., 180.

111. Ibid., 113.

112. Ibid., 193–194.

113. *Congressional Globe*, 36th Congress, 2nd session, December 10, 1860, p. 40.

114. "Republican Party Platform of 1860," The American Presidency Project, www.presidency.ucsb.edu.

115. Powell, *Nullification and Secession in the United States*, pp. 399–400.

116. In *Is Davis a Traitor or Was Secession a Constitutional Right Previous to the War of 1861?* (1866), the Southern philosopher and CSA assistant secretary of war Albert Taylor Bledsoe assures readers that the "subjugation of the Southern States, and their acceptance of the terms dictated by the North, may . . . be considered as having shifted the Federal Government from the basis of compact to that of conquest; and thereby extinguished every claim to the right of secession for the future." Bledsoe, *Is Davis a Traitor or Was Secession a Constitutional Right Previous to the War of 1861?* (Baltimore: Innes & Company, 1866), p. v.

117. Thomas H. Naylor, *Secession: How Vermont and All the Other States Can Save Themselves from the Empire* (Port Townsend, WA: Feral House, 2008), p. 78.

118. Thomas Graham Belden and Marva Robins Belden, *So Fell the Angels* (Boston: Little, Brown, 1956), p. 20.

119. Harold M. Hyman, *The Reconstruction Justice of Salmon P. Chase* (Lawrence: University Press of Kansas, 1997), p. 141.

120. *Texas v. White* 74 US 700 (1869). William Whatley Pierson Jr. wrote in his monograph *Texas Versus White* (1916), "There was in this last sentence a curious inconsistency of reasoning which destroyed the logical finality of the conclusions which Chief Justice Chase had drawn from the preambles of the Articles of Confederation and the Constitution respecting the perpetuity and indissolubility of the Union." William Whatley Pierson Jr., *Texas Versus White: A Study in Legal History* (Durham, NC: Seeman Printery, 1916), p. 58.

Here is Supreme Court justice Antonin Scalia, responding to a screenwriter's question about the legality of secession: "I am afraid I cannot be of much help . . . principally because I cannot imagine that such a question could ever reach the Supreme Court. To begin with, the answer is clear. If there was any constitutional issue resolved by the Civil War, it is that there is no right to secede. (Hence in the Pledge of Allegiance, 'one Nation, indivisible.')" The long reach of Bellamyite

Nationalism smothers Chaseian nuance. Posted by Ben Smith, www.politico.com, February 16, 2010.

121. Arthur E. Morgan, *Edward Bellamy* (Philadelphia: Porcupine Press, 1974), p. 257.

122. Edward Bellamy, *Looking Backward, 2000–1887* (New York: Oxford University Press, 2007/1888), p. 89.

123. Ibid., 122.

124. Arthur Lipow, *Authoritarian Socialism in America: Edward Bellamy and the Nationalist Movement* (Berkeley: University of California Press, 1982), p. 201.

125. Morgan, *Edward Bellamy*, p. 255.

126. Margarette S. Miller, *Twenty-three Words* (Portsmouth, VA: Printcraft Press, 1976), pp. 53–54, 64.

127. John W. Baer, *The Pledge of Allegiance: A Centennial History, 1892–1992*, www .oldtimeislands.org. See also Bill Kauffman, "The Bellamy Boys Pledge Allegiance," *American Enterprise* (October–November 2002), p. 50.

128. Kirkpatrick Sale, "The Most Desirable Option: Reeducating for Secession," *Chronicles*, January 2008, p. 18.

Chapter Two

1. David Ellis, "'Upstate Hicks' Versus 'City Slickers,'" *New York Historical Society Quarterly* 43 (1959), p. 204.

2. Stanley Walker, "New York City: The 49th State," *American Mercury* (December 1935), p. 476.

3. Read the account of the New York ratifying convention in Jonathan Elliot, *Debates in the Several State Conventions on the Adoption of the Federal Constitution* (Philadelphia: J. B. Lippincott, 1836), and marvel at the prescience of Anti-Federalists George Clinton, Melancton Smith, and Thomas Tredwell.

4. *The Correspondence and Public Papers of John Jay*, 1782–1783, vol. 3, edited by Henry P. Johnston (New York: Putnam's, 1891), p. 335. I like this summation from Stefan Bielinski's brief biography of Yates: "Yates was a localist in the literal sense of the world; rarely did his vision extend beyond the parameters of Albany and his native state." Which is to say, he was modest and understood the limits of human vision. Bielinski, *Abraham Yates, Jr. and the New Political Order in Revolutionary New York* (Albany: New York State American Revolution Bicentennial Commission, 1975), p. 56. Melancton Smith easily bested, forensically at least, the dissembling Alexander Hamilton in the debates at the New York ratifying convention. The work of this brilliant and forgotten Founder has recently been collected in *The Anti-Federalist Writings of the Melancton Smith Circle*, edited by Michael P. Zuckert and Derek A. Webb (Indianapolis: Liberty Fund, 2009).

5. Samuel Augustus Pleasants, *Fernando Wood of New York* (New York: Columbia University Press, 1948), p. 26.

6. Jerome Mushkat, *Fernando Wood: A Political Biography* (Kent, OH: Kent State University Press, 1990), p. 16.

7. Pleasants, *Fernando Wood of New York*, p. 26.

8. Quoted in Gerald Benjamin, "The Political Relationship," in *The Two New Yorks: State–City Relations in the Changing Federal System*, edited by Gerald Benjamin and Charles Brecher (New York: Russell Sage Foundation, 1988), p. 109.

9. Tyler G. Anbinder, "Fernando Wood and New York City's Secession from the Union: A Political Reappraisal," *New York History* 68, no. 1 (January 1987), p. 77.

10. Ibid., 78.

11. Pleasants, *Fernando Wood of New York*, p. 114.

12. Anbinder, "Fernando Wood and New York City's Secession from the Union," p. 87.

13. Quoted in Benjamin La Fevre, *Biographies of S. Grover Cleveland and Thomas A. Hendricks* (New York: Baird & Dillon, 1884), p. 113.

14. Mushkat, *Fernando Wood*, p. 94.

15. La Fevre, *Biographies of S. Grover Cleveland and Thomas A. Hendricks*, p. 112.

16. Anbinder, "Fernando Wood and New York City's Secession from the Union," p. 87.

17. La Fevre, *Biographies of S. Grover Cleveland and Thomas A. Hendricks*, p. 113.

18. Jerome Mushkat, "Ben Wood's 'Fort Lafayette': A Source for Studying the Peace Democrats," *Civil War History* 21, no. 2 (June 1975), p. 162.

19. Two other New York City newspapers—the *Morning Express* and the *Day Book*—supported Wood's scheme. William C. Wright, *The Secession Movement in the Middle Atlantic States* (Rutherford, NJ: Farleigh Dickinson University Press, 1973), p. 198. For a superb novella by a New York—Upstate New York, that is— writer with antiwar Democrat sympathies, see Harold Frederic's 1893 work *The Copperhead*, which is included in *Harold Frederic's Stories of York State*, edited by Thomas F. O'Donnell (Syracuse, NY: Syracuse University Press, 1966). On the draft riots, see Iver Bernstein, *The New York City Draft Riots: Their Significance for American Society and Politics in the Age of the Civil War* (New York: Oxford University Press, 1990).

20. Philip S. Foner, *Business and Slavery: The New York Merchants and the Irrepressible Conflict* (New York: Russell & Russell, 1968/1941), p. 285. August Belmont— Democrat, financier, and eponym of the famous horse race—conceded in a letter of December 19, 1860, to a friend in Alabama that "if we did only look to our own material interests and those of our city, we should not deplore the dissolution of the Union. New-York, in such a catastrophe, would cut loose from the Puritanical East and her protective tariff, and without linking her fortunes with our kind but somewhat exacting Southern friends, she would open her magnificent port to the commerce of the world. What Venice was once on the sluggish lagoons of the small Adriatic, New-York would ere long become to the two hemispheres . . ." Belmont preferred, however, that his children bear the "enviable title of American citizens" rather than "New-York merchant princes," and while the sentiment is admirable, one gets the impression that Belmont is trying hard to convince himself. *Letters, Speeches, and Addresses of August Belmont* (privately printed, 1890), p. 39.

21. Ibid., 287.

22. Ellis, Frost, Syrett, and Carman, *A History of New York State* (Ithaca, NY: Cornell University Press, 1957), p. 242.

23. Foner, *Business and Slavery*, p. 295.

24. Anbinder, "Fernando Wood and New York City's Secession from the Union," pp. 88, 90.
25. Once the states of the South cut loose, said Sickles, "then I tell you that imperial city [New York] will throw off the odious government to which she now yields a reluctant allegiance; she will repel the hateful cabal at Albany, which has so long abused its power over her; and with her own flag, sustained by the courage and devotion of her own gallant sons, she will, as a free city, open wide her gates to the civilization and commerce of the world." It doesn't sound as if Representative Sickles was exactly dreading the prospect. *Congressional Globe*, 36th Congress, 2nd session, December 10, 1860, p. 41.
26. "Koch Needles Lifestyles in *Playboy*," Associated Press, February 24, 1982.
27. David Leavitt, "Fears That Haunt a Scrubbed America," *New York Times*, August 19, 1990.
28. William Jennings Bryan, *The First Battle* (Chicago: W. B. Conkey, 1896), p. 200.
29. David Hackett Fischer, *Champlain's Dream* (New York: Simon & Schuster, 2008), p. 112.
30. Wendell Berry, "Higher Education and Home Defense," *Home Economics: Fourteen Essays* (San Francisco: North Point, 1987), p. 50.
31. Token Upstate committee member Joyce Perry of Attica complained, "The [regents] committee was actually loaded with people from Long Island and the other end of the state." Sherrie Negrea, "Rural Libraries to Be Shelved?" *Rochester Democrat and Chronicle*, September 12, 1988. See also Harold Faber, "Rural Libraries Angered by Proposed Regulations," *New York Times*, November 6, 1988.
32. Mailer, "An Instrument for the City," in *Existential Errands* (Boston: Little, Brown, 1972), p. 329.
33. Edward Noyes Westcott, *David Harum: A Story of American Life* (New York: Grosset & Dunlap, 1898), p. 284.
34. Henry W. Clune, *Main Street Beat* (New York: W. W. Norton, 1947), p. 10.
35. Mailer, "An Instrument for the City," p. 330.
36. Ibid., 328–329.
37. Ibid., 329.
38. Joe Flaherty, *Managing Mailer: A Saga of Mailer and Breslin's Siege of City Hall by Norman Mailer's Campaign Manager* (New York: Coward-McCann, 1970), p. 19.
39. Ibid., 40.
40. Mailer, "An Instrument for the City," p. 330.
41. Flaherty, *Managing Mailer*, p. 48.
42. Mailer, "Two Mayoralty Speeches," in *Existential Errands*, pp. 342–343.
43. Flaherty, *Managing Mailer*, pp. 150, 154.
44. Charles McGrath, "Norman Mailer, Towering Writer with Matching Ego, Dies at 84," *New York Times*, November 10, 2007.
45. John Buffalo Mailer, "Summer of '69," *American Conservative*, May 4, 2009, p. 15.
46. Alfred E. Clark, "Mrs. Abzug Opens Drive for 51st State," *New York Times*, June 2, 1971.
47. "Statehood-for-City Advocates Offer Data," *New York Times*, August 15, 1971.

48. Joe Flaherty, "I Hate to Say I Told You So, But . . . ," *New York Times*, February 8, 1974.

49. Emanuel Perlmutter, "Push Starts Here for 51st State," *New York Times*, June 27, 1971.

50. "Statehood Proposal for City Assailed in Report," *New York Times*, August 24, 1971.

51. Edward C. Burks, "City Hall Releases Report Hailing Plan for Statehood," *New York Times*, June 11, 1971. Secession supporters were listed in a full-page ad in the *New York Times* of June 2, 1971, headlined "Free New York City. If We Don't Make It a State, There Won't Be a City." Among them was Robert Abrams, Bronx borough president and later state attorney general. Abrams was defeated by the oily US senator Al D'Amato in the Senate race of 1992, done in by the votes of the Upstaters and Long Islanders he had wisely wanted to discard twenty years earlier. Abrams was so enthusiastic about a city-state that he even suggested a name: Stuyvesant. Not great but not bad, and something of a surprise; given the borough president's famous arrogance, one suspects the name he really had in mind for the new state was Abrams. Edward C. Burks, "Borough Presidents Split on Secession from State," *New York Times*, June 10, 1971.

52. Flaherty, *Managing Mailer*, p. 52.

53. Bella Abzug, *Bella!* (New York: Saturday Review Press, 1972), p. 192.

54. "A Massive Majority for Statehood . . . ," *New York*, August 23, 1971, p. 26.

55. "Free New York City," paid ad, *New York Times*, June 22, 1971.

56. "Statehood Demagoguery," *New York Times*, September 3, 1971.

57. Donna E. Shalala, "New York City-Statehood: An Idea Whose Time Has Passed," Report to the Executive Secretary of the Citizens Union, July 1971.

58. Albert Shanker, "Statehood for New York City?" paid ad, *New York Times*, August 22, 1971.

59. Edward Ranzal, "Petition for Vote on Statehood with 55,398 Names Rejected," *New York Times*, October 1, 1971.

60. Ralph Blumenthal, "Wagner Would Include Suburbs If City Became the 51st State," *New York Times*, June 13, 1971.

61. Washington Irving, *A History of New York*, excerpted in *Writing New York: A Literary Anthology*, edited by Phillip Lopate (New York: Washington Square Press, 1998), p. 2.

62. Howard B. Rock and Deborah Dash Moore, *Cityscapes: A History of New York in Images* (New York: Columbia University Press, 2001), p. 367.

63. Gamaliel Bradford, *Damaged Souls* (Boston: Houghton Mifflin, 1923), p. 126.

64. *Power for Sanity: Selected Editorials of William Cullen Bryant, 1829–1861*, compiled by William Cullen Bryant II (New York: Fordham University Press, 1994), p. xix.

65. Edwin G. Burrows and Mike Wallace, *Gotham: A History of New York City to 1898* (New York: Oxford University Press, 1999), p. 609.

66. Thomas Janvier, *In Old New York* (New York: St. Martins, 2000/1894), p. 1.

67. Walt Whitman, *New York Dissected: A Sheaf of Recently Discovered Newspaper Articles by the Author of Leaves of Grass* (New York: Rufus Rockwell Wilson Inc., 1936), p. 92.

68. Edgar Allan Poe, "Doings of Gotham," excerpted in *Writing New York*, pp. 96, 100–101.
69. David McCullough, *The Great Bridge* (New York: Simon and Schuster, 1972), pp. 25–26.
70. Alan Trachtenberg, *Brooklyn Bridge: Fact and Symbol* (New York: Oxford University Press, 1965), p. 74.
71. Burrows and Wallace, *Gotham*, pp. 1226, 1223.
72. "The Greater New York," *New York Times*, October 11, 1895.
73. Bird S. Coler, *Municipal Government* (New York: D. Appleton, 1900), p. 165.
74. Henry Cabot Lodge, *Daniel Webster* (Boston: Houghton Mifflin, 1886), p. 164.
75. John Tierney, "Brooklyn Could Have Been a Contender," *New York Times Magazine*, December 28, 1997, p. 23.
76. Chip Brown, "Escape from New York," *New York Times Magazine*, January 30, 1994, p. 25.
77. Kevin Sack, "If Staten Island Votes to Secede, What Will Albany Do?" *New York Times*, October 24, 1993.
78. Howard Kurtz, "A Low-Profile Borough's High-Stakes Case for Secession," *Washington Post*, February 9, 1988.
79. "Remedies of a Proud Outcast: The Legal Probability and Implications of Restructuring the Government and Boundaries of the City of New York," New York State Senate Finance Committee Staff Report, July 1983, p. i.
80. Ibid., 2–3.
81. Ibid., appendix A.
82. John Marchi, "An Independent Staten Island," *Empire State Report*, September 1983, p. 42.
83. Brown, "Escape from New York," p. 42.
84. "The Cost of Divorce to Staten Island," *New York Times*, November 4, 1990.
85. Brown, "Escape from New York," p. 44.
86. "Secessionist Turmoil," *New York Times*, February 7, 1993.
87. "Seeking Respect in Queens," *New York Times*, January 26, 1992.
88. Tierney, "Brooklyn Could Have Been a Contender," p. 20.
89. Thomas Wolfe, "Only the Dead Know Brooklyn," excerpted in *Writing New York*, p. 603.
90. Carl Carmer, *My Kind of Country: Favorite Writings About New York* (Syracuse, NY: Syracuse University Press, 1995/1966), p. 12.
91. "Upstate Should Form Own State," *Oneonta Daily Star*, April 17, 1992.
92. Those quotes not cited in the endnotes are from interviews with the author in 1994 and appear in "Smaller Is Beautiful," *American Enterprise*, March–April 1995.
93. Fredric Dicker, "Upstate Pols: Let's Oust the Big, Bad Apple," *New York Post*, March 28, 1992.
94. G. Scott Thomas, "The 51st State," *Buffalo Magazine*, August 12, 1990, p. 7.
95. "Take NYC Out of NY, Senator Says," *Rochester Democrat and Chronicle*, March 29, 1992.
96. Dicker, "Upstate Pols: Let's Oust the Big, Bad Apple."

97. "Divided New York Will Never Happen," *Elmira Star-Gazette*, undated 1992. In a Dial-a-Vote poll by the *Star-Gazette* in spring 1992, readers endorsed Upstate secession 2,813–162.

98. Jay Gallagher, "Splitting Up NY: Statute of Liberty?" Gannett News Service, undated 1992.

99. "West New York," *Syracuse Post-Standard*, April 27, 1992.

100. "Secession No Solution," *Batavia Daily News*, April 15, 1992. Long Islanders, too, liked the foretaste of self-determination. Republican assemblyman Frederick Parola, complaining that "Nassau and Suffolk [Counties] are the milk cows for the state," introduced a Long Island statehood bill. Robert Berczuk, "McGee Calls for New State Called West New York," undated, unplaced 1992. Parola's bovine metaphor calls to mind the slogan of Spain's Basque separatists, who say that "the cow of the state has its mouth in Basque country but its udder elsewhere." Paul Roberts, "The Goodbye Whirl," *New Republic*, November 21, 1994, p. 12.

101. Benjamin Sarlin, "A Secession Plan Is Floated for New York City," *New York Sun*, January 30, 2008.

102. *Congressional Record*, 92nd Congress, 1st session, June 29, 1971, p. 22570.

103. Christopher Ketcham, "News & Columns," *New York Press*, December 28, 2004.

104. Benjamin Sarlin, "A Secession Plan Is Floated for New York City."

105. Stanley Walker, "New York City: The 49th State," p. 476.

Chapter Three

1. William Allen White, *The Editor and His People* (New York: Macmillan, 1924), p. 174.

2. Quoted in Robert Smith Bader, *Hayseeds, Moralizers, and Methodists: The Twentieth-Century Image of Kansas* (Lawrence: University Press of Kansas, 1988), p. 56.

3. John Marshall, "Lawyer: Stevens County Should Secede," *Hutchison News*, February 4, 1992.

4. Linda Mowery-Denning, "United We Stand?" *Salina Journal*, May 10, 1992.

5. Don Concannon to Stevens County Board of Commissioners, January 27, 1992.

6. Author's interview with Don Concannon, December 13, 1994. See Kauffman, "Smaller Is Beautiful," *American Enterprise*, March–April 1995.

7. Marshall, "Lawyer: Stevens County Should Secede."

8. Kurt Gaston, "Stevens County Will Vote on Secession," *Southwest Daily Times* (Liberal, KS), March 2, 1992.

9. Author's interview with Bob Boaldin, December 19, 1994.

10. Kurt Gaston, "Secession 'Wildfire' Spreading, Concannon Warns Legislature," *Southwest Daily Times*, February 14, 1992.

11. "One Man, One Movement," *Southwest Daily Times*, undated (February 1992).

12. Author's interview with Robert Smith Bader, December 9, 1994.

13. Author's interview with Concannon.

14. Don Concannon letter to Thomas H. Naylor, June 4, 2001.

15. Thomas Jefferson to John Cartwright, June 5, 1824, in *The Political Writings of*

Thomas Jefferson, edited by Edward Dumbauld (Indianapolis: Bobbs-Merrill, 1981/1955), p. 101.

16. "Jerry Brown Talks," *Chronicles*, November 1994, p. 20.

17. Carey McWilliams, *California: The Great Exception* (New York: Current Books, 1949), p. 43.

18. Kevin Starr, "Three Californias: Why It's Not an Eccentric Idea," *Los Angeles Times*, June 20, 1993.

19. William Henry Ellison, "The Movement for State Division of California, 1849–1860," *Southwestern Historical Quarterly* 17, no. 2 (October 1913), p. 103. See also "Two New Californias: An Equal Division," California Assembly Office of Research, March 1992, pp. 11–27.

20. Ellison, "The Movement for State Division of California," pp. 113–114.

21. Albert L. Hurtado, *John Sutter: A Life on the North American Frontier* (Norman: University of Oklahoma Press, 2006), p. xi.

22. James Peter Zollinger, *Sutter: The Man and His Empire* (New York: Oxford University Press, 1939), p. 171.

23. Michael Di Leo and Eleanor Smith, *Two Californias: The Truth About the Split-State Movement* (Covelo, CA: Island Press, 1983), p. 26. The book is a sprightly tour of the many forms such California dreamin' has taken over the years.

24. "Two New Californias: An Equal Division," p. 21.

25. Carey McWilliams, *California: The Great Exception*, p. 55.

26. Ellison, "The Movement for State Division of California," p. 134.

27. Roberta M. McDow, "State Separation Schemes, 1907–1921," *California Historical Society Quarterly* 49, no. 1 (March 1970), p. 39.

28. Di Leo and Smith, *Two Californias*, p. 46.

29. Bernita Tickner and Gail Fiorini-Jenner, *The State of Jefferson* (San Francisco: Arcadia Publishing, 2005), p. 7.

30. Christopher Hall, "A Jefferson State of Mind," *Via*, September 2003, www .viamagazine.com.

31. Di Leo and Smith, *Two Californias*, p. 56. Jefferson presaged a later, even more mischievous secession by Kinney, Minnesota, an Iron Range town in need of a new water system. On July 13, 1977, it informed US secretary of state Cyrus Vance: "Be it resolved that the City Council of Kinney in Kinney, Minnesota, has decided to secede from the United States of America, and become a foreign country. Our area is large enough for it. We are twelve square blocks, three blocks wide and four blocks long. We will be similar to Monaco. It is much easier to get assistance as a foreign country, which we need badly, and there is no paperwork to worry about. If necessary, we will be glad to declare war and lose. However, if this is a requirement, we would appreciate being able to surrender real quick, as our Mayor works as a nurse in a hospital, and most of our council members work in a nearby mine and cannot get much time off from work." Kinney issued more than sixteen hundred passports, including one to Johnny Carson, and it got the water project, too. Kinney remained in the union. Lee Bloomquist, "Independent Spirit Thrives in Kinney," *Duluth News Tribune*, July 8, 2007.

32. Richard Reinhardt, "The Short, Happy History of the State of Jefferson," *American West* 9, no. 3 (May 1972), p. 38.
33. "Gable's Gold Coast," *Time*, April 4, 1938.
34. Reinhardt, "The Short, Happy History of the State of Jefferson," p. 36.
35. Kirk Johnson, "A State That Never Was in Wyoming," *New York Times*, July 24, 2008.
36. Reinhardt, "The Short, Happy History of the State of Jefferson," p. 38.
37. "Here Are Winner's Reasons for Suggesting Name of Jefferson," *Siskiyou Daily News*, November 24, 1941, www.jeffersonstate.com.
38. "A State of Mind," *Siskiyou Daily News*, November 27, 1941, www.jeffersonstate .com.
39. Emma Brown, "State of Jefferson: A Place Apart," *High Country News*, November 13, 2006.
40. Reinhardt, "The Short, Happy History of the State of Jefferson," p. 38.
41. Ibid., 40.
42. Hall, "A Jefferson State of Mind."
43. "Many Envoys Will Attend Mass Meeting," *Siskiyou Daily News*, December 2, 1941, www.jeffersonstate.com.
44. "It Was a Tough Battle, Men, But We Won," *Siskiyou Daily News*, November 19, 1941, www.jeffersonstate.com.
45. "District Attorney Retires at Age 87," Akron (NY) daily newspaper, undated 1950, courtesy June Chamberlain. Thanks, June—I'da voted for the Judge.
46. Tickner and Fiorini-Jenner, *The State of Jefferson*, p. 117.
47. Di Leo and Smith, *Two Californias*, p. 59.
48. Reinhardt, "The Short, Happy History of the State of Jefferson," pp. 40, 63.
49. Di Leo and Smith, *Two Californias*, p. 53.
50. Ibid., 65.
51. Edmund G. Brown, *Reagan and Reality* (New York: Praeger, 1970), p. 7.
52. Ibid., 212, 214.
53. Joaquin Miller, "The Gold That Grew by Shasta Town," *The Poetical Works of Joaquin Miller* (New York: Putnam's, 1923), p. 369.
54. S. J. Diamond, "Split Personality," *Los Angeles Times*, July 25, 1993.
55. Author's interview with Stan Statham, December 13, 1994.
56. Diamond, "Split Personality."
57. "Ten Commonly Asked Questions About Dividing California," undated handout from the office of Stan Statham.
58. Assembly Bill No. 3, California legislature, December 7, 1992.
59. "Two New Californias: An Equal Division," p. 2.
60. Di Leo and Smith, *Two Californias*, p. 201.
61. "Two New Californias: An Equal Division," pp. 2, 5.
62. Author's interview with Statham.
63. "Two New Californias: An Equal Division," p. 15.
64. Katherine Bishop, "California Dreaming, 1991 Version: North Secedes and Forms 51st State," *New York Times*, November 30, 1991.

65. Starr, "Three Californias: Why It's Not an Eccentric Idea."

66. "Two New Californias: An Equal Division," p. 2.

67. Diamond, "Split Personality."

68. Bishop, "California Dreaming, 1991 Version."

69. Frederick Rose, "Can an Entire State Have an Identity Crisis? Yes—If It's California," *Wall Street Journal*, November 16, 1993.

70. Di Leo and Smith, *Two Californias*, p. 163.

71. Joseph Kahn, "San Fernando Valley Looks to a Life After Los Angeles," *New York Times*, April 20, 2002.

72. Geoffrey F. Segal and Samuel R. Staley, "City of Angels, Valley of Rebels," *Cato Policy Report*, September–October 2002, p. 1.

73. Pam Belluck, "The New American Spirit: Divided We Stand," *New York Times*, May 31, 1998.

74. Julie-Anne Boudreau and Roger Keil, *Urban Studies* 38, no. 10 (2001), pp. 1719, 1721.

75. Ibid., 1702.

76. Matt Smith, "How to Secede from Jesusland, Without Really Fighting," *SF Weekly*, December 8, 2004.

77. Gar Alperovtiz, "California Split," *New York Times*, February 10, 2007.

78. Di Leo and Smith, *Two Californias*, p. 61.

79. Jim Gogek, "Don't Say 'Dream On': State Split Is Sensible," *San Diego Union-Tribune*, June 21, 1993.

80. Jim Evans, "Upstate, Downstate," *Sacramento News & Review*, January 2, 2002.

81. John Shelton Reed, *My Tears Spoiled My Aim and Other Reflections on Southern Culture* (Columbia: University of Missouri Press, 1993), p. 28.

82. Jason Heald, e-mail to the author, February 20, 2008.

83. Sandy Kleffman, "Jefferson Only State of Mind in Northern California," *Contra Costa Times*, September 24, 2000.

84. Brian Petersen, e-mails to the author, April 5 and 6, 2008.

85. Kevin Fagan, "A Move to Secede on California–Oregon Border," *San Francisco Chronicle*, October 5, 2008.

86. E. J. Schultz, "Ex-Assemblyman Pushes Plan to Split California into Two States," *Sacramento Bee*, February 26, 2009.

87. Ernest Callenbach, *Ecotopia* (New York: Bantam, 1990/1975), p. 3.

88. Ibid., 164.

89. Di Leo and Smith, *Two Californias*, p. 181.

90. Wendell Berry, "How to Be a Poet (to Remind Myself)," *Given: Poems* (Washington, DC: Shoemaker & Hoard, 2005), p. 18.

91. Jason Peters, "Robert Traver: Anatomy of a Fisherman," *University Bookman* 46, no. 3 (Fall 2008), p. 19.

92. Greg Kaza letter to Thomas H. Naylor, March 23, 2001. See also David Binder, "Yes, They're Yoopers, and Proud of It," *New York Times*, September 14, 1995.

93. "Texas Threat," *Time*, May 26, 1930.

94. Sam Howe Verhovek, "Serious Face on a Texas Independence Group," *New York Times*, January 24, 1997.

95. Frank Zoretich, "NM Will Secede to New Nation, Prof. Says," *Albuquerque Tribune*, February 17, 2000.

96. "Rich LI Towns Want Out," Associated Press, *Rochester Democrat and Chronicle*, November 28, 1996.

97. Doug Gross, "White Atlanta Suburbs Push for Secession," Associated Press, January 23, 2007.

98. "Descendants of Sitting Bull, Crazy Horse Break Away from US," press release, Agence France-Presse, December 20, 2007.

99. Troy R. Johnson, *The Occupation of Alcatraz Island* (Urbana: University of Illinois Press, 1996), p. 1. Thanks to Jesse Walker for steering me toward Alcatraz.

100. Adam Fortunate Eagle, *Alcatraz! Alcatraz! The Indian Occupation of 1969–1971* (Berkeley: Heyday Books, 1992), p. 112.

101. Howard Husock, "Let's Break Up the Big Cities," *City Journal* (Winter 1998).

102. Jack London, *The Iron Heel* (New York: Review of Reviews, 1917/1908), p. 117.

103. "On a Final 'Duh' Note," *Rochester Democrat and Chronicle*, April 16, 1999.

104. White, *The Editor and His People*, p. 174.

105. *Journal of the North Dakota Senate*, January 17, 1933, pp. 139–140. See also "Secession," *Time*, January 30, 1933.

Chapter Four

1. *Congressional Record*, March 11, 1959, 86th Congress, 1st session, p. 3872.

2. *Congressional Record*, June 26, 1958, 85th Congress, 2nd session, p. 12294.

3. *Congressional Record*, March 9, 1953, 83rd Congress, 1st session, p. 1782.

4. *Congressional Record*, March 10, 1953, 83rd Congress, 1st session, p. 1811.

5. Quoted in Ernest Gruening, *The State of Alaska* (New York: Random House, 1968), p. 483.

6. *Congressional Record*, June 30, 1958, 85th Congress, 2nd session, p. 12642.

7. John McPhee, *Coming into the Country* (New York: Farrar, Straus, and Giroux, 1977), p. 18.

8. Jack London, *Lost Face* (New York: Macmillan, 1910), p. 9.

9. Paul S. Holbo, *Tarnished Expansion: The Alaska Scandal, the Press, and Congress, 1867–1871* (Knoxville: University of Tennessee Press, 1983), p. 5.

10. James P. Shenton, *Robert John Walker: A Politician from Jackson to Lincoln* (New York: Columbia University Press, 1961), pp. 117, 135.

11. Ibid., 126.

12. Ibid., 186, 189.

13. Ibid., 211.

14. Victor J. Farrar, *The Annexation of Russian America to the United States* (Washington, DC: W. F. Roberts, 1937), p. 2.

15. Ibid., 14.

16. Dexter Clark and Lynette Clark, "Alaska: Legitimate State or Future Nation?" *Second Republic*, July 2004, p. 12.

17. Ronald J. Jensen, *The Alaska Purchase and Russian–American Relations* (Seattle: University of Washington Press, 1975), p. 63.

18. Glyndon G. Van Deusen, *William Henry Seward* (New York: Oxford University Press, 1967), p. 532.
19. Farrar, *The Annexation of Russian America to the United States*, pp. 111–112.
20. Ibid., 113–114.
21. Thomas A. Bailey, "Why the United States Purchased Alaska," *Pacific Historical Review*, vol. 3 (1934), pp. 40–41.
22. Jensen, *The Alaska Purchase and Russian–American Relations*, p. 85.
23. Ibid., 89.
24. George R. Stewart, *Names on the Land: A Historical Account of Place-Naming in the United States* (New York: New York Review of Books, 2008/1945), p. 398.
25. Ibid., 388.
26. Thomas Graham Belden and Marva Robins Belden, *So Fell the Angels* (Boston: Little, Brown, 1956), p. 183.
27. Jensen, *The Alaska Purchase and Russian–American Relations*, p. 92.
28. See Charles A. Jellison, *Fessenden of Maine: Civil War Senator* (Syracuse, NY: Syracuse University Press, 1962).
29. Karel D. Bicha, *C. C. Washburn and the Upper Mississippi Valley* (New York: Garland, 1995), p. 58; and *Israel, Elihu, and Cadwallader Washburn: A Chapter in American Biography*, compiled by Gaillard Hunt (New York: Macmillan, 1925), p. 367.
30. *Congressional Globe*, November 25, 1867, 40th Congress, 1st session, p. 792.
31. Jensen, *The Alaska Purchase and Russian–American Relations*, p. 114.
32. Richard E. Welch Jr., "Buying Alaska: The Myth of 'Icebergia,'" in *Interpreting Alaska's History: An Anthology*, edited by Mary Childers Mangusso and Stephen W. Haycox (Anchorage: Alaska Pacific University Press, 1989), p. 154.
33. Holbo, *Tarnished Expansion*, p. 12.
34. Donald Marquand Dozer, "Anti-Expansionism During the Johnson Administration," *Pacific Historical Review* 12 (1943), p. 259.
35. Jensen, *The Alaska Purchase and Russian–American Relations*, p. 118.
36. Farrar, *The Annexation of Russian America to the United States*, p. 95.
37. *An Alaskan Reader, 1867–1967*, edited by Ernest Gruening (New York: Meredith Press, 1966), p. 369.
38. *Congressional Globe*, July 7, 1868, 40th Congress, 2nd session, p. 3810.
39. Ibid., 3813.
40. Van Deusen, *William Henry Seward*, p. 527.
41. Dozer, "Anti-Expansionism During the Johnson Administration," p. 265.
42. Brainerd Dyer, "Robert J. Walker on Acquiring Greenland and Iceland," *Mississippi Valley Historical Review* 27 (1940–41), pp. 264, 266.
43. Dozer, "Anti-Expansionism During the Johnson Administration," pp. 274–275.
44. Quoted in Gruening, *An Alaskan Reader*, p. 380.
45. See Nancy Warren Ferrell, *Barrett Willoughby: Alaska's Forgotten Lady* (Fairbanks: University of Alaska Press, 1994).
46. Gruening, *An Alaskan Reader*, p. 384.
47. James R. Shortridge, "Planting Alaska," in Mangusso and Haycox, *Interpreting Alaska's History: An Anthology*, p. 334.

48. William M. Armstrong, *E. L. Godkin: A Biography* (Albany: SUNY Press, 1978), p. 107.

49. John S. Whitehead, *Completing the Union: Alaska, Hawai'i, and the Battle for Statehood* (Albuquerque: University of New Mexico Press, 2004), p. 48.

50. Stephen Haycox, *Alaska: An American Colony* (Seattle: University of Washington Press, 2002), pp. 167–168.

51. Mangusso and Haycox, *Interpreting Alaska's History: An Anthology*, p. 15.

52. Gore Vidal, *Williwaw* (Chicago: University of Chicago Press, 2003/1946).

53. Haycox, *Alaska: An American Colony*, p. 264.

54. Quoted in Whitehead, *Completing the Union*, p. 201.

55. Ibid., 98–99.

56. Haycox, *Alaska: An American Colony*, pp. 266, 268.

57. James J. Weston, "Sharlot Hall: Arizona's Pioneer Lady of Literature," *Journal of the West* 4 (October 1965), p. 539.

58. *Sharlot Hall on the Arizona Strip*, edited by C. Gregory Crampton (Flagstaff, AZ: Northland Press, 1975), p. 2.

59. Ibid., 3.

60. Sharlot M. Hall, "Arizona," in *Cactus and Pine* (Prescott: Sharlot Hall Historical Society of Arizona, 1989/1924), pp. 106–110.

61. Eric Gislason, "Edna Ferber's *Ice Palace*: The *Uncle Tom's Cabin* of Alaska Statehood," http://xroads.virginia.edu.

62. Edna Ferber, *Ice Palace* (Garden City, NY: Doubleday, 1958), pp. 14–15.

63. Robert B. Atwood, "Alaska's Struggle for Statehood," in *The New States: Alaska and Hawaii*, edited by William P. Lineberry (New York: H. W. Wilson, 1963), p. 17.

64. Gruening, *An Alaskan Reader*, pp. 382–383.

65. John S. Whitehead, "Anti-Statehood and Its Legacy in Alaska and Hawaii," December 1988, Alaska Humanities Forum, p. 5.

66. Quoted in "Senator Monroney Urges Commonwealth Status in *Collier's* Article," *Daily Alaskan*, February 18, 1954, www.alaska.edu/creatingalaska/newsarchive.

67. Whitehead, "Anti-Statehood and Its Legacy in Alaska and Hawaii," p. 15.

68. Ibid., 8.

69. Daniel J. Elazar, introduction to Gerald A. McBeath and Thomas A. Morehouse, *Alaska Politics and Government* (Lincoln: University of Nebraska Press, 1994), p. xvi.

70. Whitehead, "Anti-Statehood and Its Legacy in Alaska and Hawaii," pp. 22–25.

71. Gruening, *An Alaskan Reader*, p. 385.

72. Ferber, *Ice Palace*, p. 104.

73. *Congressional Record*, June 30, 1958, 85th Congress, 2nd session, p. 12643.

74. *Congressional Record*, June 26, 1958, 85th Congress, 2nd session, p. 12294.

75. *Congressional Record*, March 10, 1953, 83rd Congress, 1st session, p. 1808.

76. *Congressional Record*, May 26, 1958, 85th Congress, 2nd session, p. 9505.

77. *Congressional Record*, March 11, 1959, 86th Congress, 1st session, p. 3887.

78. *Congressional Record*, June 30, 1958, 85th Congress, 2nd session, p. 12643.

79. *Congressional Record*, June 26, 1958, 85th Congress, 2nd session, p. 12299.

80. *Congressional Record*, March 11, 1959, 86th Congress, 1st session, p. 3872.

81. Mike Coppock, "On Vogler, an Independent Alaska," www.juneauempire.com.
82. McPhee, *Coming into the Country*, pp. 316–317.
83. "Project Jukebox," Interview with Joe Vogler, March 29, 1991, University of Alaska, http://jukebox.uaf.edu.
84. Coppock, "On Vogler, an Independent Alaska."
85. Walter R. Borneman, *Alaska: Saga of a Bold Land* (New York: HarperCollins, 2003), p. 241.
86. "Project Jukebox," Interview with Joe Vogler, March 29, 1991.
87. McPhee, *Coming into the Country*, p. 317.
88. Quoted in Maria Williams, "Missing Myth—Alaska Buzzes with Theories on Maverick's Fate," *Seattle Times*, August 5, 1993.
89. Terrence Cole, "The History of a History: The Making of Jeannette Paddock Nichols's *Alaska*," in Mangusso and Haycox, *Interpreting Alaska's History: An Anthology*, pp. 465–466.
90. Clark and Clark, "Alaska: Legitimate State or Future Nation?" p. 16.
91. Ibid., 16–17.
92. "Project Jukebox," Interview with Joe Vogler, March 29, 1991.
93. Joe Vogler, "Alaska and Statehood, A Factual Primer," 1990, www.akip.org.
94. Jon Dougherty, "Alaskan Party Stumps for Independence," February 25, 2001, worldnetdaily.com.
95. Vogler, "Alaska and Statehood, A Factual Primer."
96. John S. Whitehead, e-mail to the author, May 16, 2008.
97. "Project Jukebox," Interview with Joe Vogler, March 29, 1991.
98. Williams, "Missing Myth—Alaska Buzzes with Theories on Maverick's Fate."
99. "Project Jukebox," Interview with Joe Vogler, March 29, 1991.
100. John S. Whitehead letter to the author, February 23, 2008.
101. Haycox, *Alaska: An American Colony*, pp. 280, 304.
102. McBeath and Morehouse, *Alaska Politics and Government*, p. 92.
103. Mangusso and Haycox, *Interpreting Alaska's History*, p. 5.
104. McBeath and Morehouse, *Alaska Politics and Government*, p. 145.
105. Ibid., 75.
106. Whitehead, "Anti-Statehood and Its Legacy in Alaska and Hawaii," p. 28.
107. McBeath and Morehouse, *Alaska Politics and Government*, p. 307.
108. Bill Kauffman, "Mr. Marrou Goes to Juneau," *Reason*, October 1986, pp. 33–37. I had a blast writing that piece.
109. Quoted in Dick Randolph, *Freedom for Alaskans* (Aurora, IL: Caroline House, 1982), p. 35.
110. "Project Jukebox," Interview with Joe Vogler, March 29, 1991.
111. Hal Spencer, "As Isolationism and Racism Intersect," *New York Times*, October 23, 1987.
112. Thomas H. Naylor, "Sarah Palin: America's Evita," distributed column, September 15, 2008.
113. Bill Kauffman, "Manchester Disunited," *American Conservative*, December 15, 2008, p. 35.

114. Naylor, "Sarah Palin: America's Evita."

115. Lynette Clark, e-mail to the author, March 23, 2008.

116. Lynette Clark, e-mail to the author, April 25, 2009.

117. Bob Bird, e-mail to the author, April 25, 2009.

118. Memorandum to Lieutenant Governor Sean Parnell from Sarah J. Felix, assistant attorney general, State of Alaska, February 20, 2007.

119. Paul C. Nagel, *One Nation Indivisible*, p. 106.

Chapter Five

1. Charles Callan Tansill, *The Foreign Policy of Thomas Francis Bayard, 1885–1897* (New York: Fordham University Press, 1940), p. 361.

2. George R. Stewart, *Names on the Land: A Historical Account of Place-Naming in the United States* (New York: New York Review of Books, 2008/1945), pp. 420–421.

3. Lawrence H. Fuchs, *Hawaii Pono: A Social History* (New York: Harcourt, Brace & World, 1961), p. 24.

4. Tansill, *The Foreign Policy of Thomas Francis Bayard*, p. 368. Diplomatic historian Merze Tate of Howard University concluded that "the acquisition of the islands, outside of a few personally interested New Englanders and Californians, was popular only in the southern slave holding states." Merze Tate, "Slavery and Racism as Deterrents to the Annexation of Hawaii, 1854–1855," *Journal of Negro History* 47, no. 1 (January 1962), p. 18.

5. *Congressional Record*, June 22, 1898, 55th Congress, 2nd session, p. 6230.

6. Charles W. Calhoun, *Gilded Age Cato: The Life of Walter Q. Gresham* (Lexington: University Press of Kentucky, 1988), p. 6.

7. Ibid., 22–23.

8. Ibid., 102.

9. Ibid., 135, 167–168.

10. Ibid., 135.

11. Tansill, *The Foreign Policy of Thomas Francis Bayard*, p. 404.

12. Calhoun, *Gilded Age Cato*, p. 148.

13. Grover Cleveland, "First Annual Message," December 4, 1893, www.presidency.ucsb.edu.

14. Fuchs, *Hawaii Pono*, p. 33.

15. Thomas J. Osborne, *"Empire Can Wait": American Opposition to Hawaiian Annexation, 1893–1898* (Kent, OH: Kent State University Press, 1981), pp. 147–148.

16. Calhoun, *Gilded Age Cato*, pp. 221, 171.

17. Osborne, *"Empire Can Wait,"* p. xii. This was a favorite image of the anti-imperialists. Senator Donelson Caffery (D-LA) asserted that "this Hawaiian scheme is but the entering wedge that cleaves a way open for empire." *Congressional Record*, June 29, 1898, 55th Congress, 2nd session, p. 6483.

18. *Congressional Record*, June 22, 1898, 55th Congress, 2nd session, p. 6229.

19. Osborne, *"Empire Can Wait,"* p. 7.

20. Ibid., 29.
21. George Ticknor Curtis, "Is It Constitutional?" *North American Review* 156 (1893), pp. 285–286.
22. Osborne, *"Empire Can Wait,"* pp. 39, 73.
23. Quoted in *Congressional Record*, June 22, 1898, 55th Congress, 2nd session, p. 6351.
24. "Republican Party Platform of 1896," www.presidency.ucsb.edu.
25. "Petition Against Annexation," 1897, www.archives.gov/education/lessons/hawaii-petition.
26. *Congressional Globe*, December 21, 1870, 41st Congress, 3rd session, p. 226.
27. *Congressional Globe*, January 9, 1870, 41st Congress, 2nd session, p. 386.
28. *Congressional Globe*, December 21, 1870, 41st Congress, 3rd session, p. 225. No whitewashing here. Despite his eloquent denunciation of the "spirit of greed, this land-robbing spirit" that motivated the Grant administration to propose the annexation of Santo Domingo, Senator Bayard, alas, disparaged its people as "a semi-barbarous race, the descendants of African slaves, whose attempts at self-government, continued for upward of half a century, have been but a series of blood-stained failures; whose population have dwindled away to a mere fraction of their former number in internecine strife and moral and physical degeneration. Their institutions are mere mockeries, bloody travesties of political government, and to them the presence of a strong-handed and just-minded white ruler would be the greatest blessing that Heaven could bestow." Ibid. There is an appalling ungenerosity of spirit in Bayard's remarks, but it would be dishonest to pretend he never uttered them.
29. Osborne, *"Empire Can Wait,"* p. 65.
30. *Congressional Record*, July 6, 1898, 55th Congress, 2nd session, p. 6702.
31. *The New States: Alaska and Hawaii*, edited by William P. Lineberry (New York: H. W. Wilson, 1963), pp. 46–47.
32. Fuchs, *Hawaii Pono*, p. 158.
33. Ibid., 153.
34. Ibid., 73.
35. John S. Whitehead, e-mail to the author, May 27, 2008.
36. John S. Whitehead, *Completing the Union: Alaska, Hawai'i, and the Battle for Statehood* (Albuquerque: University of New Mexico Press, 2004), p. 67.
37. *The New States: Alaska and Hawaii*, p. 49.
38. Fuchs, *Hawaii Pono*, p. 83.
39. Ibid., 379–380.
40. Whitehead, *Completing the Union*, pp. 5, 8.
41. Fuchs, *Hawaii Pono*, p. 411.
42. Whitehead, *Completing the Union*, p. 150.
43. Whitehead, "Anti-Statehood and Its Legacy in Alaska and Hawaii," p. 51.
44. Ibid., 52.
45. Testimony of Senator Kamokila Campbell, "Statehood for Hawaii," Hearings Before the Subcommittee of the Committee on the Territories, January 17, 1946, US House of Representatives, 79th Congress, 2nd session (Washington, DC: Government Printing Office, 1946), pp. 481–482.

46. Ibid., 482.

47. Ibid., 484, 490–491. The "100 percent" remark is from Kamokila Campbell, "Frank Comments by a Feminine Legislator," in *Hawai'i Chronicles III: World War II in Hawai'i, from the Pages of* Paradise of the Pacific, edited by Bob Dye (Honolulu: University of Hawaii Press, 2000), p. 192.

48. Testimony of Senator Kamokila Campbell, "Statehood for Hawaii," p. 482.

49. Ibid., 491.

50. Ibid., 499.

51. Whitehead, "Anti-Statehood and Its Legacy in Alaska and Hawaii," p. 60.

52. *Congressional Record*, March 10, 1953, 83rd Congress, 1st session, p. 1809.

53. *Congressional Record*, March 11, 1959, 86th Congress, 1st session, p. 3885.

54. Whitehead, *Completing the Union*, p. 4.

55. Fuchs, *Hawaii Pono*, pp. 412–413.

56. Ibid., 414.

57. Ibid., 82.

58. Whitehead, "Anti-Statehood and Its Legacy in Alaska and Hawaii," p. 56.

59. Ibid., 65.

60. "Hawaii at 40 Faces Midlife Crisis, Mulls Where It's Going," Associated Press, August 21, 1999.

61. Haunani-Kay Trask, *From a Native Daughter: Colonialism and Sovereignty in Hawaii* (Honolulu: University of Hawaii Press, 1999/1993), p. 66.

62. Ibid., 59.

63. Ibid., 2.

64. Ibid., 141.

65. Lilikala Kame'eleihiwa, "The Hawaiian Sovereignty Movement," in *Islands in Captivity: The Record of the International Tribune on the Rights of Indigenous Hawaiians*, edited by Ward Churchill and Sharon H. Venne (Cambridge, MA: South End Press, 2004), p. xx.

66. Milalani B. Trask, "The Politics of Oppression," in ibid., pp. 286–87.

67. Kame'eleihiwa, "The Hawaiian Sovereignty Movement," p. xxi.

68. Mark Niesse, "Hawaiian Group Demands Restoration of the Monarchy," Associated Press, June 19, 2008.

69. "A Century After Annexation, Native Hawaiians Feel Ignored," Associated Press, August 13, 1998.

70. Author's interview with Jon Olsen, November 15, 2008.

71. Kame'eleihiwa, "The Hawaiian Sovereignty Movement," p. xix.

72. Ibid., xxv.

73. "Recommendations of the Peoples' International Tribunal, Hawai'i," in *Islands in Captivity*, p. 725.

74. Quoted in Johnny Liberty and Richard Neff Hubbard, "The Rape of Paradise," *Perceptions Magazine*, March–April 1996.

75. Kame'eleihiwa, "The Hawaiian Sovereignty Movement," p. xxvi.

76. Trask, *From a Native Daughter*, p. 89.

77. John S. Whitehead, letter to the author, February 23, 2008.

78. John S. Whitehead, e-mail to the author, June 4, 2008.

79. Author's interview with Ku Ching, November 15, 2008.

80. Trask, *From a Native Daughter*, pp. 132, 146.

81. Seth Faison, "Color Taiwan Red, White and Blue? (He's Serious)," *New York Times*, August 4, 1999.

82. Joe Vogler, "Alaska and Statehood, A Factual Primer," 1990, www.akip.org.

83. Testimony of Senator Kamokila Campbell, "Statehood for Hawaii," p. 499.

84. "Report of Speech Delivered at Worcester, Mass., on Sept. 12, 1848," *Complete Works of Abraham Lincoln*, vol. 2, edited by John G. Nicolay and John Hay (New York: Francis D. Tandy, 1905), p. 94.

Chapter Six

1. William Graham Sumner, "The Fallacy of Territorial Extension," in *War and Other Essays* (New Haven, CT: Yale University Press, 1911), p. 292.

2. Paul C. Nagel, *The Sacred Trust: American Nationality, 1798–1898* (New York: Oxford University Press, 1971), p. 254.

3. *Congressional Record*, January 9, 1899, 55th Congress, 3rd session, pp. 493–502.

4. Jose Trias Monge, *Puerto Rico: The Trials of the Oldest Colony in the World* (New Haven, CT: Yale University Press, 1997), pp. 25–26.

5. Nelson A. Miles, *Serving the Republic: Memoirs of the Civil and Military Life of Nelson A. Miles* (New York: Harper & Brothers, 1911), p. 302.

6. Ruben Berrios Martinez, "Puerto Rico's Decolonization: The Time Is Now," *Foreign Affairs* 76, no. 6 (November–December 1997), p. 112.

7. Luis Munoz Marin, "The Sad Case of Porto Rico," *American Mercury* 16 (1929), p. 136.

8. Martinez, "Puerto Rico's Decolonization," p. 104.

9. Marin, "The Sad Case of Porto Rico," pp. 139–140.

10. Ibid., 141.

11. Raymond Carr, *Puerto Rico: A Colonial Experiment* (New York: NYU Press, 1984), pp. 168–169.

12. Mariano Negron-Portillo, "Puerto Rico: Surviving Colonialism and Nationalism," in *Puerto Rican Jam: Rethinking Colonialism and Nationalism*, edited by Frances Negron-Muntaner and Ramon Grosfoguel (Minneapolis: University of Minnesota Press, 1997), p. 50.

13. Martinez, "Puerto Rico's Decolonization," p. 106.

14. Jose A. Cabranes, "Puerto Rico: Out of the Colonial Closet," *Foreign Policy* 33 (Winter 1978–79), pp. 79, 82.

15. Cesar Andreu Iglesias, *Los derrotados* (*The Vanquished*), translated by Sidney W. Mintz (Chapel Hill: University of North Carolina Press, 2002/1956), p. 10.

16. Ibid., 51.

17. Ibid., 113.

18. Antonio M. Stevens-Arroyo, "Puerto Rico's Future Status: Prisoners of Many Myths," *The Nation*, January 22, 1990, pp. 86–90.

19. Martinez, "Puerto Rico's Decolonization," pp. 102, 110.

20. Carr, *Puerto Rico: A Colonial Experiment*, p. 179.
21. Jorge Amselle, "State 'Hood," *National Review*, August 11, 1997, p. 38.
22. Stevens-Arroyo, "Puerto Rico's Future Status."
23. Negron-Portillo, "Puerto Rico: Surviving Colonialism and Nationalism," p. 53.
24. Carr, *Puerto Rico: A Colonial Experiment*, p. 185.
25. "Statement by Fernando Martin, Executive President of the Puerto Rican Independence Party, Before the House Subcommittee on Insular Affairs," April 25, 2007, www.independencia.net.
26. Martinez, "Puerto Rico's Decolonization," p. 104.
27. Ibid., 102.
28. Carmelo Ruiz, "US Military Bombed Again in Puerto Rico," *Rochester Democrat and Chronicle* (via Progressive Media Project), May 29, 1999.
29. Francis X. Clines, "Protest Leader in Puerto Rico Basks in Gains," *New York Times*, December 5, 1999.
30. Stuart Taylor Jr., "Grading Sotomayor's Senior Thesis," www.nationaljournal.com, June 2, 2009.
31. Marin, "The Sad Case of Porto Rico," p. 138.
32. Ibid., 136.
33. Ibid., 141.
34. Ibid.
35. Martinez, "Puerto Rico's Decolonization," p. 110.
36. Clines, "Protest Leader in Puerto Rico Basks in Gains."

Chapter Seven

1. Mark Royden Winchell, e-mail to the author, September 20, 2007.
2. Donald Davidson, "Still Rebels, Still Yankees," in *The Attack on Leviathan: Regionalism and Nationalism in the United States* (Chapel Hill: University of North Carolina Press, 1938), p. 131.
3. John Tierney, "Disunited States of America," *New York Times*, July 4, 2006.
4. Jeffrey Rogers Hummel, *Emancipating Slaves, Enslaving Free Men: A History of the American Civil War* (Chicago: Open Court, 1996), p. 55.
5. "The Southern League, Inc.," undated early circular.
6. Unless otherwise noted, these and other comments by Clyde Wilson are taken from a series of e-mail exchanges between Wilson and the author in June 2008.
7. Clyde Wilson, "In Defense of Those 'Chicks' from Dixie," *Free Magnolia*, October–December 2007, p. 10.
8. Michael Hill and Thomas Fleming, "The New Dixie Manifesto: States' Rights Shall Rise Again," *Washington Post*, October 29, 1995.
9. Tito Perdue, *Lee* (New York: Four Walls Eight Windows, 1991), p. 85.
10. "Montgomery Declaration of Southern Cultural Independence," March 4, 2000, www.lsinstitute.org.
11. Clyde Wilson, e-mail to the author, June 2008.
12. Confidential communication.

13. Clyde Wilson, e-mail to the author, June 2008.

14. Hill's best writing is on Southern music. See, for instance, his piece on the bands of the Shoals in Northwest Alabama: Michael Hill, "Taking Down the Fiddle," *Chronicles*, November 2005.

15. Jim Auchmutey, "The New Secessionists," *Atlanta Journal-Constitution*, August 16, 1998. Said Stillman president emeritus Wynn: "I used to joke at faculty meetings that Michael was all right for a white guy. We were very close, and I was very much hurt to see him identified with the league."

16. Michael Hill, "Deconstructing Miss Dixie," *Chronicles*, September 2009, p. 16.

17. Hill and Fleming, "The New Dixie Manifesto."

18. Michael Hill, "The Symbol and the Man: A League of the South Statement," March 31, 2000.

19. "Confederate Flags Wave at Ala. Rally," Associated Press, *Rochester Democrat and Chronicle*, March 5, 2000.

20. "League of the South Statement on 'Racism,'" June 21, 2005, www.dixienet.org.

21. Kirkpatrick Sale, "On Collegiality," Middlebury Institute Paper IV, February 2007.

22. Kirkpatrick Sale, "Minimal Rights and Freedoms of Individuals in a Sovereign State," Middlebury Institute Paper V, March 2007.

23. Clyde Wilson, e-mail to the author, June 2008.

24. Richard M. Weaver, "The South and the American Union," in *The Southern Essays of Richard M. Weaver*, edited by George M. Curtis III and James J. Thompson Jr. (Indianapolis: Liberty Press, 1987), p. 251.

25. Quoted in Harry L. Watson, "The John Shelton Reed Special Issue," *Southern Cultures* (Spring 2001), p. 5.

26. John Shelton Reed, interview with the author, January 17, 2006. See "Live with *TAE*: John Shelton Reed," *American Enterprise*, May 2006, pp. 12–15. See also, among Reed's many publications, *Whistling Dixie: Dispatches from the South* (Columbia: University of Missouri Press, 1990) and *Southern Folk, Plain and Fancy* (Athens: University of Georgia Press, 1986).

27. John Shelton Reed, interview with the author, January 17, 2006.

28. *Lion in the Garden: Interviews with William Faulkner, 1926–1962*, edited by James B. Meriwether and Michael Millgate (New York: Random House, 1968), p. 60.

29. Ibid. p. 262.

30. William Faulkner, "On Fear: Deep South in Labor: Mississippi," in *Essays, Speeches and Public Letters*, edited by James B. Meriwether (New York: Random House, 1965), p. 98.

31. William Faulkner, *Intruder in the Dust* (New York: Modern Library, 1964/1948), pp. 203–204.

32. Levon Helm with Stephen Davis, *This Wheel's on Fire: Levon Helm and the Story of the Band* (New York: Morrow, 1993), p. 188.

33. Charles J. Shields, *Mockingbird: A Portrait of Harper Lee* (New York: Holt, 2006), p. 241.

34. Henry Timrod, "Sonnet: Poet! If on a Lasting Fame," *Collected Poems* (Athens: University of Georgia Press, 1965), p. 18.

35. James E. Kibler Jr., "More than Y'all: The New Southern Language," *Free Magnolia* 2, no. 1, p. 11.
36. James Everett Kibler, *Child to the Waters* (Gretna, LA: Pelican, 2003), p. 12.
37. James Everett Kibler, *Our Fathers' Fields: A Southern Story* (Columbia: University of South Carolina Press, 1998), p. 141. See also James Everett Kibler, "The Writer as Farmer," *Chronicles*, November 2005, pp. 23–25.
38. Andrew Lytle, *Bedford Forrest and His Critter Company* (New York: Minton, Balch, 1931), p. 27.
39. Ibid., 30–31.
40. August Derleth, *Walden West* (Madison: University of Wisconsin Press, 1992/1961), p. 65.
41. Daily Kos/Research 2000 Georgia Poll, April 27–29, 2009, www.dailykos.com/statepoll.
42. Author's interview with Donnie Kennedy, November 4, 2006.
43. Michael Hill, "Letter from Alabama," *Chronicles*, January 2004, p. 40.
44. Franklin Sanders, "Who Are We and What Do We Want?" League of the South Institute, March 2003, www.lsinstitute.org.
45. *The Grey Book: Blueprint for Southern Independence*, edited by Michael Hill (College Station, TX: Traveller Press, 2004), p. 161.
46. "Ray McBerry Makes Bid for Governor," Fox 5, April 22, 2009, www.myfoxatlanta.com.
47. Richard M. Weaver, "The South and the American Union," p. 238.
48. Richard Hofstadter, *The Idea of a Party System: The Rise of Legitimate Opposition in the United States, 1780–1840* (Berkeley: University of California Press, 1969), p. 240.
49. "Q&A with Ray About Issues of Importance to You," http://georgiafirst.org.
50. James Kibler, e-mail to the author, April 21, 2009.
51. *The Grey Book: Blueprint for Southern Independence*, p. xi.
52. Ibid., 1.
53. Ibid., 11.
54. Ibid., 30, 25. Also "Frequently Asked Questions About the LS," www.dixienet.org.
55. Thomas Fleming, "America's Crackup," *National Review*, July 28, 1997, p. 49.
56. William Lamar Cawthon Jr., "The South as an Independent Nation," *Southern Partisan* (3rd Quarter, 1997), pp. 18–24.
57. Clyde Wilson, e-mail to the author, June 2008.
58. Thomas H. Naylor, "The Future of the League of the South," memorandum, June 23, 2008.
59. Thomas H. Naylor, "To the League of the South with Love," open letter, July 4, 2008.
60. Clyde Wilson, e-mail to the author, June 2008.
61. Fleming, "America's Crackup," p. 64.
62. Thomas Moore, e-mail to the author, July 8, 2008.
63. Southern National Congress, "Call for Delegates," June 19, 2009, www.southernnationalcongress.org.

64. Thomas Moore, "Statement to the North American Secessionist Convention, Burlington, Vermont; November 4, 2006 by the Southern National Congress Committee."

65. Michael Hill, "Lesson for the South: Introducing Sinn Fein and the Dail Eireann," *Free Magnolia* 3, no. 1, p. 16.

66. Southern National Congress, "Call for Delegates," July 10, 2008. Moore, "Statement to the North American Secessionist Convention, Burlington, Vermont; November 4, 2006 by the Southern National Congress Committee."

67. "Southern National Covenant," adopted by the 2nd Southern National Congress on September 12, 2009, www.southernnationalcongress.org.

68. Southern National Congress, "Call for Delegates," July 10, 2008.

69. Interview with Thomas Moore, November 15, 2008.

70. Kirkpatrick Sale, e-mail to the author, December 11, 2008.

71. Thomas Moore, "Blacks and Whites Together in a Free South," *Free Magnolia* 2, no. 2, p. 7.

72. Phone interview with Thomas Moore, July 15, 2008.

73. Thomas Moore, "We Hold These Truths," July 6, 2009, www.southern nationalcongress.org.

74. Clyde Wilson, e-mail to the author, June 2008.

Chapter Eight

1. Frank M. Bryan, *Real Democracy: The New England Town Meeting and How It Works* (Chicago: University of Chicago Press, 2004), p. 20.

2. Frank M. Bryan, *Politics in the Rural States: People, Parties, Processes* (Boulder, CO: Westview, 1981), p. xvi; Bryan, *Real Democracy*, p. 33.

3. Tom Weaver, "Being Frank: A Talk with Professor Frank Bryan," *Vermont Quarterly*, Fall 2003, www.uvm.edu.

4. "An Interview with Frank M. Bryan," University of Chicago Press, 2003, www .press.uchicago.edu.

5. Frank M. Bryan, *Yankee Politics in Rural Vermont* (Hanover, NH: University Press of New England, 1974), p. 19.

6. Quoted in Frank M. Bryan and John McClaughry, *The Vermont Papers: Recreating Democracy on a Human Scale* (White River Junction, VT: Chelsea Green, 1989), p. 16.

7. Bryan, *Real Democracy*, p. x.

8. Bryan, *Politics in the Rural States*, p. 263.

9. Weaver, "Being Frank: A Talk with Professor Frank Bryan."

10. Author's interview with Frank Bryan, May 28, 2004. See Bill Kauffman, "Democracy in Vermont," *American Conservative*, September 13, 2004, pp. 18–21.

11. Weaver, "Being Frank: A Talk with Professor Frank Bryan."

12. Author's interview with Bryan.

13. Ibid.

14. Bryan and McClaughry, *The Vermont Papers*, p. 4.

15. Howard Frank Mosher, *Northern Borders* (Boston: Houghton Mifflin, 2002/1994), p. 176.

16. Howard Frank Mosher, *North Country: A Personal Journey Through the Borderland* (Boston: Houghton Mifflin, 1997), pp. 103, 42.

17. Bryan, *Real Democracy*, p. x.

18. "An Interview with Frank M. Bryan," University of Chicago Press.

19. Bryan, *Real Democracy*, pp. 15, 13.

20. Author's interview with Bryan.

21. Ibid.

22. Bryan, *Real Democracy*, pp. 83, 285.

23. Author's interview with Bryan.

24. Wallace Stegner, *Angle of Repose* (Garden City, NY: Doubleday, 1971), dust jacket.

25. Frank M. Bryan, *Real Democracy*, p. 37.

26. Frank Bryan, "Going It Alone," *Chronicles*, April 1991, p. 46.

27. Castle Freeman Jr., *Judgment Hill* (Hanover, NH: University Press of New England, 1997), p. 3.

28. For more on Craven, see Francine Latil, "Producing Change Locally: Talking with Director Jay Craven," July 2000, www.newenglandfilm.com; and Ben Beagle, "Northern Stories," *Batavia Daily News*, February 16, 2004. And rent/buy the movies!

29. Author's interview with Bryan.

30. Bryan, "Going It Alone," p. 46.

31. Author's interview with Bryan.

32. "An Interview with Frank M. Bryan," University of Chicago Press.

33. Author's interview with Bryan.

34. "About Frank Bryan: What I Believe . . . ," www.uvm.edu.

35. "The Vermont Independence Convention," Second Vermont Republic, undated 2005 circular.

36. "Our Principles," Second Vermont Republic, undated circular.

37. Thomas H. Naylor, interview with the author, October 28, 2005. See Bill Kauffman, "Free Vermont," *American Conservative*, December 19, 2005, p. 16. I met, epistolarily speaking, Thomas Naylor in 1995. He wrote to say he liked a piece I had written on secession in *The American Enterprise*. (Yes, that *American Enterprise*—flagship of Dick Cheney's think tank. It's a long story in which friendship trumps ideology, as it always should. *Not*, I hasten to add, friendship with Dick Cheney.) Naylor sent along an op-ed he had written for the *Manchester (NH) Sunday News* asking the question, "Is it Time to Downsize the US?"

38. Thomas H. Naylor, "Come to Vermont, Help Us Secede, and Escape the Empire," *Vermont Village Green*, September 1, 2009. *The Vermont Village Green* is one of several titles under which Naylor has published his columns and essays.

39. Aleksandr Solzhenitsyn, open letter to "Citizens of Cavendish, our dear neighbors," February 28, 1994.

40. Thomas H. Naylor, "Wal-Mart: Metaphor for America," *The Green Mountain Manifesto*, June 1, 2004.

41. "New Book Release: *The Vermont Manifesto*," by Thomas H. Naylor, *The Green Mountain Manifesto*, undated 2003.
42. Thomas H. Naylor, letter to the author, February 15, 2002.
43. Cathy Resmer, "Most Likely to Secede?" *Seven Days*, October 26–November 2, 2005, p. 26a.
44. Peter Holm, "Independence Day Collage," *Vermont Commons*, August 2005, p. 12.
45. Pete Sutherland with the Clayfoot Strutters, "Two Hundred Years Is Long Enough," Epact Music, 2008.
46. Resmer, "Most Likely to Secede?"; Philippe Gohier, "Vive Le Vermont Libre! Secession Finds Favour," *Montreal Gazette*, April 17, 2005.
47. Frank Bryan and Bill Mares, *The Vermont Owner's Manual* (Shelburne, VT: New England Press, 2000), p. 14.
48. Quoted in Thomas H. Naylor, *Secession: How Vermont and All the Other States Can Save Themselves from the Empire* (Port Townsend, WA: Feral House, 2008), pp. 48–49.
49. Robin Palmer, "Former Professor Argues It's Time to Leave the Union," *Barre (VT) Times-Argus*, November 16, 2003.
50. "Vermont Independence Parade & Rally," *The Green Mountain Manifesto*, June 5, 2004.
51. Naylor, *Secession*, p. 12.
52. George F. Kennan, *Around the Cragged Hill: A Personal and Political Philosophy* (New York: W. W. Norton, 1994), p. 149.
53. George F. Kennan to Thomas H. Naylor, February 7, 2001, quoted in Thomas H. Naylor, "George F. Kennan: Godfather of the Vermont Independence Movement," April 1, 2005.
54. George F. Kennan to Thomas H. Naylor, May 1, 2002.
55. George. F. Kennan, *Memoirs 1925–1950* (Boston: Little, Brown, 1967), p. 119.
56. George F. Kennan to Thomas H. Naylor, October 22, 2001.
57. George F. Kennan to Thomas H. Naylor, May 1, 2002.
58. Bill Kauffman, "Free Vermont," pp. 16–19. Quotes taken from my notes of the convention. Vermonters understand citizenship. In the great Howard Frank Mosher's novel *On Kingdom Mountain*, an eccentric mountain woman who is representing herself in a suit to keep developers from running a highway over her mountain fills the spectator seats in the state Supreme Court with carved mannequins of her ancestors and various historical personages. The Chief Justice permits it. "This might be the state capital, but it was still Vermont, and Justice Dewey, at least, was determined not to forget it." Mosher, *On Kingdom Mountain* (Boston: Houghton Mifflin, 2007), p. 186.
59. John Curran, "In Vermont, Nascent Secession Movement Gains," Associated Press, June 3, 2007.
60. Eugene D. Genovese, *The Southern Tradition: The Achievement and Limitations of an American Conservatism* (Cambridge, MA: Harvard University Press, 1994), p. 28.
61. Kauffman, "Free Vermont," p. 18.

62. Frank Bryan, "Secessionism and Vermont: Where I Stand," *Vermont Commons*, Winter 2007, p. 12.

63. Kauffman, "Free Vermont," p. 18.

64. John McClaughry, e-mail to the author, October 24, 2005.

65. Bryan, "Going It Alone," p. 46.

66. Kauffman, "Free Vermont," p. 19.

67. Rob Williams, "Beyond Barack's Bamboozling: As Obamania Fizzles, Vermonters Take a Fresh Look at Independence," *Vermont Commons*, Stick Season–Holidays 2009, p. 2.

68. "Racism? Surely You've Got to Be Kidding: SVR Co-Chair Thomas Naylor's Response to a Techno-Fascist Cyber-Smear Campaign Against the Second Vermont Republic," press release, February 26, 2007.

69. Thomas H. Naylor, phone interview with the author, 2008.

70. Thomas H. Naylor, "The Paradoxical Nature of the Geopolitics of Secession," *The Vermont Village Green*, August 15, 2008.

71. "The Chattanooga Declaration," adopted September 4, 2007, at the Second North American Secessionist Convention, http://middleburyinstitute.org.

72. Manchester quotes from the author's notes. See Bill Kauffman, "Manchester Disunited," *American Conservative*, December 15, 2008.

73. Thomas H. Naylor, "Red State–Blue State Secessionists Unite," *Vivre Le Vermont Libre!* October 15, 2007.

74. Naylor, phone interview with the author, 2008.

75. "2008 Vermonter Poll Results," UVM Center for Rural Studies, April 2008, http://vermontrepublic.org.

76. "One in Five Americans Believe States Have the Right to Secede," Middlebury Institute/Zogby Poll, July 23, 2008.

77. Naylor, *Secession*, p. 89.

78. Ian Baldwin and Frank Bryan, "The Once and Future Republic of Vermont," *Washington Post*, April 1, 2007.

79. Bryan, "Going It Alone," p. 48.

80. James Kibler Jr., e-mail to the author, April 21, 2009.

INDEX

Bill Kauffman is the author of nine books, including *Dispatches from the Muckdog Gazette*, which won the 2003 national "Sense of Place" award from Writers & Books, and *Look Homeward, America*, which the American Library Association named one of the best books of 2006. He writes frequently for *The Wall Street Journal* and *The American Conservative* and lives in his native Genesee County, New York, with his family.

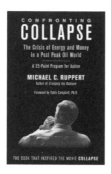

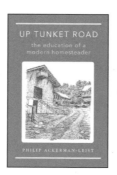